Language Handbook

Concepts, Assessment, Intervention

John R. Muma

Texas Tech University

Prentice-Hall, Inc., *Englewood Cliffs, New Jersey 07632*

Library of Congress Cataloging in Publication Data

MUMA, JOHN R. (date)
    Language handbook.

    Bibliography: p.
    Includes index.
    1. Speech disorders in children.   2. Communica-
tive disorders in children.   3. Children—Language.
I. Title.
RJ496.S7M85   616.8′55   77-18530
ISBN 0-13-522755-0

*To those true clinicians necessarily guided by intuition
but intelligently challenged by what they need to know.*

To their fortunate clients.

Printed in the United States of America

10   9   8   7   6   5

Data for Fig. 3-1 are from pp. 194–99, 255–56, 302–6, and 447–55 in *Child Development and
Personality,* 3rd Edition by Paul Henry Mussen, John Janeway Conger and Jerome Kagan.
Copyright © 1969 by Paul H. Mussen, John J. Conger and Jerome Kagan. By permission of
Harper & Row, Publishers, Inc.

Lists on pages 199 and 200 and Fig. 6-12 are from *The Development of Speech* by Paula Menyuk,
copyright © 1972 The Bobbs-Merrill Company, Inc.

PRENTICE-HALL INTERNATIONAL, INC., *London*
PRENTICE-HALL OF AUSTRALIA PTY. LIMITED, *Sydney*
PRENTICE-HALL OF CANADA, LTD., *Toronto*
PRENTICE-HALL OF INDIA PRIVATE LIMITED, *New Delhi*
PRENTICE-HALL OF JAPAN, INC., *Tokyo*
PRENTICE-HALL OF SOUTHEAST ASIA PTE. LTD., *Singapore*
WHITEHALL BOOKS LIMITED, *Wellington, New Zealand*

Contents

Preface

Language Handbook: Concepts, Assessment, Intervention was written especially for clinicians and students preparing to become clinicians. It is for those who have interests in assessment and intervention of cognitive-linguistic-communicative systems and processes. It is intended for the following clinical specialties: speech pathology, deaf education, mental retardation, reading disabilities, language arts, special education, learning disabilities, and school psychology. Although it is primarily for clinicians, parents, teachers, psychologists, and administrators will also find useful certain parts of the *Handbook*.

There are five reasons for entitling it a handbook. First, it proposes a practical, principle-oriented model to aid a clinician's conceptualization of assessment and intervention. Second, it is comprehensive, extending across cognitive, linguistic, and communicative systems and processes. Third, it integrates an extensive, multifaceted, and sometimes contradictory literature on basic processes, translating research and theory into practical applications. Clinical implications are discussed in terms of principles—some speculative and some with demonstrated value. Fourth, it provides a comprehensive list of references for further study. Finally, a glossary is provided.

Clinicians have two basic questions: "*What* do we need to know?" and "*How* should we use what we do know?" This book is organized around these two questions. Thus, it is a practical reference for basic concerns of clinicians. Unit I deals with an intervention model that defines the scope of the *what* and *how* issues. Unit II discusses basic concepts about the nature of language; cognitive, linguistic, and communicative systems and processes; and language acquisition. Unit III applies basic principles to practical issues of clinical assessment and intervention. Unit IV describes specific assessment and intervention procedures for cognitive, linguistic, and communicative systems and processes.

The *Handbook* is a practical book, written for clinicians by a clinician. The author has a background in clinical work extending over two decades. This includes experience as a public school speech therapist, university clinical supervisor, program developer for institutionalized retarded children, volunteer educator for high school dropouts, program consultant for two cerebral palsy programs, program consultant for autistic children, and program developer and research director for a parent-child infant and preschool program for lower-income families. He continues to have small demonstration groups of children at a university clinic.

This book describes complex issues as they actually are—according to the current literature—as opposed to the simplistic and often inaccurate notions which are to be found in the applied fields. This raises a fundamental issue: must the clinician deal with actual behavior in terms of systems and processes, or opt for a technician orientation with packaged materials, categories, labels, and numbers?

Finally, this book focuses on *individual differences*—a fundamental issue in clinical work.

The *Handbook* is intended for clinicians who have had little or no training in this area. Thus, it is introductory in nature. Chapter headings and subheadings, illustrations, and examples are designed to give those with no previous training easy access to the material. Inasmuch as the discussion of topics may be somewhat more complete than in some undergraduate books, this book might be considered for beginning graduate students, particularly in the following clinical fields: speech pathology, deaf education, mental retardation, reading disabilities, language arts, special education, learning disabilities, and school psychology. The *Handbook* offers useful and practical guidance for clinicians who deal with individuals having difficulty with cognitive-linguistic-communicative systems and processes. Such individuals have "delayed language," learning disabilities, mental retardation, aphasia, autism, deafness or hardness of hearing, reading problems, speech disorders, and to some extent poverty living conditions.

I have enjoyed writing the *Handbook* in its various versions over the past seven years. I only wish I could fully credit the many individuals who encouraged me and provided constructive suggestions along the way. To each of the following I express special thanks: Gene Abkarian, Alfred Baumeister, Daniel Beasley, Raymond Daniloff, Judy Duchan, Francis Griffith, Curt Hamre, Recille Hamrell, Ronald Laeder, John Locke, Rosemary Lubinski, Lynn Miner, Barry Prizant, Tom Shriner, Joyce West, and Betty Webster. I valued their comments because they are first and foremost clinicians (or individuals who offer valuable information for clinicians) and open-minded individuals who are always learning and applying something new, something better. Also, I wish to thank the many clinicians across the country who invited me to give presentations and workshops. I am grateful for their useful feedback on this material when it was in its formative stages. I of course accept full responsibility for the content as it stands, especially its shortcomings. I hope that it is a useful, practical, and comprehensive handbook for clinicians.

UNIT I
Language Intervention Model

1

Appropriate Language Intervention: A Model

Clinicians are continually faced with difficult yet challenging responsibilities in language assessment and intervention. On the one hand, they have crucial responsibilities in meeting the specific needs of each individual within their charge. On the other, the state of the art in clinical assessment and intervention is rather meager—speculative at best. Indeed, Noam Chomsky (reported in Cazden 1972a) worried that by diminishing the range and complexity of materials available to an inquiring mind and putting behavior into fixed patterns, we may disrupt natural propensities for learning. As Courtney Cazden warned in 1972a, a child may be such a powerful consumer that to teach specific primitive responses may ultimately retard the development of more advanced processes. Perhaps the best we can do is describe an individual's command of various cognitive-linguistic-communicative systems and processes to the best extent possible, then exploit such behavior.

Consider the complexity of the clinicians' problems in executing their responsibilities. First, they have very little, if any, opportunity to choose their clients. Thus, they must have a broad understanding of various clinical conditions and an in-depth understanding of the cognitive-linguistic-communicative systems and processes that manifest themselves in various combinations in clinical surroundings (Bowerman 1974).

Second, in clinical groups, individual differences are more apparent than similarities. Thus, it behooves clinicians to approach assessment and intervention with a specific orientation for each individual. This is somewhat of a departure from the usual situation, in which individuals in clinical groups are all treated alike.

Third, important developments have come from the psychological, linguistic, psycholinguistic, and sociolinguistic literature in recent years. These have important implications for clinical assessment and intervention. However, clinicians face two problems with these: limited access to the literature because of its wide dispersal, and job demands that are too great to permit necessary literature searches. Further, the basic research is rarely integrated or translated for clinical applications.

In short, clinicians have a dilemma. They must deal with a variety of conditions in which individual differences are important, yet helpful literature is dispersed and poorly oriented toward clinical applications. Obviously, there are no simple solutions. One approach is to accept authoritarian pronouncements or commercial programs at face value. This has two disadvantages: the clinician abdicates his responsibility to deal with individual needs, forcing the individual to conform to a program. Norma Rees (1973a) warned that some clinicians are too strongly oriented toward labels and assessment-intervention procedures that are absolutist or categorical in nature. The result is procedures in which individual differences are displaced by group conformity. Rees (1973a) described her feeling using the metaphor of the Procrustean bed, in which people's feet or hands were stretched or chopped off to make them fit the bed.

Another approach is to become highly sophisticated about various theoretical–conceptual positions in verbal learning and behavior, thereby enabling one to deduce or speculate about appropriate clinical implications for the individual. While this approach is undoubtedly best, it has a very serious practical limitation: most clinicians do not have sufficient time or resources to adequately familiarize themselves with the various substantive areas needed. Moreover, the literature is developing rapidly—so fast that it is difficult to keep abreast of it on a full-time basis.

Clinicians can rely to some extent on various authorities to package the available literature for clinical use in the form of books, programs, workshops, etc. However, they must be flexible in this simply because a particular assessment–intervention procedure may be appropriate for some individuals but not for others. We must always remember that authoritarian suggestions are generalities that may or may not pertain to the particular needs of a given individual. There is no such thing as *the* assessment procedure or *the* intervention procedure. Behavior is too complex, relative, conditional, and dynamic (Kagan 1967; Deese 1969). Moreover, in the clinic, individual differences are so strongly evident that it is inappropriate to expect that the same problems (i.e., mental retardation, learning disabilities, aphasia, etc.) exist for every individual in the same way within the group, or that intervention procedures should be standardized.

Given the state of the art and the complexities of carrying out clinical responsibilities, it is imperative that clinicians do two things. First, they must develop a critical but constructive attitude. With that, they will have a check against blind acceptance of authoritarian positions, and greater willingness to depart from fixed standards by placing individual needs first. This is important because clinicians are, in the last analysis, the authorities for those individuals within their charge. Second, clinicians must (to the greatest extent possible) put their knowledge into perspective and attempt to define what they do know and need to know in order to adequately assume their responsibilities. The language intervention model presented in this chapter describes a practical conceptual-operational approach regarding the *what* and *how* issues that concern clinicians.

A Relevant Language Intervention Model

Relevance is essentially a matter of deducing the particular needs of a particular person in particular situations. This is not an easy task, nor is it an arbitrary one. A relevant language intervention model is one that helps organize information with an eye to the specific concerns of clinicians as they learn about particular individuals and then implement appropriate programs.

The organization of this model, as simple as it is, gives clinicians a rational guide to determine what they need to know and do in order to devise and implement an effective, efficient, and *appropriate* assessment–intervention program. The model itself is without content; it is merely a guide to the kind of information one needs. For example, one clinician may discover that he knows a great deal about language learning but relatively little about language usage. Another may discover that he was focused almost exclusively on the structure of language and has failed to learn the importance of functions. A third may have invested most of his effort in normative assessment procedures and now has virtually no awareness of the power of descriptive procedures. A fourth may discover that he isolates linguistic systems from cognitive and communicative systems. A fifth may have thought that the only way to intervene is to carry out highly structured programs that strive to replicate first language learning, and finds there are alternatives to both structured programs and the first language learning strategy (Muma 1977a).

Interventionists, then, have a variety of backgrounds and orientations. The model proposed here serves to place these in perspective. The balance of the book provides introductory material and references for the entire model, so that interested readers may appreciate the nature and scope of the various backgrounds and orientations, as well as the available alternatives.

Figure 1-1 depicts the model. The *what* and *how* issues are important in the model. *What* has two major components: (1) what they should know about verbal learning and verbal behavior, and (2) what they should attempt to discern about an individual's needs. The first pertains to the clinician's conceptualization of verbal learning and behavior. The second pertains to what the clinician needs to know about assessment—that is, about the individuals with whom he must deal.

How issues pertain to how clinicians should use the *what* information to devise and implement appropriate intervention programs.

The major areas of conceptualization are the nature of language, underlying cognitive and memory processes, linguistic systems, communicative systems, language acquisition, and language usage. Each is described in the following chapters in an introductory manner and is then amplified with examples, illustrations, and references for follow-up reading.

The issues in the chapters on conceptualization (Unit II) have been derived from basic research in psychology, psycholinguistics, and sociolinguistics. They have

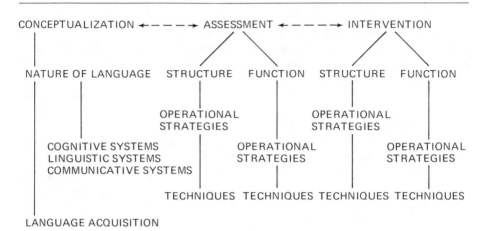

Figure 1-1 *The language intervention model.*

implications for both assessment and intervention. For example, it is now clear that approaches based upon surface structure or products of grammar are superficial. Approaches with a psychometric normative orientation are tangential to the more important issues of individual differences. *A priori* approaches that delineate categories of behavior before encountering an individual in clinical assessment or intervention (i.e., normative programs or highly structured programs) are also tangential to individual differences. Approaches based upon generative grammar (not necessarily transformational generative grammar) more adequately represent the nature of verbal behavior than do nongenerative approaches. Approaches based on the premise that cognitive systems underly verbal behavior are more productive than those which view verbal behavior exclusively as linguistic systems. Approaches that take into account covarying cultural and social systems are more relevant than those which regard verbal behavior as an entity by itself. Approaches that provide for individual prerogatives as to what, when, where, why, and how learning occurs are more effective than those which are highly structured. In summary, several conclusions from recent conceptual developments in the literature contrast with some widely accepted practices in the applied fields.

Unit III deals with general issues in clinical assessment. It stresses the importance of individual differences in clinical assessment and intervention. A number of major issues are also discussed: (1) the two basic issues of assessment—problem/no problem and the nature of a problem, (2) assessment power in terms of relevance to an individual and defining alternatives in intervention, (3) major assessment strategies (formal/informal, quantitative/descriptive, structural/functional), and (4) dynamic aspects of clinical judgments. Many clinicians are just beginning to be aware of alternative assessment strategies and some of these basic issues.

Unit IV deals with basic issues of intervention. First, a brief historical perspective on language intervention is given. The rationale is developed that the best we can do in intervention is to *describe an individual's command of various cognitive-linguistic-communicative systems and processes—to the extent possible—then exploit such behavior*. Then two contrasting philosophies of intervention are described: behavioristic and mentalistic. Major dimensions of intervention are delineated. Then six intervention strategies are presented: first language learning, second language learning, intermodality transfer, language rehabilitation, systematic variation and extension of available repertoire, and spontaneous exploration of available repertoire. There is a call for involvement of parents, siblings, and peers as effective intervention agents. Emphasis is placed on environmentally based intervention—at home, at school, on the playground, in the community, anywhere an individual typically functions. Finally, "Sesame Street" is discussed in terms of the basic principles that have been incorporated into this very successful program.

Unit V describes assessment and intervention techniques and procedures for cognitive-linguistic-communicative systems and processes. The intervention suggestions that are presented are based on the premise that assessment should not be separate from intervention. While it is understandable that clinicians want expedient procedures, they must recognize that more important issues are appropriateness and relevance to individual needs. Appropriateness and relevance are much more difficult to deal with than expediency, but are also much more rewarding since they end in more effective and efficient results. Clinicians are more challenged by the need to find the most appropriate procedure than by merely executing an easy program. A profession needs clinicians rather than technicians.

Ideologies

It is one thing to propose a language intervention model concerning *what* and *how* issues, but quite a different thing to get interventionists to incorporate it and its substantive information into their conceptual orientation and operational methods. The incorporation process not only depends on access to information, but that information must also be deemed valuable by those who may need to use it.

Ideology is one's point of view regarding the value of available information. Inasmuch as there are many points of view in language intervention, there are naturally many ideologies. As a general rule, the ideologies of many parents, teachers, and clinicians are based on expediency, emotional grounds, and authoritarianism. Naive clinicians are prone to select or dismiss intervention approaches on grounds of ease of usage, tradition, or authoritarian proclamation. They are less open to change, and too ready to categorically "evaluate" various approaches. They seek *the* answer as a subtle way of relinquishing clinical responsibilities. Sophisticated clinicians, on the other hand, strive to determine the strengths and limitations of the various approaches available, intelligently selecting alternative courses of action as the various needs arise. They are principle oriented rather than method oriented.

This is the distinction between the ideology of the clinician as "technician" and the "true" clinician. Technicians seek "cookbook" answers. True clinicians seek principles that apply to a variety of conditions in a variety of ways.

I am not implying that clinicians should avoid placing different values on the various approaches available. It is, after all, inevitable that they do so. The point is that they should recognize that they do so. They should be able to justify their positions on rational rather than emotional, categorical, or authoritarian grounds. As professionals, clinicians must strive to operate on a rational basis. They must know why they choose to adopt one particular program rather than another. The reasons should be specific to the particular needs of the individual rather than reflect a categorical position such as "poor reader," "learning-disabled," "auditory sequencing problem," "delayed language," "culturally disadvantaged," and so on.

I am reminded of an incident in which a clinician in training once asked for an outline of some assessment strategies and techniques. After several strategies and nearly thirty techniques had been discussed, she dismissed most of the information with, "All these strategies and things are nice but what I really need is some specific techniques." She selected a few and left. On another occasion, a teacher said of the same material, "All of that is too theoretical. I just want *the* specific test to tell me if he has a language problem or not." She eventually learned that there is no such test simply because verbal behavior is much too complicated. She also came to realize that verbal behavior cannot be regarded as an either/or issue. It is relative, complex, conditional, and dynamic.

Relativity

Clinicians must know and appreciate that one of the most important principles of psychology is the principle of relativity. Behaviors are related one to another. Therefore, it is necessary to deal with behavior in terms of systems and processes. Moreover, behavior is relative to the conditions under which it occurs. According to James Deese (1969), a fact of behavior is *conditional*. This implies that a behavior pattern is meaningless unless co-occurring conditions are accounted for. Behavior must always be placed in context to fully appreciate it. Urie Bronfenbrenner (1974) argued, for example, that much of the literature in developmental psychology is ecologically invalid because it is neither derived from nor translatable to natural events or conditions. Lois Bloom (1970, 1973, 1974) argued that much of what was known about language development and verbal behavior was superficial because covarying functional contexts had not been taken into account. Covarying linguistic systems can determine the performance of a target system. For example, Edward Klima and Ursula Bellugi-Klima (1969) showed that stages of development of negations and questions emerged according to co-occurring linguistic systems. Dan Slobin's famous quote, "New forms first express old functions, and new functions are first expressed by old forms" (1970, p. 2) underscores the importance of appreciating co-occurring processes in the acquisition of a target system. The litera-ture on co-articulation in phonology is based upon the premise of contextual influ-ences of co-occurring phonetic determinants (Daniloff and Moll 1968). Co-occurrence is probably important to differentiation processes in the acquisition of cognitive systems (Werner 1948; Witkin et al. 1962; Flavell 1977; Piaget 1970; Bruner 1964; Garner 1966), linguistic systems (Menyuk 1964a,b; McNeill 1970; Brown 1973b), communicative systems (Flavell et al. 1968; Muma 1975a; Glucksberg, Krauss, and Higgins 1975), and speech acts (Bruner 1975; Greenfield and Smith 1976; Searle 1969; Dore 1975).

I have shown (Muma 1973a) that the principle of co-occurring and covarying linguistic systems is important to clinical assessment. For example, it is not very important to learn that an individual is inside or outside a normative range for the acquisition of pronouns. The important information is the cognitive-linguistic-communicative conditions under which various pronouns occur, the nature of the individual's pronominal system, and its use in anaphoric reference (Waryas 1973; Ingram 1971b; Maratsos 1973c).

An appreciation of the importance of relativity has been regarded as an indicator of the maturity of a profession or discipline. Kagan (1967) held that early psychology was based upon categorical data, absolutistic thinking, and authoritarianism, with the consequent use of quantitative norms and labels. As psychology matured, it shifted away from such orientations to an appreciation that behavior is complex, relative, conditional, and dynamic. Categorical data or various taxonomies merely inventory behavior whereas relational data can potentially explain it in terms of systems and processes. Needless to say, the concept of relativity is very important in the applied fields, particularly the clinical situation, where individual differences are so strongly evident.

UNIT II
Conceptualization

2

The Nature of Language: General Perspectives

What do clinicians need to know in order to deal effectively with cognitive-linguistic-communicative problems? As a minimum, they should have some general perspectives about the nature of language. These must be consistent with the current literature. Developments have occurred in the last few years which have major assessment–intervention implications for clinicians. Indeed, they constitute a formidable challenge to many currently held notions in the clinical fields. Some of the more basic and pervasive of these notions will be discussed in this chapter.

Some General Properties of Language

Hockett (1960) delineated several basic properties of language:

1. *Vocal-auditory channel:* The vocal-auditory channel is exclusively utilized in human language, thereby leaving much of the body free for other simultaneous activities.
2. *Broadcast transmission and directional reception:* Everyone within earshot can get the message. Transmission is not to a specific point.
3. *Rapid fading:* The message is fleeting. It is transmitted but rapidly fades away.
4. *Interchangeability:* Individuals can interchange between transmitter and receiver.
5. *Total feedback:* A speaker receives everything he transmits. This makes possible an internalization of communication.
6. *Specialization:* Language is for the specific purpose of conveying messages.
7. *Semanticity:* A message conveys particular meanings because there are relatively fixed associations between a message and objects, actions, relationships, and events in the communicative context.

8. *Arbitrariness:* The associations between linguistic devices and their meanings are arbitrary. Thus, there is virtually no limit to what can be communicated.

9. *Discreteness:* Language functions on a discrete set of units—phonemes. However, the human vocal mechanism can produce a huge variety of sounds, only some of which are regarded as phonemes.

10. *Displacement:* Humans can talk about things that are remote in time or space from present time and actual space.

11. *Productivity:* It is the ability to say and understand something novel. New information can be transmitted.

12. *Traditional transmission:* A language is transmitted to new individuals through learning and teaching and not through heredity.

13. *Duality of patterning:* Meaningful units—words—are arrangements of smaller differentiating units—phonemes. Languages have constraints about the arrangements of meaningful units and of differentiating units.[1]

These properties portray verbal behavior as active and dynamic. The applied fields, on the other hand, have implicitly regarded language as somewhat fixed and static (H. Clark 1973b). People were supposed to "correct" errors and learn "Standard English."

Bolinger (1975) has also outlined basic properties of language. He considers language to be:

1. *Human.* Humans are uniquely able to learn and use symbolic systems in adept ways (notwithstanding the accomplishments of the great apes in recent research [Limber 1977]).

2. *Behavioral.* Language is not an entity but a behavior, the product of underlying grammatical systems. It is performance in a competence-performance comparison.

3. *Composed of sound patterns.* The medium of language is sound. Speech and listening are thus its primary modalities. Reading and writing are modalities that serve to preserve the spoken one.

4. *Hierarchical.* There is a nonlinear structural organization of verbal elements.

5. *Changeable.* Language is both receptive and resistant to change. Its parts are intricately interwoven, which maintains language. But language is also separable and its parts are recombinable.

6. *Embedded in gesture.* Language is not simply verbal utterance but also action patterns. Audible gestures constitute a paralanguage, and visible language is body language. There are also audible and visible learned and unlearned gestures. Learned audible gestures are lexical, and include not

[1]From "The Origin of Speech," by Charles F. Hockett. Copyright © 1960 by Scientific American, Inc. All rights reserved.

only words but near-words like "Uh-huh" for "Yes," "Huh" for "What," "Hmm" for "I wonder," "Tsk-tsk" for disapproval, and so on. Visible gestures include waving a hand for "Good-bye," a shrug for "I don't know," and a finger on the lips for "Be quiet." Another type of gesture is iconic—an imitation of a sound such as a snore, sound of a machine gun, or a visible gesture such as a motion of the hand for "Put it down." Another main type of gesture is instinctive, e.g., a laugh, smile, cry, blink. These are initially involuntary but become voluntary. They tend to synechdochize (part disappears while another part stands alone, as in the pronounced intentional intake of air in a gasp of dismay or startle).

7. *Arbitrary and nonarbitrary.* The sound patterns of a language could name anything—"tree" is a sound pattern that is arbitrary and could name anything. But the arrangement of words in utterances is not so arbitrary. The use of a language relies to some extent on a certain degree of expectation. Once a language has established that degree of expectation it loses degrees of freedom or arbitrariness.

8. *Horizontal and vertical.* Horizontalness is a string of words in a written sequence, or phonemes in a syllabic organization in speech. Verticalness pertains to alternate equivalences in a string.

9. *Possessing structural similarities.* Languages are related to each other genetically, culturally, and typologically. Genetically, they have a lineage in which one language evolves from another. Cultural changes may precipitate a language, as in the case of pidgin or Creole English. A typological relationship between languages identifies their similarities regardless of origin.

10. *Heard as well as spoken.* Both encoding and decoding functions occur.

The Dynamic Property of Verbal Behavior

Verbal behavior is very powerful because it is dynamic. People do not memorize a fixed set of sentences to be selectively used, they acquire a grammatical system that, as Chomsky puts it, allows them to produce or generate novel utterances of their language. These utterances are specific to an occasion. Verbal behavior is dynamic because novel yet appropriate utterances can be produced and understood.

Verbal behavior is dynamic in another sense also. As Roger Brown (1973a,b), George Miller (1962), and many others have shown, a person can use one word for many referents or one referent can have many labels. To illustrate, the word *dog* can have many referents: dog *A*, dog *B*, dog *C*, etc. One referent, for example, dog *A*, can have many labels—"Pax," "mutt," "my dog," "Irish Setter," etc. This is a fundamental principle of verbal behavior: specific utterances can be selected from a number of possible alternatives. Selection is in terms of the particular form that seems to be most appropriate to the occasion.

This has a number of implications for language assessment in the applied fields. It means, for example, that the old notion of a one-to-one correspondence between thought and language is unwarranted. The current literature shows some correspondence between the development of cognitive underpinnings of language—such as awareness of object permanence as a precursor to object labelling (Bloom 1973; Greenfield and Smith 1976; Bates 1976; Nelson 1973, 1974)—but clearly, dynamic form-referent relationships rule out a direct one-to-one correspondence between thought and language. This undermines the adage that if one speaks nonstandard English, he must be retarded or in some way mentally deficient. Those who believe this reveal wholesale ignorance of both cognition and language.

The dynamic property of language underscores another principle—the difference between surface and deep structure, or form and function. It also underscores the principle of the difference between the knowledge of linguistic systems and the knowledge of their selective use.

There is an interesting parallel between motor, mental, and linguistic systems. This is their dynamism. The more one uses a motor, mental, or linguistic system, the more adept one becomes. The less it is used the less it is available. For the motor system, an athlete trains to reach a maximum level of performance, but when he or she stops training, the performance level diminishes. Motoric behavior is dynamic. An extreme case is when someone is confined and has little motoric activity. Contractures and even atrophy can occur. In cognition, a similar process appears to operate. The more one uses memory the more one *can* remember; the more one learns, the more one *can* learn.

Verbal behavior is dynamic not only in terms of producing and understanding novel utterances and form-referent relationships but also in underlying cognitive systems and processes, and communicative systems. Perception, conception, and memory are dynamic because they continually change with new experiences. Perception is a function of what we know (Garner 1966). Conception, according to Jean Piaget (1954, 1963, 1970), is a continuous redefining of existing schemata through assimilation (incorporation of new information into an existing schema) or accommodation (reorganization of an existing schema to incorporate new information). While there may be differences in theory between experts in cognition, they acknowledge that conceptualization is dynamic. Indeed, the pervasive principle of differentiation is a dynamic one. This principle is discussed in the chapter on language development.

Memory capacity is not fixed or static as is often implied or stated in the applied fields. It is dynamic (Jenkins 1973, 1974). The more one uses it, the more one can remember, since increasingly more efficient chunking and rehearsal occur.[2] Switching operations in verbal behavior are other ways of appreciating dynamism.

---

[2]Chunking is a psychological process whereby one segments experience into units consistent with his concepts. Rehearsal is a psychological process for transferring information in short-term storage into long-term storage.

The Difference Between Language and Grammar

What do I mean by language and the meaning of language in relation to other related topics, such as verbal behavior, grammar, cognition, and communication?

Language pertains to linguistics, psycholinguistics, sociolinguistics, and other related fields. Language can be regarded as the product of *grammar*. As Miller put it (1973, p. 7), "a language is all the conceivable sentences that could be generated according to the rules of its grammar." However, this definition is too restrictive because it is sentence oriented. As indicated above, language extends to gestures. A functional definition may be better. According to Miller (1973, p. 7), language is "a socially shared means for expressing ideas."

Language is an abstraction because an infinite number and variety of sentences can potentially be expressed by the mutual grammars of innumerable people. Subgroups of people who have similar grammars are said to speak *dialects* of a language because their grammars vary in similar ways. At the individual level, the products of one's grammar comprise his or her *idiolect*. With the current emphasis on the functions of language-speech acts, it is necessary to de-emphasize a sentence oriented definition of language and to stress the *functions* of language. As Bruner (1975) put it, ". . . language is a specialized and conventionalized extension of co-operative action." He indicated that ". . . language is acquired as an instrument for regulating joint activity and joint attention."

Grammar is a set of rules for coding one's thoughts, ideas, and emotions for the purpose of conveying an intent to someone else. A grammar entails an active process which must be activated at will, with intent or purpose, and is selectively utilized. This is a definition of grammar which is intentionally general enough to allow for such things as utterances, gesture language, body language, architectural language, and even the grammar of play. Recognizing that speech is the primary mode of language, we can define grammar as "a set of rules that describes how the realm of sound is related to the realm of meaning" (Miller 1973, p. 7). Other explicit, succinct definitions have been given by Chomsky (1957, 1965a,b, 1968). Paraphrasing his various definitions, a grammar is a finite set of rules that provide the ability to produce or generate (and comprehend) an infinite number and variety of sentences in a language without also producing nonsentences.

Chomsky's definition of language revolutionized both the theoretical fields—linguistics, psycholinguistics, sociolinguistics, philosophy, theoretical mathematics—and the applied fields—English education, language arts, anthropology, speech pathology, deaf education, mental retardation, special education, and learning disabilities. In the clinical fields, major psycho-sociolinguistic concepts have given birth to new perspectives. These concepts have important assessment and intervention implications. Hitherto, the prevailing attitude was that grammar was essentially the same as language. Grammar was thought to be a set of rules regarding correct sentences. Everyone was taught (a) to emulate such correct sentences, (b) to diagram or parse sentences to discern their grammar, and (c) to learn Standard English. Chomsky (1957, 1965a,b, 1968), on the other hand, defined grammar from a psychological standpoint rather than as a list of sentence types with criteria for correctness. Chomsky discussed grammar in terms of a capacity to produce and understand an infinite number and variety of novel utterances of a language, within a finite set of rules. Chomsky's definition places an inordinate emphasis on the structure of language. Relatively recent approaches subordinate structure to function by accounting for communicative intent, available reference and coding alternatives in the realization of speech acts. Chomsky's definition has major implications in the applied fields because it points out how approaches based on products of language are rather superficial. Rather than concern ourselves with sentence types and scores, it behooves clinicians to focus on specific cognitive, linguistic, and communicative systems as they operate across sentences and in referential contexts.

Relationships Among Cognition, Language, and Communication

Cognition is a more generic term than language or communication. Chomsky believes that language is but one aspect of cognition. Verbal behavior is the product of underlying perceptions, thoughts, and mental operations. Linguistic systems are governed to some extent by various cognitive constraints. Thus, language can be said to have cognitive underpinnings. This means that clinicians dealing with verbal behavior must deal with cognitive systems and processes as the underpinnings of verbal behavior.

The primacy of cognition is most clearly apparent in the early stages of language development (Piaget 1961; Bloom 1970; Bruner 1964; Werner and Kaplan 1963; Brown 1973b; Sinclair-deZwart 1969). However, this primacy appears to wane to the point that verbal behavior can facilitate cognitive development *and* cognition can facilitate language development. This shift away from a cognitive primacy to a dual function is what Bloom (1972, 1975) regarded as *crossover*. Chafe (1970, p. 31) indicated that concept and symbol became "freed from each other to the extent that change could modify either one without affecting the other." Apparently Vygotsky (1962) was referring to this dual function in his account of "spontaneous" and "scientific" word learning strategies. In a spontaneous strategy a word serves to consolidate experience by labeling things that had previously been spontaneously deduced from experience. The meaning of the word becomes spontaneously evident. In a scientific strategy a word or label leads to hypotheses about its alternative meanings. McNeill's (1970) concepts of horizontal and vertical strategies in word learning parallel Vygotsky's concepts of spontaneous and scientific strategies. The crossover relationship between cognition and language seems to occur well after attainment of object permanence, probably early in the Piagetian preoperational stage. The crossover function gives an individual considerable cognitive power to deal with his world. As Bruner (1964, p. 4) put it,

> In effect language provides a means, not only for representing experience, but also for transforming it. . . . Once the child has succeeded in internalizing language as a cogni-

tive instrument, it becomes possible for him to represent and systematically transform the regularities of experience with far greater flexibility and power than before.

Language or linguistic systems are only one of several communicative devices. An individual must also know and appropriately use nonlinguistic, paralinguistic, and metareferential devices in communication. One cannot deal with language without considering communicative processes and the roles that linguistic systems play in communication. The study of verbal learning and verbal behavior extends to underlying cognitive systems and processes, as well as communicative systems and processes.

Clinicians must recognize that understanding cognition is basic to any attempt to deal with language assessment or intervention. Similarly, such efforts must also deal with communicative systems and processes. Any attempt to deal with language without taking into account its cognitive underpinnings is superficial. Any attempt to deal with language without considering communicative intent is weak and vulnerable to distortion (Schlesinger 1971; Bowerman 1973; Bruner 1975; Dore 1974; Halliday 1975; Searle 1969). Clinicians need to keep these relationships in mind as they consider the various assessment and intervention programs that are available in the applied fields. As a rule of thumb, procedures that isolate and segment verbal behavior into categories are more vulnerable than those which provide patterns of performance about systems and processes. Perhaps interrelationships among cognition, language, and communication can be appreciated by knowing the scope of grammar.

The Scope of Grammar

Clinicians have had to reorient themselves to new concepts of language and grammar. Traditionally, language and grammar were virtually synonymous and pertained to sentence building or syntax. Today, however, the scope of grammar is much broader and more encompassing. It can be viewed in two complementary ways—structurally and functionally. According to Cazden (1971a, p. 1167), the scope of grammar from a structural point of view extends from one's underlying thoughts, meanings, or communicative intents to making the sound patterns of one's language (see Fig. 2-1). Notice that this is an elaboration of Miller's definition of grammar. It is evident that cognition is basic to grammar—an elaboration in which semantics is on one end and phonology the other with syntax as a formal realization of meaning (Halliday 1975). In this perspective, form is subordinate to function. It is basic because meaning pertains to one's underlying concepts, these concepts must be formulated into a linguistic code, and mental operations are needed to produce a linguistic code in speech sound patterns. The scope of grammar embraces three domains of language structure: semantic, syntactic, and phonological. These are inextricably related. For example, it is impossible to consider syntax independent of semantics or phonology independent of syntax without distortion. This is a very common error in the applied fields. Speech articulation and concept formation are frequently thought of as sepa-

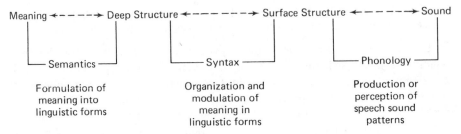

Figure 2-1 *The scope of grammar: structure. (Adapted from Cazden, "The Psychology of Language,* in Handbook of Speech Pathology and Audiology, *Lee Edward Travis, ed., © 1971, p. 1176. By permission of Prentice-Hall, Inc.)*

rate from language. Grammar extends from thought to the production of speech sound patterns.

Additionally, the scope of grammar can be viewed from a functional perspective. Functional perspectives are of two types: intrapersonal and interpersonal. Figure 2-2 illustrates these. Psycholinguistics deals with *intra*personal language functions. There seem to be two main types of these: mediation and representation. Halliday (1975) regards intrapersonal functions as ideational (representative, referential, cognitive). Language can facilitate concept development, conversion of information in short-term memory to long-term memory, or problem solving. These are mediational functions. When language serves these functions, it is said to have mediated a concept, provided a rehearsal strategy, or given a solution. Students find that one of the best ways to study is to discuss the material with someone else. Talking it over helps them understand an issue better than if they simply memorize it. Sometimes language can interfere with concept development, problem solving, and even language learning (Courtright and Courtright 1976), depending upon such things as learning level, competing stimuli, cognitive-emotional set, etc. When language facilitates cognitive processing, it is said to *mediate.*

The other main type of intrapersonal function is representation. *Representation* is the use of language to code or map one's thoughts. This is done for two reasons: (1) to categorize or classify one's experiences in an efficient way in order to integrate various experiences and remember such experiences, and (2) to convey intended meanings to someone else. This is an *inter*personal language function, called communication. The field of sociolinguistics deals with interpersonal language functions. Halliday (1975) indicated that interpersonal language functions are expressive-

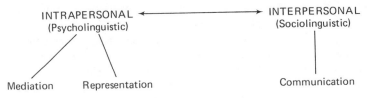

Figure 2-2 *The scope of grammar: functions.*

conative,[3] stylistic, and social. Cromer (1976) summarized both mediational and representational functions of language by indicating that language speeds up representation, transcends immediate time and space, and provides a means of dealing with many things at once.

Clinicians have generally been unaware of the mediational and representational functions of language. While they have recognized the communicative function, they have been rather remiss in appreciating mapping and coding functions. The applied fields have traditionally approached language as sets of words and sentences to be mastered virtually independent of one's intent to code a particular idea for a particular purpose. Much of what has been done in the applied fields deals with language out of communicative context. Students and clients have been trained to learn "core vocabularies" and build sentences in an academic, nonfunctional way. An appreciation of both intrapersonal and interpersonal functions should go a long way toward rectifying the traditional practice of dealing with language out of its natural functional context.

Intrapersonal and Interpersonal Constraints

Theoretically, anyone who knows a language can produce an utterance of infinite length and complexity or an infinite number of utterances. However, we do not do it that way. Utterances are specific to a particular occasion. Rather than display our grammatical capacities, a variety of constraints operate which result in limited performance.

Nelson (1974) held that a young child is coping with several kinds of constraints: attention, memory, inference, knowledge, and strategy. Carroll (1964) and Cazden (1967) have delimited intrapersonal constraints which influence and determine the particular utterances that are spoken. Figure 2-3 was adapted from Cazden (1967). There are both long- and short-term intra- and interpersonal constraints. The long-

[3]Expressive-conation refers to the use of language in sharing one's thoughts and ideas with someone and in the process realizing other thoughts and ideas.

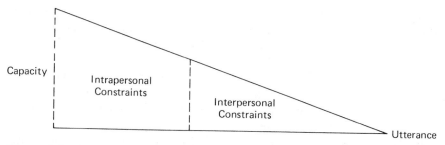

Figure 2-3 *Intrapersonal constraints and interpersonal constraints. (Adapted from Cazden 1967.)*

term ones include mental retardation, physiological disturbances, deafness, and aphasia. Short-term intrapersonal constraints include temporary illness, fatigue, intoxication, and distraction. Long-term interpersonal constraints include socioeconomic status and ethnic cultural influences. Short-term interpersonal constraints pertain to perceived roles, personal relationships, etc. Given the various constraints that serve to determine a particular utterance, it is a fallacy to take a single language sample as evidence of an individual's verbal capacities.

Very young children have considerable difficulties with memory constraints, particularly with memory processing capacity and with certain types of memory (Slobin 1970; Olson 1973; Ervin-Tripp 1973). Contrary to a prevailing idea in the applied fields, young children do not have as much difficulty with memory span as with processing capacity. Indeed, memory span data are rather trivial compared to type of memory, processing strategies, and chunking operations. As long ago as 1938, Blankenship demonstrated that digit memory span is hopelessly confounded and virtually meaningless. Its cousin, mean length of utterance (MLU), is also hopelessly confounded for children older than four years of age: above the age of four, MLU reflects situational and status variables more than developmental variables (Shriner 1969; Hunt 1964). Yet, the applied fields continue to value digit memory span as an index of memory capacity and mean length of utterance as an index of linguistic development in children over four years of age.

The Difference Between Language Knowledge and Use

It is one thing for children to learn the linguistic systems, mechanisms, or devices of their language, dialect, and idiolect, but quite a different matter to learn their appropriate use. Except for some rather subtle aspects of language learning, children have acquired essentially adult knowledge of their language by about four or five years of age (Bloom 1975; Palermo and Molfese 1972). This is a remarkable feat because of what is learned in only a few years with only brief, somewhat fragmentary contacts with one's language (Nelson 1974). It is all the more remarkable because they have to acquire a cognitive basis for language learning before learning linguistic systems, mechanisms, and devices (Macnamara 1972; Nelson 1973, 1974). Yet they do not develop their cognitive systems completely before they engage in language learning. They engage in both cognitive learning and language learning simultaneously. *The Original Thinking Game* (Bruner 1974) and *The Original Word Game* (Brown 1958b) are closely related processes going on simultaneously in the child, although there appears to be somewhat of a lag in which the former is antecedent to the latter. Thus, it is through development in both underlying cognitive systems and a developing awareness of linguistic mechanisms that children obtain the essentials of language knowledge by preschool age.

Further language learning will of course occur. The purpose of language learning will then be to reconcile certain inconsistencies and to discover rather subtle nuances (Cromer 1976; Chomsky 1969; McNeill 1970; Rosenbaum 1967; Palermo and Molfese 1972; Bloom 1975). Language learning continues throughout life in the semantic domain through continuous differentiation and reorganization of concepts through continued experience (Nelson 1973, 1974). Important developments beyond the preschool period, such as the concrete-operations stage and the formal-operations stage, are yet to be realized in cognition (Piaget 1954, 1962, 1970). In adolescence the acquisition of cognitive skills obviously entails dialectics (Riegel 1975). While preschool children may have vestigial communicative skills, this area evidences the greatest amount of growth from then to about age ten or twelve. During this time, children learn to be efficient in coding messages, develop a role-taking attitude that is used to perceive listener cues in communication, and develop selection rules for coding the best message for a perceived context. Thus preschool children have assimilated a great deal, but they have a great deal more yet to learn.

It has been demonstrated that preschool children know virtually all of the rules of adult language except for some subtle nuances (Menyuk 1964a,b). Yet there is a considerable difference between the language of preschool children and that of adults. Aside from vocabulary, the difference is facility or use of language. Preschool children are not as adept in language use as adults. They need to learn the rules of language use from two different perspectives: *efficiency* and *appropriateness*. They tend to string out a series of utterances in which small or slight changes are made from one utterance to the next. A young child might say, "Mommy, I saw a kitty. The kitty was pretty. The kitty was soft. The kitty is Tom. Mommy, the kitty has tiny fingernails. The kitty has sharp fingernails." An adult would be much more efficient, saying, "I saw a pretty cat named Tom with soft fur and sharp claws." Of course, such an utterance would be addressed to another adult. This raises the issue of appropriateness.

Speakers have options concerning not only what they want to talk about but also how they can code a message in a particular context for a particular effect. They use *selection rules,* which pertain to the psychosocial dynamics of a situation. This is sociolinguistics or pragmatics. Children need to learn how to selectively produce the appropriate code for a particular context; they need to know the rules of language usage. This is very complex. Susan Ervin-Tripp (1971, p. 37) put it, ". . . everything that can be said about linguistic rules can be said about socio-linguistic rules." We are all aware that children are sometimes startlingly frank. We sometimes attribute this to honesty. But it is probably not honesty so much as it is a child's inability to select an alternative code that would be more propitious or appropriate to the particular circumstance.

The distinction between language knowledge and language usage is very important in both assessment and intervention. It is imperative to obtain language samples in several varied contexts in order to sufficiently assess the individual's command of language. If a clinician relies on only a single language sample of an arbitrary length, usually fifty or one hundred utterances, the probability is high that the sample reveals more about language usage than language knowledge.

Switching in Language

Verbal behavior is very versatile. We can have not only different referents for a given message, but different messages for the same referent. This is important because if one code does not work then a speaker can switch to another. Speakers spontaneously change to new codes in the course of reconciling communicative obstacles (Muma 1975a; Longhurst and Reichle 1975; Glucksberg, Krauss, and Higgins 1975).

Speakers and listeners switch not only codes but also modalities, both in oral and in written behavior. It is easy for humans to change from speaking to listening, reading to writing, listening to writing, speaking to writing, writing to speaking, etc. However, switching modalities between input and output is very difficult for nonhumans because it is very difficult for them to transfer information via intermodal cortical tracts (Geschwind 1965a,b; Cromer 1976). That is, nonhumans have considerable difficulty learning something in one modality, visually for example, then transferring the information to another modality, say auditory.

Another form of switching occurs in verbal style. An adult can readily switch from a formal style of speaking to an informal style, and vice versa. We can speak technically to a colleague, but in the next instant switch to a very casual style.

Still another form of switching is the use of language to convey rational thought and to express emotive states. Humans can express concepts, ideas, and logic. Further, we can express love, anger, happiness, fear, and many other emotional states. Only humans—and to a limited degree specially trained chimpanzees (Kellogg 1968; Gardner and Gardner 1969; McNeill, 1970; Limber 1977)—can switch the use of language in conveying thoughts and emotions.

Finally, switching occurs between coding systems according to which one coding system or another has priority in conveying a message. A message can be conveyed in several ways—linguistically, nonlinguistically, paralinguistically, contextually, and even metareferentially. These coding systems and devices occur in combination. Rarely, if ever, do they occur in isolation. However, the priority of coding systems or devices varies from message to message and circumstance to circumstance.

Perhaps it is best to consider what these coding systems and devices are like before illustrating the switching of priorities. Linguistic coding systems and devices are those which issue from the semantic-syntactic-phonological/graphemic mechanisms of language. They produce sentences and partial sentences. They are more elaborate, versatile, and referentially powerful than nonlinguistic coding systems and devices, which include such things as body language or kinetics, gestures, facial expressions, eye contact, touching, holding, and movement in special relationships to people and things. Several reviews of nonverbal communicative behaviors are available (Maclay and Osgood 1959; Duncan 1969; Birdwhistell 1970; Mehrabrian 1972; Wiener et al. 1972; Franklin 1973; Knapp 1972; Rochester 1973; Boomer 1965; Bruneau 1973). Paralinguistic devices are coding mechanisms that are superimposed on a linguistic message. These include pausing and other hesitation phenomena, unusual stress or intonations, rate variations, and possibly aspirations and certain gestures. Mahl (1958), Kasl and Mahl (1965), and Goldman-Eisler (1972) demonstrated psychological-behavioral distinctions between ''ah'' and ''non-ah'' hesitation phenomena in spontaneous speech. ''Ah'' behaviors indicate information processing whereas ''non-ah'' behaviors indicate anxiety states. Meta-referential devices draw attention to the code itself by notifying listeners that in the maze of competing coding devices they should specifically attend to a particular element. Listeners may use such metareferential utterances as: ''Tell it like it is''; ''Don't give me any of that jive''; ''Don't gimme any of that highfalutin stuff''; ''Talk like us, not like a politician.'' Speakers can also make metareferential comments that prepare the listener: ''I'm going to use a technical term—deixis.'' Notice that these statements are admonishments concerning one's willingness to adapt to the needs of another in overcoming certain communicative obstacles. Metareferential acts have been described by Rosenberg and Cohen (1966).

These systems and devices can be readily illustrated. Linguistically, someone might say, ''I liked that movie.'' But nonlinguistically, he may produce a facial expression, nod his head, or make a gesture that gives quite a different message than what was coded linguistically. Paralinguistically, the same utterance may contain an unusual pause, stress, or intonation to convert a declarative statement to a negative, interrogative, or emphatic one.

Clearly, linguistic codes do not stand alone. They are cast into a matrix of other coding devices and shifting priorities in the use of these devices. The various switching mechanisms in verbal behavior provide further evidence that such behavior is dynamic.

Clinicians have been prone to think that linguistic devices are the only important aspects of verbal behavior. Many programs are directed toward linguistic performance alone, with little, if any, attention given to alternative coding devices, and virtually no recognition that a linguistic code appears in a matrix of other codes which are specific to a particular communicative intention and context. Clinicians must perceive the ''big picture'' by regarding the entire communicative process rather than the small incremental view on sentence building and vocabulary size.

Language Modalities

Language can take many forms. We generally speak of expressive and receptive modalities of language. Figure 2-4 depicts these primary expressive and receptive modalities. Expressive modalities are speech and writing; receptive modalities are listening and reading. Speech and listening are regarded as the primary modalities because they are usually acquired first and used most, except by the deaf.

A common misconception is that these modalities are unique and rather independent. While there are obvious differences, and modalities are only semi-independent (Bolinger 1975, p. 478), they are more alike than different, more

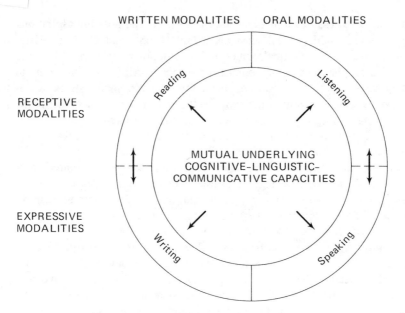

Figure 2-4 *Schematic indicating interrelations between language modalities.*

intimately related than independent. They share mutual underlying cognitive-linguistic-communicative systems and processes, that in their essentials are the same for all modalities but differ in surface features. For example, the pronominal system is the same for speech, listening, reading, and writing. The only difference is whether the surface form of the pronominal system will be in *phonemes* (speech sound patterns) or *graphemes* (printed or written language patterns). When we think in these terms, the similarities between modalities are considerable and the differences seem rather minor.

Knowledge of this interrelatedness has considerable implications for the applied fields. Rather than attempt to identify relative modality performance, which, of course, is the basic strategy in using the *Illinois Tests of Psycholinguistic Abilities* (ITPA) (Kirk, McCarthy, and Kirk 1968), one should deal with underlying cognitive-linguistic systems—a more substantial psycholinguistic inquiry. This is not to say that intermodality performance is not important. It is. But there are more fundamental psycholinguistic questions that underlly such performance.

Verbal Style

Speakers of a language have options not only about what to say, but also about how to say it. Someone who wishes to talk about a horse winning a race, for example, has innumerable ways of doing it. He might say any one of the following:

"He won!"
"Big Daddy did it."
"I won!"
"The chestnut bay won!"
"I'll be hog-swallowed."
"Damn it, he won."

The point is that speakers have many choices about the verbal forms they use. A person might speak formally on one occasion, less formally on another, technically on another, and very informally on another, perhaps even swearing or cursing. Yet all of these may be about the same event, such as winning a horse race. These options are called stylistic options. A formal style is called an *acrolect,* everyday speech is called a *mesolect,* and vulgar speech is a *basolect.*

The most important determinants in the use of different styles are the social dynamics of a situation and their influence on a speaker's selection rules in generating utterances. The applied fields have been somewhat remiss in appreciating stylistic variations.

Communicative Intent

Speakers do not produce just any utterances. They selectively produce those which they believe appropriate to a topic and which fulfill their communicative intentions. Verbal behavior is to a large extent determined by this intent (Schlesinger 1971; Bowerman 1973). Children do not do as well with language when communicative intent is removed (Slobin and Welch 1971; Bloom 1974).

A common problem in the applied fields is the attempt to deal with language in the absence of communicative intent. Clinicians must be aware whether or not communicative intent is operating, for verbal behavior varies significantly thereby.

Available Reference

Available reference is also an important determinant of what is said. Available reference means those referents, actual or presumed, that a message is about. An individual may utter a partial message because he thinks it is the best way to convey his intent in a particular situation. But he must take into account the referents that may be coded in a message. He could say "the pencil" if a pencil and a pen were the referents available. However, if the referents were two pencils, "the pencil" is not an adequate code; it would be necessary to say "the long pencil," or "the nearest pencil," if those are the salient attributes for the referents. The point is that the utterances one makes are not simply products of one's knowledge of cognitive-linguistic systems and processes. They are also determined by communicative intent and perceived available reference (Olson 1970, 1971). As Brown (1958a) argued, names and other labeling behavior—objects, actions, relationships, and emotions in words, phrases, and sentences—do not depend on the most frequently occurring labels but on appropriateness and efficiency in the context of available reference and communicative intent.

Most efforts to deal with language in the applied fields do not ascertain the relationships between a code and available referents or communicative intent. This is particularly true in language assessment where language samples are taken and analyzed without due consideration for available referents and underlying intents. Olson (1970), Bloom (1970, 1973), Schlesinger (1971), and Bowerman (1973) have demonstrated that to consider the form of utterances without considering the underlying meaning or intent in the context of available referents is to misconstrue the essence of language. Such practices lead to distortion and misrepresentation.

Linguistic and Referential Contexts

Communicative intent pertains to communicative context. Available reference pertains to referential context. Language functions (see Fig. 2-2) pertain to both communicative context and referential context. Additionally, we can speak in terms of linguistic context. In all of these, the most general or generic term is *context*.

Contexts are very important in verbal behavior. The more behavior is segmented and extracted from various contexts, the more vulnerable clinicians become to distortion and misunderstanding. Language is most fully understood in communicative context (Lakoff 1972; Halliday 1975; Bates 1976; Bruner 1975; Schank 1972; Winograd 1972; Dore 1975). Any behavior becomes distorted when it is removed from natural contexts. For this reason, much of what is known about child development is "ecologically invalid" (Bronfenbrenner 1974, 1977; Proshansky 1976; Brooks and Baumeister 1977).

Verbal learning and verbal behavior are strongly influenced by contexts. The applied fields can no longer afford to rely on frequency counts or to segment verbal behavior into isolated elements such as single words or phonemes. While for certain purposes it may be necessary to deal with verbal behavior out of its communicative context, it is important not to neglect other contextual influences. It is important to maintain contextual information by looking at the patterns of behavior rather than reducing behavior to normative categories or quantitative units. Contextual information must be maintained by accounting for co-occurring and covarying behaviors.

Apparently co-occurring systems are important determinants in the acquisition and early use of new grammatical forms and functions. Again Slobin's statement is pertinent: "New forms first express old functions, and new functions are first expressed by old forms" (1970, p. 2). *Linguistic context* pertains to various co-occurring semantic-syntactic-phonological systems in an individual's utterances. These systems may vary somewhat. The variations are constrained not only by language but also by one's knowledge and early usage. Thus, linguistic context is very important in clinical assessment and intervention. While developmental sequences are highly stable within grammatical systems (Brown 1973a,b; Brown, Cazden, and Bellugi-Klima 1969), co-occurring systems in language learning and usage vary from individual to individual. Such variations raise questions of using normative assessment and structured intervention.

Individual covarying systems in language learning and usage go a long way to explain the dampened oscillatory function in error reduction reported by Menyuk (1964a). Language learning in this respect might be similar to socioemotional development, in which young children need to establish a security base from which they can extend themselves cognitively and socially. A young child will first play next to his mother, then venture away from her in discovering new things. But he will retreat to the security base under stranger-anxiety or in anticipation of separation-anxiety (Ainsworth 1969; Bowlby 1969; Antonucci 1976).

In language learning, co-occurring systems and functions apparently constitute a security base from which an individual can extend himself. A dampened oscillatory function is a sequence in which at first many errors occur, followed by a swing of increasingly fewer errors, then a rise again to more errors, though not as many as before, since something has been learned. Presumably the increase of errors is precipitated by venturing away from a secure linguistic base to a new system, while probably maintaining to a certain degree the secure base by co-occurring systems. The reduction of errors phase reflects a "linguistic retreat" to known systems in known co-occurring contexts. Linguistic ventures can be made by extending a target system or by varying co-occurring systems—extending structure while maintaining function, or extending function while maintaining structure (Slobin 1970).

It is possible that a child may be extending from a linguistic base in those cyclic interactions between parent and child, in which after two or three exchanges the child varies his production (Brown and Bellugi 1964; Ervin-Tripp 1966). Bloom (1972) held that a child may need one or two opportunities to orient himself to a linguistic event in cyclic exchanges between child and parent. This may be a function of spontaneous imitation (Bloom, Hood, and Lightbown 1974; Ramer 1976).

Certain pronominals will appear in the context of some co-occurring systems in early language learning and usage. The particular co-occurring systems will vary from individual to individual. It behooves clinicians to identify co-occurring systems for their target systems, because such information provides very useful alternatives for exploiting an individual's behavior in intervention (Muma 1973a,b). Since children apparently control structure while attempting something new in function—and vice versa—it is necessary to carry out clinical assessment and intervention by mapping *referential context* in terms of semantic functions and relationships (Brown 1973a,b; Schlesinger 1971; Bowerman 1973; Halliday 1975; Chafe 1970; Lakoff 1972a,b). Clinicians have begun to adopt this strategy (Leonard 1975a,b; Miller and Yoder 1974; Ruder and Smith 1974; Duchan and Erickson 1976). Referential context also pertains to available reference, actual or presumed.

Linguistic and referential contexts offer clinicians a great deal of assessment and intervention power, since they are directly relevant to individual differences and are ecologically valid. However, they are relatively new concepts to clinicians. Clinicians who have used them find them valuable; those who have not say they are too difficult or too time consuming to warrant the effort. Although it is desirable to have a technical orientation to identify co-occurrence patterns, it is not necessary. I have had students with no special training in linguistics who were very successful in extracting them. It is a time-consuming process, but more powerful than any normative test. It is this type of information that is needed to deal with the individual differences so evident in clinical assessment and intervention. Linguistic and referential context procedures redirect clinical work from a *data* orientation to an *evidence* orientation.

As to the time question, the amount of time spent is not prohibitively long. Within half a day we are able to identify co-occurrences for three or four target systems—more than enough information to keep a clinician productively directed in intervention. Crystal, Fletcher, and Garman (1976) also report that a satisfactory linguistic analysis can be obtained in about a half a day. And, of course, such procedures are selectively used for certain individuals. It is not wise to categorically dismiss a procedure because it may be time consuming. Such a statement could be a way of dismissing one's responsibilities and thus be evidence of the calibre of the professional. What would happen if one came with an appendicitis attack to a medical doctor and was told, "It takes too much time. Today I'm treating only colds or illnesses that require pills." Some clinical conditions today are being treated with "pills" when they need "operations."

Status and Process Orientation

A *status orientation* views an individual's verbal behavior in terms of grammatical products—e.g., mean utterance length, sentence type, and vocabulary size—and uses various qualification measures such as norms. A *process orientation* views an individual's verbal behavior in terms of systems or processes—e.g., pronominal system, auxiliary system, adjectival systems, transitive systems, negations, determiner systems, etc. A process orientation accounts not only for target systems but for co-occurring systems and developmental sequences as well.

Psychology and linguistics have process orientations. The applied fields have a rather strong status orientation by virtue of their commitment to normative measures. However, in recent years there has been a marked shift in the applied fields toward a process orientation.

Important Theoretical Positions About Grammar and Language

Clinicians typically do not have sufficient time or opportunity to know all the various theoretical positions on grammar. However, they should be aware of the major theoretical orientations and shifts of orientations. It would also be useful to have some understanding of why these theoretical shifts occur.

Around the turn of the century, taxonomic and structuralistic orientations prevailed. A *taxonomic orientation* is one that deals with categories, e.g., "parts of speech," sentence types, etc. A *structuralistic orientation* is one that deals with inventorying and cataloging language forms. Structuralism is a rather elaborate form of a taxonomic orientation. The traditional views of language were essentially structuralistic. Their primary goals seemed to be to identify and delineate languages in terms of their forms or structures. In the instance of American English, structuralism provided a definition of Standard English and "correctness" that became the traditional but somewhat mythical goal of American education.

The traditional orientation on Standard English gave way to a psycholinguistic orientation (Roberts 1964). This happened for several reasons, which are summarized and compared below:

Traditional	*Psycholinguistic*
(a) Imitative model	(a) Generative model— novel utterances
(b) Language products	(b) Grammatical processes
(c) Grammar equals language structure	(c) Grammar equals psychological capacity
(d) Atheoretical-empirical	(d) Theoretical-descriptive, explanatory
(e) Inventory of structural types	(e) Generative mechanisms
(f) Performance	(f) Competence and performance
(g) Form	(g) Form and function

In the early 1960s there was considerable interest in transformational generative—or TG—grammars. These had two major dimensions: phrase structure or base rules, and transformational operations. TG grammars were structuralistic in that they were addressed to syntactic generative capacities for producing an infinite number and variety of sentences of a language, but not nonsentences. TG grammars were superior to taxonomic ones because they were theoretical (Tuniks 1963) and dealt with concepts of verbal capacity and usage rather than inventories of language, or verbal products. However, TG grammars had two major limitations: an inordinate focus on syntax (to the virtual exclusion of semantics) and a failure to provide explanatory adequacy, although they were quite successful in providing descriptive adequacy. Miller (1962, 1965); Bateman and Zidonis (1966); O'Donnell, Griffin, and Norris (1967); and Frank and Osser (1970) held that transformational operations were mental increments in sentence complexity. However, the work of Clifton and Odom (1966) discounted this proposition. The studies by Johnson (1965, 1966) and Yngve (1960) indicate that underlying hierarchical structures extend to transformational operations. Transformational descriptions have been very useful in portraying language development (Brown 1968; Menyuk 1964b, 1969; O'Donnell, Griffin, and Norris 1967), and continue to have a valuable potential for describing clinical conditions (Muma 1971a; McDonald and Blott 1974; Jacobs and Rosenbaum 1968; Engler et al. 1973; Quirk and Greenbaum 1973; Crystal, Fletcher, and Garman 1976).

At the end of the 1960s two major shifts of orientation occurred. TG grammars were found to be seriously lacking, because they were almost exclusively about language *structure*. They had little or nothing to do with language *functions*. Bloom (1970, 1973) showed that the referents of an utterance are needed in order to understand its referential functions. Accordingly, a major shift occurred in which structure became subordinate to function. Functions were viewed as semantic and relational. Utterances were analyzed in terms not so much of their syntactic structures but of their semantic and relational functions. This emphasis on language from a functional point of view was espoused by Fillemore's (1968) case grammar. Various elaborations on case grammars or generative semantic theories have emerged in recent years (Lakoff 1972a,b; Chafe 1970; Ingram 1971a; Halliday 1975; Perfetti 1972). And, of course, semantic theories extend into underlying cognitive development—most notably in the applications of Piagetian psychology to language learning (Sinclair-deZwart 1969, 1970, 1971; Bloom 1970, 1973; Nelson 1973, 1974; and to some extent E. Clark 1973a,b).

The second major shift was to view language from a broad perspective-communicative context. This shift focused on the role of communicative intent (Schlesinger 1971; Bowerman 1973), the emergence of referential skills in the communicative process (Flavell et al. 1968; Glucksberg, Krauss, and Higgins 1975), available reference (Brown 1958a; Olson 1970), and the psychology of speech acts (Searle 1969; Sadock 1974; Halliday 1975; Dore 1974, 1975; Wells 1974; Bruner 1975; Bates 1976). Thus, the study of verbal behavior has seen major shifts away from language structure to function—an emphasis on cognitive underpinnings for emerging communication skills.

Parenthetically, behaviorists—particularly behavior modificationists and associationists (S-R theorists)—have attempted to apply their concepts to verbal behavior. These concepts have been largely discounted despite Skinner's (1957) bold effort and various behavior modification studies (Guess, Sailor, and Baer 1974; Guess et al. 1968). Behavior modification may be effective in altering performance, but there is some question as to its effect on language learning. The repeated failure of generalization and "reversal learning" justifies this conclusion. Behavior modification is waning as an influential procedure (Krasner 1976). As for associationists, it is noteworthy that three of the most prominent associationists—Jenkins (1974), Palermo (1971), and Deese (1970)—concede that S-R theories are inadequate to account for verbal behavior.

Furthermore, in principle, such S-R analyses of language behavior can never adequately account for the acquisition and maintenance of language (Palermo 1971).

If we were to argue that a sentence is nothing more than a complicated kind of conditioned response (as has been suggested; see Mowrer, 1954, for example) or a set of associations, or some more complicated version of these via the principle of mediation (see Osgood, 1968), we would be asserting (1) that each element in a sentence is a reaction to some preceding stimulus, and (2) these reactions are chained together in a string. There are several ways of showing that these two propositions are false (Chomsky 1956, in Deese 1970, p. 5).

These operations—which constitute the result of generative theory—cannot be accounted for, derived from, or otherwise interpreted within the traditional psychological points of view about intellectual processes. They are particularly difficult for any theory that reduces cognition to associations between elements (Deese 1970, p. 42).

Inasmuch as the information processing model (Shannon and Weaver 1949; Osgood 1957) underlies some widely used clinical assessment and intervention procedures, perhaps something should be said about it. This model deals with the input, association, and output components of information processing. In clinical assessment, this model underpins the following tests: *Illinois Tests of Psycholinguistic Abilities* (Kirk, McCarthy, and Kirk 1968), *Examining for Aphasia* (Eisenson 1954), *The Language Modalities Tests for Aphasia* (Wepman and Jones 1961), *Minnesota Test for Differential Diagnosis of Aphasia* (Schuell 1965; Schuell, Jenkins, and Jimenez-Pabon 1964). Unfortunately, the clinical application of the information processing model reduces to modality performance—auditory sequencing, visual sequencing, etc.—which is secondary to underlying cognitive-linguistic-communicative capacities. The clinical applications of the information processing models deal with superficial aspects of verbal behavior.

Myths About Imitation, Comprehension, and Production (ICP)

It is commonly thought in the applied fields that imitation is easier than comprehension and that comprehension is easier than production. Studies by Fraser, Bellugi, and Brown (1963), and Lovell and Dixon (1967) support this view, and the *Northwestern Syntax Screening Test* (Lee 1969) is based upon it. However, there is some question whether there is indeed a relative difficulty between imitation, comprehension, and production.

The production task is actually delayed imitation in the studies cited; it lacks both available referents and communicative intent. Recent studies on the imitation of spontaneous production have revealed very different findings (Bloom 1974; Slobin and Welsh 1971). Children's spontaneous productions may exceed imitative performance, especially if imitation is outside of a communicative context, i.e., free of available referents and intent. Moreover, comprehension varies as a function of available referents, linguistic complexity, intent, and so on (Bloom 1974; Huttenlocher 1974; Winograd 1972; Schank 1972; Ingram 1974a). It appears that the notion of ease of processing between imitation, comprehension, and production has been too simplified in the applied fields. It is necessary to understand the entire communicative context.

What Is Simple?

What may be simple to adults may not be simple to children. Unfortunately, a prevailing attitude in the applied fields is based upon the contradictory proposition, that what is simple for adults is also simple for children. This, however, is probably not the case.

Adults intuitively believe that simplicity in language is defined by beginning with the smallest unit and building up to the most complex unit. This is probably correct. The difficulty is knowing the simplest starting point. There are several views in the applied fields on this. One appears in phonology: first sound in isolation, then syllable, word, phrase, and sentence. Another crops up in cognition, where the following sequence is frequently given: sensation, discrimination, perception, and conception. In syntax, this sequence is often encountered: nouns, verbs, adjectives, noun-verb combinations, adjective-noun-verb combinations, noun-verb-noun combinations, etc. Another version in syntax is that individuals learn a core vocabulary by labeling activities and then combine these words to make sentences.

However, the developmental literature does not support these notions of simplicity. Indeed, it indicates that much of what is done in the applied fields probably (and unwittingly) makes things more difficult! To reduce sentences to single words in which labels rather than referents are provided and in which communicative intent is omitted increases the difficulty considerably. Even the sequence of noun-verb, adjective-noun-verb, and so on is contradictory to the most prevalent sequence in the developmental literature, verb-noun, verb–modified noun, noun-verb–modified noun (Brown, Cazden, Bellugi-Klima 1969; Limber 1976). In short, the applied fields have some assumptions that should be reexamined and possibly replaced by more justifiable principles.

Summary

Clinicians need to have basic concepts about the nature of language and verbal behavior. They should realize that process orientations are more powerful than normative orientations in clinical assessment and intervention. They should deal with verbal behavior from the broad perspective of cognitive, linguistic, and communicative systems and processes, rather than the narrow perspective of categories. They should, to the extent possible, keep verbal context intact because it allows the opportunity to appreciate co-occurring systems, communicative intent, available reference, and communicative skills. They must realize the primacy of language functions over structure. In short, the new viewpoints appearing in the literature have major implications for clinical assessment and intervention.

3
Cognitive Systems

Language and verbal behavior are first and foremost cognitive behaviors. Our verbal behavior is determined by what we know, by what we perceive and think in a given circumstance, and by the cognitive operations in production and comprehension. Clinicians who deal with retarded, aphasic, and autistic persons, and those with learning disabilities, are keenly interested in cognitive systems. Anyone who undertakes language assessment or intervention must deal with cognitive systems. "Language is used to express the child's cognitions of his environment—physical and social . . ." (Slobin 1973).

Cognition and Language: A Piagetian Perspective

The Piagetian theory is unquestionably the most fully elucidated and studied theory of cognitive development. Scholars of language development have found it offers a great deal in accounting for cognitive underpinnings in language development (Sinclair-deZwart 1969, 1971, 1973a,b; Inhelder 1969; Bloom 1973; Nelson 1973, 1974; Macnamara 1972) and in language learning itself (Sinclair-deZwart 1969, 1973a,b), particularly in disclosing similar developmental processes in cognitive and linguistic development and the separation of sign and signal in the emergence of symbolic functions.

Piagetian theory is *biological* because it rests on the proposition that developmental stages are invariantly manifest as an individual passes through maturational stages. It is also *pragmatic,* because it places an emphasis on the active processing of experience, at first motorically and later cognitively, through assimilation or accommodation. A central concept in the theory is *adaptiveness,* which refers to the processes whereby we learn to deal effectively with the various conditions we encounter. Infants are essentially nonadaptive; they are at the mercy of virtually any circumstance they meet. However, infants begin very early to develop a repertoire of motoric, social, and emotional behaviors that provide increased command over themselves, others, and their environment. The differential crying of infants is *instrumental* because it causes changes in their environment. One cry brings a warm and comforting mother, another occasions a change of diapers, yet another wanes into sleep, and so forth. As infants learn to intentionally grasp, crawl, walk, and talk, they obtain increased power over their surroundings, which constitutes a measure of adaptiveness. *Adaptiveness* is not only power but flexibility, efficiency, and effectiveness in deducing and employing the best means to the best solution or compromise in any particular situation. Adaptiveness may mean action in one circumstance and thought or word in another.

The theory deals with the developmental stages in cognition that lead to increased adaptiveness. According to Piaget, the acquisition of adaptive skills or capacities occurs through two processes: assimilation and accommodation. *Assimilation* is the incorporation of new information into existing schemata or concepts. *Accommodation* is the reorganization of existing schemata or the creation of new ones in order to incorporate information that does not readily correspond to existing ones.

> In assimilatory process reality is modified to match internal organization (or structure) in the brain. In accommodatory process, internal structures are modified in accordance with environmental influence. The former guarantees that reality is not passively copied, and the latter assures that cognitive structures do not have some correspondence to the real world. Assimilation in its extreme form is best seen in fantasy and symbolic play, which are more responsive to the internal structures of the child than to environmental factors. Accommodation, on the other hand, is best exemplified in imitation, which is maximally responsive to environmental influence and can function relatively independently of inner structures. Imitation, then, is a kind of hyperadaptation, while play signifies relaxation from the demands of adaptation (Morehead and Morehead 1974, pp. 154–55).

Figure 3-1 summarizes the Piagetian developmental stages. Piaget states that perception develops differently from cognition. The former develops in a continuous manner, the latter in stages. Each stage involves a period of formation and a period of attainment.

The sensorimotor stage is based upon action patterns that infants at first issue in unintentional reflexive acts, but later in a developing progression of intentional ones. These begin with intrinsically motivated activity and are followed by stereotypic actions to see what happens, behaviors that are produced to achieve a specific goal, and various action patterns toward a goal. Finally, at the end of the sensorimotor stage, children begin to use imagery or mental representation as a means of dealing with their environment, rather than relying exclusively on action-patterned schemata. Early cognitive development comes about through a child's acting on his environment for several reasons—discovering alternative means, alternative solutions, causality, object permanence, and so on. The sensorimotor stage is marked by learning through doing. In the next stage learning occurs primarily through doing plus seeing or hearing—conceptualizing.

The preoperational stage is one in which symbolic behavior begins to emerge. Earlier, a child's schemata consist of both action patterns and imagery, but toward the end of the preoperational stage mental representations become functional. Imagery is a perceptual event in which one cognitively records a picture or image of something.

Figure 3-1 *Summary of Piaget's developmental stages.*

I. *Sensorimotor stage (birth to 18–24 months)*
   A. *Reflexive behavior (birth to 1 month)*
      Innate reflexes prevail; child fused to environmental stimuli.
   B. *Primary circular reactions (1 to 4 months)*
      Repetition intrinsically motivating; lacks intent and purpose; is not aware of environmental effects; reflexive sensory and reflexive motor schemata; begins coordination first within and then between sensory modalities.
   C. *Secondary circular reactions (4 to 6 months)*
      Begins freeing himself from environment by sitting; begins intentional activity; early awareness of causality; coordinates vision and movements of arms and hands; acts on objects; repeats activity because it results in an interesting effect on environment; begins awareness of subject/object action patterns; stereotypic action patterns; "out of sight, out of mind."
   D. *Coordination of secondary reactions (6 to 10 months)*
      Begins problem solving; uses a behavior to obtain a goal whereas previously he produced a behavior just to see what would happen; object permanence; aware that others are sources of action; grasps with thumb apposition; creeping at the middle and end of period; explores.
   E. *Tertiary circular reactions (10 to 18 months)*
      Walking; explorer; active trial-and-error experimentation; vary behavior toward the same object or goal; act and object or means and end clearly differentiated; alternative actions toward an object to discover its potentialities; enjoys novelty; anticipatory behavior—prerepresentational.
   F. *Representation and invention (18 to 24 months)*
      Internal representation and manipulation of reality begins; deferred imitation; mental events freed from action patterns; mental imagery begins.
II. *Preoperational stage (18–24 months to 7 years)*
    Previously schemata were action patterns, now they are symbolic units; toys represent things; only rudimentary classifications—surface features; egocentric or centered; uses words and language but not fully developed concepts and rules; lacks mental representation.
III. *Concrete operations (7 to 12 years)*
     Obtains mental representations—conceptual maps; conservation of relationships; relational terms; degree and contrast rather than absoluteness; class inclusion and categorization, serialization as in sequencing big to little.

Figure 3-1 *(continued).*

IV. *Formal operations (12 years and over)*
Aware of alternatives; develops a hierarchical strategy for solving a problem; deductive thought; will attempt to solve a make-believe or abstract problem; generalized orientation toward problem solving; decentered.

In the early stages, children have difficulty in separating figure/ground relationships (Witkin et al. 1962). Subsequently, they can isolate specific attributes or even clusters of attributes that pertain to a specific figure, topic, or subject. Imagery orientation can be identified by showing children three pictured items, two of which are similar in color (red bird, red cross), two others similar in shape (cross, airplane), and the remaining two similar in function (bird, airplane). When asked to pick two that go together, children in the preoperational stage will pick two items on the basis of color or shape whereas children at the end of this stage will pick two that have similar function.

In the concrete operations stage, children are able to deal effectively with mental representations; they can reconstruct a map of their activity from memory. They can deal effectively with conservation tasks—the ability to maintain the necessary relationships between covarying dimensions even though the dimensions may have been transformed. Thus, a child at this stage would regard two balls of clay as equivalent in mass even after one had been squashed flat. Also, if he saw water poured from a short, wide glass into a tall, narrow glass he would conserve quantity by regarding the total amount of water as remaining the same. Before this stage, children believe there is more water in the taller glass. Figure 3-7 illustrates conservation for liquids, mass, and quantity.

By the formal operations stage deductive thinking has developed. Here, children develop elaborate logical relationships. Moreover, they not only have alternative solutions to a problem but place them in a hierarchy. Thus, given a task, a child in the formal operations stage would develop an elaborate hierarchy of alternative solutions. Riegel (1975) believes there is yet another stage of cognitive development called *dialectical operations*. This, as best I can deduce, means a critical scientific orientation in which the child questions the basic premises and assumptions of things in order to understand them better. Youniss (1974) argued that while Riegel has some important criticisms, they are misplaced. Possibly dialectics is only a different orientation to higher-order cognitive activities.

How does Piagetian theory help us understand language development? First, it shows some interesting parallels between cognitive and linguistic development. Sinclair-deZwart (1971) indicated that (a) spatial and temporal ordering is also manifest in linguistic organization; (b) classifications of objects, actions, and relations have linguistic counterparts in constituent structure; (c) cognitive relationships and states are linguistically coded as subject/predicate, topic/comment (Gruber 1967), or modal/argument (Langacker 1967), modality and proposition (Fillmore

1968), and theme and rheme (Hinds 1975); and (d) embedding and conjoining action schemata. Eventually, concepts have linguistic counterparts in recursiveness and conjunction. Sinclair-deZwart (1969) reported that a partial isomorphism seems to exist between language and logic. Other researchers, including Greenfield, Nelson, and Saltzman (1972) and Goodson and Greenfield (1975), have also shown some parallels between cognition and language. These are consistent with the weak version of the Sapir-Whorf hypothesis espoused by Brown (1956), in which language does not determine thought but predisposes it. Reviews of the Sapir-Whorf hypothesis can be found in Slobin (1971), Carroll (1956), and Cromer (1976).

Second, Piagetian theory underscores the cognitive underpinnings of language development. "The Piagetian position, then, is that language acquisition cannot begin until certain operations of the sensorimotor period have been acquired" (Cromer 1976, p. 306). Sinclair-deZwart (1969) indicated that the first verbal utterances—words—are intimately linked to and contemporaneous with symbolic play, deferred imitation, and mental images as interiorized imitations. These appear at the end of the sensorimotor stage. Thus, the sensorimotor stage, and to some extent the preoperational stage, are very important to language learning. Causality, anticipation, object permanence, and reversibility are essential to concept knowledge, and eventually word knowledge.

Causality is an awareness that cause and effect relationships exist. Some causes are intrinsic—reflexive and volitional activity. Others are observable— actions of oneself toward something or someone and actions of other things toward something or someone. Much later, implied or apparent causative agents and alternative or sequential cause and effect relationships can be deduced. *Anticipation* is a preparedness to deal with an event. One's preparedness indexes his representations of previous relevant experiences. *Object permanence* is the child's awareness of contours in figure/ground perspectives of things about himself, and his ability to form a mental representation of things so that when they are displaced the mental image is retained. The phenomenon of "out of sight, out of mind" does not occur. This is the initial phase of knowing objects rather than actions. *Reversibility* is the ability to appreciate attributes of things without reliving action patterns. This frees one from original learning and establishes a potential for generalization. Sinclair-deZwart (1969) suggests that intellectual operations are actions that have become interiorized and reversible. Studies by Inhelder (1969) and Ferreiro and Sinclair (1971) have shown that nonconservers also have difficulty with spatial reversibility (altered order of sticks by length) and temporal reversibility (altered order of events in time). Moreover, they could not code reversibility in language before they could do it cognitively.

The Piagetian position is that, as cognitive development occurs, the child becomes increasingly able to free himself from direct experience to rely more on representations of experience. This is known as *cognitive distancing*. Infants are "fused" to their environment and subject to environmental stimulation. They are cognitively proximal. Adults, on the other hand, are cognitively distant. They operate from a complex matrix of cognitive representations of past experiences. Sigel (1971a) showed a cognitive distancing continuum from objects to pictorials to words. Pictures are cognitively more distant or representational than objects (actual as opposed to representational objects) and words are cognitively more distant than pictures (Kelly and Tomlinson-Keasey 1976; Beckwith and Thompson 1976). Presumably cognitive distancing can thus be an index of task complexity. If children are having difficulty dealing with words, perhaps it would be wise to shift them to pictures or objects.

I once observed an autistic child and a teacher play with a play house. The child's play was inappropriate for the representational furniture and dolls. However, we switched the situation to an actual kitchen and her behavior became significantly more appropriate. We have had similar experiences with aphasic and learning-disabled individuals.

Sinclair-deZwart (1973b) defined an important principle underlying both cognitive and linguistic development: both contrastive and complementary changes occur in cognition and in language acquisition. Cognitively,

> A logical structure is more powerful, when it becomes more general and less linked to a particular context, whereas understanding of object properties is more powerful, when it becomes more specific and differentiated. We are tempted to think that syntactic structures and lexicon follow similar opposite and complementary directions, with here, too, a close link between the two so that new acquisitions in either lead to new acquisitions in the other (1973b, p. 14).

According to this view, syntactic knowledge is more powerful when it becomes more general, and semantic and phonological knowledge is more powerful when it becomes more specific.

The Piagetian view is that language is part of symbolic function: "The symbolic function can be defined essentially as the capacity to represent reality through the intermediary of signifiers that are distinct from what they signify. The important term in this definition is the word *distinct*" (Sinclair-deZwart 1969, p. 318). *Distinct signifiers* are words, gestures like pointing, or anything that stands for but is separate from a referent. A *signifier* is something that could be a part of what it stands for, such as a motor act. Distinct signifiers are of two types: symbols and signs. *Symbols* have a link of resemblance with an object or event. They are personal, often being invented in play, and are mostly isolated—though within the context of symbolic play. *Signs* are typically words. They are arbitrary, social in that they are shared by others, and form linguistic systems. Distinct signifiers have their roots in imitation. At the end of the sensorimotor stage, symbolic orientation begins; thought becomes representational or detached from action. It is a time when cognitive distancing becomes released from direct stimulation, distinct signifiers begin to appear, and the cognitive underpinnings for verbal behavior have been laid down and a child is about to launch a career of learning linguistic systems, processes, and devices.

According to Cromer (1976, p. 306), "Language is especially important in that it allows three developments to occur." These are: (a) it speeds up representation over what can be done through sensorimotor representation, (b) it provides an ability to transcend immediate space and time, and (c) it provides a means for representing many things simultaneously. Thus, language increases cognitive power.

Piaget and Inhelder regard language as

> A ready-made system that is elaborated by society and that contains, for persons that learn it before they contribute to its enrichment, a wealth of cognitive instruments (relations, classifications, and so on) at the service of thought (1966, p. 69).

Sinclair-deZwart (1969) elaborated:

> The knowing person expressed his "knowledge" in this code. As such, language takes the place of symbolization in the relationship knower-symbolization-known. But this code is itself an object of knowing; as such, it takes the place of the "known" in the knower-known relationship. Piaget stresses mainly the first aspect; most psycholinguists pay attention only to the second (Sinclair-deZwart 1969, p. 326).

Interested readers are directed to the following references: Athey and Rubadeau (1970); Elkind (1967a,b); Elkind and Flavell (1969); Furth and Wach (1974); Ginsburg and Opper (1969); Lavatelli (1970); Sharp (1969); Mussen, Conger, and Kagan (1969); Evans (1973); Issacs (1960); Piaget (1954, 1961, 1962, 1963, 1970); Piaget and Inhelder (1963); Inhelder and Piaget (1964); Inhelder (1969); Sinclair-deZwart (1969, 1971, 1973a,b); Flavell (1963); Furth (1969); and Furth and Youniss (1976). Jon Miller (University of Wisconsin, Madison), Gerald Chappell (University of Wisconsin, Stevens Point), and Donald Morehead (California State University) have developed excellent in-service training sessions on the applications of Piagetian psychology to language learning and clinical practice.

Before leaving the Piagetian orientation it is appropriate to say something about the development of spatial perception. Piagetian theory is heavily grounded in sensorimotor acts. Its position is that the development of perception, being continuous, differs from other aspects of cognition, which develop in stages.

Piaget and Inhelder (1963) show that awareness of perceptual space occurs in different ways according to the type of perceptual space and the awareness *within* and *between* perceptual domains. Awareness within a perceptual domain (visual, auditory, tactile, kinesthetic) always exceeds awareness between domains. A child has much more awareness of the visual domain alone than of the visual and tactile domains together. As for types of perceptual space, Piaget contends there is a developmental sequence in the learning of topological space, projective space, and Euclidean space. *Topological* space is awareness of a point in space or figure/ground relationship. By knowing topological space, one can segment the boundaries of events, as well as part/whole relationships. *Projective space* is the spatial relationship of two or more objects seen from a viewer's perspective. Something has a right side, left side, top, bottom, front, and back with respect to how the viewer perceives the world. What is right or left for the viewer is also right or left for the object perceived, etc. *Euclidean space* is the awareness of the perceptual orientation of another as separate from that of the perceiver. Figure 3-2 depicts the differences between topological, projective, and Euclidean perceptual awareness.

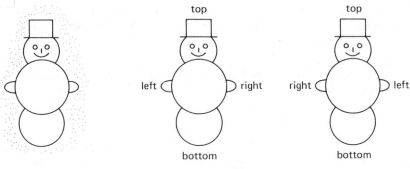

TOPOLOGICAL AWARENESS	PROJECTIVE AWARENESS	EUCLIDEAN AWARENESS
(a) Snowman/background	Viewer's perspective	Viewer's perspective rotated
(b) "body parts"		to conform with that which
(c) hat/snowman		is perceived

Figure 3-2 *Topological awareness, projective awareness, and Euclidean awareness of "snowman."*

Perceptual Space and Time

H. Clark (1973a) holds that awareness of space and time has some interesting patterns of development. These are the symmetry and asymmetry of various perceptual planes. He contends that perceptual space or P-space is discerned before symbolic representations of space, which he calls L-space or language space. He contends that there is a one-to-one relationship between them. He calls this the *correlation hypothesis*. According to it, word meaning is broken down into units of semantic features that correspond to "fundamental categories" of perception. Moreover, Clark suggests that awareness of physical space precedes that of temporal space in development. Thus, terms for physical space can be used in metaphoric ways to refer to temporal space, e.g., "It was a *long* stick." "It took a *long* time."

What does this mean to clinicians? Perhaps an illustration will make the point. Figure 3-3 has one horizontal plane (*A*) and two vertical planes (*B* and *C*) that segment physical or spatial awareness. Plane *A* is a horizontal surface above which is "up" and below which is "down." Note that verticality is asymmetrical in most of our experience, since "up" is above a horizontal plane. Plane *B* shows front-back. This is also asymmetrical in that most of our perceptual experiences are "front." Plane *C* shows right–left-sidedness. Unlike verticality and front-back, right–left-sidedness is symmetrical. It is through experience, conditioning, and possibly cortical wiring, that one may show a preference for sidedness. But perceptually, the right and left sides are equipotential. The anatomical location of the various sensory modalities, coupled with the way we move through space (front to back), defines the perceptual orientations of verticality and front-back as asymmetrical. Of what importance is this? Asymmetry is a means of learning about space and spatial orientation. Moreover, it foretells how temporal relationships are learned. The dynamics of learning about

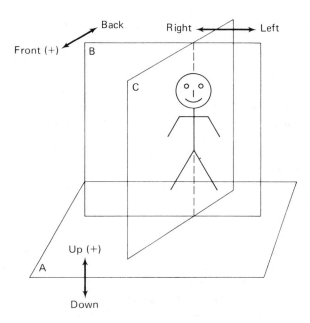

Figure 3-3 *One horizontal (A) and two vertical planes (B and C) that segment spatial awareness. (Derived from H. Clark 1973.)*

space and time determine how spatial and temporal terms are learned. Spatial terms are *dimensional adjectives* such as more, big, tall, fat; and *relational adjectives,* which are various prepositions.

The correlation hypothesis says that as spatial and/or temporal awareness is acquired an individual can learn appropriate terms. However, the acquisition of terms entails further complications, according to the *complexity hypothesis* (H. Clark 1973a) or the *semantic feature hypothesis* (E. Clark 1973). These state that when two terms share the same semantic features, the one with the fewest will be learned first. Learning proceeds from the most general (unmarked) to the most specific (marked). For example, the following paired terms share semantic features: big/little, long/short, more/less, tall/short, and thick/thin. The first term of each pair is unmarked, indexing a dimension, or general semantic function. The second term indexes not only a dimension but a specific, or marked, aspect of it. According to the hypotheses, the positive or unmarked term is learned before the contrastive or marked term.

A correlate of the hypothesis predicts that adult antonyms will be treated as synonyms by the child before the child acquires the most specific semantic features of the antonym pair (Eilers, Oller, and Ellington 1974, p. 196).

However, H. Clark indicated that these hypotheses may not hold in production as they purport to in comprehension. Specifically, although unmarked terms should precede marked in comprehension, marked may precede unmarked in production.

A considerable amount of research has been done in this regard (see the appropriate section in chapter 6). However, the evidence only partially supports these hypotheses. Eilers, Oller, and Ellington (1974) indicate that they need to be refined to provide for alternative strategies for learning marked and unmarked terms. Friedman and Seely (1976) suggest that they were inadequate because (1) the metaphoric relationship between acquisition and spatial and temporal awareness may be too simplified, (2) neither the priority of spatial terms over temporal terms nor the priority of positive (unmarked) terms over marked terms were supported but the findings may be in the *kinds* of semantic features studied, (3) they do not deal with the reorganization of semantic features that inevitably occur, and (4) they do not take into account contextual influences on word meaning.

H. Clark (1973a) also introduced the concept of *canonical encounter.* Canonical encounter is a situation in which two individuals are in the most optimal position for perceiving information from each other. This occurs when they are facing each other in close proximity.

Duchan (1976) has introduced an interesting concept, called *cognitive bias,* that pertains to a child's perceptual awareness and his verbal terms for that perceptual awareness. Cognitive bias is similar to what might be called response preference. Children may have a bias toward objects in terms of their usual action pattern in a Piagetian sense, or perceptual awareness in the E. Clark (1973a) and H. Clark (1973a) sense. Thus, they are biased to relate to objects as they are perceived or can be acted upon, irrespective of verbal cues that may be given. Response bias may account for some of the behavior reported on the acquisition of relational terms (dimensional adjectives, spatial prepositions) such as *in, on, under, more/less, big/little,* and so on. A child may not use a linguistic term to cue the idea of putting something into a container if his cognitive bias already predisposes him to do so. Under cognitive bias, a child is likely to put something in a box whether he is given a linguistic cue or not. Thus, it may be necessary to demonstrate linguistic knowledge for atypical acts. Duchan delineated some stages in the transfer from behavior that is cognitively biased to behavior that is regulated linguistically. First, a child operates exclusively with a cognitive bias interpretation. Verbal cues have no effect. Second, a partial linguistic intrusion occurs on cognitive bias. This appears similar to what Bruner et al. (1966) reported. Specifically, a verbal cue may activate behavior, but momentum of the activity occurs such that a verbal cue will not terminate the behavior. However, Duchan indicated that the partial linguistic intrusion is as Cazden (1972a) put it: a word acts as a cue to draw attention to another instance of a concept. And third, a child operates with a semantic interpretation from which he can be directed through language to do novel things with known objects.

Perception becomes very complex, especially after the acquisition of basic perceptual awareness and the achievement of a symbolic orientation. This may occur at the end of the preoperational stage but more likely in the Piagetian concrete operations stage or Bruner's symbolic stage. It is certainly not unidimensional (pure tone), nor is it unimodal (auditory). Perception is not a complex set of discriminations, but is rather based upon categorization or classification abilities. We perceive on the basis of how we classify or represent experience. According to Garner (1966), we perceive according to what we know. An auto mechanic and I can listen to the car motor with the same auditory mechanisms, but he can deduce a sound pattern that something is amiss, whereas I cannot. With a symbolically oriented person, perception is as much the product of one's experiences as it is the presentation of and response to stimuli. This, of course, has many implications for clinical audiology and generalizing from performance in highly controlled conditions with noncontextual materials to everyday performance. Interested readers may wish to look at the recent work on comprehension, especially the works by Carroll and Freedle (1973), Bever (1970, 1973), Winograd (1972), Schank (1972), Huttenlocher (1974), Bransford and McCarrell (1974), and Bloom (1974). It is necessary for the applied fields to revise some overworked notions about discrimination, perception, and comprehension. Indeed, the evidence to date suggests that comprehension is multideterminant (Bloom 1974; Ingram 1974a) and follows at least a three-stage sequence in language acquisition: rudimentary semantic strategy fused to available references, syntactic strategy, and semantic strategy (Bever 1970, 1973; Macnamara 1972; Bransford and McCarrell 1974; Muma, Adams-Perry, and Gallagher 1974; and Huttenlocher 1974).

Development of Attending Patterns

Kagan's theory of cognitive development parallels Piaget's speculations on schema development. Kagan and others (Kagan 1969, 1970, 1971; Kagan and Lewis 1965; Lewis and Goldberg 1969; Lewis, Kagan, and Kalafat 1966; Lewis 1967, 1970; McCall 1967; McCall and Kagan 1967a,b, 1969) have sought to account for cognitive development in terms of the development of attending patterns. They regard the conditions under which infants and young children attend to stimuli as a means of understanding the genesis of cognitive growth. Attending patterns are a function of the relationship between the status of available stimuli and one's underlying knowledge, or schemata. This theory reveals that cognitive development is not simply a matter of stimulation or enrichment of the environment. One must be conceptually ready to attend and process available stimuli (Hunt 1969). Readiness and enrichment are not enough. One must for some reason physically or conceptually engage the stimuli (Bruner 1961; Anglin 1973). Moreover, available stimuli to be compelling must not correspond exactly with previously held schemata nor contrast too greatly. This is an interesting concept. *Discrepancy* is a compelling stimulus feature (Melton and Martin 1972; Munsinger and Kessen 1966; Gaines 1970). What may be discrepant for one child may not be for another. Like Piaget, Kagan acknowledges individual differences, active processing of available stimuli, and dynamic relationships between one's underlying knowledge and varying available stimuli.

Kagan (1968, 1971) proposes a three-stage theory that predicts when a stimulus will attract and maintain an infant's attention. The first stage is *all-or-none*. The infant will notice an event when the stimulus pattern is changed from absent to present or vice versa. He will attend to his mother when she appears at the door or to the door area when she leaves. However, the infant will "lose interest" in a few minutes, to be "won over" by some other compelling stimuli. Attention is relatively brief and directed toward major changes of stimuli. The second stage is *discrepancy*. A child (even an adult) has a partial schema or concept and encounters something that corresponds only partially with previously acquired schemata. The new set of stimuli are discrepant with the old schemeta. Discrepancy is very potent in getting and maintaining attention. It is one of the mechanisms that was employed so successfully in "Sesame Street." Poor children attend to "Sesame Street" rather intently. Prior to the development of the program, it was widely thought by both educators and psychologists that it was virtually impossible to capture and maintain the attention of poorer children. Discrepancies are intentionally built into the program by varying concepts, rate, and sequence for the purpose of getting and maintaining attention. The third stage is *density of stimuli*. An individual draws new relationships between concepts in order to integrate and reorganize them, establishing a means for generalizing to new or transformed experiences.

Kagan, McCall, Zelazo, and others have provided evidence on the discrepancy theory. They had a set of carefully controlled and manipulated conditions which enabled them to conduct a series of systematic inquiries into this theory for infants as young as three months. I was fortunate to participate in the execution of these studies with infants in a poverty program. Our work was under the supervision of Dr. Phil Zelazo, then at Harvard and now at the New England Medical Center Hospital. It was amazing how well we could demonstrate predictable attending patterns in the age range of three months to three years. And in a free play situation, it was amazing how well evidence in cognitive development relates to things like tempo of play from the toddler to the early school ages. Zelazo developed these procedures with Kagan and has adapted them with Kearsley for use with infants having varying degrees of developmental difficulties including severe neuromotor handicaps and speech delays.

One of the most fascinating parts of this work occurred at the Harvard laboratory, where the researchers were looking not only at overt attending behaviors (such as eye tracking, smiling, body orientation, pointing, and fretting as functions of stimulus onset, duration, offset, and repetition), but at covert behavior as well. The most intriguing and reliable index of internal processing was cardiac rate. When a discrepant stimulus was initially presented, an infant responded with an *orienting response*. Overtly he ceased other activity and became oriented to the stimulus. Covertly, cardiac rate decelerated in proportion to the degree of discrepancy between the infant's schema (conceptualized past relevant experience) and the stimulus. Interestingly enough, when a discrepancy is relatively small, cardiac deceleration is large, and vice versa. Of course, if a discrepancy is too large the infant would probably not attend at all, and therefore would evidence neither a covert nor an overt response. After the orienting response, infants have what is regarded as a *hypothesis testing period* in which they presumably try to resolve discrepancies between what they perceive and what they know. This process corresponds to Piaget's concepts of assimilation and accommodation. Overtly, attending patterns are maintained in eye orientation, often accompanied by smiling and vocalization. Smiling is apparently an important overt manifestation of information processing (Zelazo 1971, 1972; Zelazo and Komer 1971; McCall 1972). The literature on the importance of smiling and laughter in cognitive development is summarized by Sroufe and Waters (1976). Covertly, cardiac rate accelerates. The work of Lacey et al. (1963) and Lewis (1971) has demonstrated that covert activities indeed mark specific information-processing activities.

Enactive, Iconic, and Symbolic Systems

Bruner (1964, 1966) and his colleagues modified and substantiated a developmental model advocated by Werner (1948) and Werner and Kaplan (1963). Basically, it describes developmental hierarchical relationships for the emergence or acquisition of cognitive processing systems.

The emergence of cognitive processing systems is in three major stages: enactive (motoric), iconic (imagery), and symbolic (representational). The enactive stage appears in early infancy. An infant processes experiences primarily by motoric means. He mouths, touches, fingers, pats, kicks, and in various ways physically manipulates things. As he becomes mobile (crawling, creeping, toddling, and walking), he acquires a much greater range of motoric processing. His mobility allows him to convert distant stimuli into proximate stimuli, affording him more opportunities for enactive processing. Enactive processing corresponds somewhat to Piaget's sensorimotor stage. Piaget holds that infants launch their concept development in action patterns; Bruner contends that it issues from motoric engagement.

Iconic processing is perceptual or image processing. In the early phase, it is in terms of undifferentiated imagery. According to Witkin et al. (1962), figure-ground distinctions are rather vague and unarticulated. A child tends to repeat action patterns in an effort to reestablish past experiences. In Piaget, this occurs in the early part of the sensorimotor stage. As figure-ground distinctions become clearer, iconic processing separates more clearly from enactive processing. At the toddler and preschool ages, iconic processing is in terms of *perceptual attributes*. These include color, shape, size, quantity, and position.

Symbolic processing means a child's ability to represent experiences in prototypes or categories. From past experiences, the child can extract, organize, and define salient attributes into categories (Nelson 1974). New experiences are perceived in terms of prototypes or categories (Garner 1966) rather than direct stimulation. Symbolic processing depends upon the child's conceptual categories. Symbolic processors can select two items as comparable because they function in similar ways, such as the bird and airplane in Fig. 3-4. Iconic processors, given the same choice, will match items according to perceptual properties (Vespucci 1975; Kelly 1976). If

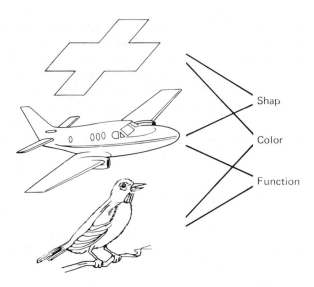

Figure 3-4 *Pairs of items that share perceptual attributes (shape or color) or function. (Adapted from Vespucci 1975.)*

the bird is the same color as another item, iconic processors are inclined to ignore the airplane and match the bird with the item of the same color, or same shape, size, etc. They can identify one or two attributes of things, but they have difficulty integrating them (Bruner 1964).

Thus, enactive or motoric processing appears very early in development, then iconic processing appears, which in turn is superseded by symbolic processing. This occurs about the time a child begins school. Even early on, rudimentary symbolic behavior such as labeling and early word combinations appears. However, the dominant cognitive processing systems are enactive processing in infancy and iconic processing in early childhood. Enactive and iconic processing are retained throughout life, but much greater reliance is placed on symbolic processing.

Apparently, increased reliance is placed on symbolic processing because it is much more powerful and efficient than either enactive or iconic processing. According to Bruner (1964), symbolic processing allows one not only to represent experience with language but also to transform it.

> Once the child has succeeded in internalizing language as a cognitive instrument, it becomes possible for him to represent and systematically transform the regularities of experience with far greater flexibility and power than before (1964, p. 4).

With respect to memory, it is much easier to store and retrieve information that is symbolic rather than iconic in nature. Moreover, more information can be stored in symbolic form. This topic is more fully treated in the section on memory.

Thus far, I have merely made a series of assertions about a three-stage emergence of cognitive growth that provides a role for language. Let us examine some evidence for these assertions. Bruner (1964) reported an interesting observation concerning a residual priority of motor behavior over iconic and symbolic behavior. An aphasic individual could not name an egg, but his gesture (motoric) language was rich in displaying alternative uses of eggs. Bruner concluded, "He cannot identify objects without reference to the action he directs toward them" (1964, p. 3). Similarly, facility in naming and word recall in aphasia can be helped by shifting from symbolic to visual, tactile, or gestural modes. Interestingly enough, experienced clinicians report that on occasion these "facilitatory techniques" also have interfered with recall.

Bruner (1964, 1966) was interested primarily in the developmental transition from iconic to symbolic representation. A series of studies document this transition. Bruner cited studies by Emerson (1931) and Werner (1948) concerning body orientation to a task. Both young and older children achieved good performance on a task. But when the task was varied (rotated about an axis), younger children had poor performance, whereas the older ones maintained good performance. The younger children operated perceptually, whereas the older operated conceptually. The younger children's imagery made them field dependent; the symbolic orientations of the older children were field independent (Witkin et al. 1962). When the field was rotated the younger children rotated their bodies to realign their perceptual image with the rotated field. Older children performed this rotational operation mentally. Bruner cited a study by Mandler (1962) in which subjects only obtained visual images after a series of overpracticed successful trials. Apparently the motor plan for doing skilled motor activity is a type of imagery. This is reminiscent of the interest in imagery dominance in the early 1900s, in which it was thought that some people were supposedly dominant in visual imagery while others were dominant in motor imagery, auditory imagery, etc.

Bruner and Kenney (1966) had children between five and seven years of age reconstitute a double classification matrix that was scrambled. The matrix varied size on the rows and height on the columns. The children had no difficulty reconstituting the matrix. The older children were faster than the younger, but all were successful. Then one object was placed in a cater-cornered position and the children were asked to reconstitute the matrix around this item. This required that the matrix be rotated to correspond to the displacement. Most seven-year-olds succeeded but most five-year-olds did not. "The youngest children seem to be dominated by an image of the original matrix" (Bruner 1964, p. 5). The older children, on the other hand, considered alternatives and made hypotheses about solutions to the problem, frequently in overt fashion: "This should go here. And this here. . . ." The older saw it as a problem requiring reckoning, whereas the younger simply tried to copy the original image. The older approached the task from a representational perspective in which they had prerogatives for resolution. The younger tried to deal with the problem in terms of the original stimulus.

Interestingly enough, the language of the children reflected perceptual versus symbolic conceptualizers. The children employed three types of language—dimensional, global, and confounded. Those who used confounded language (which is not organized and fails to separate the salient dimensions such as, "That one is tall and that one is little") had the greatest difficulty. Language did not appear to act as an aid in the transposition task. Bruner concluded:

> First, that children who use iconic representation are more highly sensitized to the spatial-qualitative organization of experience and less to the ordering principles governing such organization. They can recognize and reproduce, but cannot produce new structures based on a rule. And second, there is a suspicion that the language they bring to bear on the task is insufficient as a tool for ordering (Bruner 1964, p. 5).

Somewhat later, children use language to *activate* cognitive processing. This appears in the child's ability to state the salient dimensions of a task, and in so stating, be led to a solution. Bruner contended that if a young child was prevented from using an iconic representation, "there would be less likelihood of a perceptual-iconic representation becoming dominant and inhabiting the operation of symbolic processing" (Bruner 1964, p. 6). The child would draw upon symbolic representation and thereby perform much better. Bruner reports a study by Frank that illustrates the effects of saying before seeing.

Frank (1966) attempted to make nonconservers conserve by verbalizing. Young children commonly fail to realize that the volume of a liquid remains the same even though the liquid is poured into a different-sized container. Such children are called nonconservers, because they do not operate on the critical principle of volume; instead, they operate on height. Frank had some four- to seven-year-old children participate in a conservation task. She poured a liquid into a new container in the presence of each subject, with the water level screened from view. The children were asked to estimate the level in the new container. There was a striking increase in the number of conservers. At the four-year level, for example, the increase went from zero to 50 percent, and they verbalized their judgments. Then the screen was removed. The four-year-olds changed their minds. "The perceptual display overwhelms them and they decide that the wider beaker has less water" (Bruner 1964, p. 7). Virtually all of the five-year-olds stuck to their judgments, even though some were previously nonconservers. All of the six- and seven-year-olds stuck to their judgments. Then, after several minutes, Frank repeated the original unscreened conservation task. The four-year-olds were unaffected by their prior experience. The five-year-olds, however, showed a marked increase from 20 percent (pretest) to 70 percent (posttest) in conservation response. The six- and seven-year-olds increased 50 percent and 90 percent, respectively. A control group on pre- and posttests had no significant improvement.

Nair (1963) studied the verbal processes children use in resolving a conservation task. She reported that three types of arguments are used: perceptual, action, and transformational. Two-thirds of the successful conservers used nonperceptual arguments. "It is plain that if a child is to succeed in the conservation task, he must have some internalized verbal formula that shields him from the overpowering appearance of the visual displays . . ." (Bruner 1964, p. 7).

Enactive, iconic, and symbolic processing concepts have many implications for the applied fields. Mentally retarded children seem to have predominantly enactive and iconic processing. The American Association of Mental Deficiency published a special monograph edited by Garrison (1966) that presented the Bruner model as a potentially useful approach to understanding cognitive processes in mental retardation. This monograph also advocated the application of Piagetian psychology and the Guilford model of multidimensional intelligence, which are also useful in understanding learning disabilities and autism (Prizant 1975).

Parenthetically, there is a striking similarity between the developmental hierarchies in the Bruner model and those in the acquisition of skilled motor acts (Bruner 1973). Late acquired cognitive or motoric abilities override early acquired ones, but the early ones can reappear as the result of a loss of the later abilities. Early motoric stages are marked by reflexive behavior followed by the gradual control of large muscle groups and, subsequently, the attainment of fine muscle groups with attendant sensorimotor coordinations. Though many reflexive behaviors are "outgrown," they are not actually lost. Higher motor operations in the central nervous system override earlier motor behaviors. Cerebral palsy, particularly spasticity, is a condition in which early reflexive behaviors continue to be manifest, often exaggerated, because the higher functions for voluntary control are not operating to override them. Thus, one can become cerebral palsied if higher cognitive functions are destroyed by illness or traumatic injury. Thus, there seem to be some interesting parallels in motor and cognitive development. Earlier functions are not entirely lost but are overridden by more advanced ones. Similarly, there seem to be some interesting parallels between cognitive development and language development (Goodson and Greenfield 1975).

Bruner and his colleagues have an interesting view of the course of cognitive growth. Language is an important dimension of cognition. It provides the ability to liberate oneself from immediate stimuli and operate effectively in a representational world. Bruner's three stages suggest that one proceeds from actions to images to symbolic representations. With symbolic representation, one has the capacity for extension and elaboration of concepts, or thought. One also has the capacity to shape these thoughts into an organized code that is shared by others—grammar. Bruner seems to regard language in a broad sense—encompassing much, if not all, of thought, but not all of cognition—since he separates iconic and symbolic functions.

Others regard language as limited by a grammatical system. On first thought, this view may appear to be narrow. However, as our knowledge of cognitive and semantic categories has increased, it has become more and more evident that a line between language and cognition is difficult to establish and maintain (Bowerman 1976). Bloom (1970) described linguistic competence as the overlapping of cognitive-perceptual development, nonlinguistic experience, and linguistic experience. She maintained that competence develops as a function of the degree and rate at which these components attain overlap. Cognition is the more generic. In language, words and various grammatical devices are used to index, code, or map referents in one's underlying conceptual framework. These trigger similar cognitive structures in listeners. Thus, language functions in an interpersonal sense as a vehicle of communication, transmitting thought by coding shared reference.

Cognitive Distancing

According to Piaget, a basic premise of development is cognitive distancing, which is the ability to be increasingly free from direct environmental stimulation while being more reliant on symbolic representations of events. As Piaget put it, infants are fused to their environment but adults are cognitively independent of it.

Sigel (1971a) defined cognitive distance in terms of the levels of representation of things, actions, and relationships. He held that things cognitively less distant are easier to process than those more distant. He used this model to show that disadvantaged children could learn better with material that was cognitively close. This construct would be useful in the applied fields, particularly in the clinical arena, dealing with aphasia, autism, mental retardation, learning disabilities, etc.

Sigel proposed three levels of representation: objects, pictorials, and words. Real as opposed to representational objects afford direct experience. As Piaget would say, objects allow a child to develop action patterns toward them. However, if the object is itself a representation, such as a toy truck, there is no assurance that "truckness" will be learned through action patterns. Nevertheless, objects are low in cognitive distance and therefore relatively easy to process through action patterns. Compared to objects, pictorials are moderate in cognitive distance. Accordingly, pictorial representations of objects would be more difficult to process than actions on objects. It is not clear whether line drawings or actual pictures are cognitively more distant. I would say that line drawings are easier to process because figure/ground segmentations are easily discerned, the contours tend to highlight salient attributes, and they more nearly approximate prototypes.

The developmental sequence in the Bruner model describes cognitive distancing. His three stages of development provide the cognitive capacities to cope with the world in ways increasingly removed from the original stimulus—proximate to distant to representational; present to past and/or future; response to immediate environment to delayed response to alternative response, etc. Sigel (1971) called this emergence capacity the *distancing hypothesis*. As Bruner (1964, p. 14) put it, "Once language becomes a medium for translation of experience there is a progressive release from immediacy." Paraphrasing Bruner (1964, 1966), language as a cognitive system permits one to represent experience and act on the representations rather than the immediate environment. Paraphrasing Dale (1972, p. 203), language is a liberating force, freeing the mind from dependence on the immediate environment.

Much is gained by going from images to representational functions. Representations can be manipulated. They can be abstracted in terms of features and attributes. These abstractions can, in turn, be reorganized for the formulation of new concepts. At the symbolic stage, one's conceptual world is a dynamic system based upon classes and subclasses integrated by hierarchical structures or rules. This allows the selective storage and retrieval of functionally useful concepts. An image, on the other hand, is an all-or-nothing proposition linked to a specific context by association.

The symbolic system is more powerful than the motoric and iconic systems. It has the ability to extend stimuli. It allows an individual to deal with stimuli that are removed or invented—past, future, abstract, etc. An individual is not bound to an immediate environment. Responses are not limited to a given circumstance, but are responses to all that one brings to a situation (cognitive past), deduces in a situation (cognitive present), and forecasts or ramifies (cognitive future). A symbolic system is dynamic, continually changing one's conceptual world as the result of new experiences.

In short, the motoric and iconic stages are responses to primary stimuli in the immediate environment. These are proximate or distant in nature. They reflect the perceptual world but do not exhaust it (Garner 1966). In the symbolic stage one both responds to and invents stimuli. These are in continual flux as a function of various new experiences.

Perception and Figure/Ground Differentiation

Perceptual processes, although relatively low on a cognitive hierarchy, are still very complex in their own right. They have functional ranges in which they operate. If a stimulus exists outside a given functional range, an individual will not sense it. Functional ranges are determined not only by the range of potential responses of any particular sensory system but also by the psychological set at any particular moment.

This can be readily illustrated. The human ear is normally responsive to sounds in the frequency range of 64 to 10,000 cycles per second or hertz (Hz). Responsiveness varies along this continuum. Humans are most responsive to frequencies within the speech range (125 to 4000 Hz). Intensity of sound is perceived as loudness. There are levels of intensity (decibel or dB level) beyond the response range of an individual. The lowest level at which one can hear a sound is his acuity threshold. Hearing, like all other sensory processes, is dynamic. One's acuity threshold is never constant, but fluctuates (Green and Swets 1966). The threshold for perceiving a 1000 Hz pure tone may be -5 dB on one occasion, and -7 dB, -4 db, 0 dB, or even $+2$ dB on other occasions. If an audiologist uses an ascending technique, he will get a "higher" threshold than if he uses a descending one. Thus, perceptual set influences the range for sensing stimuli. The upper (loud) end of a functional auditory range also fluctuates. Very loud sounds can significantly, though temporarily, alter thresholds for perceiving very quiet sounds. This is known as the temporary threshold shift phenomenon. Thus, the response ranges of hearing reflect very complicated sensory response systems. Complex meaningful sound patterns, such as speech sound patterns, are easier to perceive across a functional range than simple pure tones. These observations indicate that sensory systems are not simple responses to external stimuli, but are also governed in significant ways by higher cognitive processes.

Garner (1966, p. 19) showed that perception entails very complex cognitive processes:

> To perceive is to know. It is to know and comprehend the nature of a stimulus; it is to know the nature of the alternatives to a stimulus; and it is to know the structure and organization of sets of stimuli. Furthermore, the perception of stimuli as existing in sets

and subsets is an active process for the perceiver, one in which he will define and organize sets of stimuli which he may never have experienced, if the nature of a stimulus clearly requires such an inference in order for it to be known.

Given the complexity of sensation and perception, it is imperative that clinicians do not place a premium on acuity levels or discrimination measures. Above all, they should realize that aberrant scores suggest a problem rather than define it, and nonaberrant scores do not necessarily mean "normal." Performance within a normal range does not define a process as normal, particularly for the crude measures presently available—especially auditory discrimination measures (Locke, n.d., circa 1976). The validity of speech discrimination testing and training in an attempt to deal with deviant speech articulation has been questioned by Rees (1973b) and Ingram (1976). Clients may be able to perceive subtle distinctions in the speech of clinicians but be unable to perceive important distinctions in their own speech (Aungst and Frick 1964). The traditional approach of attempting to tap acuity, discrimination, and perception has been crude almost to the point of being nonproductive. Clinicians should not underestimate complex psychological processes and overvalue gross information.

Figure/ground differentiation is important in perception (Goldman 1962; Gibson and Gibson 1955; Maccoby and Bee 1965; Zaparozhets 1965; Bower 1966; Witkin et al. 1962; Witkin et al. 1966). As Goldman (1962) pointed out, three-year-olds are whole-perceivers who see few details. At four and five they notice component parts. By nine they synthesize and integrate. Birch and Lefford (1964) showed a developmental trend for normal children: discrimination to analysis to synthesis. They showed that some brain-injured children did not follow this sequence. Farmham-Diggory (1967) gave similar evidence.

Studies of eye movements of infants and young children indicate that they look at things with a single fix. Older children and adults scan contours. When children between three and five are taught to pay attention to contours, they show significant improvements in copying, whereas training in motor skills does not lead to improved performance. This suggests that the acquisition of figure/ground differentiation can be improved at this age with intervention.

Maccoby (1967) has shown that children can differentiate simple geometric forms at very early ages, but the reproduction of this skill is much slower to develop. The lag in motor behavior development behind perception may be linked in some way with mediation and production deficiency.

Memory and Chunking

The applied fields are woefully misled and dated in regard to the understanding of memory. Digit memory span is still regarded as a good index of memory capacity. However, Blankenship (1938) provided an extensive review of memory span both from the substantive and from the methodological points of view. She concluded that memory span is hopelessly confounded between both intra- and interpersonal factors, so much so that it is virtually useless. Her conclusions are still valid today, yet the applied fields continue to make something of digit span data.

There are some important concepts about memory that clinicians should know. First and foremost, memory capacity is not static or fixed, but dynamic (Jenkins 1974; Inhelder 1969; Melton and Martin 1972). The more you know the more you can know; the more you remember the more you can remember. The applied fields have taken Miller's (1956) classic paper on mental capacity too literally. Miller held that humans have a fixed mental capacity to deal with seven (plus or minus two) units or chunks of information at any one time. In the applied fields, this was taken to mean seven digits, numbers, geometric forms, instructions, etc. This presumably provided a method to measure digit memory span. Unfortunately, the applied fields overlooked an extremely important point: Miller was talking about *units* or *chunks* of information. It turns out that units or chunks in memory are defined psychologically, not extrinsically. This is also true for "stimulus," "response," and "reinforcement" (Kagan 1967). Thus, what might be a unit or a chunk to one person may not be to another. There is no one-to-one correspondence between external stimuli (a digit, for example) and a cognitive processing unit. Given a list of digits, one person may try to remember them independently, another in pairs, and a third in some other chunk. The nature and size of the chunk is determined by the nature and complexity of the underlying cognitive organization brought to bear on the information (Simon 1974).

The phenomenon of symbolically perceiving and representing experience has been variously described as differentiation and restructure, schemata and structure, concepts and systems, concepts and hierarchies, categories and rules, bins and structures, classes and hierarchies, or simply chunking (see Fig. 6-10). Chunking usually refers to verbal behavior but can as easily be used to mean conceptual behavior. It seems to be the best generic term for how memory capacity can be increased.

Chunking is related to memory load. As memory load is increased, it becomes increasingly necessary to chunk events in more efficient ways. Through chunking, one can successfully deal with large amounts of information with minimal difficulty in storage and retrieval. Chunking provides a way of representing information so that it conforms with one's conceptual units and organization.

The most fundamental characteristic of chunking is that perceptual and conceptual chunks have an underlying hierarchical structure (Gagne 1965, 1967; White 1965). Concept formation follows a sequence of differentiation and reorganization. Heider/Rosch (1971, 1973a,b) (Rosch is Heider's married name) demonstrated that semantic categories are conceptually organized in a hierarchical system of features. Items with the most basic set of features are "focal" items; those with only a few features are "peripheral" items. By systematically varying focal and peripheral items with different cultural groups, she showed that there are certain natural categories in hierarchical organization.

Chunking is a fundamental process in language. It occurs in speech perception, speech production, and comprehension. Speakers do not process all of the acoustic patterns that strike their ears. There are numerous noises that compete with the signal. Yet listeners readily detect the desired signal in the maze of noise. They do not need the same pattern to conclude that a given sound was produced; they operate with a cognitive set that allows for variation within a tolerable range. Thus, several acoustic patterns could be judged as the same speech sound (Peterson and Barney 1952; Miller 1965). Moreover, the production of sounds is also variable within certain tolerable ranges and subject to contextual influences (McDonald 1964; Daniloff and Moll 1968; Daniloff and Hammarberg 1973). Both the perception and production of sounds is essentially under psychological control, evidenced by their contextual nature—signal to noise ratio, tolerable variation in acoustic signal, motor performance, etc.

In perception and comprehension it is possible to "get" the wrong signal because target utterances are embedded in a maze of nonfluent utterances—false starts, repetitions, partial sentences, etc. Normal listeners have little difficulty in sorting out the "necessary" from the "unnecessary" because they are operating under a system that chunks information according to the categories of language. If certain bits of information do not "fit" a chunk, it is either placed in another chunk or cast aside as not pertaining to the grammatical system. A linear system would not operate this way. It would strive to account for all information in the order in which it occurs.

Humans are versatile. We will try any of several rehearsal strategies. The important issue is which strategy we will rely on in various circumstances. If the material has an underlying structure, we are prone to use that structure to remember the information. If we do not deduce a structure, we spontaneously assign one. Sometimes the rehearsal strategy we try works well and sometimes not, but in every instance we attempt to discern and/or assign structure to information which is to be placed in memory. There are no external rules. We rely on past experiences, categories, and organizations. We assign categories and organization to the events we encounter (Garner 1966; Nelson 1973, 1974).

According to Bruner (1964, p. 2), the most important issue in memory is retrieval:

> To dismiss this problem as mere memory is to misunderstand it. For the most important thing about memory is not storage of past experience, but rather the retrieval of what is relevant in some usable form. This depends upon how past experience is coded and processed, so that it may indeed be relevant and usable in the present, when needed. The end product of such a system of coding and processing is what we may speak of as a representation.

He argues that if information is not retrievable, the 1unction of memory is not served. This sounds like a circular argument, but it is not. It has important implications for the applied fields.

There are several types of memory, but iconic and symbolic storage are the two types that we rely on the most. Iconic storage is through imagery. It is relatively inefficient and the memory can easily be overloaded. With respect to retrieval, it has two serious limitations: a relatively short life—it is difficult to maintain an image for very long—and difficulty of retrieving information unless retrieval takes place soon after the information was stored.

On the other hand, symbolic memory is very efficient. In fact, the more that it is used the more it increases in efficiency. This efficiency has two aspects: the amount of information placed in memory and the ease of retrieval. The more one uses symbolic memory the more one can remember and the easier it becomes to retrieve information. It is important to remember that symbolic memory has an underlying hierarchical organization rather than a linear one. Iconic memory does not have a hierarchical structure. Increased symbolic memory means an increased organization of the underlying hierarchy, whereas increased iconic memory merely means the addition of more information. This hierarchical organization is why symbolic memory is so efficient. See the works of Gagne (1965, 1967) and White (1965) on the significance of hierarchical structure in cognition. Bruner (1964) posited that the most significant characteristic of language and cognition is hierarchical structure.

The difference between iconic and symbolic memory can be readily illustrated. Figure 3-5 shows several forms, some of which require iconic storage and retrieval and others storage and retrieval either iconically or symbolically. The forms on the right are usually stored and retrieved symbolically and the ones on the left iconically. Assume that the forms have equivalent sizes, amounts of ink, and relationships and proximity to each other. Since we have usually had past experience with the geometric forms on the right, we probably have well-established categories, concepts, and labels for them. We use these categories and labels to place their information in memory. It would be relatively difficult to place the forms on the left side in memory and retrieve them later, but relatively easy to store and retrieve the ones on the right, even over very long periods of time. Further, it would be easy to overload iconic memory by adding more items, whereas it would require many, many more items to overload symbolic memory. Indeed, if retrieval depended not upon maintaining juxtaposed relationships (an iconic dimension) but simply upon the number and type of geometric forms, it would be difficult to overload symbolic memory. Clearly, symbolic memory surpasses iconic memory.

It is much more difficult to put information into memory, store it, and recover it

Figure 3-5 *Iconic or symbolic storage and retrieval.*

ICONIC MEMORY   SYMBOLIC MEMORY

when it has little in common with previous information. Language is perhaps the most powerful and convenient way of facilitating both storage and retrieval processes. To repeat Bruner:

> The most important thing about memory is not storage of past experiences, but rather the retrieval of what is relevant in some usable form. This depends upon how past experience is coded and processed so that it may indeed be relevant and usable in the present, when needed. The end product of such a system of coding and processing is what we may speak of as a representation (Bruner 1964, p. 2).

Language facilitates memory in both ways—getting information in and getting it out in a usable form.

It is easier to code and store meaningful material than nonmeaningful material. And, of course, it is easier to retrieve meaningful than nonmeaningful material. As Glucksberg (1966, p. 8) put it, "This irregular geometric form is difficult to reproduce from memory unless it is given a verbal description." He added, "The greater the complexity of the original figure, the greater the potential influence of verbal processes" (p. 9). The classic study by Carmichael, Hogan, and Walter (1932) showed that when a particular set of labels was given, recall of a set of figures was consistent with these labels; and when the labels were changed, recall changed in ways consistent with the new labels.

Adults rely much more on symbolic than iconic memory. The shift in reliance away from iconic processing to symbolic processing occurs at about five years of age. Some clinical groups, particularly involving the retarded, used iconic more than symbolic memory. This may be a fundamental problem with autistic children and aphasic individuals. West has been doing research on iconic and symbolic processing of aphasic patients at the Manhattan Veterans Administration Hospital in New York City. She reports that certain types of aphasics have particular difficulties with iconic and symbolic processing. She has devised a therapy program to help these patients overcome this problem (West 1971). Her work has been reported at several conventions of the American Speech and Hearing Association, and she has prepared an interesting workshop package.

In addition to iconic and symbolic processing, it is imperative that clinicians know about both short- and long-term memory and how they pertain to primacy-recency functions in memory processing (Atkinson and Shiffrin 1970; Craik and Lockhart 1972). Apparently, the primary function of short-term memory is to hold information in momentary abeyance and to possibly transform it to conform to one's long-term storage mechanisms (assimilation), or change the long-term storage mechanisms to conform to the new information (accommodation). It appears that in verbal behavior the *form* of a message is handled by short-term storage and the *function* is dealt with in long-term storage. Information must pass through short-term storage in order to get to long-term storage. However, the reverse is not so. The different functions of short- and long-term storage provide a selector mechanism for what and how information will be stored. We place a telephone number in short-term memory because we need it only for specific and immediate occasions. Then we either forget it, write it down, or rehearse it to put it into long-term storage. Other more useful information is put directly into long-term storage.

Up to this point memory has been viewed from three perspectives: iconic and symbolic, storage and retrieval, and short- and long-term. Clinicians should have a fourth perspective: *primacy-recency functions*. These functions appear in what is known as a *serial learning curve*. An individual is given a series of items—one every second—then asked to recall as many as he can. At first glance, it appears to be a digit memory task, but it is not. It is necessary to overload the memory with items that have no discernible underlying pattern. Typically, fifteen to twenty letters of the alphabet are used with adults, fewer with children. Under these conditions, primacy-recency effects occur. Notice in Fig. 3-6 that the items recalled occur at certain locations in the string. Those at the beginning and end of the string are recalled and those in the middle are forgotten. The items most recently placed in memory (the last items in the string) are usually reported first. They comprise the *recency* end of the serial learning curve, and are usually reported first, presumably to clear short-term storage. They must be either dumped from memory or placed in long-term storage via rehearsal. When the storage part of the task is over, most individuals dump the recency items first.

The items that begin the string are recalled much better than those in the middle and comprise the *primacy* end of a serial learning curve. These intial items have been subjected to rehearsal and placed into long-term storage. They are recalled because they have been rehearsed much more than the others. Primacy effects result from rehearsal (long-term storage), and recency effects are the result of short-term storage.

Primacy-recency effects can be altered by giving a reference point around which to orient rehearsal, or by providing material that contains explicit or inherent structure. A reference point can be introduced by inserting a novel item in the list or by something as subtle as a smile or a cough during the presentation of items. The novel item and immediately adjacent items are recalled. However, the response to structure is much more important, for if an individual deduces underlying structure and uses it as a rehearsal strategy, primacy-recency effects will dissipate in favor of the inherent structure. Recall will follow the pattern of the material. This is very important for assessment, for if an individual treats patterned material as if it were nonpatterned he will evidence a primacy-recency effect. Moreover, if recency effects are stronger than primacy effects, there is reason to believe the individual has serious cognitive processing problems. Echolalic behavior in autistic, retarded, and schizophrenic individuals frequently shows a recency function. Echolalia is often on last words: a teacher might say, "Okay, Johnny, let's go outside." He may reply, "Outside."

Figure 3-6 shows primacy-recency effects for material with different levels of structure—numbers, words, and a sentence. These are from actual responses of a normal adult. Notice that primacy-recency effects are clearly evidenced for numbers, somewhat evidenced for words, and dissipated for a sentence. In the instance of words, *clustered recall* can be expected. This occurs (Bousfield 1953) when an individual recalls items in clusters, usually two or three, for a given class, i.e., two animate nouns, three inanimate nouns, two adjectives, etc.

In the literature on language learning, there are occasional references to *recency*

Figure 3-6 Recall of strings containing 18 items each but with varying degrees of underlying structure.

Stimulus	Underlying Structure	Primacy									Recency								
Random Numbers	Very Low Recall:	46	13	91	27	74	58	86	39	62	17	34	96	73	52	29	68	41	84
		−	−	+	+	+	−	0	−	−	−	−	−	0	+	−	+	+	+
Single Syllable Nouns	Low Recall:	man	bone	frog	shoe	ice	chair	meat	ball	horse	boy	door	ant	store	dog	sky	hat	soup	bear
		+	+	+	−	+	+	−	−	−	−	−	−	−	+	+	+	+	−
Sentence	High Recall:	Five	men	in	the	crew	that	sailed	around	the	world	asked	for	leave	soon	after	the	incident	occurred.
		+	+	+	+	0 (boat)	+	+	+	+	+	+	+	+	+	+	−	−	−

− = not recalled
0 = distortion; approximation
+ = recalled

functions in cognitive processing. These are somewhat different from recency *effects* and refer to the most recent cognitive operation in formulating and issuing a behavior. Inasmuch as hierarchical structures pervade cognitive-linguistic systems, recency functions would be those operations that were last in the hierarchical organization. In a subject-verb-object (transitive) sentence, the object is the last to be formulated and issued. Brown, Cazden, and Bellugi-Klima (1969) report a recency function in the acquisition of subject-verb-object sentences. They report that the object phrase becomes developed first and more elaborately than the subject phrase. Oller and Kelly (1974) reported a recency function in the acquisition of speech articulation. Ervin-Tripp (1973), Olson (1973), and Slobin (1973) have identified several primacy-recency functions in language acquisition (see chap. 6).

Parents, teachers, and clinicians should know about storage and retrieval, iconic and symbolic memory, short- and long-term storage, and primacy-recency effects in memory. They should realize that memory is dynamic, varies rather than is fixed, and is hierarchical rather than linear. They should be concerned about what an individual brings to a task, the nature of the task, and the storage and retrieval strategies employed, rather than the simplistic notion of digit span.

Verbal Activation and Interference in Cognition

Clinicians should realize that verbal behavior can activate or interfere with cognition. Bruner (1964, 1966) and his colleagues showed that children with more advanced language usage were more successful in problem solving than children less advanced. For example, children at the "appropriate functional features" level of concept development could verbalize the rules for correctly solving tasks. These behaviors spanned tasks (object sorting, equivalence judgments, induction, solutions by implications). However, this is essentially correlational evidence. Increased cognitive performance occurred with increased verbal performance. Perhaps language activates cognitive mechanisms, perhaps cognitive mechanisms activate linguistic mechanisms, or perhaps other variables may be operating. Activations may be possible in both directions. Indeed, it is very likely that bidirectional activation occurs at the adult level; this would be consistent with Vygotsky's notion that language and thought first develop in parallel but merge in early childhood. It would also be consistent with Bloom's (1972) notion of "crossover."

Bruner and his colleagues have also given direct evidence of language functioning as a cognitive activator. This was shown in the studies by Bruner and Kenney, Frank, and Nair, all reported in Bruner (1964, 1966). Children who are nonconservers become conservers by verbalizing the task before visualizing it. Except for the four-year-old children, the older children (five–six–seven) maintained their judgments during a visual posttest. The exception of the four-year-olds may mean that verbal activation will not work if the child is not cognitively ready. For example, Bruner and Kennedy concluded that language was insufficient as a tool for ordering with some young children. This is consistent with Duchan's (1976) developmental stages regarding a release from a cognitive bias (see p. 44).

Cazden (1972, p. 231) summarized work by Sinclair-deZwart (1969) and Inhelder et al. (1966) concerning the relationship between language and the cognitive capacity for conservation. Cazden indicated that conservers used relational terms (more than, less than), differentiated terms (long/short, fat/thin), and coordinated descriptions for two dimensions (more marbles, but, smaller). Nonconservers, on the other hand, did not use contrast in their descriptions, but only "big" and "small" for size, and mentioned only one dimension.

We know neither the genesis nor the mechanisms of language activation, but apparently around four years of age self-activation is realized. Moreover, we do not know the relationships that undoubtedly exist between cognition and the mapping of conceptual events into language.

Palermo and Lipsitt (1964) summarized a series of studies concerning language mediation and activation, and DeCecco (1967) summarized a similar series. Goss (1961) summarized and criticized much of this literature in an article entitled *Verbal Mediating Responses and Concept Formation.* Kaplan's (1961) review also dealt with the relationships between symbolic activity and other activities, particularly perception and concept formation. Other relevant papers include Meichenbaum and Goodman 1969; Gusinov and Price 1972; Blank 1974; Rees 1973b.

These and other studies show that a verbal label facilitates learning. Words can serve to cue a common underlying attribute of seemingly different things. For example, "animal" cues the animalness attribute of ants, kangaroos, and fish. This is referred to as *learned equivalence* by Dollard and Miller (1950, p. 101). Words can also cue distinctive attributes of previously undifferentiated concepts. This is called *learned distinctiveness.* Thus, the act of labeling can lead to increased generalization or discrimination depending upon how the label cues one's conceptual response. Notice that these forms of response to verbal labeling correspond closely with two styles (or, according to Guilford, operations) of thought: divergent and convergent (Guilford 1967; Carroll 1968; Messick 1968). Referring to Vygotsky, Cazden (1972a, p. 29) said, "the word first functions as an invitation to a concept, calling attention to yet another instance. Later the word comes to symbolize the concept itself as a condensation of the child accumulating experience." Brown (1958a,b) referred to the same process, when he indicated that a word acts as a lure for cognition by drawing attention to another instance.

Labels that are themselves similar do not facilitate learning to the same degree as do labels that are more distinctive (Norcross 1958). Labeling associated with the functional use of the label facilitates learning of a nonverbal response (Spiker, Gerjuoy, and Shepard 1956). Labels used while learning one discrimination problem helped in a subsequent problem. This is similar to evidence on reversal and nonreversal shift problems in discrimination learning (Kendler and Kendler 1959; Kendler 1971). Discrimination learning was also facilitated when names were used (Dietze 1955). Again in the context of Vygotsky's views, Cazden (1972a, p. 229) said, "If one has no name for a phenomenon, one may not notice it." DeCecco's (1967) critique of a study by Gagne and Smith (1962) sums up much about the activating influence of labeling and verbalizing in concept learning, principle learning, and problem solving. The subjects verbalized principles themselves. Gagne and Smith found that subjects who verbalized took more time to make successive moves.

> Verbalization may develop a set or disposition for analytical thinking and may result in more successful problem solutions. Gagne and Smith suggest that verbalization may simply force subjects to think (DeCecco 1967, p. 350).

While labeling may indeed act in cognitive activation, we must not lose sight of developmental factors. Verbal activation may not be effective unless a child is developmentally ready (Hunt 1969). Moreover, verbalization may interfere by disrupting skilled behavior. Weir and Stevenson (1959) found that verbalization interfered with performance at about seven to nine years of age. They reasoned that the older subjects spontaneously verbalized solutions to themselves. Overt verbalization seemed to interfere with internal formulation. Interestingly enough, Macnamara (1967) and Macnamara and Kushner (1971) have shown that when a person attempts to understand another dialect or language and verbalizes the code, his comprehension is hindered. Courtwright and Courtwright (1976) found that overt verbalization interfered with one aspect of language learning.

In reporting the results of studies by Keeney, Ganizzo, and Flavell (1967), Dale (1972, p. 214) indicated that kindergarten children did not have the skill to integrate certain functions for facilitating memory, yet they demonstrated component skills. They named, rehearsed, and used the names for recognition, but they did not integrate them. Older children, on the other hand, readily exhibited integrated mnemonic behavior. Flavell, Beach, and Chinsky (1966) provide further study. These younger children were said to have a *mediation deficiency* but not a *production deficiency*.

Verbalization may serve to direct behavior. As a child talks about what he is doing he formulates a course of action. This is called a *regulatory function* of language (Luria 1961; Kohlberg, Yeager, and Hjertholm 1968). This is somewhat different from the "talk it through" behavior adults use to organize thoughts. The child operates in one mode at a time. He thinks and then acts, but does not think and act simultaneously. Single mode performance can interfere with cognition. In early childhood, a command may activate a motor or perceptual activity but not stop it. A kind of momentum follows in which verbalization does not seem to effect a change. Thus, the original verbalization may actually interfere with the shift in perceptual-conceptual behavior. Bruner et al. (1966, p. 45) said,

> hypermotoricity interferes with "reflectiveness" in young children, seeming to delay language development and the development of linguistic ability. When a child cannot inhibit the motoric acting out of responses, he cannot organize a central pattern sufficient for language—or at least for any language more complicated than the immediate holophrase.

Bruner indicated that the period beginning with the first word and ending with the first combination of words (usually about six to nine months in duration) may be a period for steadying and overlearning—presumably of motoric behavior. While this is a possibility, Bloom (1970, 1973) and Greenfield and Smith (1976) have shown that this is a very important period of cognitive-linguistic growth.

Moreover, there are undoubtedly other influences on cognitive development besides verbal mediation or activation. Bruner (1957) argued that one's needs are significant determinants of perception. Obviously, environment is also a strong determinant, as are past experiences as constituted in underlying cognitive representation and cognitive styles for assimilation and accommodation (Garner 1966).

Perceptual set can be a powerful promoter or inhibitor of learning. The studies by Piaget and Kagan on schemata development strongly indicate that previous learning defines to a large extent what can be learned. Hunt's (1969) notion of *cognitive match* apparently is very real. This states that learning occurs when there is an optimal match between one's conceptual development and a given opportunity. Apparently, an optimal match is one in which relevant discrepancies occur. Perceptual set is influenced by past experiences not only on a conceptual level but on an emotional one as well. Indeed, emotional influences can, and generally do, override cognitive influences. When one is faced with information that is emotionally-laden, it can be conceptually denied. Previously I had indicated that new information would be accommodated or assimilated. Now I am saying that new information may not be comprehended at all because of an insufficient cognitive match, or it may be denied on emotional grounds. The cognitive dissonance theory (Festinger 1957) posits some formal dynamics of these possibilities.

Verbalizations can consolidate conceptual classes, cue figure/ground relationships, override emotive dimensions, change perceptual set, etc. The tip-of-the-tongue condition (Brown and McNeill 1966) illustrates that a verbal label (a word) is somewhat independent of, yet somewhat dependent on, an underlying conceptual system organized on features and attributes. In this state one cannot think of a particular word, yet is quite aware of the semantic features of the word, such as its initial sound, number of syllables, part of speech, etc. The tip-of-the-tongue condition is common in aphasic individuals. There is reason to believe that in aphasia this kind of problem represents a faulty memory system. West (1971) and Swinney and Taylor (1971) are studying aphasia and devising therapeutic procedures specifically aimed at altering some memory processes (specifically short-term memory and iconic storage) in the hope of overcoming word-finding difficulties. Kellas, Ashcraft, and Johnson (1973), and Ellis (1970) are studying storage and retrieval strategies and capacities of the retarded in an attempt to understand some of their cognitive processes. Kavanagh and Mattingly (1972) have dealt with short-term memory processes in learning to read.

Production Deficiency and Mediation Deficiency

Clinicians should know about production deficiency and mediation deficiency. Flavell and his colleagues (Flavell, Beach, and Chinsky 1966; Keeney, Caninizzo, and Flavell 1967; Corsini, Pick, and Flavell 1968; Moely, Olson, Halves, and Flavell 1969) have conducted several studies on these topics.

Production deficiency refers to a situation in which an individual fails to use a label (and possibly an interiorized action pattern) to recall items. And when an individual is able to label or demonstrate the functions of items yet is not able to appropriately categorize them in an object sorting task or cluster them in a memory task, the problem is called *mediation deficiency,* because labeling and/or demonstrating does not mediate or precipitate the appropriate categories.

Some children or adults with clinical problems (aphasia, mental retardation, learning disabilities, etc.) may show production deficiency and/or mediation deficiency. A common strategy in the applied fields is to develop naming or labeling behavior. The literature on concept development clearly shows that labeling is only one aspect of word knowledge and usage. Intervention that ends at word learning or the labeling of single referents falls considerably short. Words must be used in the context of intra- and interpersonal language functions if intervention is to have lasting significance.

Technology of Reckoning

Piaget, Bruner, and others have observed that there is a developmental sequence in which one can deal cognitively with increasingly complex stimuli. Early on, young children can identify single attributes; subsequently they can deal with clusters of them. A young child will point to the *red* ball, the *blue* ball, the *big* ball, etc. Subsequently, he will choose a *red* ball and a *green* ball, or even a *red and green* ball. These, however, are only combinations of attributes. A much more advanced cognitive skill is the ability to integrate attributes into a higher order. This is what Bruner (1964, 1966) called the technology of reckoning, because it is an ability that allows one to effectively deal with varied experiences in one's world. Experiences are not reducible to single attributes or clusters of attributes. They are perceived and dealt with as complex, highly integrated events (Nelson 1974). Once one can integrate and reorganize attributes into higher orders, he has achieved a great deal of cognitive power in living in the real world. That is why the famous Piagetian tasks on conservation are so important.

Figure 3-7 illustrates conservation tasks for liquids, masses, and quantities. A child is shown two identical containers holding the same amount of liquid. He is asked to confirm that the same amount of liquid is in both containers. The liquid in one container is then poured into a new container which is either taller and thinner or shorter and wider. The child is then asked if he thinks there is ''more,'' ''less,'' or ''the same'' amount of liquid in the new container compared to the original one. Nonconservers will probably be able to say that the liquid is high or low, wide or narrow, or even high and narrow or low and wide, but they would conclude that the new container held ''more'' or ''less'' liquid. They would not see the necessary relationship between height and width to conclude that ''the same'' amount of liquid is in both containers. Similarly, a nonconserver would conclude that a flattened ball of clay is ''less'' than the original ball, and pennies spread out are ''more.'' Conservers, on the other hand, maintain correct relationships, even though transformations occur.

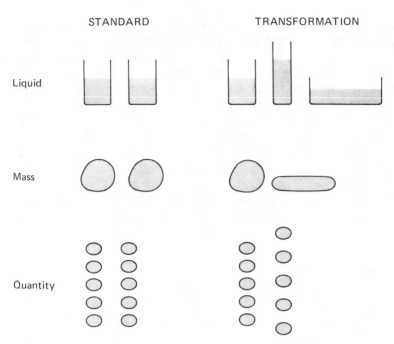

STANDARD   TRANSFORMATION

Liquid

Mass

Quantity

Figure 3-7 *Conservation for liquids, mass, and quantities.*

Daily experiences are not exact repetitions of previous experiences. They are, by and large, transformed versions of other experiences. Technology of reckoning allows us to cope with new events in effective ways by generalizing and integrating from past to present.

There are two major problems with conservation tasks. One has to do with the way the task is carried out and the other with its language or terminology. Bruner (1964, 1966) contended that if the task were changed slightly different results would be obtained. He held that the task was essentially a symbolic task and if a young child was strongly influenced by iconic processing he would perform as a nonconserver when in fact he could conserve. Bruner placed a screen between a child and the container that differed from the standard. He allowed the child to see the containers beforehand and to see the act of pouring, but prevented the child from seeing the entire container after all of the liquid was poured into it. He reasoned that if the child saw the new container with the liquid, the child would have an iconic response that would override any symbolic reponse available to him. Sure enough, Bruner and his colleagues were able to show that some children who were nonconservers became conservers when the iconic dimension was controlled.

The use of the words "more," "less," and "same" also presents some problems. Studies by Donaldson and McGarrigle (1970), Maratsos (1973a), Palermo (1973), E. Clark (1973a,b, 1974, 1975), and H. Clark (1970, 1973a) indicate that children learn such words first to indicate dimension and subsequently to indicate contrast. Performance of young children on conservation tasks may reflect a child's awareness of these linguistic terms more than his awareness of conservation.

Dimensional Salience and Set Shifts

An interesting developmental change occurs in cognition during the preschool years. It is a change in performance on reversal and nonreversal shifts in two-choice discrimination learning (Brier and Jacobs 1972). The Kendlers (H. Kendler 1971; Kendler and Kendler 1959, 1970a,b) have done many studies on this change. Figure 3-8 illustrates it. Children are shown a series of cards, each of which contains two geometric forms (one large and one small, one red and one white) and asked to guess which of two forms the examiner is thinking of. They are told whether they guessed right or wrong for each pair of forms. After a few guesses, older children and adults quickly discover which of the two variables and which criterion the examiner is using. They discover a rule for the activity. Young children, on the other hand, do not approach the task in terms of a rule-governed activity. They must be conditioned until they learn the correct set. It usually takes longer for young children to be conditioned to the initial set than older children and adults to deduce a rule, but in both cases they learn to choose the desired forms consistently. They have learned the initial set. Then, without saying so, the examiner changes either the criterion of the variable (from large to small on the "size" variable or from red to white on the "color" variable) or the variable (from size to color or vice versa). The former is called a *reversal shift* and the latter a *nonreversal shift*. The question is how many trials it will take to learn a reversal shift or a nonreversal shift. Preschool children need to be conditioned to the task whereas older children and adults regard the task as rule-governed. Adults find the reversal shift relatively easy to learn because it is based upon a rule they learned in the initial set. The only difference is a change in criterion. Young children find the reversal shift about as difficult as the initial set because they must be reconditioned to a new set. However, the opposite holds for the nonreversal shift. Adults find the

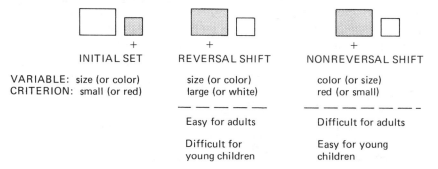

VARIABLE: size (or color)   size (or color)   color (or size)
CRITERION: small (or red)   large (or white)   red (or small)

Easy for adults   Difficult for adults

Difficult for young children   Easy for young children

Figure 3-8 *Performance on reversal and nonreversal set shifts for young children and adults.*

nonreversal shift rather difficult because they resist abandoning a rule that has worked so well. Young children, on the other hand, perform the nonreversal shift much better than both the initial set and the reversal shift, because they are easily reconditioned to still another set. Thus, performance on reversal and nonreversal shifts identifies whether a person is rule-governed in cognitive processing. Figure 3-8 illustrates the changes and criteria for the reversal and nonreversal shift and the relative performance of children and adults on these tasks. Kramer (1976) modified the regular Kendler materials so the tasks contained pictorials of functional items such as cakes, flags, trees, and boats.

A recent development has changed this procedure somewhat. It has been shown that if the task begins with the dimension that is most prominent or salient, it takes fewer trials for the initial set and possibly the reversal shift, but not the nonreversal shift. This is due to the influence of dimensional preference or perceptual salience. *Perceptual salience* is a phenomenon that occurs with preschool and early school-aged children who show a strong orientation to perceptual variables (Odom and Corbin 1973; Odum 1972; Odum and Guzman 1970, 1972; Caron 1969). The orientation is so strong that it can override other cognitive processing. Moreover, perceptual salience seems to vary on a daily basis. If a child shows a preference for size, the initial set should begin with the variable of size. If a child shows a preference for color, the initial set should begin with color.

Models of Intellect

American education has had a tradition of determining the level of cognitive performance. This tradition appears in intelligence and achievement test performances and the labeling processes attendant to such performances—mental retardation, underachiever, cultural-familial retardation, learning disability, etc. However, in recent years educators have realized that level of performance on intelligence and achievement tests has been misleading and that the attendant labeling processes have been very unfortunate to equitable opportunities in education and society (Mercer 1972a,b, 1974; Hobbs 1974a,b). (See "On the Rights of Children," *Harvard Educational Review* 1973, 1974, and "Challenging the Myths: The Schools, the Blacks, and the Poor," *Harvard Educational Review* 1971.) One has only to survey class action suits across the country to find that an inordinate number of minority students have been labeled retarded on the basis of performance on intelligence tests which for one reason or another were biased against them. It has become increasingly evident that the level of cognitive performance is not a good index of overall cognitive abilities (Wechler 1975; Guilford 1967; Cattell 1963; Scarr-Salapatek 1971).

Intelligence test performance is as much the product of extrinsic as intrinsic variables, and may reflect such similarities and differences between tester and testee as sex, socioeconomic status, ethnic affiliation, and language or dialect. Performance can be seriously altered by the test situation (Sroufe 1970). Aside from tester-testee differences, socioeconomic status and ethnic affiliation may be major determinants of performance (Lesser, Fifer, and Clark 1965; Stodolsky and Lesser 1967). Notice that all these are external to the individual. They are certainly not his specific mental abilities. It is no wonder that efforts at defining levels of performance on intelligence tests are so vulnerable to class action legal suits.

It is also no wonder that the most recent definition of mental retardation (Grossman et al. 1973) has come under attack (Baumeister and Muma 1975). This definition provides that a person must perform two standard deviations below the mean on a recognized test of intelligence, demonstrate behavior that is adaptively inappropriate according to the *AAMD Adaptive Behavior Scale* (Nihira et al. 1974), and have arrested development to a level under that which would be normal by eighteen years of age. Operationally, adaptiveness is defined by the *American Association of Mental Deficiency Adaptive Behavior Scale* (Nihira et al. 1974). This scale delineates an extensive array of adaptive domains but unfortunately has bastardized the notion of adaptiveness by quantifying behaviors rather than describing them in context. For example, in the area "Resists following instructions, requests or orders" one is asked to indicate whether a child's resistance is "occasional" or "frequent" according to the following: (a) gets upset if given a direct order, (b) plays deaf and does not follow instructions, (c) does not pay attention to instructions, (d) refuses to work on assigned subject, (e) hesitates for long periods before doing assigned tasks, (f) does the opposite of what was requested, and (g) other (specify). Such data have virtually nothing to do with adaptiveness! An appropriate question should be, "Under what *conditions* do these behaviors occur?" They may be adaptive in some conditions but not in others. The crucial information—conditionality of behavior—is omitted. Needless to say, the American Association of Mental Deficiency needs to avail itself of the current psychological literature both in defining mental retardation and in dealing with adaptiveness. The Piagetian approach to adaptiveness and the models proposed by Anderson and Messick (1974) provide excellent approaches. Psychologists have recognized the pitfalls and fallacies of composite cognitive measures. Indeed, Wechsler (1975) acknowledged that cognition is multidimensional and relational.

Perhaps it is appropriate at this point to give an overview of the different perspectives of intellect, since these challenge the notion of the quantification and summation of mental capacities.

Messick (1968) discussed several models of intellect: a dimensional model, a hierarchical model, a morphological model, and a sequential model. *Dimensional models* depict cognitive dimensions as sets of vectors in multidimensional space (Osgood, Suci, and Tannenbaum 1957). A *hierarchical model* is addressed to subordinate and superordinate relationships between intellectual capacities (Gagne 1965, 1967; Kofsky 1966). This model proposes a general or "g" factor of intellect. The *morphological model* (Zwicky 1957) portrays intellect in terms of matrices of functions, operations, and substantive areas. The *sequential model* describes intellectual functioning in terms of sequential events. The information feedback loop is an example (Miller, Galanter, and Pribram 1960; Reitman 1965).

Guilford's theory of the structure of intellect deserves particular attention because it is both widely known and more highly elaborate than most. It is probably the most highly developed example of the morphological approach, and is addressed to an operational–informational view of intellect. It posits a three-dimensional matrix: *operations* (evaluation, convergent production, divergent production, memory, and cognition); *products* (units, classes, relations, systems, transformations, and implications); and *content* (figural, symbolic, semantic, and behavioral). Carroll (1968) pointed out that the Guilford theory represents cognitive functions by a matrix of the three coexisting primary dimensions. Messick (1968) indicated that the theory could extend to sensory modes (auditory, visual, kinesthetic, etc.) and provisions for individual differences (response set, stylistic, and personality variables). Nevertheless, the Guilford theory provides an extensive integrated summary of the known and potential factors of intellectual functioning. As Messick (1968, p. C-6) put it, the Guilford theory offers "a kind of periodic table of the mind" in which the unfilled cells suggest areas of test construction for unexplored areas of intellectual performance.

Guilford's theory is a *logical* model, derived from a conceptual analysis of relationships. Hierarchical models, on the other hand, are frequently *psychological*, derived from empirical evidence about relationships. Burt (1949) has offered a hierarchical model for levels of intellectual functions that is probably familiar to most clinicians. He posited four levels below the *General Intelligence ("g") Level:*

Relations: logical and aesthetic thought processes
Associations: memory and habit formation; imagery, verbal abilities, and practical abilities
Perceptions: perceptual discrimination; complex perceptual processes and coordinated movement
Sensations: simple sensory processes and movements

He also provided for certain general processes that affect mental functions at all levels, such as speech, attention, etc.

Another major hierarchical theory of intellect is Cattell's theory (1963). This theory holds that, rather than a single "g" factor, there are two general intellectual abilities: "fluid" and "crystallized" intelligence. Fluid intelligence is the basic hereditary component; crystallized intelligence is the "capacity to perceive limited sets of correlates as a consequence of prior learning" (Damarin and Cattell 1968, p. 6). Messick (1968) pointed out that Cattell's theory is one of a few that provides for motivation, immediate reinforcements, transfer of training, and relevant personality traits. Although the Guilford model is classified as morphological, its elaborations incorporate hierarchical functions, sequences, and complexity.

It is noteworthy that the American Association on Mental Deficiency published a special monograph on cognitive models that seemed to offer an increased potential for understanding and managing retarded individuals. This monograph (Garrison 1966) presents three theories: Piaget's, Bruner's, and Guilford's. Stephens et al. (1971) have applied Bruner's model to a study of mental retardation. It should be stressed that while the above theories provide for verbal systems, they fall considerably short of an integrated theory for language and thought.

Chomsky's transformational generative theories (1957, 1961, 1965a,b) were attempts to deal with verbal capacity. Moreover, Chomsky (1968) held that verbal behavior is cognitive behavior. Verbal behavior maps or indexes underlying thought. Obviously, thought is primary and language secondary—certainly in the early stages of development. An understanding of language and verbal behavior must entail cognition. It is apparent that available models of intellect, although of considerable interest to teachers and clinicians, are not sufficiently elaborated nor directly relevant to verbal behavior to offer useful implications in assessment or intervention. It behooves clinicians to deal with cognitive systems and processes. The efforts of Piaget (1961), Sinclair-deZwart (1973b), Inhelder (1969), Ervin-Tripp (1973), Nelson (1973, 1974), Goodson and Greenfield (1975), Greenfield, Nelson, and Saltzman (1972), Bowerman (1976), Bloom, Hood, and Lightbown (1974), Bloom (1970, 1973), Slobin (1970), and various attempts to deal with generative semantics and speech acts go as far as we can go presently in understanding the relationships between cognition and language.

Cognitive Style

The literature in cognitive development indicates that cognitive processes are multidimensional and individuals have cognitive alternatives. Cognitive alternatives in conceptualization and problem solving put quite a different perspective on cognition than the traditional notion of level of performance, which can occur in a variety of ways. Thus, it becomes important to know the alternative cognitive processing styles at one's disposal and the conditions of their use.

There is a considerable literature on cognitive style. The classic study by Bruner, Goodnow, and Austin (1956) was influential in developing this literature. Three prominent viewpoints on cognitive processing style are cognitive tempo, analytic and synthetic thinking, and divergent and convergent thinking. It must be recognized that the use of these styles is a matter of choice rather than a limitation of cognitive capacity. It is presumed that older children and adults have the capacity to use alternative cognitive styles. However, we have preferences about the styles we use. These preferences can dominate us to the degree that we rely on some strategies to the virtual exclusion of others, and do so in circumstances where they may be least effective.

Cognitive tempo refers to the rate of processing. Impulsivity and reflectivity are two contrasting cognitive styles. *Impulsivity* entails a commitment to a solution before considering alternatives. It is as if one chooses to solve a problem according to the first thing that comes to mind, no matter if appropriate or not. Impulsivity is characterized by quick responses. Because alternatives are not fully considered, impulsivity very often leads to incorrect or inappropriate responses. *Reflectivity,* on the other hand, entails a careful consideration of alternatives before commitment to a particular solution. Accordingly, the deliberation period is more time consuming but it is also more efficient and effective. Kagan indicated that at about five, six, or seven years of age children undergo a change in cognitive functioning that includes the ability to inhibit acts and to select appropriate ones. Rather than taking an impulsive approach to problem solving, a child at this age becomes

> more planful in his play and in his attack upon problems. One of the processes common to many of these changes is an increase in reflection, an increased tendency to pause to consider the differential validity or appropriateness of a response, the ability to select the right response rather than emitting the one that happens to sit on top of the hierarchy when an incentive stimulus appears (Kagan 1972, p. 21).

As one would imagine, the degree of familiarity with a problem or the principles of a problem is closely linked to whether or not impulsivity or reflectivity will be used. If one encounters a relatively novel problem, he is likely to be somewhat impulsive simply because he does not have the necessary experience to deduce appropriate alternatives. On the other hand, he may choose to defer the problem to someone else. Deferring a problem is a reflective solution. As one becomes more familiar with the issues, he will likely take more time to ponder alternative solutions. If he is familiar with a problem, he can consider alternatives relatively swiftly and still accurately solve it. Clearly, familiarity is intimately related to the application of style. If one perseverates, he will be slow in solving a problem. However, perseveration is not active problem solving. Accordingly, it should not be equated with reflectivity (Kagan and Messer 1975).

Cognitive tempo is evidenced in the style of play as well as concept development (Ault 1973; Bush and Dweck 1975; Kagan 1965; Kagan, Pearson and Welch 1966). The number of toy changes per unit of time is an index of tempo of play. Many changes indicate an impulsive style; few indicate reflectivity. The toys should be relatively novel.

Cognitive tempo can be modified (Yando and Kagan 1968, 1970; Zelniker, Cochavi, and Yered 1974; Baird and Bee 1969; Egeland 1974; Denny 1972; Briggs and Weinberg 1973). Impulsive students become more reflective when they have reflective teachers, but reflective students do not modify their cognitive style when they have impulsive teachers. Impulsivity is evident when an individual is quick to indicate he likes or dislikes someone or something, or when someone "jumps to a conclusion" without knowing the circumstances or understanding the reasons.

Analytic and synthetic thinking style (Kagan et al. 1964; Kagan, Pearson, and Welch 1966; Kagan and Kogan 1970) are closely related to convergent and divergent thought (Guilford 1967). *Analytic thought* is going from whole to part whereas *synthetic thought* entails going from part to whole. Convergent thought leads to conventional responses. Divergent thought leads to unconventional or novel responses. Divergence deals with creative potential. Most cognitive tasks deal with convergent thinking; only a few deal with divergent thinking. Chapey, Rigrodsky, and Morrison (1976) showed that divergent thinking is a problem in aphasia.

Cultural and socioeconomic profiles reveal another kind of cognitive style. Lesser, Fifer, and Clark (1965) and Stodolsky and Lesser (1967) have shown that there are distinctive cultural and socioeconomic profiles of cognitive performance over a battery of tests. Four ethnic groups (Chinese, Jewish, Negro, and Puerto Rican), with high and low socioeconomic levels for each group, participated in a series of tests. These included arithmetic, similarities, vocabulary, and motor performance. Two very important findings were reported. First, ethnic groups had distinctive patterns of performance. The Chinese performed differently all across the tests than did the other three groups. Each group had distinctive patterns of performance. Second, socioeconomic level was consistently reflected within each ethnic group. The high socioeconomic subgroup scored consistently and significantly above the respective low socioeconomic subgroup. These findings are important because they reveal a pluralistic society in which no particular ethnic group is superior to another in cognition, and because they show that both cultural and environmental advantages are powerful.

Summary

Clinicians interested in language must deal with cognitive systems. The systems surveyed in this chapter provide them with several basic concepts, most of which are significant alternatives to such traditional notions as intelligence, memory span, and sensation-discrimination-perception-conception.

Cognitive systems are complex, dynamic, relative, and conditional. They entail active processing. Clinicians should have a basic understanding of Piagetian psychology, especially the sensorimotor period, because it provides a useful framework for understanding some cognitive prerequisities for language learning. Similarly, the development of cognitive awareness of space and time is important to an understanding of the acquisition of dimensional adjectives, relational terms, and temporal terms. The development of attending patterns and the importance of discrepancy learning constitute an area with major clinical implications: the importance of variation in assessment and intervention. The Bruner model of enactive, iconic, and symbolic cognitive processing systems provides a major framework for assessment and intervention. Cognitive distancing offers clinicians a useful perspective with which to view the hierarchical relationship among objects, pictures, and words. Perception and figure/ground differentiation are active dynamic processes governed in significant ways by an individual's experience and the particular conditions with which he must deal. Memory is also dynamic. Clinicians should regard memory from three viewpoints: iconic/symbolic memory, short-term/long-term memory with their attendant rehearsal and retrieval strategies, and primacy/recency functions. Interestingly, verbal behavior can both facilitate cognition and interfere with it, depending on the situation. Clinicians should realize that an individual may have difficulty with a task because of a production and/or mediation deficiency. Additionally, issues such as a limited technology of reckoning, constraints of nonrule-governed learning, and dimensional salience may singly or compositely account for various problems in verbal behavior.

Clinicians should know that psychologists have shifted away from intelligence testing or level-of-performance measures to alternative models of intellect that deal with cognitive systems and cognitive style. Intelligence testing is crude, misrepresents various cognitive systems, and begets categorization and labeling. It is more important to know *how* an individual functions cognitively than *what* score he got on an intelligence or achievement test. Accordingly, clinicians should know that assessment and intervention should be in terms of process models (Bruner, Piaget, Guilford, Kagan, etc.) rather than status models (psychometric tests: Wechsler, Binet, etc.). Clincians should deal with an individual in terms of his cognitive style (tempo, divergence-convergence, analytic-synthetic), rather than make him conform to a group through a normative comparison. Unfortunately, the current definition of mental retardation and the AAMD Adaptive Behavioral Scale perpetuate the psychometric notion and bastardize adaptiveness.

4

Linguistic
Systems

The purpose of this chapter is to describe the nature of various linguistic systems. In keeping with the outline of the scope of grammar, linguistic systems are presented for the semantic, syntactic, and phonological domains. It must be emphasized, however, that these domains are inextricably related. Indeed the semantic and syntactic domains are difficult, if not impossible, to separate (Bowerman 1976; Lenneberg and Lenneberg 1975; Ross 1974). Before discussing these domains, it is helpful to give a brief historical perspective and to repeat (a) the difference between surface and deep structure in verbal behavior, (b) the versatility of verbal behavior, and (c) the importance of contexts.

Historical Perspective

The traditional view of language held that it was exclusively linguistic. The modern view is that language is cognitive-linguistic-communicative. Traditionally, language was viewed almost exclusively in terms of linguistic forms—parts of speech, sentence types, diagrams of the structure of sentences, "correctness" and "grammatical standards," etc. This view was formally espoused by Bloomfield in the early 1900s. It held sway for about half a century—a period regarded as the Bloomfield era in American linguistics. It was also known as *structuralism.* The structuralist movement had a kind of scientific sanction by virtue of employing the empirical or data-gathering procedures advocated in American psychology by Watson. It is interesting to note that classical empiricism had a life span that closely corresponded with the Bloomfield era. Empiricism is not gone, but it has been redefined so that evidence is sought on *process* rather than *status* variables, on *systems* rather than *states,* and on *individual differences* rather than *group norms.*

The applied fields were heavily influenced by structuralistic and empirical traditions. These became so pervasive in American education that "correctness of grammar" or Standard English was an accepted goal for everyone, and norms were required as necessary for appraising performance.

We commonly think of language as a set of sentences, but this is only partially true. Language (more generally verbal behavior) encompasses not only a set of sentences but a variety of other behaviors that symbolically represent messages in regulating joint attention and joint activity (Bruner 1975). These include linguistic messages as well as paralinguistic, nonlinguistic, and metalinguistic messages. Moreover, the particular set of communicative devices employed in any given circumstance is directly related to the perceived communicative context and motivation for engaging in verbal behavior. Thus, contrary to tradition, a consideration of language must extend beyond sentences or utterances (Dore 1975). It entails cognition (thoughts and concepts underlying verbal behavior, perception of the communicative circumstance, mental processing), motivation (intent or desire to verbalize or code one's communicative intent), grammar (an ability to employ verbal mechanisms), and communicative functions (an ability to know which verbal message to employ to obtain the most desired effects for a particular circumstance). The study of verbal behavior is much more than the study of language forms. It has become a study of speech acts (Searle 1969; Bruner 1975; Dore 1975).

Chomsky (1957, 1961b, 1965a,b) is largely responsible for redefining language and verbal behavior in psychological rather than structuralist terms. It is interesting to note that Chomsky derived his basic views from the works of Von Humbolt, de Saussure, and other nineteenth century scholars. In addition to Chomsky, many others, particularly from Harvard University, have been instrumental in developing psychological views of verbal behavior. They include Brown, Miller, Bruner, Carroll, Lenneberg, Slobin, McNeill, Bellugi-Klima, Cazden, Ervin-Tripp, Bever, Fodor, Katz, Bowerman, Greenfield, P. de Villiers, and J. de Villiers. The University of Minnesota has several influential contributors, including Flavell, Jenkins, Masters, Moely, Palermo, Deese, Chinsky, Corsini, and Maratsos. Many others have made significant contributions to an understanding of verbal behavior, but this is not the place for an extended list.

Chomsky's work was addressed primarily to syntax. Bloom (1970, 1973) redefined Chomsky's views to include referential context. Schlesinger (1971) and Bowerman (1973) extended the study of verbal behavior to include communicative intent. Hymes (1967), Labov (1966, 1972), Ervin-Tripp (1971), Fishman (1970), and many others established the field of sociolinguistics. Searle (1969), Bruner (1975), Dore (1975), Greenfield and Smith (1976), Bates (1976), Halliday (1975), and others have defined the importance of verbal functions in realizing communication. Flavell et al. (1968), Glucksberg, Krauss and Higgins (1975), Rosenberg and Cohen (1966), Muma (1975a), and Longhurst and Sigel (1973) have dealt with role taking in playing the communication game. Currently, the perspectives of verbal behavior are based on underlying semantic relations, cognitive processes, concept development, communicative processes, communicative intent, linguistic contexts, and referential contexts.

Perhaps the single most important departure from traditional notions is an interest in language, more particularly grammar, as a psycho-sociological enterprise rather than as a structural entity in itself. The traditional view sought to describe the nature of language in terms of linguistic forms—the products of grammar. The generative view sought to describe and explain human capacities in producing utterances of a language—a theory of grammar rather than a study of the *products* of grammar. More recently, generative concepts have been redirected away from an emphasis on structure to an emphasis on cognitive and communicative functions.

Surface and Deep Structure

Clinicians should know the distinction between surface and deep structure in order to better understand the relationships among semantic, syntactic, and phonological domains. This distinction underscores the principle that verbal behavior is a product of cognition. Such products serve as a code through which cognitive behaviors can be shared by regulating joint attention and joint action.

Verbal behaviors merely index or code underlying thoughts. They are issued in particular forms in the hope of realizing desired effects. The behaviors themselves are surface forms and their organization is the surface structure. The traditional views of language dealt with its surface structure. The more important aspects, however, are the underlying concepts, thoughts, emotions, or intents that have been coded—the deep structure. There are several ways of showing not only that surface and deep structure are distinct but that deep structure has a certain psychological priority over surface structure. Language *function* is more important than *form*. Structure or form is in the service of function.

One way to reveal surface and deep structure is through ambiguity. According to Deese (1970, p. 7), "Nothing provides better evidence than ambiguity that sentences, like icebergs, have their larger and more significant portions hidden beneath the surface. Ambiguous sentences clearly carry more than their superficial structure indicates." In referring to alternative forms and meanings for ambiguous sentences, Cazden (1971, p. 1165) concluded, "Such factors as these have led transformational grammarians to postulate two distinct structures for each sentence: a deep (underlying abstract) structure, and a surface (superficial and perceptible) structure."

Sentence (1) gives a clear example of ambiguity.

(1) They are eating apples.

There are two apparent meanings to the same surface structure. One refers to a type of apples—eating apples. The other refers to the act of eating apples. The way one disambiguates this sentence is by knowing the appropriate communicative *referent*. The important point is that there are two structures to a sentence. The surface structure is its *form;* the deep structure pertains to its *function* and *meaning*.

Another way to demonstrate that sentences have a surface and a deep structure is to compare two sentences that appear in their surface structure to be similar but whose deep structure proves them to be very different. The classical examples are sentences (2) and (3).

(2) John is easy to please.
(3) John is eager to please.

On superficial inspection one would conclude that these two sentences are the same type. However, when one attempts to paraphrase them it becomes apparent that they are different in underlying meaning. Sentence (4) is a paraphrase of (2), and (5) is an ungrammatical paraphrase of (3).

(4) It is easy to please John.
*(5) It is eager to please John.

Similarly, sentences (6) and (7) show a different subject-object relationship.

(6) The Apache are easy to kill.
(7) The Apache are eager to kill.

"The attitude of the cavalry would be more determined by the deep structure of the sentences than by the surface structure" (Wales and Marshall 1966, p. 70).

Also, alternative sentence structures can convey the same meaning. Sentences (8), (9), and (10) convey the same essential thought but in different forms.

(8) The man carried a pail.
(9) A pail was carried by the man.
(10) It was a pail that the man carried.

Clearly, sentences have deep and surface structures. Moreover, deep structure apparently has cognitive priority over surface structure. This can be readily substantiated. First, it is at the deep-structure level that ambiguity is resolved. When ambiguous sentences are placed in the context of referents they can be more easily resolved. However, some ambiguous sentences are not recognized as ambiguous sentences, a common ploy used in advertising. This evidence is for ambiguous sentences. Evidence can be readily shown for other sentences, too. Indeed, Bloom (1970) argued that contextual referents (actual or presumed) are needed to interpret *all* sentences. Winograd (1972) and Schank (1972) have also argued on the importance of contextual referents in comprehending utterances.

Second, deep structure evidences priority in sentence recall. When asked to recall sentences, we remember the gist of them much better than the form (Slobin 1971; Fillenbaum 1966; Sachs 1967). In immediate recall, adults usually have very little trouble recalling surface form completely and correctly. However, in delayed recall, surface structure or form is lost before deep structure. Adults can report what a sentence was about even though they cannot report the exact wording. Thus, it appears that surface structure is cognitively subordinate to deep structure (meaning and function). It is as if the surface structure of an utterance provides a format or key with which meaning can be effectively cued. Once processing begins, however, surface structure is cast aside in favor of deep structure.

Third, both the development and complexity evidenced in comprehension reflect a distinction between surface and deep structure. I have outlined a three-stage developmental sequence in attaining language comprehension: rudimentary semantic strategy fused to the environment, syntactic strategy, and semantic strategy (Muma, Adams-Perry, and Gallagher 1974). The latter two rest on the proposition that surface and deep structure are distinct and intimately related, although not independent. A syntactic strategy relies on surface forms to discern meaning. A semantic strategy relies on deep structure to discern meaning. Macnamara (1972) held that in early language learning, children strive to discern deep structure first and use it to get at the subtle aspects of surface structure. Bruner (1975) made a similar point when he indicated that a child infers the mode of expression and regards prosodic information as an envelope or matrix into which morphemes go. As sentence complexity increases, the correspondence between surface and deep structure becomes increasingly difficult to discern. In some literary works, particularly by Faulkner and Joyce, certain sentences are so complex that it is very difficult to know what they are about. Studies by Forster (1966), Marks and Miller (1964), Martin and Roberts (1966, 1968), Turner and Rommetveit (1967), and Lahey (1974) have demonstrated that as sentence complexity increases it becomes increasingly more difficult to discern meaning.

A somewhat different point can be made about complexity. Complexity may also be a function of available referents (Olson 1970). Bloom (1974) and Ingram (1974a) held that comprehension may be more difficult for certain conditions even though the complexity of surface structure remains the same. That is, a sentence out of context is more difficult than one in context (Bransford and Johnson 1972; Slobin and Welch 1971; Bloom 1974; Winograd 1972; Schank 1972; Lakoff 1972a).

The distinction between surface and deep structure has important implications for clinicians. One major consideration is that language intervention should always be carried out with full recognition of an underlying referential system. A grammatical system is contextual. Language training should occur in a communicative context. Witness the success of foreign language learning when students are placed in a functional context that demands performance versus the relatively limited success of learning by vocabulary and building sentences. Teachers and clinicians should weigh the issue of surface and deep structure when they consider using "core" vocabularies. At the very least, such vocabularies should be either in the context of an object or a picture or established in the oral vocabulary before being taught in a written modality. Moreover, they should include *functionally* relevant words and alternative meanings of words.

What are the implications of this for speakers of a nonstandard dialect? One is that it reveals the naiveté of teachers who ostracize speakers for saying things like "I bes here" rather than "I am here." The deep structure is essentially the same for both sentences. It is absurd to label a nonstandard dialect speaker as uncouth, inferior, or stupid for using such phrases. In fact, it is bigotry. Baratz (1968, 1969a,b, 1970), and others have discussed this issue in terms of differences rather than deficits.

Transformational operations play a primary role in casting surface structure from deep structure in the production of a sentence. The disparity between deep and surface structure can be characterized in terms of transformational operations and their semantic constraints. It should be apparent to clinicians that the distinction between deep and surface structure is important, that deep structure has priority in cognitive processing by fluent adult speakers, and that deep structure is acquired before surface structure.

Versatility of Verbal Behavior

The hallmark of verbal behavior is versatility. Several aspects of versatility were described in Chap. 2. Versatility is basic to verbal behavior, yet the prevailing attitude in the applied fields is that language is rather static (H. Clark 1973b). Rarely is adequate provision made for versatility. Another attitude is that if a client can learn to make sentences, that is all we need to teach him. This is a superficial view of verbal behavior. The more important ability is a versatile command of language—the ability to recode messages in essentially equivalent forms when necessary.

The principle of versatility is that one referent can be coded in many ways, and one code can have many referents (Olson 1970). This is important to understanding linguistic systems because it raises the issue of essentially equivalent forms, which are not equivalent so much in surface structure as in deep structure. For example, "the boy," "he," "my brother," "Jimmy," "the guy in the blue jeans" are linguistically equivalent in the sense that they can function similarly in the context "_____ ate the pie," or "_____ drove a car." Also, they can have the same referent. Equivalencies of this sort are what clinicians should be concerned about, for they provide a considerable command over language.

The ability to switch the functional use of a code is very important. We use language to express emotional states, rational thoughts, and ideas. The same code can be used for one or all these purposes. A person might say, "I want to go home," and the statement can mean many things, only some of which are an actual desire to go home. It could also mean just the opposite under certain circumstances. The actual words used are not always the best indicator of a message. The tone of the utterance may indicate an emotional message quite different from the linguistic message. Linguistic systems do not stand alone; the communicative context is central to their function.

The ability to switch modalities of language has a number of implications for the understanding of linguistic systems. The linguistic systems we use in one modality are essentially the same in others. Underlying grammatical systems operate in the same fundamental ways in both the spoken and written modalities. Just as sentences are marked by punctuation, utterances are marked by intonations, inflections, pauses, stress, etc. The written modalities use a graphemic system in which alphabetical forms (letters) represent the speech sounds (phonemes) of the oral modalities. Nouns function linguistically the same way in written language and in spoken language. The differences that occur between modalities are relatively minor compared to the similarities.

Importance of Contexts

A fundamental mistake in the applied fields has been a failure to adequately recognize the importance of linguistic and referential contexts. Linguistically, words are not always nouns, verbs, etc. Words become nouns only when they function as nouns in linguistic context. Sometimes the linguistic functions of words entail special devices to denote a function, i.e., *-tion* denotes a noun, *-ize* denotes a verb, *-ly* denotes an adverb, etc. Sometimes the words are not marked by a linguistic device. Their function can be deduced from how they are used. For example, the words "house," "tree," and "horse" are nouns in sentences (11), (12), and (13), but are adjectives in sentences (14), (15), and (16).

(11) I bought a *house*.
(12) The *tree* had split into three parts.
(13) My *horse* is fast.
(14) The *house*boat sank.
(15) The *tree*house was falling apart.
(16) Give me the *horse* collar.

Moreover, only certain co-occurring structures can appear in linguistic contexts prescribed by one's grammar. Children control co-occurring systems when they attempt to extend their knowledge to other systems. Accordingly, evidence of co-occurring structures, or their absence, is useful in assessment (Muma 1973a,b). The literature on coarticulation deals with contextual influences that operate in the production of speech sounds (Daniloff and Moll 1968; Daniloff and Hammarberg 1973; Ingram 1974b, 1976). This literature shows that many determiners operate in phonetic contexts to influence the production of speech patterns, and that to regard phonemes as entities (which is the prevailing view in the applied fields) is to greatly underestimate the significance of phonetic context.

In addition to linguistic context, it is necessary to consider referential context, which pertains to coded available referents (real or presumed), alternative coexisting codes, and communicative intent. These are all needed in order to deduce underlying meaning. The literature in recent years has defined the importance of referential context (Bloom 1970, 1973, 1974; Olson 1970; Schlesinger 1971; Bowerman 1973; Wieman 1976; Hinds 1975).

Semantic Systems

Semantics is the dimension of grammar pertaining to meaning. According to Cazden, "Semantics refers to the relationship of that syntactic system to the nonlinguistic world of objects, events, and ideas that we talk 'about' " (1972a, p. 8). Semantic theory attempts to account for *sense,* or connotation, and *reference,* or denotation. *Connotative meaning* pertains to subjective meaning—that which one attributes to or feels about a word, phrase, or utterance. *Denotative meaning* pertains to objective meaning—that which is inherently indexed by a word. Denotative meanings are given in dictionaries. The connotative meaning for "home" may be a place of warmth, security, and pleasure for one person, and a place of hostility, fear, and anxiety for someone else. According to *Webster's Dictionary,* the denotative meaning of "home" is "one's dwelling place; abode of one's family." Needless to say, daily speech contains both connotative and denotative meanings. Moreover, meaning is not simply the sum of the meanings of all the words contained in an utterance, but what is coded by the organization of the entire message.

Semantics has been studied from three major approaches—word meaning, sentence meaning (semantic functions and relations in utterances), and speech acts. The first approach has been largely unproductive, simply because meaning is determined by linguistic and referential contexts (Olson 1970, 1971; Macnamara 1972; Brown 1958a; Bruner 1975; Schlesinger 1971; Gruber 1967; Hinds 1975). Clinicians are most generally familiar with the notion of vocabulary size as a crude index of word knowledge. Vocabulary size has traditionally been gauged by the Thorndike and Lorge (1944) word frequency counts. A more recent reference to word usage by children has been published by Carroll, Davies, and Richman (1971). More formal approaches for studying word meaning include word associations, clustering, and semantic differential. Selected references for these approaches appear below:

1. *Associations:* Deese 1965; Miller 1969; Brown and Berko 1960; Entwisle 1966a,b; Entwisle, Forsyth, and Muus 1964; McNeill 1963; Fillenbaum and Jones 1965; Jenkins and Russell 1960; Jenkins et al. 1971; Ervin 1961; Palermo and Jenkins 1964; Gallagher, Baumeister, and Patterson 1970; Francis 1972; Postman and Keppel 1970.
2. *Clustering:* Bousfield 1953; Bousfield, Esterson, and Whitmarsh 1958.
3. *Semantic differential:* Osgood, Suci, and Tannenbaum 1957; diVesta 1966; Snider and Osgood 1969.

Experience underlies meaning. What we know and believe from experience are the primary determinants of what we code and comprehend in language. Thus, meaning (or more formally, semantics) is intimately tied to cognition. As Nelson put it, "Categorization of sound patterns and of objects and events in the real world is basic to learning a language" (1973a, p. 21). Brown regarded first language learning as "a process of cognitive socialization [involving] . . . the coordination of speech categories with categories of the nonlinguistic world (1956, p. 247). Lenneberg held that cognition, specifically concept-formation, is central to an understanding of meaning. "The abstractness underlying meanings in general . . . may best be understood by considering concept-formation the primary cognitive process, and naming (as well as acquiring a name) the secondary cognitive process" (1967, p. 332–33).

From this viewpoint, vocabulary is relatively unimportant, or at least a subordinate aspect of semantics. The more important issue is the various alternative meanings one has for each word. *Vocabulary* is merely the number of words one knows. In linguistics, vocabulary and alternative meanings of words constitute one's *lexicon*. The issue of alternative meanings is perhaps more important than the number of lexical items or words. While vocabulary is important, its use and alternative meanings are much more so.

This has the following implications for the applied fields: first, semantics deals with intimate relationships between cognition and language (Bowerman 1976). Various aspects of cognition, such as concept-formation, organization, storage and retrieval, and processing, are fundamental to language. This does not mean, however, that there is a one-to-one correspondence between thought and language, like that posited by the Sapir-Whorf hypotheses of linguistic determinism and linguistic relativity. These hold that one's language determines one's thought. Perhaps there is a partial isomorphism as described in the Piagetian section, but the evidence supports the contrary view, that thought determines one's language—at least in the early stages before "crossover." Second, "word" learning is not as important as concept learning. Third, concepts should always be learned in context rather than in isolation. Fourth, the most potent learning arrangement is when referents are contextually *functional* for an individual. By functional I refer particularly to utility, saliency, and, early in cognitive development, cognitive bias. This means that clinicians probably should refrain from reducing contextual referents to a minimum. The opposite strategy—providing rich and varied contexts—will probably afford greater opportunity for alternative referents to become functional. Certainly, the role of clinicians should be one of active engagement within the context of various referents. Perhaps selective parallel talking about events will sufficiently cue categories and attributes: ". . . new words function mainly as a means of categorizing observed phenomena" (Halliday, 1975, p. 251).

Fifth, the concept of vocabulary changes drastically from an inventory or word count to an appreciation of a dynamic lexicon. A *lexicon* is a catalogue of lexical items (words) that carry clusters of alternative meanings. Thus, words are labels used to index any of several meanings. When words are incorporated into a sentence, they bring syntactic and semantic properties. Words in context reduce alternative referents to a few or a single referent, thus facilitating communication (Olson 1970, 1971; Brown 1958).

It is a *dynamic* lexicon for two main reasons. First, one's lexicon is continuously acquiring new attributes (assimilation), and new concepts are invented or previously acquired concepts are revised (accommodation). Apparently there are organizational changes in the acquisition of a lexicon. Differentiation and reorganization are common in concept learning and label acquisition (Nelson 1973, 1974; Brown 1973a). A major organizational change seems to occur at about seven years of age as indexed by the syntagmatic-paradigmatic shift (Brown and Berko 1960; Entwisle 1966a,b; Entwisle, Forsyth, and Muus 1964; McNeill 1966b; Miller 1969; Francis 1972). This will be discussed in the chapter on language acquisition.

Second, it is a dynamic lexicon because of the alternative ways referents can be indexed. A word not only has many referents, but referents have several words. The word "build" has several meanings. A single referent, such as a particular person, can be designated by "Joe," "a man," "a soldier," "a son," "a student," and so on. This implies that vocabulary counts are not really informative about a child's word knowledge. Moreover, there is the implicit suggestion that the organization of a lexicon is in terms of a catalogue or dictionary of word meanings. However, a lexicon can be organized in terms of attributes or in some other way.

Perhaps I should pause briefly to make a few comments about the dynamics of change for concepts, since one's concepts constitute the substantive basis of semantics. Flavell (1970) indicates that concepts are subject to three aspects of development: increased validity, increased status, and increased accessibility. Validity is the degree to which one's concepts match those of the larger community. A person's concept for "play" may be limited and unique. As he encounters more instances of "play," his concept acquires increased definition—increased status. As a definition conforms more to that of others, it acquires increased validity. The status and accessibility of a concept are close-linked to validity. As alternative referents are incorporated into a concept, it becomes more defined; the status is regarded as more clearly developed. As it acquires increased definition, it is more readily accessible for use.

Increased validity, status, and accessibility are easily seen in a school setting. Witness the redefinition of concepts in "show and tell" or a field trip to the police station. In the case of a visit to the police station, a child's prior concept of a policeman may be very narrow. However, the field trip will probably (a) enhance the child's concept of policemen, (b) increase the status by providing new dimensions, and (c) increase accessibility, as evidenced by an increased usage of the concept after the visit.

While the word-oriented approaches to meaning have essentially run their course with no substantial contribution to the understanding of semantic systems, two other approaches have shown considerable promise, especially in understanding semantic processes in early language acquisition. These are *sentence meanings* in terms of semantic and relational functions entailed in utterances, and *semantic functions* of speech acts. Fillmore's (1968) case grammar was largely responsible for the former and Searle's (1969) speech acts for the latter. Both approaches have received considerable attention and have been substantially modified. The case grammar (or generative semantic) approach has been modified and advanced by Schlesinger (1971), Bloom (1970, 1973), Brown (1973b), Chafe (1970), Greenfield and Smith (1976), Edwards (1974), Ingram (1971a), and Perfetti (1972). Clinicians will be happy to know that semantic functions have proven very useful in accounting for the early stages of language learning (one-, two-, and three-word utterances) for both normal language learning and language acquisition with clinical groups (Chapman and Miller 1975; Suci and Hamacher 1972; Golinkoff 1975; Freedman and Carpenter 1976; Duchan and Erickson 1976; Leonard, Bolders, and Miller 1976). The speech acts approach has been advanced by Bruner (1975), Dore (1975), Greenfield and Smith (1976), Greenfield, May, and Bruner (1972), Ryan (1974), Edwards (1974), Bates (1976), and Halliday (1975).

There are two important reasons why clinicians should use a case grammar approach in assessment and intervention. First, it is especially useful in dealing with the early stages of language acquisition. This is an important period in dealing with nonverbal individuals and individuals with very limited language. For example, this approach (and the speech acts approach) is very useful in making the transition from sensorimotor acts to speech acts (Greenfield and Smith 1976; Bates 1976; Bruner 1975; Dore 1974, 1975; Greenfield, May, and Bruner 1972; Edwards 1974; Halliday 1975; Sinclair 1970). Second, it is virtually structure-free. The form of an utterance is not important. What is important is what the individual is trying to do with his utterances or his functions. A variety of forms can be used for any function. Early language learning centers on the kinds of functions an individual is attempting to perform with his utterances.

Semantic relationships are closely linked to underlying concepts and attributes. As a child deduces objects separate from him, he will code semantic categories that reflect this distinction. When he deduces animate and inanimate objects, he will be able to code semantic categories that reflect the distinction. As he learns that some things initiate action and others receive it, he will code semantic categories according to that distinction. As he learns different actions, states, and relationships, he will code them in language. The current semantic theories are addressed to identifying the various cognitive-semantic functions and relationships that individuals attempt to code in language.

Basic substantive functions at the single word level include the following (Miller and Yoder 1974):

1. Comments or greetings (attaching a linguistic label to a perceived event)
2. Vocatives (call for someone)
3. Agent (person or thing responsible for action)
4. Object (recipient of action)
5. Action (type of action or state)
6. Possession (objects associated with or belonging to someone or something)

Relational functions of single word utterances include

1. Recurrence (return or recurrence of something missing)
2. Nonexistence (expect the occurrence of something)
3. Disappearance (comment that something or someone just disappeared)

4. Rejection (deny existence of something present)
5. Cessation (an event stopped)
6. Existence (objects, people, events noticed or discovered)

Thus, at the single word level, a considerable amount of learning occurs. The cognitive basis for language is well underway.

The semantic categories delineated by Ramer (1976) provide a useful framework for clinical work. These categories appear in Fig. 4-1.

Figure 4-1   *Semantic categories.*

Semantic Category	Description	Utterance	Relevant Context
Genitive	Indication of possession.	"Mommy bun"	Child observed mother eating a bun. Is asked, "Whose bun is it?"
Attributive	The first element specifies an attribute of the second element.	"Rubber ball"	Child selected a rubber ball from a collection of balls.
Locative	Indication of location.	"In bed"	Child's response to the question "Where's Mommy?"
Temporal	Indication of time.	"Heavy now"	Child tried to lift a bin of blocks.
Manner	Indication of the way in which an action occurred.	"Other way"	Said after child tried to put a block into the wrong part of the shape box.
Instrumental	Indication of inanimate causal object.	"Nail in hammer"	As child pounded a toy nail with a hammer.
Explicit deixis	Specific indicator or pointer.	"That one"	When asked, "Which book do you want?" child pointed to a specific book.
Quantitative	Indication of number.	"Two spoon"	Child played with several spoons.
Recurrence	Indication of repetition.	"More juice"	Child finished his juice and held out his cup to his mother.
Dative	Indication of indirect recipient of action.	"Give me this"	Child to observer when he couldn't reach the hammer.
Agent	Indication of animate initiator of action.	"Mommy hit"	When mother spanked child.
Action	Indication of action.	"Baby fall"	When a doll fell off the bed.
Patient	Indication of direct recipient of action.	"Eat soup"	As child is eating soup.
State	Indication of state of being.	"Sleep now"	Child pretends to sleep by placing head on bed.

Figure 4-1 *(continued).*

Semantic Category	Description	Utterance	Relevant Context
Indicative	Taking note of an object or person.	"See ball"	Child notices a ball in corner of room.
Rejection	Refusal of offered object or action.	"No banana"	Mother asks, "Do you want a banana?"
Nonexistence	Indication of the absence of an object or person that had previously been present.	"Ball gone"	A ball rolls under the sofa.
Denial	Indication of the falsity of a previous statement.	"No pot"	Child plays with a pot pretending it is a pool. Observer calls it a pot.
Conjunctive	Indication of more than one referent or simultaneous aspects of same referent.	"Shoe sock"	Observer asked "What do you wear on your feet?"
Disjunctive	Indication of either/or relationship between two referents.	"Bunny either"	Child imitated the observer's statement, "Don't give it to me from the cat or the bunny either."

(Ramer 1976, p. 705)

The speech acts approach is a fresh and potentially very productive way of studying verbal meaning in terms of various functions. Unlike the sentence oriented approaches that deal with semantic functions and relations, the speech acts approach is not limited to lexical material—words or word constructions (Dore 1975). It attempts to deduce the roles of utterances in terms of ongoing events and presumed communicative intent. A child may have a pragmatic intent—a desire to communicate for some reason. He may issue a verbal or nonverbal act in an attempt to realize this intent. The verbal act may be words, differentiated cries, or an idiosyncratic sound pattern. The function of the act can be deduced from the events. Thus, the speech acts approach is tied to what is happening in the communicative context. It deals with dynamic events.

Several approaches proposed in recent years indicate that a primary function of speech acts is to code dynamic events. Nelson (1973, 1974) indicated that a child will label things that change. Dynamic attributes are labeled. If objects change, nouns are given. If actions change, verbs are given. If relationships change, their naming is described by the old information–new information theory of Chafe (1970) and Wieman (1976), which bears on similar theories, such as theme and rheme (Firbas 1964; Hinds 1975), topic and comment (Gruber 1967), mode and argument (Schlesinger 1971), and mode and proposition (Fillmore 1968). The *context* (theme, topic, mode) refers to old information whereas *variations* in context (rhemes, comments, arguments, propositions) constitute new information. A *mode* is the kind of utterance an individual makes—comment, question, declarative, etc. An *argument* or *proposition* is the constituent of an utterance that defines its specific nature in terms of semantic functions and relationships. Ingram (1971a) indicated that a proposition contains transitivity and predication. Transitivity is a semantic reference to the verb, and predication pertains to the semantic functions of transitivity (Perfetti 1972).

Speech acts are instrumental in regulating joint activity and joint attention. The concept of speech acts facilitates an understanding of the transition from the sensorimotor period to representation (Bates 1976; Bates, Camaioni, and Volterra 1975; Greenfield and Smith 1976; Greenfield, May, and Bruner 1972; Bruner 1975; Edwards 1974; Dore 1974, 1975; Sinclair 1970). According to Greenfield and Smith (1976), nonverbal events such as actions and perceptions become known in terms of semantic functions—agent, action, object, location, etc. "Words" (sometimes invented or idiosyncratic) become situationally combined by the contiguity of nonverbal events and verbal acts. Such words do not have the referential meaning of adult speech. As Bloom (1973, p. 113) put it, "Children develop certain conceptual representations of regularly recurring experiences, and then learn whatever words conveniently code such conceptual notions." Word learning is not central to speech acts; speech acts concern language functions.

Children come to realize semantic functions and relationships through action or experience. Motivated to have joint awareness of these functions and relationships, they employ whatever devices they can. This leads to a reliance on linguistic devices. Linguistic devices are potent and efficient for regulating joint attention and joint action. "Language is a specialized and conventionalized extension of cooperative action" (Bruner 1975, p. 18). "Language is full of 'hints' about how to proceed from sound to sense. But we should also should bear in mind that joint experience and joint action are also full of hints as to how we should proceed from sense to sound" (Bruner 1975, p. 18). Bruner outlined the following list of semantic relations:

Universals
1. Agent-action (Mommy push)
2. Action-object (Eat pie)
3. Possession (Mommy sock)
4. Demonstrative marker (That doggy)
5. Feature marker (Big doggy)

Semi-universals
6. Location marker:
   a. Object (Daddy home)
   b. Action (Eat here)
7. Negation (No car)
8. Recurrence (More cookie)

9. Greeting notice (Hi spoon)
10. Recipient of action-experience (Show me book, or, Hear horn)

Brown (1973b) has a similar list: agent-action, action-object, agent-object; and initial semantic functions included: nomination, nonexistence, recurrence, location, possession, and attribution. Greenfield and Smith (1976) and others have extended the list of early semantic functions: vocative, object of demand, action performed by agent, inanimate object of action, action of inanimate object, affected person, instrumental agent. Figure 4-1 provides an operational framework of semantic functions and relations for clinical use.

Dore (1975) delineated nine primitive speech act functions. They appear in Fig. 4-2, and entail labeling, repeating, answering, requesting (action), requesting (answer), calling, greeting, protesting, and practicing. Halliday (1975) regarded early language development as a child's progressive mastery of a functional potential. He indicated that in the initial phase of learning functions, each expression or utterance has only one function. He found in studying the acquisition of one child, the following functions were acquired in essentially this order, with the last function significantly last:

1.	Instrumental	I want—
2.	Regulatory	Do as I tell you
3.	Interactional	Me and you
4.	Personal	Here I come
5.	Heuristic	Tell me why
6.	Imaginative	Let's pretend
7.	Informative (representational)	I've got something to tell you

Figure 4-2 *Nine primitive speech acts.* [a]

Primitive Speech Act	*Description*
Labeling	Segmented or categorized experiences are labeled, but for no apparent communicative intent
Repeating	Imitation of an available word or utterance
Answering	Response to an inquiry, "What's this?"
Requesting (action)	Seeking instrumental assistance with something
Requesting (answer)	Labeling with a question intonation seeking verification of a label
Calling	Utterance for the purpose of notice or proximal interaction
Greeting	Utterance to acknowledge presence of another
Protesting	Utterance to deny or reject
Practicing	Labels in the absence of a reference

[a]Adapted from Dore (1975, p. 31)

The descriptors on the right are exemplars in the adult sense. They provide the essential dimension. These functions are evident in early language learning by single words or sound patterns (even gestures) cast in a matrix of events and actions. In early language learning, a child

> can use language to satisfy his own material needs, in terms of goods or services (instrumental); to exert control over the behavior of others (regulatory); to establish and maintain contact with those that matter to him (interactional); and to express his own individuality and self-awareness (personal). Moreover, any one option may have a very considerable range, not only in the sense that it can be used very frequently . . . but also, and more significantly, in the sense that many of the options are very general in their applicability (Halliday 1975, pp. 246–48).

Speech acts become coded in conventional ways by learning the vocabulary or lexicon, word combining mechanisms, and word marking mechanisms (or morphology) of a language. Thus, vocabulary and structure are in principle the same thing (Halliday 1975).

Syntactic Systems

The syntactic domain deals with the form, structure, and organization of words (more technically morphemes) in the formulation of sentences. Early one- and two-word utterances convey basic semantic functions and relations but are relatively barren of syntactic systems and processes (Bowerman 1976). Linguistic systems provide an elaborate means for making semantic functions and relations explicit. For example, a child might say "cookie" to mean a number of things, depending upon available referents and communicative intent. However, a child who knows various syntactic systems may be more explicit in several ways: "My cookie," "Give me another cookie," "Give me the oatmeal cookie," "Give me the oatmeal cookie that Mommy baked," "Give me the oatmeal cookie that Mommy baked yesterday," etc. Explicitness in coding intent in the most appropriate way reduces ambiguity and increases communicative power—efficiency and effectiveness.

Syntactic systems are very complex, and intimately related to semantic functions and relationships, as well as to phonological systems. While syntactic systems pertain to language *form* or *structure,* semantic functions and relationships pertain to underlying *intent* or *functions.*

Clinicians should know about the morphological system, the hierarchical structure attendant to phrase structure, transformational operations, recursiveness, and derivation. Moreover, they should have some basic understanding of major syntactic systems, suprasegmental systems, and co-occurring systems.

The *morpheme* is the basic unit of meaning (Bolinger 1965, 1975). It is the basic unit in formulating and modulating meaning in a sentence. Through syntax, morphemes are combined, changed, ordered, and tagged to code meaning in an intended way. Morphemes are inextricably related to both semantics and syntax and are intimately related to phonology. For example, a plural morpheme might be /z/ or /s/ depending upon the phonological context.

There are bound and unbound, or free, morphemes. *Unbound morphemes* can stand alone—"tree," "supper," "zipper," "table," and so on. *Bound morphemes* must be connected with another morpheme, bound or unbound. They pertain to the affix systems. *Affixes* are word markers or tags that indicate form class or alter the semantic state of words. Those that appear in the initial part of a word are called *prefixes* and those that occur at the end of a word are called *suffixes*. Suffixes can be either derivational or inflectional, but prefixes are always derivational.

Derivational mechanisms can change word forms and convert sentences into words and phrases. For example, the morphemes "regulate," "lazy," and "verbal" can be used to create or derive "regulation," "laziness," and "verbalize." And, "A bird is black" can be turned into "a blackbird." "The man is mad" can be converted into "a madman." More elaborately, "She is lovely" can be converted into "*That she is lovely* seems obvious." Derivational mechanisms are very powerful because they provide a means for creating verbal forms without having previously heard the forms. Derivational rules are apparently limited in number because they operate on grammatical classes and constituents, i.e., change nouns to verbs, verbs to nouns, adjectives to nouns, nouns to adjectives, count nouns to mass nouns, etc. Derivational systems that replace constituents such as nominals are somewhat more complex than those that change form classes of words (Lees 1965; Rosenbaum 1967). The *Roberts English Series* (New York: Harcourt Brace Jovanovich, 1967) places an emphasis on derivational systems. Bolinger (1975) had two major categories of morphemes, lexical and grammatical. Lexical morphemes produce words whereas grammatical morphemes tag or index words. Grammatical morphemes are function words (articles, demonstrations, prepositions, conjunctions, and inflectional suffixes).

Inflectional mechanisms change the state or increase the explicitness of morphemes. Nouns can be made plural or show possessiveness. Adjectives can show comparative (*-er*) and superlative (*-est*) relations. Verbs can have tense markings. Subject and predicate agreement can be shown. The following are some examples of inflectional mechanisms:

Plural: duck*s*, shoe*s*, zipper*s*
Possessive: Bill'*s*, *his*, *mine*
Tense: cook—*cooked*, see—*saw*, save—*saved*
Subject-predicate agreement: She wait*s*, I wait

Figure 4-3 outlines a taxonomy of morphemes.

The acquisition of inflectional morphemes was studied by Cazden (1968) and Palermo and Eberhart (1968). The developmental sequence for inflectional morphemes appears in Chap. 6. Inflectional rules begin to appear in Brown's Stage II (1973a,b).

Clincians should appreciate phrase structure, since it carries the hierarchical organization for the constituents or units of syntax and defines sentence types. *Phrase structure* is that part of grammar which delineates the basic underlying organization of a sentence. Sentence constituents are organized in hierarchical struc-

Figure 4-3 *Taxonomy of English morphemes.*

Bound, Affix

    Prefix: *per*ceive, *un*known, *dis*count, etc.
    Suffix:
            Derivational—happi*ness*, happi*ly*, etc.
            Inflectional—cak*es*, Ann'*s*, open*ed*, etc.

Unbound, free

    Simple: dog, apple, laugh, big, etc.
    Bound + bound: conclude, uncouth, perfect, etc.
    Bound + free: impractical, actor, building, etc.
    Free + free: hotdog, bookstore, sidewalk, etc.

---

tures that begin with a general rule which is differentiated into increasingly more specific rules until specific lexical classes are delineated and specific morphemes identified. The most general unit is the sentence. The next level is the subject and predicate, or subject noun phrase and verb phrase. The units are in turn differentiated further until all of the constituents in the phrase structure of a particular sentence are delineated.

What follows is an extended illustration of how phrase structure rules operate from general to specific in hierarchical organization. These rules serve that purpose:

      S →   sentence
    NP →   noun phrase
    VP →   verb phrase
      N →   common noun
    art →   article
    det →   determiner
  dem →   demonstrative
    ( ) →   optional

The most general phrase structure rule for adult grammar is

    S→ NP + VP

This is read, "Sentence should be considered as a noun phrase (subject) and a verb phrase (predicate)." NP and VP can also be rewritten according to more specific replacement rules:

    NP→ det + N

This is read, "Noun phrase should be considered as a determiner and a common noun." The determiner can be rewritten to show that it contains a pre-article and article, or genitive, or demonstrative, and postdeterminer in that order, but only one genitive, demonstrative, or article is required and permitted, whereas the remainder is optional. After each of these have been "rewritten" until all morphemes are identified for a particular sentence, several variations of determiners can be made.

The following are only a few examples:

$$Det \rightarrow (\text{pre-article}) + \begin{matrix} \text{art} \\ \text{dem} \\ \text{gen} \end{matrix} + (\text{postdet})$$

(pre-article) +	art dem gen +	(postdet)		
many of	the those these my	ten first six		+ boy(s)
some of	his	best		

Notice that each of these alternative determiners complies with the determiner rule and can be used to make a noun phrase with "boy(s)." Phrase structure rules can be successively rewritten until one reaches a lexical class, thereby affording an opportunity to choose a particular item, i.e., a morpheme. This item is then read into the slot.

For example, follow the series of rewrite rules to obtain a lexical item such as "son."

S→ NP + VP
NP→ Det + N
N→ Common N
Common N→ Count N
Count N→ Animate N
Animate N→ Class X
Class X→ brother, father, *son,* etc.

The phrase structure rewrite rules presented thus far are only illustrations. They neither go through all the necessary rewrite rules nor show the complete set of rules. They merely illustrate rewrite rules for particular lexical or grammatical items. The important information in the illustration is that specific units are derived from more general units and that a single item at a time is rewritten. These are two properties of a phrase structure grammar.

The derivation of subunits from more general units is the hallmark of a hierarchical structure. Phrase structure rules are hierarchical. Figure 4-4 illustrates the underlying hierarchical arrangement for the phrase structure in sentence (17):

(17) The car would stop.

Notice that Fig. 4-4 can describe an enormous number of intransitive sentences merely by replacing words at the bottom of the hierarchy (within the same terminal classes). For example, it would yield sentences like the following:

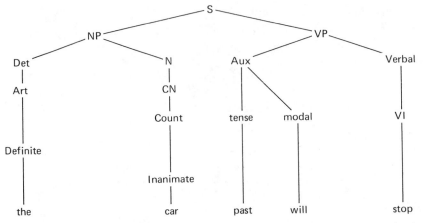

Figure 4-4 *Underlying hierarchical arrangement for phrase structure in the sentence "The car would stop."*

The *clock* would stop.
The boat *will* stop.
The *train* would *run*.
The *toy* would stop.
The *plane will go*.

Or, if alternatives were taken at a higher level, the following sentences would be permissible:

A boat would stop.
The girl smiled.
The monkey will scratch a flea.
The rabbit will cost two dollars.
A boat will sail.
The man had eaten.
Most of the boxes were here.

Again at a higher level, many more alternatives are available.

Somebody opened the icebox yesterday.
Ruth asked for the money.
She sat on the sofa.

At a still higher level, the following sentences (with the necessary transformations) are permissible:

Cooking is fun.
His promising to come kept us here.
It was easy for him to swim.

The point of this illustration is that phrase structure rules have an organizational structure that is hierarchical in nature. More generalized rules lead exponentially to more sentences. Ultimately, an innumerable number and variety of sentences can be produced, limited only by the number of entries available in the terminal classes of the hierarchies. In view of the fact that many classes contain a virtually unlimited number of entries, an astronomical number of sentences could be generated by phrase structure rules. This indicates that a hierarchical structure is very powerful in producing a large number of sentences.

Hierarchical structure is also very powerful in facilitating memory. Rather than a vast number of rules for the production of sentences, a hierarchical structure requires relatively few, though they must be organized to account efficiently for sentences. From a memory standpoint, it is much more efficient to have a few highly organized rules for producing sentences than to learn a large number of loosely related rules for producing those same sentences.

Clinicians should know the basic sentence types of English. Sentences are classified by type in two ways: structure and function. Harris (1965) and Thomas (1965) have outlined English sentence types according to structure or form. Muma (1971a) has consolidated their views. Figure 4-5 shows the main constituents of the basic sentence frames of English.

The main constituents are numbered according to position in the sentence. These positions only index a gross surface structure, which does not show the actual hierarchical relationship of sentence constituents. Position One contains the subject noun phrase. Position Two contains the auxiliary and main verb. Position Three contains the verbal elements required by each verb type. Position Four contains optional adverbial elements. The classes of the main verbs (with their attendant constituents in position Three) serve to distinguish sentence types. Developmental evidence (Muma 1971a) gives some construct validity to this representation. The evidence shows that there are differential patterns of transformation according to sentence type (excluding those processes specific to certain sentence types).

Figure 4-5   *Constituents of basic sentence frames of English (Muma 1971a).*

		Constituents		
1	*2*	*3*	*4*	*(Example)*
1. NP[a]	aux BE	Adjectival	(Adverbial)[b]	He is nice (today).
2. NP	aux BE	NP	(Adverbial)	He is a cook (today).
3. NP	aux BE	Adverb-place	(Adverbial)	He is here (today).
4. NP	aux VI		(Adverbial)	He sleeps (today).
5. NP	aux VT	NP	(Adverbial)	He reads a book (today).
6. NP	aux Vh	NP	(Adverbial)	He has a book (today).
7. NP	aux Vs	Adjectival	(Adverbial)	He seems nice (today).
8. NP	aux Vb	Substantive[c]	(Adverbial)	He becomes a cook (today).

[a]NP is noun phrase.
[b]Parenthesis means optional.
[c]Substantive may be either a noun phrase or an adjectival.

Another way of considering sentence types is with respect to the various general functions of utterances. These are declarative sentences, yes/no and wh-questions, negations, passives, iterations, elliptical sentences, exclamations, imperatives, etc. Transformational operations reveal that underlying basic strings can be changed into these types of sentences. Through *transformational operations*, one can appreciate the interrelatedness of such sentence types.

The earlier versions of transformational generative grammar (Chomsky 1957, 1961, 1965a,b; Miller 1962; Thomas 1965; Harris 1965; Roberts 1964) proposed a kernelization process in which it was thought that basic "kernel" sentences were produced, on which transformations were superimposed. Chomsky then abandoned the concept of kernelization, because "kernel sentences play no distinctive role in generation or interpretation of sentences . . ." (1965b, p. 18). He went on to say that kernel sentences should not be confused with the basic strings that underlie them. His revision is probably due to the difficulties that have arisen trying to demonstrate a psychological priority for kernel sentences over transformed sentences. The early psychological evidence was promising (Miller 1965) but was eventually contradicted by other evidence (Clifton and Odum 1966; Johnson 1965, 1966; Lakoff 1972b). Bever (1968) suggests that the concept of kernelization may have psychological reality even though the linguistic evidence is equivocal. Deese (1970, pp. 42–44) presents both positions.

Clinicians need not concern themselves about transformational increments in memory load and kernelization. They should, however, be aware of sentence types and the transformational operations of sentences as one way of describing an aspect of contextual relationships in grammar. Rarely are sentences produced in basic forms. They usually contain a variety of structures which are not directly attributable to an underlying hierarchical structure. These sentences are thought to be transformations on underlying basic forms. Phrase structure grammars account for increased complexity through patterns of increased differentiation. Thus, a multimodified noun phrase would have a hierarchical structure with several levels of differentiation. This makes it difficult to describe not only the differentiating levels and units but also memory processing. A *transformational approach* describes operations beyond phrase structure that are incorporated into sentences. Thus, it is simplified because there is no need to specify hierarchical structures beyond the basic phrase structure for a sentence type. Additional structures are presumably incorporated by operations *on* the sentence rather than resulting from differentiation *within* its constituents. Moreover, transformational operations account for open-endedness, or recursiveness, by allowing for recurrent applications of transformations.

Further, transformational operations provide a way of showing the interrelatedness of sentences. *Interrelatedness* is a strong index of simplicity of grammar, and refers to the mutual application of transformations to all sentences, regardless of their past derivational history. That is, except for certain local transformations (such as the passive and objective), transformations apply to all sentences and can be used repeatedly in any single sentence.

There is evidence pro and con that transformational operations apply to the whole sentence rather than its specific constituents. Two types of evidence support this notion. First, certain transformations occur significantly more frequently with certain sentence types—exclusive of those which are specific to certain sentence types, such as passive, elliptic, iteration, there, etc. (Muma 1971a). Since most transformations can theoretically apply to any sentence type, it would be reasonable not to expect selectivity if the operations were on constituents *within* sentences. But this is not the case. Second, it would appear that a recursive use of transformations would allow both the same transformation several times and several transformations in the same sentence. In adult grammar, both situations are "allowable," but this is not the case with early child grammars. There is a period in which multiple transformations in a single sentence occur only with *different* rather than the *same* transformations (Menyuk 1969, p. 96). Figure 4-6(a) illustrates transformations loaded on a sentence in different ways. This evidence supports a phrase structure account as well. Sometimes multiple use of the same transformation is on the same constituent. When this happens, the constituent must be differentiated into increasingly lower levels of specificity, which means increased "depth" in memory processing. Phrase structure grammars have successfully accounted for sentences that presumably contain transformational operations (Johnson 1965, 1966).

Figure 4-6(a)   *Three transformations (TR) spread across a sentence, loaded within a constituent, and repeated within a constituent.*

The man cut down a tree.
TR across a sentence: The *big* man cut down *and hauled off* the *rotten* tree.
TR loaded on a constituent: The *big* man *in the red hat, my uncle,* cut down a tree.
TR repeated within a constituent: The *big, fat, old* man cut down a tree.

In general, phrase structure grammars appear to be powerful in accounting for sentences relatively low in complexity (both structurally and psychologically). Transformational grammars, on the other hand, appear to be less powerful in accounting for such sentences, but more powerful in accounting for high-complexity sentences. "Powerful" is used here to refer to both descriptive adequacy and explanatory adequacy (an account of cognitive processing). For example, phrase structure grammar apparently provides the best account of pre-noun modifiers and relative clauses (Johnson 1965, 1966). Transformational grammars provide the most attractive accounts of embedding and conjoining. Phrase structure grammars can account for left recursive sentences but not very satisfactorily for right recursive and self-embedded sentences. Transformational grammar, on the other hand, accounts for all three. *Recursiveness* refers to a property of grammar in which rules can be used again and again within a sentence. It is most easily seen in the repeated use of adjective modifiers—big tree, big old tree, big old rotten tree, big old rotten oak tree, etc. The numbering system is a recursive one. We count to ten, mark ten, count to ten again, mark twenty, count to ten again, etc. Theoretically, we can count to infinity because recursive systems are open-ended.

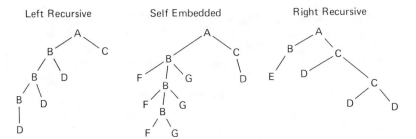

Figure 4-6(b) *Types of recursive sentence structures. (Adapted from* Noam Chomsky *by John Lyons. Copyright © 1970 by John Lyons. Used by permission of The Viking Press.)*

Right recursiveness, self-embedding, and left recursiveness are shown in Fig. 4-6(b). It shows that certain parts of the sentence are held in memory while other parts are resolved. In the case of left recursiveness, pre-noun modifiers of the subject obtain several levels of resolution while other aspects of the sentence are held in memory. In self-embedding, post-noun modifiers are expanded. In right recursiveness, the direct object or verb complements are expanded. Forster (1966) has shown that left recursive, right recursive, and self-embedded sentences are treated differently in memory. Sentences (18), (19), and (20) exemplify left recursiveness, self-embedding, and right recursiveness:

(18) The young brown and white cocker spaniel barked all night.
(19) A squirrel that ran into the nest on the right lost its tail.
(20) The men ate peanut butter sandwiches and stale chocolate candy bars.

Sentence (20) was not only right recursive but, from a transformational point of view, conjoined—two underlying sentences, (21) and (22), were joined to form (20):

(21) The men ate peanut butter sandwiches.
(22) The men ate stale chocolate candy bars.

There is a dispute concerning the needs and adequacies of phrase structure grammars and transformational grammars. As the dispute continues, the applied fields can obtain new useful insights. Transformational grammar has already proven useful. Menyuk (1964a,b, 1969, 1971); Menyuk and Looney (1972a,b); Morehead and Ingram (1973); Hass and Wepman (1969); Engler et al. (1973); and Leonard (1972) have shown that a transformational model provides increased definitions of clinical disorders such as "delayed language." Menyuk (1969) has also shown that it provides an increased definition of language acquisition. O'Donnell, Griffin, and Norris (1967), Brown, Cazden, and Bellugi-Klima (1969), Brown (1971), and others have shown that the concept of transformational operations is useful in appreciating language acquisition and usage.

Transformational operations make changes on underlying phrase structure, generating thousands of additional sentences that could not be made by phrase structure rules alone. Transformational rules can produce an infinite number and variety of sentences. For example, transformations on underlying sentence base (23) could result in sentences (24) through (29), as well as hundreds more.

(23)	The dog ate the bone.	(Underlying sentence base)
(24)	The bone *was* eat*en by* the dog.	*Passive transformation*
(25)	The dog *did not* eat the bone.	*Negative, do transformations*
(26)	*Did* the dog eat the bone?	*Yes/no, do transformations*
(27)	*What did* the dog eat?	*Yes/no, do, wh-transformations*
(28)	The dog ate the bone *and* some meat.	*Conjunction transformations*
(29)	The dog can eat *and* run today.	*Conjunction transformations*

Transformations can be classified according to

1. Types of change on underlying base or phrase structure
2. Objects of change
3. Constraints of change

There are transformations that perform order, addition, and deletion changes (and various combinations of these) on phrase structure. Examples of these for sentence base (30) are given in sentences (31) through (35).

(30)	Some birds can fly.	(Underlying sentence base)
(31)	Can some birds fly?	*Order change*
(32)	Some birds can fly and swim.	*Addition change*
(33)	Some birds can.	*Deletion change*
(34)	Can some birds fly and swim?	*Order and addition changes*
(35)	Can't some birds fly and swim?	*Order, addition (not), and addition (and) changes*

There are two transformational categories for objects of change: simple or single base, and general or double base. Simple transformations are those applied to a single underlying sentence of varying complexity. General transformations combine underlying sentences. Examples of simple and general transformational operations on underlying sentence base (36) are given in sentences (37) and (38).

(36)	The dog tracked the rabbit.	(Underlying sentence base)
(37)	*Did* the dog track the rabbit?	*Simple change*
(38)	The dog *that won the field trials* tracked the rabbit.	*General change*

Notice that in (38) two underlying sentence bases were combined. The sentence base, "The dog won the field trials," was inserted into (36). Thus, (38) was made by a general transformation.

The 1965 version of Chomsky's theory posits local transformations as well. These operate on alternatives—hopefully binary (Halle 1957)—at the phrase structure level: object he/him, passive, etc.

There are two types of transformations according to the constraints of change: *optional* and *obligatory*. An optional transformation has no constraint. A speaker may use it or not according to how he wants to say something. On the other hand, other transformations are obligatory, and a language or dialect requires them. For example, sentence (40) has an optional transformation applied to underlying sentence base (39).

(39) He carried the suitcase.
(40) He carried *his* suitcase.

Notice that either is an acceptable sentence. However, (40) is more explicit. It states ownership of a particular suitcase. An example of an obligatory transformation is provided for underlying sentence base (41) in sentence (42).

*(41) I gave he a nickel.
(42) I gave *him* a nickel.

These transformations were on surface structure (they showed the resulting sentences). One should appreciate various structural descriptions (requirements and constraints) involved in the execution of transformations. Several lists of transformations with structural descriptions are available (Roberts 1964; Chomsky 1965a,b; Menyuk 1964a,b; Lees 1965; O'Donnell, Griffin, and Norris 1967; Hunt 1964; Bateman and Zidonis 1966; Jacobs and Rosenbaum 1968; and Muma 1971a). Even though the Roberts material is now dated because of revisions on the theory, it is recommended as an introduction because it is readily understood and contains a programmed learning text for both phrase structure and transformational rules. Jacobs and Rosenbaum (1968) provide an updated and easily read discussion of English transformational grammar.

The examples above showed classifications of transformations. These were not mutually exclusive. For example, sentence (44) is the result of a transformational operation that is optional, general, and makes an addition change on underlying sentence base (43).

(43) The clown has funny ears.
(44) The clown had funny ears and a big nose.

Moreover, the order of utilization of transformations leads to different sentences. This is referred to as the traffic rules of transformation.

Clinicians will find the concept of transformations useful in understanding a child's verbal behavior, and in programming activities and materials in language intervention. I have already mentioned that transformational usage provides a good index of language acquisition. Menyuk (1964b) showed that the distinction between optional and obligatory transformations is developmentally significant. She also showed that multiple transformation within the same sentence is developmentally significant in terms of both number and variety (1969, p. 96). An increased number of transformations indicates greater maturity. Repeated use of the same transformation in a sentence indicates even greater maturity, and in the same constituent of a sentence still more maturity (see Figure 4-6a). Mellon (1967) devised a sentence combining activity (double base transformations) to teach written composition in the junior high school. His approach was much more successful than the typical English lessons dealing with "parts of speech" and various other parsing procedures.

Because an understanding of transformational operations leads to an appreciation of the interrelationships of sentences, clinicians have a powerful tool for understanding a child's verbal behavior. The following sentences illustrate this point. Sentence pairs (45) through (50) are intimately related.

(45) The team can play ball well.
(46) *Can't* the team play ball well?
(47) It was silly.
(48) *For him to touch the wire* was silly.
(49) She is the daughter *of Mrs. Brown.*
(50) It is Tom'*s* dog.

Sentences (45) and (46) share the same basic underlying sentence except for the following transformations on (46): yes/no and negation. Sentences (47) and (48) share the same basic underlying sentence except that (48) contains a nominal expansion in the form of a for–to transformation. Sentences (49) and (50) do not contain the same basic underlying sentence. They are related, however, because they are the same sentence type (BE + NP) and contain a possessive transformation.

Perhaps I should pause here to reiterate and expand some terminology: the morpheme is the basic semantic-syntactic unit. However, there are larger units in syntax called sentence constituents. In sentence hierarchy, any of the various units from the most general (subject and predicate) to the class from which a particular morpheme is selected are constituents of the sentence. Figure 4-7 illustrates some hierarchical constituents for sentence (51) below. These are shown for surface structure in the middle of the figure, and for hierarchical structure on the right side.

(51) The girls rode a horse.

An *immediate constituent* analysis is one in which constituents are derived according to the constituents which are immediately superordinate (more generic). Thus, the constituents of article and noun in Fig. 4-7 are derived from NP_1 and NP_2 for the subject and object respectively.

Similar derivations of constituents are shown in Fig. 4-7, and other terms are sometimes used for constituents. *Verbal, nominal, adverbial,* and *adjectival* are

Figure 4-7 *Hierarchical constituents of sentence (51).*[a]

Sentence:	*The girls rode a horse.*	S
Clauses	*The girls rode a horse.*	NP_1 + VP
and	*The girls (past + ride) a horse.*	NP_1 + aux + VT + NP_2
Phrases:	*The girls (past + ride) a horse.*	art. + N + aux + VT + NP$_2$
Words:	*The girls (past + ride) a horse.*	art. + N + aux + VT + art. + N
Morphemes:	*The girl + plural (past + ride) a horse.*	art. def. + N + plural + past + tense + VT + art. indef. + N

[a] Adapted from Cazden (1972a, p. 16).

terms of major constituents of sentences. The concepts of verbal, nominal, adverbial, and adjectival replace the traditional notion of "parts of speech." Syntactic categories are not discrete. Various syntactic categories overlap, or as Ross (1974) put it, "squish" with other categories. Bolinger (1975, pp. 152–53) provides a table showing the overlap of the major syntactic categories, nouns, verbs, adjectives, and adverbs.

Verbal pertains to the entire predicate system except for the auxiliary. Depending upon the type of predicate system, the verbal may range from a single morpheme to an elaborate system of them. The verbal is italicized in sentences (52) through (57).

(52)	Some horses *are fast*.	NP aux *BE adj*
(53)	Those stones *appear old*.	NP aux *Vs adj*
(54)	Most of the players	
	had a cold.	NP aux *Vh* NP
(55)	They *pulled the log*.	NP aux *VT* NP
(56)	Somebody *laughed*.	NP aux *VI*
(57)	No one *knew the first*	
	thing about canoeing.	NP aux *VT* NP

Nominal pertains to any forms that can replace a noun phrase. Nominals can be a single morpheme or a complex pattern of morphemes as shown by the italicized segments of sentences (58) through (61).

(58)	*Everyone* can swim across	
	the pool.	NP aux VI prep NP
(59)	*Tom* sold *it* to the *men*.	NP aux VT NP prep NP
(60)	*Rowing* is difficult.	NP aux BE adj
(61)	*His running all summer*	
	helped *his team*.	NP aux VT NP

Adverbial pertains to any forms that function as an adverb constituent. As with nominals, verbals, and adjectivals, adverbials can be a single morpheme or a complex pattern of morphemes. The italicized segments of sentences (62) through (65) show adverbials.

(62)	He slept *yesterday*.	NP aux VI *adv*
(63)	We took him *home*.	NP aux VT NP *adv*
(64)	Somebody turned it *too*	
	tight.	NP aux VT NP *adv*
(65)	I asked for it *so I*	
	could ride easier.	NP aux VT NP *adv*

In sentence (65) there is an embedded sentence which contains an adverbial.

Adjectival pertains to forms that function as an adjective constituent. The following sentences illustrate some adjectivals.

(66) The *big* turtle was *about*
        one hundred years old.   NP aux BE *Adj*
(67) Those boys played foot-
        ball in the *wrong* league.   NP aux VT NP *adv*
(68) The *onion* soup tasted *good.*   NP Vs *adj*
(69) The man *with a blue hat*
        told some *funny* stories.   NP *adj* VT NP

Notice that adjectivals were appearing in nominals and adverbials. This is a general property of nominals, verbals, adverbials, and adjectivals. That is, the open-ended property of grammar allows for various constituents to be embedded in other constituents. Transformational operations provide systematic ways for embedding and conjoining various constituents. Accordingly, transformational operations provide for a considerable variety of sentences. Remembering that a generative grammar provides for an infinite number and variety of sentences (under the restriction of a finite memory), one realizes that transformational operations play a major role because there are relatively few transformational operations, yet they can be used to produce an infinite number and variety of sentences. Recursiveness (open-endedness), hierarchical structure (phrase structure), transformations, and derivations are major generative mechanisms. Appendix B shows semantic and relational functions, phrase structure rules, morphological rules, major transformations, and some clues for identifying loci of learning for syntactic systems of English.

The *pronominal* system is unique because each form is learned individually and because its primary function is anaphoric reference. *Anaphoric reference* is the use of a pronominal to carry or maintain previously established reference. In sentence (70), both uses of "their" provide respective anaphoric reference to "the boys," and "them" is an anaphoric reference to "their lunches."

(70) The boys carried *their* lunches in *their* pails so the teachers did not see *them.*

Waryas (1973) has described the distinguishing features of various pronouns of English. Her description is presented in Fig. 4-8.

I have discussed co-occurring structures in the section on the importance of contexts and elsewhere, particularly in reference to establishing a security base from which a child can extend himself in language learning. It is because co-occurring structures define syntactic context in which language learning occurs that clinicians should understand them. *Co-occurrences* are unique both for an individual and for the particular linguistic systems he tries to learn. Thus, it is not possible to discuss specific co-occurrences. It is the principle of co-occurrence that is important.

Every utterance that contains more than one verbal system contains co-occurrences. In sentence (71) several linguistic structures co-occur.

	Speaker	Listener	Other	Singular	Subjective	Reflexive	Possessive	Replacive
me	+	−	−	+	−	−	−	−
I	+	−	−	+	+	−	−	−
myself	+	−	−	+	−	+	−	−
my	+	−	−	+	−	−	+	−
mine	+	−	−	+	−	−	+	+
us₁	+	+	−	+	−	−	−	−
we₁	+	+	−	−	+	−	−	−
ourselves₁	+	+	−	−	−	+	−	−
our₁	+	+	−	−	−	−	+	−
ours₁	+	+	−	−	−	−	+	+
us₂	+	+	+	−	−	−	−	−
we₂	+	+	+	−	+	−	−	−
ourselves₂	+	+	+	−	−	+	−	−
our₂	+	+	+	−	−	−	+	−
ours₂	+	+	+	−	−	−	+	+
you₁	−	+	−	+	−	−	−	−
you₁	−	+	−	+	+	−	−	−
yourself	−	+	−	+	−	+	−	−
your₁	−	+	−	+	−	−	+	−
yours₁	−	+	−	+	−	−	+	+
you₂	−	+	+	−	−	−	−	−
you₂	−	+	+	−	+	−	−	−
yourselves	−	+	+	−	−	+	−	−
your₂	−	+	+	−	−	−	+	−
yours₂	−	+	+	−	−	−	+	+

	Speaker	Listener	Other	Singular	Human	Male	Subjective	Reflexive	Possessive	Replacive
them	−	−	+	−			−	−	−	−
they	−	−	+	−			+	−	−	−
themselves	−	−	+	−			−	+	−	−
their	−	−	+	−			−	−	+	−
theirs	−	−	+	−			−	−	+	+
him	−	−	+	+	+	+	−	−	−	−
he	−	−	+	+	+	+	+	−	−	−
himself	−	−	+	+	+	+	−	+	−	−
his	−	−	+	+	+	+	−	−	+	−
his	−	−	+	+	+	+	−	−	+	+
her	−	−	+	+	+	−	−	−	−	−
she	−	−	+	+	+	−	+	−	−	−
herself	−	−	+	+	+	−	−	+	−	−
her	−	−	+	+	+	−	−	−	+	−
hers	−	−	+	+	+	−	−	−	+	+
it	−	−	+	+	−		−	−	−	−
it	−	−	+	+	−		+	−	−	−
itself	−	−	+	+	−		−	+	−	−
its	−	−	+	+	−		−	−	+	−

Figure 4-8 Semantic and syntactic features of lexical entries for pronouns. (Reprinted from Waryas 1973.)

(71) The mouse ate some moldy cheese.

The sentence contains a subject noun phrase and a transitive verb phrase, which in turn contains an object noun phrase. The subject noun phrase consists of a determiner which is the definite article *the* and an animate common noun. The transitive verb *ate* contains an auxiliary system that is marked by a past tense marker on "eat." The object noun phrase has a determiner which is an indefinite article, an adjectival modifier, and a mass noun. Sentence (71) contains a large number of co-occurring syntactic structures. Utterances can also be described in terms of co-occurring semantic functions and relations. Sentence (71) contains the following: agent-action-object-attributive. Any one aspect of an utterance co-exists in structural and functional context with the others. This is important to the clinician focusing on a specific syntactic system or semantic function. Clinicians do not need to know the technical jargon to identify most of the co-occurring structures and functions in utterances.

A clinician may choose to identify syntactically the linguistic contexts in an individual's sentences. In sentence (71), the co-occurring structures for the definite article *the* are all of the other structures mentioned above. Co-occurrences in several sentences would reveal that the definite article appears in only a limited set of other structures in early language acquisition. For example, one child might attempt only to use "the" in subject noun phrases of transitive sentences. Another child's might be the past tense of the auxiliary system. Still another child's co-occurrence might be a definite article with animate nouns. Many patterns of co-occurrence are possible.

Functionally, sentence (71) shows that agentive co-occurs with action, object, and attributive. The definite article co-occurs with agent. This co-occurrence between form and function pertains to Slobin's statement, "New forms first express functions, and new functions are first expressed by old forms" (1970, p. 2).

Prosodic features of language are structural in nature, much in the same way as are vocabulary and other syntactic dimensions. Prosodic features are sometimes called *suprasegmentals* because they mark major constituents of utterances, providing access to the identification of phonemes, or segments. However, perception of phonemes is probably not direct. There seem to be intervening units that define the phoneme. Prosodic information provides an envelope or matrix into which a child "knows" that morphemes go (Bruner 1975). A syllable is a basic phonetic unit (Stetson 1951; Stevens, House, and Paul 1966; Moskowitz 1970; Ferguson, Peizer, and Weeks 1973; Ferguson and Garnica 1975), and a morpheme is a basic semantic-syntactic unit (Bolinger 1965, 1975).

Prosodic features include intonation, stress or accent, pausing, rate, and certain inflections. Intonation patterns denote the mode of an utterance, i.e., declarative, question, emphatic, etc. Children first mark a question by an intonation pattern that converts a declaration into a question. This is called a tag question. Tag questions can also be made by producing a yes/no question marker outside of a declarative statement: "Daddy go. Right?" Pausing marks constituent structure. Unusual pauses may reveal linguistic difficulty or uncertainty. Stress patterns emphasize elements for stylistic or other reasons.

Infants may not be able to say speech sounds and words, but they can produce vocalizations with intonational contours like sentences. Moreover, they respond to utterances based on intonational contours. According to Crowder (1972), infants have a "preliminary acoustic storage" that allows them to deal with pitch, voice quality, location, and loudness. Between two and four months, they respond differentially to angry and friendly, familiar and unfamiliar, and male and female voices (Kaplan and Kaplan 1970). Menyuk (1974) reports that at four or five months, infants show an orienting rather than reflexive response to noise. Between five and eight months they seem to distinguish declarative statements and questions. At six months behaviorial responses are differentiated between speech and nonspeech. At eight to ten months they will localize a sound source.

Phonological Systems

The human vocal mechanism is capable of producing a large variety of sounds, only some of which are regarded as speech sounds. *Phonology* deals with sound patterns that are phonemic—carry meaning for a language—and with how these sound patterns are produced. The study of the identification and perception of sound patterns of a language is called *phonemics,* and the study of speech sound production is called *phonetics.* Speech sounds are called phonemes, though Winitz indicated that phonemes are more than speech sounds. "Phonemes are often thought to be speech sounds like /i/ or /t/. The phoneme, however, has quite a different meaning in linguistics; it is defined as a unit of a spoken language that signals semantic distinctiveness" (1969, p. 2). This is the *phonemic principle* of languages. Those aspects of the sound system that index meaning are phonemic.

According to phonemic principles, languages are said to be arbitrary, because specific sound patterns are informative for some languages but not others. Aspiration is a case in point. Some sounds, particularly plosive and stop consonants, are made in such a way that a release of air can be heard (aspiration). For example, the /k/ in "make" is aspirated, but it is not aspirated in "make-up." In English, aspiration is nonphonemic—it makes no difference to the meaningfulness of sound patterns. However, aspiration is significant in other languages, such as Spanish. In these, aspiration alters the meaning of words. Aspiration is phonemic in some languages, but not English.

In semantics and syntax, the morpheme is the basic unit of a sentence. In phonology, the *phoneme* is the basic unit of a syllable (Stetson 1951; Stevens, House, and Paul 1966; Moskowitz 1970; Winitz 1975). Phonemes in English are classified as *vowels, consonants, liquids,* and *glides.* These are partially defined by the type and degree of vocal tract narrowing, as shown in Fig. 4-9. Vowels are produced with a relatively open vocal tract. Liquids and glides are produced with

Figure 4-9 *Degree and type of narrowing for vowels, liquids, glides, and consonants.*

Phonetic Category	Narrowing	
	Type	Degree
Vowels	Open	) (
Liquids and glides	Approximation	) (
Consonants	Obstruction	)(
Consonants	Occlusion	(

approximations of the tongue to various aspects of the vocal tract. Liquids are the /r/ and /l/, as in "rat" and "look," respectively. Glides are /h/, /w/, and /j/. Consonants are produced with obstructions and occlusions.

Consonants are classified in terms of the place and manner of their articulation in the oral cavity, particularly by the tongue, as shown in Fig. 4-10. Vowels are classified according to place of articulation in the *vowel triangle,* shown in Fig. 4-11. *Stop consonants* momentarily impede air flow. These are classified according to which articulators stop the air flow:

Figure 4-10   Place and manner classification for English consonants.

Manner	Bilabial	Labiodental	Dental	*Place* Alveolar	Palatal	Velar	Glottal
Stops							
Voiceless	p			t		k	
Voiced	b			d		g	
Fricatives							
Voiceless		f	θ	s	š		h
Voiced		v	ð	z	ž		
Affricates							
Voiceless					č		
Voiced					ǰ		
Nasals							
All voiced	m			n		ŋ	
Lateral				l			
Semivowels	w			r	y		

Adapted from *Aspects of Language,* Second Edition, by Dwight Bolinger © 1975 by Harcourt Brace Jovanovich, Inc. and reprinted with their permission.

Figure 4-11   Vowel triangle for general American English vowels.

Tongue Elevation	*Tongue Position*		
	Front		Back
High	/i/ beat		/u/ cooed
	/I/ bit		/ʊ/ could
Mid	/e/ bait	/ ə / roses	/o/ code
	/ ɛ / bet		/ ɔ / cawed
Low	/æ/ bat	/ ʌ / but	/a/ cod

Adapted from *Aspects of Language,* Second Edition, by Dwight Bolinger © 1975 by Harcourt Brace Jovanovich, Inc. and reprinted with their permission.

Category	Articulators	Examples
Bilabial	Two lips	*b*ig, *p*in
Alveolar	Alveolar ridge (upper front gum)	*t*wo, *d*og
Velar	Velum region (upper back)	*c*an, *g*o

Consonants made by an obstruction create turbulence in the air that results in a hissing sound. These are called *fricatives*. The following chart describes fricatives in terms of articulators.

Category	Articulators	Examples
Labiodental	Lower lip—upper teeth	*f*our, *v*ase
Dental	Tongue between teeth	*th*in, *th*en
Alveolar	Alveolar ridge (post dental)	*s*ee, *z*ebra
Palatal	Hard palate region upper front	*sh*ow, vi*s*ion
Glottal	Glottis (larynx)	*h*elp

Consonants made by a momentary stop and a relatively slow release are called *affricates*. There are two of these in English: a combination of /t/ and / ʃ / sounds, as in *chew*, and /d/ and / ʒ /, as in *juice*. Both of these are alveolar. *Nasal* consonants are those in which air is released through the nasal cavity. All are voiced. There are bilabial nasal consonants (*m*ake), alveolar nasal consonants (*n*o), and velar nasal consonants (si*ng*). Consonant pairs that vary in only one feature are called *cognates*. /p/ and /b/, /f/ and /v/, /t/ and /d/, and /k/ and /g/ are cognates; the only difference between the two members of each pair is voicing.

Most clinicians account for speech sound articulation in terms of "place and manner." However, there are problems with place and manner descriptions. They describe phonemes as entities, but phonemes are psychological categories perceived in a maze of acoustic patterns and produced in a variety of ways. Speech perception and production are dynamic processes. A given phoneme is rarely if ever produced the same way repeatedly, and certainly not in varying contexts. There is a range of acoustic and phonetic patterns that could be regarded within a particular phonemic boundary (Peterson and Barney 1952; Miller and Nicely 1955). A third problem is that consonants are separated from vowels; that is, different descriptions are used for consonants than vowels. Halle indicated that distinctive feature approaches overcome this problem.

A further difference between most standard systems and the distinctive feature system lies in the treatment of two major classes of segments, the vowels and the consonants. In most standard systems these two classes are described in terms of features which are totally different: consonants are described in terms of "points of articulation," whereas, vowels are described in terms of the so-called "vowel triangle" (1965b, p. 327).

The *distinctive features* approach is an attempt to overcome some of the problems of place and manner approaches. Phonemes are regarded as syllable segments containing bundles of features that portray their acoustic and phonetic status. Features of a phoneme are distinctive when they contrast with features in another segment. This is illustrated in Fig. 4-12. Note here that some aspects of the place and manner approach are retained. Halle indicated that another benefit of distinctive feature systems is that they can be used to account for both the acoustic and the phonetic aspects of articulation.

> In the preceding, the distinctive features have been utilized for two separate purposes. On the one hand, they have been used to characterize different aspects of vocal tract behavior, such as the location of the different narrowings in the vocal tract, the presence or absence of vocal cord vibration, lowering or raising of velum, and so forth. On the other hand, the features have functioned as abstract markers for the designation of individual morphemes. It is necessary at this point to give an account of how this dual function of the features is built into the theory (1965b, p. 332).

Figure 4-12 Cluster of phonetic features for each of three phonemes (/p/, /b/, and /m/).

Phonetic Features	/p/	/b/	/m/	Distinctive Features
Closure				
Open	−	−	−	
Approximation	−	−	−	
Obstruction	−	−	−	
Occlusion	+	+	+	
Place				
Vertical	2	2	2	
Horizontal				
bilabial	+	+	+	
labio-dental	−	−	−	
lingua-dental	−	−	−	
lingua-alveolar	−	−	−	
lingua-palatal	−	−	−	
lingua-mid-palatal	−	−	−	
uvular	−	−	−	
glottal	−	−	−	
Manner				
Voiced	−	+	+	*
Oral	+	+	−	*
Continuant	−	−	+	*
Duration	−	−	−	
Movement	−	−	−	
Fusion	−	−	−	
Lateral	−	−	−	
Labialization	−	−	−	

Several different feature systems have been published. The Chomsky and Halle (1968) and Halle (1965a,b) features are undoubtedly most widely cited in the applied fields (McReynolds and Engmann 1975; McReynolds and Huston 1971; Menyuk 1968, 1972; Crocker 1969; Compton 1970; Pollock and Rees 1972; Winitz 1969, 1975; Singh 1976; etc.). A major limitation of the Chomsky and Halle features is that they are for adult speech. They do not take into account variations frequently found in the clinical articulation of children (Walsh 1974; Ingram 1974b, 1976). Other feature approaches have been developed by Jakobson, Fant, and Halle (1963), Ladefoged (1972a,b), and Vennemann and Ladefoged (1973). The Ladefoged material seems easier to understand than others.

Most of the distinctive feature systems have a great deal to offer the applied fields, but the terminology is rather difficult. Cynthia Jacobson and I attempted to "reduce" various feature procedures to a manageable level in regard to terminology and acoustic-phonetic distinctions. From time to time Jack Irwin contributed, but the overall direction and critique of this and a related effort dealing with syllabication came in consultation with Ray Daniloff, Art Compton, and Kim Oller. The result was the distinctive phonetic features described in Appendix C. These describe *target articulatory movements or states* in which a variety of positions can be obtained, depending upon coarticulatory influences. "Targetness" denotes the dynamic character of speech articulation (Curtis 1964; Spriestersbach and Curtis 1964). "Movement" and "state" denote the dynamic mechanism in which any given articulatory position is momentarily obtained while passing from one to the next articulatory movement. By using the phrase "target articulatory movements or states," a variety of phonetic approximations can obtain in the realization of a given bundle of phonetic features, or phoneme. Targetness is apparently under substantial kinesthetic control, since various sensory blocks of the articulatory mechanism strongly affect efficiency (Putnam and Ringel 1972; Scott and Ringel 1971).

Figure 4-13 shows the phonetic feature states of English phonemes in isolation. These may not be obtained for phonemes in connected speech where coarticulatory influences are strong (Daniloff and Hammarberg 1973). Again, a phonetic orientation is physiologically based, whereas a phonemic orientation is acoustically based. Distinctive feature systems deal with both. Clinicians are interested primarily in a phonetic feature orientation because they want to assess and change speech articulatory patterns.

Phonemes appear in syllabic structure. Stetson (1951) defined the syllable as the basic or morphological unit of speech. Stevens, House, and Paul (1966) indicate that a syllabic account of articulatory behavior overcomes some of the problems of isolating phonemes in a dynamic process. Fudge (1969), Moskowitz (1970), and Fergusen, Peizer, and Weeks (1973) regard syllabic influences as important in phonology. According to Stetson, all syllables have: (a) a releasing factor, (b) vocal channel shaping factor(s), and (c) an arresting factor. Releasing and arresting factors can occur in two ways: by the chest providing a vocal airstream, and by consonantal actions in the vocal channel. Stetson used the symbol "O" to stand for

Example	Segments	Open	Approximation	Obstruction	Occlusion	Vertical	Bilabial	Labiodental	Lingua-dental	Lingua-alveolar	Lingua-palatal	Lingua-mid-palatal	Velar	Glottal	Voice	Oral	Continuant	Duration	Movement	Fusion	Lateral	Labialize	
b<u>ea</u>t	i	+				1					2				1	+	+	+				3	
b<u>i</u>t	ɪ	+				1					2				1	+	+					3	
b<u>ai</u>t	e	+				2					2				1	+	+	+				3	
b<u>o</u>t	ɛ	+				2					2				1	+	+					3	
b<u>a</u>t	æ	+				3					2				1	+	+					3	VOWELS
f<u>a</u>ther	ɝ	+				2						+			1	+	+	+					
aft<u>er</u>	ɚ	+				2						+			1	+	+						
b<u>u</u>t	ʌ	+				2						+			1	+	+						
c<u>o</u>d	a	+				3							+		1	+	+	+				1	
c<u>aw</u>ed	ɔ	+				3							+		1	+	+					1	
c<u>o</u>de	o	+				2							+		1	+	+					1	
c<u>ou</u>ld	u	+				1							+		1	+	+					1	
c<u>oo</u>ed	ʊ	+				1							+		1	+	+	+				1	
<u>c</u>up	k				+	1							+		3	+							CONSONANTS
<u>g</u>o	g				+	1							+		1	+							
<u>t</u>wo	t				+	1				+					3	+							
<u>d</u>og	d				+	1				+					1	+							

Figure 4-13 *Phonetic feature chart for "isolated" English phonemes.*

mechanisms of the chest, "C" for consonantal actions, and "V" for vocal channel shaping. With these he delineated the basic syllable types of English:

Syllable Type	Example
OVO	eye
OVC	up
CVO	key
CVC	cup

Vowels always occur between releasing and arresting factors. Consonants never occur in a medial position or in isolation. They can occur in the medial position of words but not in syllables. A word, however, is not a speech unit but a semantic-syntactic unit.

Syllabic structure is not easily discernible. Indeed, it varies from dictionary to

PHONETIC FEATURES

Example	Segments	Open	Approximation	Obstruction	Occlusion	Vertical	Bilabial	Labiodental	Lingua-dental	Lingua-alveolar	Lingua-palatal	Lingua-mid-palatal	Velar	Glottal	Voice	Oral	Continuant	Duration	Movement	Fusion	Lateral	Labialize	Class
pail	p					2	+								3	+							CONSONANTS
ball	b					2	+								1	+							
four	f			+		2		+							3	+	+						
vase	v			+		2		+							1	+	+						
thin	θ			+		2			+						3	+	+						
there	ð			+		2			+						1	+	+						
see	s			+		2				+					3	+	+					3	
zoo	z			+		2				+					1	+	+					3	
show	ʃ			+		1					1				3	+	+					1	
vision	ʒ			+		1					1				1	+	+					1	
chew	tʃ			+	+	1				+					3	+				+		3	
juice	dʒ			+	+	1				+					1	+				+		3	
man	m				+	2	+								1	+							
not	n				+	1				+					1	+							
sing	ŋ				+	1							+		1	+							
long	l		+			2					1				1	+	+		+		+		LIQUIDS
run	r		+			2					1				1	+			+			1	
hill	h	+				1								+	2	+	+	+					GLIDES
way	w		+			1									3	+			+			1	
young	j		+			1						+			1	+			+				

Only the salient feature states are given.

Figure 4-13 *(continued).*

dictionary on many words. Moreover, there is considerable disagreement between dictionaries regarding stress patterns. Muma and Muma (1973) conducted a dictionary search for words containing /s/ according to a syllable structure code I devised based on the work of Stevens, House, and Paul (1966), Fromkin (1966), Fudge (1969), Bondarko (1969), Moskowitz (1970), and Venneman (1972). The code is illustrated in Fig. 4-14.

Slots 1 and 11 mean word boundary. Slots 2 and 10 mean syllable boundary with the phoneme at the indicated boundary juncture. Slots 3, 4, 5, and 7, 8, 9, provide for consonants and consonant clusters, prevocalically and postvocalically, respectively. Slot 6 indicates the vowel. The syllabic structure for "stock" in "stockyard" is 1–3–4–6–7–10.

Figure 4-14 *Syllabic structure code for the syllable "stock" in "stockyard."*

1 2 3 4 5   *1* 2 3 4 5
no. of syllables   target syllable

stockyard   stress: *1* 2 3 4 5
word
stok' / yard /   /   /
 # / > / c   c   c   v   c   c   c / <   #
 ✓   s   t   a   k   y
 1   2   3   4   5   6   7   8   9   10   11

Consonantal clusters are multiple factors in either releasing or arresting syllable pulses. Consider the following examples:

Syllable	Example
CVC	cup
CCVC	stop
CCCVC	street

Stetson defined four types of consonants:

Simple	CVO	see
Compound	CCVC	stop
Abutting	CCCVC/CVC	streetcar
(Double)	CVC/CVCC	cupboard

Notice that the last two consonantal types deal with two syllables. A double consonant is merely a special case of abutting consonants, in which the arresting and releasing factors are the same. In this example it is a bilabial arrest and release.

The literature on child speech indicates that syllabic factors account for certain aspects of deviant articulation. This is a new concept for the applied fields. Ingram (1974b) showed that some articulation patterns were a function of weak syllable deletion, syllabic reduplication, or a syllabic voice process. Wicklegren (1966, 1969) indicated that variations in syllabic structure attendant to short-term memory processing are reflected in articulatory behavior. Renfrew (1966) and Panagos (1974) also held that syllabic complexity was influential for instances of an *open syllable*. This was defined by Renfrew (1966) as deletions of final consonants. Ingram (1976, p. 29) indicated that children tend to reduce words to a basic CVO syllable by employing (1) deletion of final consonants, (2) cluster reduction, (3) unstressed syllable deletion, and (4) reduplication. The child phonology literature is showing not only that syllabic structure relates to child variations and aberrant articulation, but that there are apparently important correlates traceable to other aspects of grammar (Leonard and Ritterman 1971; Shriner, Holloway, and Daniloff 1969; Winitz 1975; Menyuk and Looney 1972a,b; Panagos and Hofmann 1971; McNutt and Keenan 1970; Whitacre, Luper, and Pollio 1970).

The literature on coarticulation deals with contextual influences on phonemes. Speech production is dynamic. Phonetic features influence each other such that *feature spreading* occurs in natural speech. "The locus of the influence is the segment, and the element of influence is the articulatory feature" (Daniloff and Hammarberg 1973, p. 242). The study of these influences is the study of coarticulation. Daniloff and Hammarberg define coarticulation "as the influence of one speech segment upon another; that is, the influence of a phonetic context upon a given segment. Phonetic context is most varied within connected conversational speech. Thus, coarticulation is most extensive in running speech" (1973, p. 239). Coarticulation entails feature spreading from one segment (phoneme) to another. Coarticulatory influences are bidirectional: left-to-right ones are known as forward or carryover coarticulations. Right-to-left ones are backward or anticipatory. These apparently result from different processes. Both effects are influenced by variables such as phonetic context, stress, juncture, and rate. These effects can extend beyond adjacent phonemes and even across syllabic boundaries.

One type of coarticulation is accommodation, which effects smooth transitions between individual segments. There seem to be two types of accommodation. "First, when two adjacent sounds are produced with the same articulator, their points of articulation tend to become identical. For example a /d/ followed by a / θ /, as in *width,* becomes dental, like the / θ /. A difference that canonically was one of both point and manner of articulation has been reduced to manner only" (Daniloff and Hammarberg 1973, p. 243). "Secondly, where two adjacent sounds are made with different articulators [we regard different parts of the tongue as different articulators—along with Oehman (1966)] the 'unused' articulator assumes the position it should have for the adjacent sound" (p. 244). Daniloff and Hammarberg (1973) cite several studies indicating that coarticulatory effects are important for the smooth and easy flow of articulatory movements and for perceiving natural speech.

The coarticulation theories have raised many important issues about the dynamic mechanisms of speech production. The literature on coarticulation will play an increasing role in the assessment and intervention of articulation disorders. Most clinicians are presently oriented on rather mundane notions such as omission, substitutions, and distortions of phonemes, and initial, medial, and final word positions of phonemes. Some clinicians have become oriented on distinctive feature approaches. The Chomsky and Halle (1968) approach is more limited than the Jakobson (1941, 1971) approach, because the former deals with adult features whereas the latter deals with the emergence of features in child phonology. Two major developments in phonology will have far-reaching effects in clinical assessment and intervention. They are coarticulation theories because they place phonemes in phonetic context and phonotactic theories because they have identified phonological processes unique to child phonology that have considerable application to clinical work. Daniloff and Moll (1968) have compared and evaluated some of the coarticulation theories. They favor those by Henke (1967) and Kozhevnikov and Chistovich (1965), which propose articulatory-syllables containing forward planning across phonemes. Ferguson and Garnica (1975) provide an excellent critique of behaviorist theories (Mowrer 1952; Winitz 1969; Murai 1963; Olmsted 1971), structuralist theories (Jakobson 1971; Jakobson and Halle 1956; Moskowitz 1970), natural phonology theory (Stampe 1969) and prosodic theory (Waterson 1971).

Whichever theoretical model proves most productive is ultimately of interest to language interventionists because such models provide the fundamental conceptual orientation for assessment and intervention. The coarticulation approach can handle forward planning; the distinctive feature approach cannot.

The child phonology literature has recently seen some very interesting child variations that account for some articulation problems that had previously been overlooked or too grossly accounted for in using the initial, medial, and final position of sounds in words, and in omission, substitution, and distortion descriptions. These variations have appeared in many articles, sometimes under the rubric of phonotactic rules. They are summarized nicely by Ingram (1974b, 1976). He described the following child variations: reduplication, diminutive, weak syllable deletion, cluster reduction, voicing, and assimilation. *Reduplication* usually occurs when a child attempts a polysyllabic word but is unable to correctly repeat the second or subsequent syllables. The child compensates by repeating the initial syllable—"daddy" becomes "dada." *Diminutive* is a process whereby a child will add [i] to the end of a word, i.e., "Mommy," "Daddy," "Spotty," etc. "Reduplication and diminutive do not have morphological value but are attempts to represent syllabic noise" (Ingram 1974b, p. 54). "*Weak syllable deletion* generally applies to two-syllable words when the initial syllable is unstressed, and to unstressed syllables in three-syllable words" (Ingram 1974b, p. 57). Examples of weak syllable deletion are: [bana] for "banana" and [madu] for "tomato." Cluster reduction is the simplification of consonantal clusters, i.e., [dap] for "stop" and [bun] for "spoon." *Voicing* is an intriguing phenomenon in child phonology: "In its purest form, voicing is a process whereby the child voices all the initial consonants and unvoices final ones" (Ingram 1974b, p. 59). This occurs in a brief period in a child's normal phonological development. Examples are [ba] for "pie," [mat] for "mud," and [zup] for "soup." *Assimilation* is very much like backward and forward coarticulation except that a sound may replace another. For example, a child might say [g∧k] for "truck," [gɔk] for "dog," and [gɜk] for "duck." Information of this kind gives the clinician valuable new insights into phonological disorders.

Child variations have considerable implications for clinical speech disorders. Locke (1976) has analyzed published speech discrimination tests. He concluded that the kinds of discriminations on these tests are irrelevant to the kinds of discriminations that children need to make between what their speech is like—child variations —and what they need to learn. Moreover, a study by Aungst and Frick (1964) indicates that speech discrimination should be done in such a way that a child monitors his own speech rather than that of someone else.

The current literature has a great deal to offer clinicians. The most important departure from the traditional articulation approach is that phonemes are no longer thought of as entities but as products of coarticulatory influences, and possible other kinds of grammatical influences. Moreover, the traditional notions of sounds in initial, medial, and final word position are displaced by sounds in syllabic context. Further, the traditional notions of omission, substitution, and distortion are replaced by distinctive features and child variations. All in all, clinicians now have more powerful ways of accounting for deviant articulatory behavior.

Summary

Clinicians should have a basic understanding of linguistic systems. There have been major shifts of thought about them in recent years. Taxonomic or "parts of speech" approaches have given way to transformational generative grammar approaches. By the late 1960s, syntactic approaches had given way to semantic and language function approaches, particularly speech acts. Phonology has shifted away from the phoneme as an entity to dynamic phonetic events in a context of other events and influences. Phonology has shifted from an adult distinctive feature system to child variations. All of these developments have important implications for clinical assessment and intervention.

Linguistic systems cannot be viewed as products such as vocabulary size, mean length of utterance, sentence types, etc. It is necessary to deal with the systems and processes themselves in order to get at the versatile, dynamic nature of verbal behavior. It is imperative that clinicians deal with both the structural and the functional dimensions—semantic functions and relations, speech acts, etc. They must deal with verbal behavior in context—semantic-syntactic contexts pertain to available reference, linguistic context, communicative intent, semantic relations; speech acts and phonological contexts pertain to coarticulation, distinctive features, child variations, syllabic structure, and prosody.

5

Communicative Systems

Communication is the primary function of language. It is realized not only through verbal codes but also through a matrix of complexly integrated coding mechanisms in a communicative context. This context, actual and presumed, is the primary determinant of what, when, where, why, and how something is said and/or done. Communication is not unidirectional—a speaker talking to a listener. It involves the concerted needs and efforts of both encoder and decoder. Both functions are usually assumed by all participants.

The what, when, where, why, and how issues of communication are traceable to social systems and group dynamics (sociolinguistics) and to an individual's prerogatives in communication (pragmatics). Since clinicians deal with individual problems, we are here concerned primarily with pragmatics. It is helpful to place pragmatics in the context of a general model of communication and an overview of sociolinguistics.

A Communication Model

The communication model described below presupposes the necessary perceptual-cognitive-linguistic development that enables productive engagement in dynamic communication. The rudiments of communicative skills appear in infancy (Greenfield and Smith 1976; Halliday 1975; Dore 1974, 1975; Bates 1976; Bruner 1975). Differential crying by the infant and differential stress and inflection between old (or evident) and new information in one- and two-word utterances (Wieman 1976; Bates 1976) are early vestiges of communicative efforts predicated by communicative context. However, these efforts are narrowly adaptive (Brown 1973b, p. 65) because they are context bound and depend upon an interpreter with special qualifications for knowing an infant's repertoire and its use. Moreover, early speech acts, such as labeling, may be extended sensorimotor acts rather than true representations (Dore 1974, 1975; Bruner 1975; Greenfield and Smith 1976; Bates 1976).

By about four years of age, children know the basic linguistic mechanisms of their language, although some aspects (particularly subtle ones) are yet to be acquired (C. Chomsky 1969; Cromer 1976; Palermo and Molfese 1972; Bloom 1975). Young children perceive and talk about the here and now. Communicative repertoire is limited virtually to "talk to" behaviors, possibly accompanied by simple emotive displays for immediate need gratification. When faced with communicative obstacles, they usually either repeat or abandon their efforts. The egocentric speech of young children lacks the volitional and motivational character of adult speech.

By eight years of age, most children have successfully played the "original word game" (Brown 1958b), in which one's knowledge of his world becomes socialized in language (Halliday 1975) and the "original thinking game" (Bruner 1964; Bruner et al. 1966), in which one is released from direct experience to rely on representational or symbolic experience. Thus, eight-year-olds have essentially acquired the grammatical and referential machinery of their linguistic community. However, it is one thing to know something but another to use one's knowledge in adept ways (Hammond and Summers 1972). "What is crucial is not so much a better understanding of how language is structured, but a better understanding of how language is used, not so much what language is, as what language is for" (Hymes 1972b, p. xii). These children are not yet communicatively competent, though some vestiges appear at preschool ages (Shatz and Gelman 1973). "They must still learn to play the communication game to ascertain the message best suited to a particular situation and thereby realize effective and efficient communication" (Muma 1975a).

By eight years of age, the dimensions of communication have changed in several important respects. Issues about the nature of language no longer pose significant obstacles. Topics are more adult. Communication is primarily, but not exclusively, representational. Most important, eight-year-olds have lost an exclusively egocentric orientation. They have become aware that effective communication can occur only if they consider the other participants in the process. They realize that a decoder is not merely to be talked to but a partner in finding the message best suited for a particular situation. The awareness of the encoder-decoder partnership in communication provides a way of becoming fully adaptive in playing the communication game. Awareness of the encoder-decoder partnership in communication has been variously called *role taking* (Flavell et al. 1968; Miller, Kessel, and Flavell 1969), *role of the other* (Mead 1934), *edited social speech* (Glucksberg and Krauss 1967), *speaker sampling and comparison* (Rosenberg and Cohen 1966), *social speech* (Piaget 1954, 1961, 1962, 1963, 1970), and *communicative speech* (Vygotsky 1962). This literature has been reviewed by Glucksberg, Krauss, and Higgins (1975).

Communicative competence is the capacity not only to conceive, formulate, modulate, and issue messages but also to perceive the degree to which intended meanings are appropriately coded in a matrix of referential codes and conveyed (although not necessarily accepted). Thus, communication is much more than issuing and receiving a message. *Interpersonal communication* is issuing a message in the most appropriate way(s) for conveying intended meanings to a particular person for particular effects. It is more complicated than an active speaker talking to a passive listener. Both encoder and decoder are active participants in formulating, perceiving, and revising codes in ascertaining not only essential meaning but the ways in which meaning can be effectively conveyed. Consideration must be given to the form or nature and type of code, reference or representation, and acceptability or communicative license. Moreover, the participants must be able to switch between producing or *dumping* intended messages of presumed best fit for a particular circumstance and *playing* the communication game to resolve obstacles (Muma 1975a). This means that they must frequently be able to interchange encoding and decoding roles.

Dumping denotes the product of underlying mental operations in which one's communicative intent is coded in a *message of presumed best fit* for a particular situation. Assuming that a message of best fit is dumped or issued, the probabilities are high that only essential meaning rather than complete, accurate, or faithful meaning is conveyed. This is because encoding represents only selected aspects of an intent and decoding is naturally biased. Thus some distortion is inevitable. No matter what level of agreement may result between encoder and decoder regarding form, reference, and acceptability, the message will be unwittingly distorted to some degree. Some distortions are merely incidental to a message, but others could seriously jeopardize it. Unintentional influences may overshadow the message: "It wasn't so much what he said but how he said it." Distortions are likely when a message differs significantly from one's values, beliefs, or morals: "I can't believe what I hear." Conflicts between what one knows and perceives in a message can result in a cognitive dissonance problem (Fetsinger 1957). Perception alone can screen out information, thereby creating a distortion, since perception is to a great extent governed by what one knows (Garner 1966). All in all, the probabilities of distortion are very high even though consensus may have been established as to form, reference, and acceptability.

A message of best fit is a complex matrix of referential codes. These are linguistic, nonlinguistic, paralinguistic, and, in resolving communicative obstacles, metareferential. Linguistic codes are obviously more complicated, versatile, and powerful than the others. The particular combination of coding devices employed in any particular situation is intimately tied to topic and context in addition to a host of sociological influences (Bernstein 1970; Shuy 1970; Labov 1972) and available reference (Olson 1970, 1971; Brown 1958a). Nonlinguistic devices include postures, pointing, facial expressions, situational designs, head nodding, eye contact, holding, touching, movement and proximity in space, and figure/ground orientation. Paralinguistic devices are typically superimposed upon a verbal utterance. These include pausing and other hesitation phenomena, intonations, inflections, rate variations, aspiration, and certain gestures. Kasl and Mahl (1965) identified psychological distinctions between "ah" and "non-ah" hesitation phenomena in spontaneous speech. "Ah" behaviors indicate information processing whereas "non-ah" behaviors indicate anxiety states. Several reviews of nonverbal communicative behaviors are available (Maclay and Osgood 1959; Duncan 1959;

Birdwhistell 1970; Knapp 1972; Bruneau 1973; Mehrabrian 1972; Wiener et al. 1972; Rochester 1973). Metareferential devices signal communicative obstacles: "Tell it like it is." "Don't give me any of that jive."

The linguistic code is not always the most important. Other devices can override or subordinate it. For example, "I like the movie" may mean someone likes a particular movie. However, the utterance may be made with a facial grimace and shaking head to indicate exactly the opposite. Or, the word "I" could be stressed to mean that, while someone else may not have liked the movie, the speaker did.

Communicative competence pertains to one's capacities to function as either encoder or decoder for a complex matrix of codes in communicative context. The *encoding function* involves the ability to perceive the communicative context in terms of actual and presumed reference, and through linguistic and other coding devices, produce a message appropriate to the encoder's communicative intent and the decoder's needs for information. An encoder tries to produce the message of best fit for his perception of the situation, his intent, and the listener's needs. Cognitively, an encoder attempts to take the role of his decoder in determing the message of best fit. The *decoding function* entails the ability to decipher available codes (linguistic and otherwise) to discern intended meanings. Brown (1965) called the decoding function an ability to "cash words into referents." The decoding function presupposes a perceptual-cognitive-linguistic system essentially similar in nature and use to that of the encoder. The decoder can ascertain meaning as if he were the encoder. The decoding function also involves the recognition and identification of communicative obstacles. We can selectively appraise the encoder of these obstacles—and their nature—so the encoder can revise his code to produce a message of best fit.

The identification and resolution of communicative obstacles is what Muma (1975a) called *playing* the communicative game. The communicative game has two major components: dump and play. Dumping a message means the perceptual-cognitive-linguistic operations of encoders in producing a message of presumed best fit for a particular decoder and situation. If the code is consistent with one's communicative intent, deals with available referents (actual or presumed), and is in an appropriate form, the decoder will be able to discern the meaning of an intended message. However, if these requirements are not met, intended meaning may not be conveyed. If the decoder recognizes this and indicates it to the encoder, they may play the communication game to identify the nature of the problem and reconcile it. "I don't understand _____." "Huh, what did you say?" "Don't beat around the bush, tell me what you want to say." Figure 5-1 outlines this model.

The encoder-decoder model has received considerable attention in recent years. The works of Flavell et al. (1968), Glucksberg, Krauss, and Higgins (1975), Bearison and Cassel (1975), Rosenberg and Cohen (1966), Longhurst (1974), Longhurst and Reichle (1975), Longhurst and Siegel (1973), Longhurst and Berry (1975), Garmize and Anisfeld (1976), Keller (1976), Maratsos (1973b), Shantz and Wilson (1972), Clark and Delia (1976), Bates (1976a,b), Mueller (1972), Fry

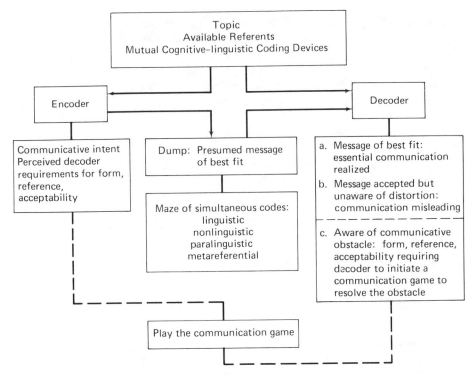

Figure 5-1 *Outline of encoder and decoder functions in dumping messages and playing the communication game.*

(1969), and many others have documented the dynamic nature of the encoder-decoder processes in communication. The encoder-decoder processes should not be linked to or associated with the traditional notion of expressive and receptive language. This notion has separated verbal processes that are inextricably related (Bloom 1974). It has led to arbitrary distinctions in the applied fields that have been unfortunate in clinical assessment and intervention, because it tries to make differences more important and similarities less important than is the case in natural behavior. The same fallacy has occurred regarding modality differences and similarities. The clinical fields have tried to make much of modality differences when in fact similarities are more substantial—indeed, fundamental—to clinical assessment and intervention. Again, encoding and decoding in a communicative model should not be compared to the notions of expressive and receptive language. Such comparisons will only perpetuate some capricious notions in the clinical fields (see Chaps. 7 and 8).

The terms "message," "code," and "map" are used interchangeably. An encoder strives to make a message, code, or map that brings a decoder to think or behave in intended ways. "Map" means that it directs one to think an intended way. "Code" means that something is cued in the decoder that corresponds to what was intended by the encoder. "Message" has similar connotations to "code" and "map."

A coding or mapping function is especially salient to early child language. Recent studies (Greenfield and Smith 1976; Nelson 1974; Bates 1976; Wieman 1976 and Bruner 1975) have shown that early one- and two-word utterances and stress patterns are not of nouns, verbs, or adjectives as had previously been held, but of new information in the context of old information. A child will label actions if actions vary, things if things vary, and attributes if attributes vary. Nelson (1974) indicated that young children are more inclined to attend to and label dynamic attributes because they vary; subsequently the children will name static attributes. Kagan (1971) and McCall (1972) have shown that it is easier to get and maintain attention in infants (and adults) with discrepancies than repetitions. Thus, early labeling and stress variations on new information occur in the context of old. An infant is truly mapping, coding, or indexing what is new for him. This has considerable implications for clinical assessment and intervention. It means that clinicians cannot rely on norms in assessment or highly structured programs in intervention. Both assessment and intervention are context-specific and vary as a function of the underlying concepts or schemata the child brings to the context. Assessment and intervention must take into account dynamic communicative contexts; to do less is to render assessment and intervention superficial.

Sociolinguistics

Sociolinguistics deals with language usage—usage related to, and possibly caused by, various social dynamics. Early sociolinguistic studies dealt with such variables as geography, social status, sex, age, race, style, situation, interface between languages, psychology, pedagogy, and assessment. More recently, there has been a shift away from seeking status variables to a study of process variables in ongoing dynamic social systems. Bernstein's (1970) theory of language as an indicator of social systems is a good example of this. The fascinating study by Labov, Cohen, Robins, and Lewis (1968) of language as an indicator (and possibly a mediator) of roles in adolescent gangs in New York City is another good example. The various studies of mother-child interaction in language development are also sociolinguistic in nature (Reichle, Longhurst and Stepanich 1976; Broen 1972; Lewis 1972; Lewis and Freedle 1973; Olim 1970; Bee et al. 1970; Nelson 1973b; Phillips 1973; Snow 1972; Jones 1972; Clark-Stewart 1973; Martin 1975; Bearison and Cassel 1975; Moerk 1974, 1976).

According to Shuy (1970), sociolinguistics deals with three basic issues: linguistic continuum, linguistic variable, and linguistic situation.

1. *Linguistic continuum.* Speakers have options whether to use their acrolect, mesolect, or basilect; that is, they can talk formally, informally, in techni-

cal jargon, swear, etc. Individuals from different socioeconomic backgrounds can communicate effectively if they choose to speak in a manner somewhere in the linguistic continuum that is comfortable to both. The degree to which linguistic continua overlap is the degree to which communication will be relatively free from confusion.

2. *Linguistic variable.* Labov (1966, p. 15) systematically attacked the concept of free fluctuation or free variation, and in so doing formulated the concept of the linguistic variable. Free variation refers to presumed exceptions to grammatical rules. This means that not all speakers may always speak the same way. Thus, one may study and write various rules of a dialect, and discover that some rules are in free variation. Labov discovered that it was possible to account for much of free variation by social characteristics rather than grammatical rules. "In formulating the linguistic variable, Labov sought to correlate matters hitherto dismissed as free fluctuation with such social characteristics as social status, race, age, sex, and style" (Shuy 1970, p. 339).

3. *Linguistic situation.* We are only beginning to appreciate the dynamics of a linguistic situation. In the past decade we have become increasingly aware that situational variables play a major role in the nature of language. This is an embarrassment, because some conclusions have been made that appear to reveal the biases of the examiners rather than the abilities of an examinee.

For example, mean length of utterance is rather easy to compute. It has been used to assess verbal development. Unfortunately, after four years of age, mean length of utterance reflects situational variables stronger than developmental ones (Shriner 1969; Brown 1973b). Sroufe (1970) has outlined other situational variables that operate in test situations. A variety of factors in the linguistic situation have led to unwarranted conclusions in educational and clinical assessment. Three special issues of the *Harvard Educational Review* documented some of the unfortunate things that have happened, especially to minority students. These special issues are (1) *Challenging the Myths: The Blacks, the Schools, and the Poor* (1971), (2) *The Rights of Children, Part I* (1973, vol. 43), and (3) *The Rights of Children, Part II* (1974, vol. 44).

Probably the main emphasis of sociolinguistics is on linguistic behavior as it relates to social class. This takes primarily the form of an inquiry into the verbal behavior of the lower classes. Sociologists are also interested in attitudes about linguistic forms as a means of understanding sociological systems. They are interested in the phenomena of change when dialects come into contact, the dynamics of linguistic switching, and other issues related to verbal behavior. "Sociolinguists assume that language, or a variety of language, used by a given speech community is adequate to meet the needs of its user relative to the demands of that community. They assume, furthermore, that children learn the language of their peer group, and that dialects, even nonstandard dialects, are systematic in nature" (Shuy 1970, p. 347).

Ervin-Tripp (1971) outlined three general types of sociolinguistic rules: alternation rules, co-occurrence constraints, and sequential rules for speech events. An *alternation rule* is one in which a choice between linguistic alternatives depends on social variables. For example, a child who selectively says "please" or "gimme" according to whether he is talking to his grandmother or to his playmates demonstrates a sociolinguistic alternation rule. A *co-occurrence constraint rule* occurs when speakers assume various roles. For example, a speaker of a nonstandard dialect may choose to use Standard English. The various dimensions of grammar in Standard English that contrast with his dialect constrain what he might say. *Sequential rules* for speech events refer to routinized utterances expected of various social situations, for example, "Hi, how are you?" "What's happening?" "Good morning." "Right on."

Labov (1970b, pp. 301–2) gave four reasons why speakers of nonstandard dialects may resist learning and using Standard English:

1. *Structural interference.* Structural differences between one's dialect and Standard English may be confusing.
2. *Opposing motivations.* Consonant with the attitude that "Black is beautiful" and the motto "Tell it like it is," many dialect speakers do not want to learn a "jive" dialect. They want to "do their own thing." In this case, doing their own thing is speaking their own dialect rather than that of someone else.
3. *Teacher-student interaction.* Teacher-student interactions are often so strained that students resist any effort to change behavior in the direction of a teacher's goals. This is especially the case for boys from disadvantaged environments. Cazden (1966a), Plumer (1970), and Entwisle (1968) indicate that desirable attitudes toward learning are likely to occur when there is minimal contrast in ethnic and socioeconomic backgrounds between teacher and student. Sroufe (1970) made the same point about testing. Effective teaching entails much more than a good awareness and presentation of content. It extends into the whole domain of interpersonal affairs. Teachers and clinicians should try to identify with their students in order to facilitate teacher-student interaction.
4. *Resistance in peer groups.* Most students are highly influenced by peer values. They strive to do things in cliques, even establishing fads and lingo or jargon. Rather than run the risk of peer alienation, they resist learning and using Standard English. Accordingly, dialect speakers often choose to be quiet rather than subject themselves to criticism of their way of talking and living.

Verbal behavior of ghetto children is rather rich and well developed. Labov et al. (1968) delineated several verbal skills of inner city adolescent gangs. These skills are important because individuals who are most skillful are usually high in the power structure of a gang. The skills are sounding, playing the dozens, signifying, toasting, rapping, running it down, jiving, shucking, copping a plea, and rifting.

Sounding is a verbal attack, characteristically with increasingly obscene remarks, on the family (usually the mother) of an individual to which the sound is addressed. Even though obscenity is displayed, the participants do not respond to it personally. Indeed, a participant who becomes angry and resorts to physical activities is regarded as a poor sounder. Labov (1972) indicated that one individual begins by directing a sound to another. The other is challenged to rebut by producing another sound directed at a family member of the first. It is necessary that others be around to give immediate feedback on each sounding effort (Kochman 1972). Others may intercede to pick up the challenge of a sounder. Labov (1972) indicated that there is considerable symbolic distance in sounding, which insulates this activity from other kinds of verbal interaction.

Playing the dozens is a special type of sounding that uses rhymed couplets, usually a dozen lines. The purpose of the dozens is to humiliate one's opponent verbally through cleverly rhymed verses loaded with invectives toward his family or a family member. The winner of the dozens is the individual judged by his peers to have the largest store of couplets on hand, the best memory, the best delivery, and the best improvisation and creativity. *Signifying,* according to Abrahams (1970, p. 264), is an effort to "imply, goad, or boast by indirect verbal or gestural means." Burling (1973) regards signifying as teasing or taunting speech that may include boasting. Unlike sounding and the dozens, signifying is intended to provoke feelings of embarrassment, shame, or aggression. A player tries to come down on his opponent while at the same time standing up to his opponent's attacks.

Toasts are oral epic poems, widely recited and admired on the street corners. They have rhyme and rhythm and are recited with a slightly musical style. Typically, only men give toasts. A skillful toaster can aptly turn a phrase and vary his pitch, volume and speed of delivery for special effects. Muhammad Ali has demonstrated skillful toasting: "dance like a butterfly, sting like a bee . . ." *Rapping* is talking to as opposed to interacting with another. Rapping is used to give an extended historical perspective of something, or by men in male-female introductions to tell a woman of one's positive features. *Running it down* is used to ask for more information or clarification. When a listener is so impressed with a delivery that he wants to hear it again, he will say, "Run it down again," or "Lay it on me again." *Jiving* is used to put someone on. One's audience perceives that it is a hoax or impractical: "Man, stop that jiving." *Shucking* is a special kind of jiving—jiving "the Man" (the white establishment). The individual plays a role, saying the kind of things the establishment expects, thereby following a line of least resistance. The establishment is thus duped and misled. *Copping a plea* was succinctly described by Abrahams and Gay (1972, p. 204): "When one cops a plea, he acclaims the superiority of another, and makes an appeal for pity, mercy, or some other form of sympathy. Whether this appeal is authentic or merely a play on one's sympathies and ego is virtually impossible to determine by someone who is unfamiliar with the styles of verbal behavior prevalent among Black Americans." *Rifting* is a formal display of occult or "heavy" knowledge of the Black Muslim religion. Certain substantive words are given extra stress and spaced at regular intervals. The last line is often drawn out for emphasis.

Switching from dialect to dialect is different from switching from one style to another within the same dialect. The differences seem to have stronger implications in the motivational arena than in the linguistic one. Often only subtle grammatical differences constitute a shift in dialects. Baratz (1969b) described some dialect or code differences between Black English and Standard English.

1. *Numerical quantifier.* When one has a numerical quantifier such as two, seven, fifty, etc., he doesn't need to add the morphemes for plural, e.g., fifty cent; two foot.
2. *Possessive marker.* The use of possessive markers differs with the situation involved. The nonstandard speaker would say, "John cousin." The possessive is marked by the contiguous relationship of John and his cousin.
3. *The conditional.* This is expressed by word change rather than by "if." Standard English: "I asked *if* he wanted to go." Nonstandard English: "I asked *did* he want to go."
4. *Third person.* The third person singular has no obligatory morphological ending in nonstandard English. "She works here" becomes "She work here."
5. *Verbal agreement* differs with usage. A Black adolescent might say, "She have a bike" or, "They was going."
6. *The use of the copula is not obligatory.* "I going." "He a bad boy."
7. *Rules of negation.* The double negative is used a great deal. "I don't have none."
8. *Use of "ain't."* "Ain't" is used mainly in the past tense. "I didn't go yet" becomes "I ain't go yet."
9. *Use of "be."* "Be" is used to express habitual action: "He workin' right now" becomes "He be workin' every day."

Labov (1972) determined the following phonological differences between Black English and Standard English:

1. *R-lessness.* the semi-vowel /r/ is replaced by a prolonged vowel or glide:

guard ⟶ god
sore ⟶ saw
par ⟶ pa
court ⟶ caught

The intervocalic /r/ becomes a schwa:

Carol ⟶ Cal
Paris ⟶ Pass
terrace ⟶ test

2. *L-lessness.* /l/ is replaced by a back rounded glide:

help $\longrightarrow$ hep
fault $\longrightarrow$ fought
toll $\longrightarrow$ toe
all $\longrightarrow$ awe
fault $\longrightarrow$ fought

3. "One of the most complex variables appearing in black speech is the general tendency towards the simplification of consonant clusters at the ends of words" (Labov 1972, p. 15):

past $\longrightarrow$ pass
rift $\longrightarrow$ riff
meant $\longrightarrow$ mean

4. Weakening of the final consonant:

boot $\longrightarrow$ boo
feed $\longrightarrow$ feet
seat $\longrightarrow$ see

5. Final fricative /θ/ becomes /f/:

tooth $\longrightarrow$ toof
death $\longrightarrow$ deaf

The syntactic and phonological differences between Black and Standard English have lead some linguists to regard Black English as a derivative of Standard English—a pidgin or a creole language. A *pidgin* language is a reduced, simplified, and often mixed language, usually evolved for trading purposes by speakers with no common language. A *creole* language is a pidgin language that has become the native language of a speech community and has therefore expanded and acquired all the functions and characteristics of a full natural language (Trudgill 1974).

Not knowing these and other rules of Black English, psychologists and educators have construed these *differences* as *deficits*. Their assumptions in assessing language and cognitive skills of the ghetto community appear to have evolved because they do not know the difference between *what language is* and *how it functions.*

Differences and Deficits

Unfortunately, certain myths about language have pervaded American education. These center around the notion of Standard English—a legacy of Bloomfield's notions of correctness. They reflect the Sapir-Whorf hypotheses that language determines thought. They are unfortunate in several ways. First, they are so pervasive. The prevailing attitude of educators and the public is that children should learn Standard English. Bloomfield's notions of correctness have become institutionalized. Second, both Bloomfield's notions and the Sapir-Whorf hypotheses are open to question. Linguists do not agree what Standard English is, but they do agree that everyone speaks some dialect of a language. As for linguistic determinism—the Sapir-Whorf hypotheses—an underlying premise is that there is a one-to-one correspondence between language and thought. However, a fundamental principle of verbal behavior easily dispatches that premise: one referent can have many words and one word can have many referents. Possibly there is a partial isomorphism between what one knows and what he says, but inasmuch as a speaker has alternative ways of saying the same thing and alternative meanings for what is said, it is inappropriate to conclude that a one-to-one correspondence holds between thought and language (Sinclair 1969).

Third, and most important, large numbers of students—typically minority students—have unfortunately had their educational careers compromised by these myths. Inordinately large numbers of minority students have been placed in the least desirable program tracks—even being labeled "cultural familial mentally retarded" (Grossman, Warren, Begab, Eyman, Nihira, and O'Connor 1973)—because their dialects jeopardized performance on intelligence and achievement tests or significantly conflicted with the dialects of their teachers. Many states are now in the throes of class action suits because of this. American education must reexamine the assumption that students should conform to a single standard—the standard of middle-class whites.

Sociolinguists have shown that nonstandard speech is highly developed and reflects a grammar that is merely different from that of a standard speaker. Educators and psychologists have contended that nonstandard speech is uncouth, incorrect, and reflects an inferior or underdeveloped language. They imply that nonstandard speech is deficient and its speakers should be given remedial or compensatory education. An extension of this idea is that if one's language is deficient, then one's thought processes are also deficient: a nonstandard speaker *and* his culture are inferior. This is known as the *deficit* position.

Labov (1970) gave the following six ideas naive educators and psychologists turn to in "reasoning" that minority students are in some ways inferior to middle-class Standard-English-speaking white students.

1. The lower-class child's verbal response to a formal and threatening situation demonstrates his lack of verbal capacity.
2. This verbal deficit is a major cause of the lower-class child's poor performance in school.
3. Since middle-class children do better in school, middle-class speech habits are necessary for learning.
4. Class and ethnic differences in grammatical form are the same as differences in the capacity for logical analysis.

5. Teaching the child to mimic certain formal speech patterns used by middle-class teachers teaches him to think logically.
6. Children who learn these formal speech patterns are thinking logically and will do much better in reading and arithmetic in later years.

Well-intended but naive educators and psychologists turn to the use of norms to vindicate their position. They argue that test norms provide a functional standard by which everyone can be measured. There are some awesome ramifications of this use of norms. First, one must be certain that such norms are indeed appropriate. Too often, inappropriate norms are used to determine aberrance. Indeed, it is easy to find a significant difference when the wrong norms are used (Baratz 1969a). Second, and more telling, norms derived from one dialect tell us virtually nothing about the competencies or capabilities of an individual speaking another dialect. Such evidence is hopelessly confounded with a host of performance variables. Thus, to claim propriety because norms are used is merely to displace the issue rather than resolve it.

The *difference* side of the controversy holds that American society is polycultural and education should be responsive to a variety of sociocultural needs. The *deficit* side holds that there is essentially one culture—the "melting pot" notion—and education is a socializing process in which students are brought to conform to one standard. The difference side recognizes dialectic variation and multiple standards. The deficit side recognizes one standard and anyone who does not use that standard runs the risk of being regarded a linguistically and possibly intellectually and culturally deficient—he may even lose the educational opportunities for making it in society.

The deficit position is arbitrary and traditional; the difference position is rational and relevant. The deficit position is arbitrary because it is based upon what Bloomfield and other early prescriptive grammarians proclaimed was correct or Standard English. However, these criteria do not even correspond with today's "Standard English," let alone nonstandard English. Linguists not only disagree about what Standard English is but regard the issue as unimportant since *speakers* of a language or dialect determine what it will be—no one can arbitrarily delimit correct language. The history of language is full of efforts to standardize language; none have succeeded. They have failed because (1) languages are continually changing, (2) people have linguistic variations—dialects and idiolects, (3) the mobility of people tends to both confound and gloss variations, undoubtedly influencing the rate and nature of language change. The end result is that America has a polycultural-polylinguistic society. The difference position is the more rational because it acknowledges this culture.

The deficit position has become the traditional one because Standard English was established as a fundamental American educational goal: "Every child will speak and write correctly." If an American child did not speak or write "correctly," he was considered deficient. When differences were found between a child's verbal behavior and Standard English, the child was made to conform, to learn and use a linguistic system foreign to his own. While this policy was fine for English teachers because they taught the same thing to all children, it was disproportionately difficult for children from diverse backgrounds. The deficit position resulted in an educational system that had the built-in defect of offering the best education to those who could best deal with the arbitrary standards—middle- and upper-class whites—while withholding from those who had to translate from their primary dialect to the pedagogical language.

The difference position is more relevant because it deals with the situation as it is: polycultural-polylinguistic. The deficit position established arbitrary standards to which children had to conform. The difference position acknowledges the complexity of the society the schools must accommodate.

The deficit notion led to the notion of compensatory education. This was formalized in the Head Start program, under the premise that deficits could be alleviated by starting the educational process during the preschool years. There were fallacies in this premise. First, most middle- and upper-class children already go to some form of preschool, so at best Head Start could only try to match what those children got. Second, Head Start needed a health and nutritional program to "underwrite" the educational program. Third, the curriculum of Head Start was a misconceived "readiness" curriculum that dealt with the products of education (naming letters, counting, colors, etc.) rather than the processes of education (exploration, enjoyment, alternatives, socialization, etc.). Fourth, and not surprisingly, the anticipated benefits of Head Start did not last. There are two obvious reasons: (1) products rather than processes were taught, and (2) the kind of assessment done was not very relevant, e.g., normative measures of intelligence, achievement, and vocabulary. While easy to administer, they were not appropriate. The *ETS-OEO Longitudinal Study of Head Start* (Ball and Bogatz 1970) showed that desirable results occurred when process measures were used. These resulted even though the early stages of the curriculum concentrated on products and the early (and premature) study by the Westinghouse Corporation contained disquieting data (Cicirelli 1969). The problems with Head Start resulted in two additional programs, *Follow Through* and *Parent-Child Centers,* later called *Parent-Child Development Centers.* Follow Through was conceived to follow the Head Start children into school with a curriculum continuous with the Head Start program. Thus the educational careers of poorer children would be shaped from preschool to the third grade. The curriculum continued to be product rather than process oriented. Parent-Child Centers were conceived on the premise that parents are the primary intervention agents of young children. Thus, properly training parents would lead to desirable early learning in children. I was affiliated with the Parent-Child Center program for a little more than two years as the research director of a very large program. While very nice things could be done in consultation with the top authorities in child development across the country, the national and local administrators were woefully incompetent, undermining the program at almost every turn. Conceptually the Parent-Child

Center program (Muma 1971c) was an excellent idea; functionally, it was a tremendous waste of taxpayers' money. The program model was not followed, the curriculum was rended, and there were serious problems with administration, particularly in reporting data.

"Sesame Street" and "The Electric Company" are two other programs that have realized their expected potential in educating preschool and early school-aged poverty children. The evaluation of "Sesame Street" by the Educational Testing Service (Ball and Bogatz 1970) yielded impressive results. Both of these programs are under continuous evaluation.

Both "Sesame Street" and "The Electric Company" reflect a polycultural-polylinguistic society. Gerald Lesser is one of the early founders of "Sesame Street." His research (Lesser, Fifer, and Clark 1965; Stodolsky and Lesser 1967) provided important evidence regarding ethnic and socioeconomic *differences* rather than *deficits* in mental behavior. Similarly, Moore (1971) argued that poor children have different cognitive styles than middle-class children. Accordingly, educational programs should be focused on cognitive style rather than level.

The *difference* viewpoint has major implications for education. Plumer (1970) recommended major changes in reading instruction and the virtual abandonment of English courses. She reasoned that since English education courses have been notoriously ineffective, they should be omitted or revised (Bullock Report 1975). The reasons for a greater commitment to reading instruction are that reading skills are very important for advancement in educational programs and that it is unlikely that publications will appear in nonstandard English. This is not to say that reading instruction will be *only* in Standard English. Plumer (1970), Baratz (1970), and others argue that it is probably better to teach a nonstandard speaker to read in his dialect (his own speech) first and then teach him to read in Standard English. Moreover, a rich and varied language experience is apparently essential for successful reading (Plumer 1970; Entwisle 1971; Thorndike 1971; Smith 1971).

The *difference* view has considerable implications for complications in comprehension. Cazden (1966a, p. 188) summarized some difficulties a child might encounter:

> The child who speaks a nonstandard dialect may have difficulty understanding his teacher and his schoolbooks. The evidence on this point is unclear. Cherry (1965) reports a pioneer attempt to use the Cloze technique to "evaluate the extent to which information is successfully communicated from teachers to pupils of various social backgrounds and the degree of effective communication among children from different social backgrounds (p. 23)." Words were deleted according to a predetermined sequence from samples of teacher and peer-group speech, and the child's comprehension was measured by his ability to replace the exact word or suggest a substitute that made semantic or grammatical sense. Despite methodological problems in oral presentation of the speech samples and in the reliability of the scores, there were three major results: (1) social-class differences in understanding teacher speech were more apparent among fifth-graders than first-graders, but this effect was not maintained when intelligence was controlled statistically; (2) there were no social-class differences among fifth-graders in comprehending lower-class peer speech, but middle-class children were significantly

superior to lower-class children in comprehending middle-class peer speech, and this effect was maintained even when intelligence was controlled; (3) Negro-white differences in these receptive language skills were virtually absent. In interpreting these results, we should note that while lower-class fifth-graders had more trouble understanding middle-class peer speech, the decreased comprehension across social-class lines was not reciprocal. The middle-class children understood lower-class children.

Following from the difference/deficit controversy, a solution for comprehension problems is two sided. "They [students] should learn to comprehend the teachers' standard dialect better, or teachers need to learn to speak the dialect of disadvantaged children" (Plumer 1970, p. 270). The onus for change and accommodation should be on both the teacher and the student.

I had a rather clear experience in which dialectic contrasts interfered with comprehension. I attempted to give instructions to a teacher who spoke a different dialect. It was a situation in which a standard speaker wished to give instructions to a nonstandard speaker about a reading program for her child. In the course of instruction, she repeated aloud certain words of each of my utterances. The instructions were brief and the materials were at hand, yet she failed to comprehend them. I realized this failure was not because of intelligence, since she was considerably above average. As I reviewed this, I concluded three things: (1) her re-auditorizations were a translation process from my dialect to her dialect, (2) they controlled my rate of speaking, and (3) their frequency (and/or the complexity of translation) constituted a significant interference in comprehension. Courtwright and Courtwright (1976) reported similar behavior. This experience underscores the need for teachers to uphold their end of the responsibility to realize that performance failures may not be due to an inadequacy in students, but to inappropriate communication in which both teacher and student have a part.

The role of educators and psychologists should be determined by the *difference* rather than the *deficit* rationale. "To devalue his language or to presume Standard English is a 'better system' is to devalue the child and his culture and to reveal a naiveté concerning language. Our job, then, is to teach a second language system (or a dialect) without denying the legitimacy of his own system" (Baratz 1968, p. 145).

Williams (1970) suggested the following guidelines in resolving these sociolinguistic issues in a productive manner:

1. *We must avoid confusing language* **differences** *with* **deficiencies.** Careless interpretations of standardized tests have caused many of the problems involved on this point, with bias on the part of researchers and techniques accounting for the rest.
2. *It is a reasonable and desirable goal that all children in the United States be able to function linguistically in Standard English in addition to whatever dialect they have learned at home.* It is important that Standard English be developed parallel to or be built upon the home language, rather than at the expense of it.

3. *We must develop new strategies for language instruction* by focusing on preschool children and using materials that build on what the child has learned in his home environment. The overall approach is to incorporate the social context of language acquisition into the instructional context.
4. *We must increase our research efforts in the study of language differences in the United States and the interrelation of these with different social and family structures.* This can be achieved by increasing our commitment to sociolinguistic field studies and to studies of the role of language in child socialization.
5. *Language programs for the poor should incorporate evaluative components.* We must evaluate language concepts and usage relative to the social environment involved.

Interested readers may want to read the following: Baratz (1968, 1969a,b, 1970); Labov (1972); Hymes (1967); Shuy (1965); Quay (1971). Bernstein has recently revised his work.

Elaborated and Restricted Codes

Bernstein's sociolinguistic theory (1970) has stimulated considerable interest. It is important that we realize the background of this theory so we can have a better appreciation of it.

There are three major issues underlying Bernstein's theory. First and foremost, it is a theory of social systems as opposed to a theory of language or intellectual competence. The fundamental issues pertain to social dynamics such as underlying roles, language functions, context, etc. Second, it was initially derived from the Sapir-Whorfian hypothesis that language conditions one's perceptions of and responses to his environment. Whorf focused on the structure of language whereas Bernstein focused on the structure of the communicative context of language. Hymes (1964, p. 20) indicated that the latter is the more fundamental question: "What chance the language has to make an impression upon individuals and behavior will depend upon the degree and pattern of its admission into communicative events." Third, Bernstein's theory is just that—a theory. We do not have sufficient data to determine its value.

This brief commentary is necessary, because according to Baratz (1969b) and Cazden (1966a), Bernstein's theory has been bastardized or misinterpreted. Attempts have been made to attribute a one-to-one correspondence between elaborative codes—high levels of competence (Bernstein's theory), and restricted codes—low levels of competence. Concepts of this sort might be regarded as ways of institutionalizing middle class values while subordinating other ones. Consequently, Cazden (1966a), Baratz (1969b), and Bernstein (1970) addressed themselves to the misinterpretations of the concepts of elaborative and restricted codes. Indeed, Bernstein repeatedly admonished against their misuse. He held that both codes could be used by disadvantaged groups. In 1970 he wrote, "The uses (or abuse) of this distinction has sometimes led to the erroneous conception that a restricted code can be directly equated with linguistic deprivation, linguistic deficiency, or being nonverbal" (1970, p. 26).

Bernstein's theory can be summarized in terms of the "restricted" and "elaborated" codes that reflect contrasting socializing conditions. Prominent sociological influences are family, peers, school, and co-workers. These determine how one uses language. The use of codes in social systems can occur in several ways. First, certain codes are used according to perceived contextual demands. One might use a restricted code for interactions at home but an elaborated code at school. Second, one rarely, if ever, uses only a restricted or an elaborated code. Codes are predominantly restricted or elaborated depending on the social conditions of a situation. Third, while most speakers usually *know* restricted and elaborated codes, they usually *use* one or the other. When the context calls for switching back and forth, there is often resistance. The span of restricted and elaborated codes is very large. To ask someone who identifies with one end of this span to perform on the other end is to invite resistance even though he may *know* what to do. This is particularly true of individuals who ordinarily employ a restricted code. Fourth, the criteria appearing in Fig. 5-2 are not linguistic criteria. They pertain to communicative functions of language—a sociological factor.

Fig 5-2 summarizes the contrasting sociolinguistic features underlying the use of restricted and elaborated codes. "Communal" means the code is shared with several others. "Individual" means that utterances are new or novel. A communal code is laden with clichés and contains highly predictable utterances. An individual code is not so routinized. "Positional" means a code that exemplifies a given status of a speaker within a given social context. In a "positional and personalized form of social control" this is not so. In a position-oriented family, a member functions in terms of his formal position or assigned role. There is a clear separation of roles, usually in terms of male/female, adult/child, familial structure, etc. In a person-oriented family, on the other hand, psychological qualities of an individual rather than formal status are the primary determinant of performance.

A "closed" communication system is one in which alternatives are inherent in

Figure 5-2 *Polar features for elaborated and restricted social codes: Bernstein's current model.*

Restricted Code	Elaborated Code
Communal	Individual
Positional	Positional and personalized form of social control
Closed	Open
Substance	Elaboration of process
Here-and-now	Exploration of motives and intentions
Limited alternatives	Wide range of alternatives
Rigidly organized	Flexibly organized

Figure 5-2 *(continued)*

General Category	Specific Sub-types of Category	

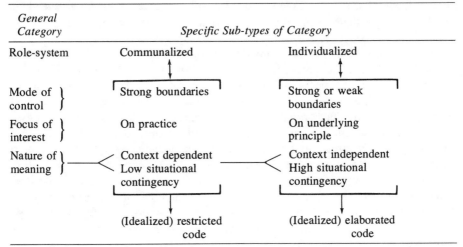

From B. Bernstein, A sociolinguistic approach to socialization: with some reference to educability. In F. Williams, *Language and Poverty* (Chicago: Markham, 1970). Copyright © 1970 by the Institute for Research on Poverty.

the roles. Thus, communication is limited to areas delimited by one's role. Families that verbalize very little generally exhibit closed communication systems and positional orientations. An "open" communication system is usually found in a person-oriented family. Open communication means not only more talking, but talking that involves a variety of alternatives for a situation. An individual in a person-oriented family with open communication is actively coping with his environment on his terms, defining his role rather than having it assigned to him.

A "substantive" code is oriented primarily on context and products. An "elaboration of process" code deals with mechanisms underlying behavior or products. A "here-and-now" code deals with the present, whereas an "exploration of motives and intentions" code deals with underlying motives. A "limited alternatives" code is one in which a few of several possible versions are employed. A "wide range of alternatives" code is one that employs many versions. A "rigidly organized" code is limited to a few frequently used and limited alternatives. A "flexibly organized" code offers a wide variety of alternatives. Bernstein's theory, then, is concerned with socialization of language as opposed to the structure of language.

Lawton (1963, 1968) and Williams and Naremore (1969a, b) have conducted research on Bernstein's hypothesis. Plumer indicated that although these studies yield findings about restricted and elaborated codes as proposed by Bernstein, they have not yet dealt with the heart of his theory—a study of the socialization processes that presumably underly the codes. Plumer felt there are three fundamental problems in the study of the socialization processes. The first is a suitably objective definition of the linguistic distinctions between restricted and elaborated codes. Bernstein (1970) has emphasized that he does not want to establish linguistic criteria for them. He is more interested in social referents than linguistic ones. Plumer indicated that the linguistic referents employed by Lawton (1963, 1968), and Robinson (1970) differed from Bernstein's and from each other. Perhaps what is needed is an orientation on social theory rather than an attempt to remold sociological issues into linguistic ones.

The second problem is the lack of consistent theoretical grounding for the codes and their features. Again, the issues of socialization theory stand out. It is apparent that a cornerstone of socialization theory is the contextual referents for observed events. Differential verbal behavior reflects contextual variables. Labov (1965, 1972) has demonstrated this.

The third problem concerns representative—optimal performance. Again, it is a sociological issue. Representative performance corresponds closely with socialization principles. One chooses to behave in accordance with the performance standards of the social group he identifies with and is motivated by. Optimal performance, on the other hand, is contrived, unnatural, and foreign. It is removed from the heart of social theory, one's functional environment. Perhaps Plumer was referring to a range of verbal alternatives as an index of optimal performance. To this end, Labov (1966) conducted a series of ingenious techniques within one's regular environment.

Pragmatics

As Hymes (1972b) indicated, knowing what language is for is more crucial than knowing what language is. A child can code his intent in language, but it is quite a different matter to play the communication game efficiently and effectively. A child must have not only a cognitive base for language plus a knowledge of linguistic systems, but also be adept at using this knowledge in formulating utterances, employing nonlinguistic, paralinguistic, and metareferential systems, and perceiving and reconciling obstacles as he plays the communication game. Obviously, language usage is a complex matter. As Ervin-Tripp put it, "everything that can be said about linguistic rules can also be said about sociolinguistic rules" (1971, p. 37).

Communicative competence pertains to both knowledge and the use of knowledge. "Competence is understood to be dependent upon two things: (tacit) *knowledge* and (ability for) *use*" (Hymes 1971, p. 16). Hymes described long- and short-range views of competence. The short-range view is an unfolding or realization of innate capacity in the early years of life. The long-range view is an unfolding of sociological or environmental influences throughout life.

Pragmatics is the set of sociolinguistic rules one knows and uses in determining *who* says *what* to *whom, how, why, when,* and *in what situations. Who* refers to the identity of a speaker, his personality, self-concept, and the constellation of emotional and sociocultural influences that bear on him. *What* refers to his communicative intent cast into a matrix of coding devices and possible functions in the context of available referents. *Whom* refers to the perceived decoder, his identity, and his function in playing the communication game. *How* refers to the matrix of coding devices used, a hierarchy of functions within the matrix, and the requirements of the medium for conveying a message. *Why* refers to the selection processes in arriving at a particular message of presumed best fit from among alternatives. *When* refers to the timeliness of a message for a particular effect. *Situation* refers to the influences of a situation that determine a particular code. Olson (1970) indicated that the available reference is a primary determiner of a code.

Theoretically at least, individuals have an unlimited number and variety of ways to say something. They must become adept in selecting the most appropriate code for a particular function in a particular circumstance. "The child finds a great many different linguistic mechanisms for saying essentially the same thing; his intention can be constant while his linguistic forms vary" (Church 1971, p. 75). An individual can switch to alternative forms should the need arise.

Hymes (1971, p. 12) provided the following outline for a theory of language users and language use:

1. Whether (and to what extent) something is formally *possible*.
2. Whether (and to what extent) something is *feasible* by virtue of the means of implementation available.
3. Whether (and to what extent) something is *appropriate* in relation to a context in which it is used and evaluated.
4. Whether (and to what extent) something is in fact actually *performed,* and what its doing entails.

The issue concerning "formally possible" pertains to grammaticality. It deals with whether or not a given form is admissible. "Admissible" in this context means within the generative capacity of one's grammar. "Feasibility" is in some ways synonymous with what Cazden (1966a), Hymes (1971, p. 17), and Carroll (1964, p. 4) call intrapersonal variables. These include memory constraints, perception, coding complexity, and so on. "Appropriateness" pertains to identification and motivation. If a speaker and listener identify with the topic and comment and are motivated to communicate, appropriate messages will be coded and recoded as needs arise. Simple explosure is not enough. "The point is that identification and motivation are what count, not explosure" (Hymes 1971, p. 17). A speaker makes various judgments about the appropriateness of an utterance according to his identity and motivation, and they are to a certain extent constrained by the communicative context. Ervin-Tripp put the issue of *appropriateness* in the following way: ". . . coming to say the right thing in the right way at the right time and place as defined by their social group" (1971, p. 37). Notice that appropriateness varies according to sociological influences.

Theories of language use must take into account (1) the personnel, (2) the situation, (3) the function of the interaction, (4) the topic and message, and (5) the channel (Ervin-Tripp 1967). Another way of indicating the scope of language use is (1) the language one hears, (2) patterns of interaction one engages in, and (3) the nonlinguistic environment or context.

One very interesting aspect of pragmatics is proxemics. *Proxemics* is the proximity or physical distance one has as he interacts with another. Apparently, there are developmental stages in proxemics. Figure 5-3 outlines developmental stages proposed by Wood (1976, p. 239). In another, similar table, Wood added sex differences, which she claims appear at ten years of age (possibly six years for white middle-class children). I suspect that developmental stages in proxemics will reveal other important influences so that it will be a rather complex picture. The reason that these stages are expected to be complex is that the literature on sex differences in infancy (Maccoby and Jacklin 1974; Bem 1975; Hutt 1972; Flerx, Fidler, and Rogers 1976), security base, separation anxiety, and stranger anxiety (Bowlby 1969; Ainsworth 1969; Antonucci 1976; and many others) indicates movement in proximal-distal dimensions. (See Chap. 10 concerning proxemics of the nonverbal child.)

Clearly, pragmatics is very complex. It pertains to encoding and decoding skills of individuals in the communication game. Moreover, it is intimately related

Figure 5-3   *Children's acquisition of territorial zones.*

Age	Zone*	Explanation
Birth to three years	Intimate	Children learn the closeness of communication with their mothers, other members of their family, and caretakers. They touch, desire hugging, and profit from "close" communication.
Three to seven years	Personal	With the acquisition of language, children become full-fledged communicators. They talk to others, usually on a personal basis. Much of their activity is self-centered (egocentric), and they have not acquired an understanding of socialization to any great extent.
Seven years and older	Social	When children become more social, as opposed to egocentric, they form strong social relationships. They learn how to behave in social settings, and they can understand social relationships.
Seven years and older	Public	Older children acquire an awareness of a "public" type of communication, particularly if the school setting offers the opportunity for performing in a public situation.

*If proxemic zones are acquired in a zone-by-zone fashion, we might assume that the zones learned first are retained while further learning takes place.

From Barbara S. Wood, *Children and Communication: Verbal and Nonverbal Language Development,* © 1976, p. 125. By permission of Prentice-Hall, Inc., Englewood Cliffs, New Jersey.

to communicative context. Meaning is inherent not so much in the words of a message as in the linguistic and referential context of the words. Thus, Bates was motivated to say that *"all* of semantics is *essentially* pragmatic in nature" (1976, p. 426). Halliday (1975) indicated that language comes to occupy the central role in the processes of social learning. Brown regarded first language learning as "a process of cognitive socialization" (1956, p. 247). And Bruner (1975) indicated that language is instrumental in regulating joint attention and joint action.

Summary

Clinicians need to know about communicative systems, ranging from speech acts (Chap. 4) to what is entailed in the communication game. They should have a general understanding of sociolinguistic parameters and pragmatics—who, what, when, where, why, how. They should have an appreciation of the deficit-difference positions, elaborated and restricted codes, proxemics, and other basic sociolinguistic issues. They should realize that communication is not just an active speaker talking to a passive listener, nor an encoder producing a series of linguistic codes, but a complex dynamic matrix of various kinds of codes. Realizations of these kinds should convince clinicians that assessment and intervention endeavors should be derived primarily from actual communicative events. This can ensure a certain degree of ecological validity in their enterprise.

6

Language Acquisition

Much of what is done in assessment and intervention is based upon what is known about language acquisition. Thus, developments in the language acquisition literature have important ramifications for assessment and intervention. Clinicians generally have a traditional understanding of language acquisition. However, developments in recent years have altered these older views.

Traditionally, it was held that psychometric norms gave the best evidence of language development. Even today, the most widely used assessment procedures are based upon this premise. Also, it was traditionally thought that development could be explained in vocalization and verbalization stages. Verbalization was thought to begin with the production of the first word. Mean length of utterance was considered the best measure of language acquisition and imitation the primary means of language learning. Accordingly, intervention was based upon stages of vocalization, sentence building, mean length of utterance, imitation, etc. Evidence to date suggests that many of these notions were gross, vague, and misconstrued important language learning processes. As these came to be translated into intervention, procedures came into existence that were deficient in comparison to what we now know about language learning. Let us examine some of the more pervasive of these notions, and compare them to current views.

The Vocalization-Verbalization Notion

Traditionally, there are two major periods of language acquisition: first, vocalization, then verbalization. The vocalization period was thought to begin with the reflexive birth cry and to last about twelve months, ending when a child produces his first word. Further, it was thought that there were two intervening stages: babbling, then echolalia. Reflexive vocalizations are the result of changes of state in the infant, i.e., hunger, temperature, discomfort, pleasure, etc. Babbling is sound play that is intentional and intrinsically motivated. Echolalia is vocalization or verbalization imitating someone else. A child tries to imitate what has just been heard. These are not clearly discernible stages. Babbling occurs after as well as before echolalia, and echolalia occurs after as well as before the first word has been produced.

At least three important functions (in addition to the development of cognitive underpinnings) begin to come into play during the first year. These are (1) sensorimotor coordination of the oral mechanism, (2) discrimination, or the categorization of phonemic patterns and intonations, and (3) the functional realization of differential sound patterns. Sensorimotor coordination of the oral mechanism begins as an infant selectively vocalizes in certain ways for certain circumstances. He continues throughout the course of learning to produce the sound patterns of his language. It takes most children about seven years to learn the sound patterns of English (McDonald 1964; Templin 1957). Presumably it takes about this long for children to learn the sound patterns of other languages as well, which suggests a maturational function (Salus and Salus 1974). Truby, Bosma, and Lind (1965) report that infants acquire increased control of the vocal mechanism in the first six months. As Menyuk summarized, "cry and noncry vocalizations become stabilized during this period, and the sudden changes in pitch and amplitude . . . no longer occur" (1974, p. 214). She indicated that complete closure of the vocal tract to produce sounds occurs and consonantal production or babbling follows. Nakazima (1962) reported that infants about eight or nine months old can imitate intonational patterns produced by their mothers, but not words, syllables, or phonemes. As Menyuk (1974) put it, infants first observe *suprasegmental* aspects of utterances rather than *segmental* ones, and relate these suprasegmental aspects to communicative contexts. Bruner (1975) held that a child becomes aware of prosodic patterns and regards them as envelopes or matrices in which morphemes go. During the babbling period, utterances increase in frequency and length and their segmental and syllabic content changes. As Menyuk further reports from a study by Nakazima, infants from six to eight months have repetitive babbling that is done for play: "At nine months, however, there is a decrease in repetitive babbling and a reorganization of babbling . . . simpler sequences are produced and sounds are used as evocation and response to voice stimuli" (Menyuk 1974, p. 217).

While the development of babbling is interesting, its communicative aspects are even more so.

> In addition, Bruner casts doubt upon the use of babbling, at least using only its phonetic aspects as an adequate base for searching for language prerequisites. To this we must concur; rather than study the phonetic aspects of babbling as critical, it is in the communicative aspect of babbling in interaction with other infant behaviors and the mother's behaviors that precursors may be found (Lewis and Freedle 1973).

At two to four months, infants respond differentially to angry and friendly, familiar and unfamiliar, and male and female voices (Kaplan and Kaplan 1970; Turnure 1971). According to Crowder (1972), infants can only analyze and store auditory aspects concerning pitch, voice quality, location, and loudness. Morse (1974), Eimas et al. (1971), and Eisenberg (1970) would undoubtedly disagree. At four to five months, infants show an orienting response to an auditory stimulus. Menyuk (1974) indicated that between five and eight months, infants seemed to respond differentially to statements and questions. At six months, they seemed to distinguish speech from nonspeech, and a female voice produced increased vocalizations. By eight or nine months, they imitate the intonational patterns of their mothers. At eleven to fourteen months, conventional words and word approximations appear. At thirteen months a child will produce utterances of more than one syllable. Nakazima (1970) concluded that at the early stages of word production, speech perception and production are not yet integrated. "Labels and particular objects are also not definitely associated" (Menyuk 1974, p. 218).

Parenthetically, smiling and vocalization during infancy have been found to be useful indices of (a) cognition—specifically hypothesis testing (Zelazo 1971, 1972; Kagan 1971; McCall 1972; Sroufe and Waters 1976); (b) socialization (Todd and Palmer 1968; Siegel 1969; Bowlby 1969; Ainsworth 1969; Antonucci 1976); and (c) a conceptual link between cognitive-social development (Kagan 1969a; Zelazo 1971, 1972; Zelazo and Komer 1971; Sroufe and Waters 1976).

Discrimination-categorization of phonemic patterns and intonations begin to be acquired very early. Studies by Eimas et al. (1971), Clifton and Meyers (1969), Clifton, Graham, and Hatton (1968), Trehub and Rabinovitch (1972), and others have shown that a speech receptor mechanism is activated as early as four months, and possibly even one month. This literature is rather extensive. It has been reviewed by Eisenberg (1970) and Morse (1974). Much of this research is based upon cardiac deceleration to auditory stimuli. This reflects an orienting response to a stimulus (Sokolov 1963). More recently, the degree of cardiac acceleration following the orienting response has been shown to be a function of perceived discrepancy of a stimulus. This period of cardiac acceleration has been regarded as the hypothesis testing period in which discrepancies are resolved (Kagan and Lewis 1965, McCall 1967; McCall and Kagan 1967a,b, 1969; Melton and Martin 1972). In addition to cardiac rate, voice-onset time has been used to study the differential perception of voiced consonants and voiceless stops (Liberman et al. 1961). High amplitude sucking has also been used (Sigueland and DeLucia 1969). Other techniques such as EEG and skin galvanic responses apparently are not productive for research of this type.

Very young infants apparently not only attend to suprasegmentals but also make distinctions about phonemic categories. This means that early speech perception is not merely discrimination, but categorization. Moreover, the perceptual context is essential to categorization: "depending upon context the *same* acoustic cue will be perceived as different and *different* acoustic events will be perceived the same. This invariance problem is the basis of the whole issue of complex linguistic perception. It makes speech special and apparently requires the postulation of some specific decoder" (Morse 1974, p. 42).

Very early on, at about one month of age, an infant discovers that vocalizations have instrumental functions. This means that they can get things from others through vocalizing; therefore, an individual does not have to do it for himself. An infant discovers that if he cries a certain way, his mother will give him certain kinds of attention and care. When he makes certain sound patterns, particularly those resembling "mama" or "papa," he gets special benefits. Somewhat later, as he makes various word combinations, he discovers even greater instrumental power.

According to Menyuk (1974), though differential patterns of cry appear very early, differential patterns of noncry appear only at about six to eight months. Attempts to emulate intonation patterns also appear at this age. Vocalizations to persons and responses to calling occur at about nine months (Nakazima 1970).

Clearly, to describe vocalization solely in terms of reflexive behavior, babbling, and echolalia is to misconstrue what is happening. Similarly, to define the onset of verbalization as the time when a child produces his first word is to misrepresent the learning process (Huttenlocher 1974). The distinction between vocalization and verbalization is false and arbitrary, and is misleading in intervention. Most of the vocal acts in infancy are essentially rule governed (Bruner 1975a,b; Dore 1974, 1975; Bates 1976a,b; Wells 1974; Greenfield and Smith 1976; Halliday 1975). Verbal behavior occurs well before the first word is produced. Moreover, many instances of a first word are unstable "complexive" labels, and many others are not (Bowerman in press a,b). Lewis and Freedle (1973) indicate that infants have differentiated their environment as early as twelve weeks. Moreover, it is almost impossible to know when a child produces his first word. Word approximations may occur, but there is no assurance that they are labeling with communicative intent, nor of knowing the extent of meaning for a label when it does occur. Early labeling behavior is unreliable. First labels are often names of complexes (Vygotsky 1962). Their meanings vary from event to event until a child obtains an awareness of object permanence (Bloom 1970, 1973). Moreover, a child needs several varied instances to realize the features of a prototype (Rosch and Mervis 1975; Smith et al. 1974; Bowerman in press a,b). Several instances of labeling in communicative context are needed before we know with assurance that the label was indeed used with communicative intent. Even then it may be limited to idiosyncratic knowledge. Most instances of the "first word" are when anxious but loving parents attribute meaning to a vocal pattern. The literature on the onset of the first word is inconclusive (Darley and Winitz 1961). As Menyuk put it, "We do not in fact know when the child ceases to babble and produce 'real' language" (1969, p. 29).

The period of verbalization from about the first to the fourth year is fascinating. It is a remarkable period of cognitive-linguistic learning. Elaborate cognitive and linguistic capacities and systems are acquired in an amazingly short time, with only meager and fleeting contacts with one's language. The salient aspects of language are seldom if ever made explicit, yet young children spontaneously discern its inherent mechanisms. This spontaneity of learning and ability to discern complex mechanisms with virtually no overt assistance leaves no other conclusion than that a biological process unique to humans is operating. Brown (1973a,b) concluded this about language learning and Piaget (1954, 1970, 1962) concluded it about cognitive development.

The period from one to four has been regarded as the critical language learning period (Lenneberg 1967), because learning occurs with relative ease. Indeed, a child can learn more than one language with no apparent detrimental effects (Mazeika 1971). Lenneberg (1967, pp. 128–30) has shown that other important maturational and physiological developments also occur during this period. Brown (1973a,b), Bloom (1973), Halliday (1975), Bruner (1975a,b), Wells (1974), Bates (1976a,b), and Greenfield and Smith (1976) have shown that the period from the production of the first word to two- and possibly three-word combinations is a period of major cognitive-linguistic development. Interestingly enough, the traditional view of this period was that it is a dormant one in which some new words were added to a meager vocabulary.

By four, a child has acquired the basic knowledge of his linguistic system. He still must resolve some subtle nuances (C. Chomsky 1969; Cromer 1970; Palermo and Molfese 1972; Bloom 1975) and a major change seems to occur in the semantic system at about seven (Brown and Berko 1960; Ervin 1961; Emerson and Gekoski 1976; Entwisle, Forsythe, and Muuss 1964; Francis 1972). Major changes occur in language usage and functions. Thought becomes highly representational (Bruner 1964; Piaget 1954, 1962). Children become skillful in the organization and complexity of their utterances, and intermodality transfer occurs (Kavanagh and Mattingly 1972). Intermodality transfer is the transferral of intuitive knowledge of language in one modality (speech/listening) to explicit knowledge in another (writing/reading).

Figure 6-1 is a profile of verbal development (A) for the first ten years, and (B) over ninety years. This shows the rate of language learning and highlights some general dimensions in the development timetable. Profile (A) shows that the verbalization period begins early in the first year, and a truly remarkable rate of learning occurs between the first and fourth years, with a slower but substantial amount of learning between the fourth and eighth years. Most children have acquired an adult grammar by about the eighth year (McNeill 1966a, 1970; Menyuk 1969; C. Chomsky 1969). The dotted lines indicate the variability of learning over these ages. There is a great deal of variability at an early age, but it diminishes until there is virtually none in adulthood. However, semantic development seems to be continuous through adult life as new concepts are learned and old ones revised. Profile (B) shows attainment and degeneration of language capacity over roughly ninety years. This second profile is an attempt to integrate the earlier profile with the reduced language function attendant to aging (deAjuriaguerra and Tissot 1975). Figure 6-1 is a normative statement only. One should be extremely cautious about interpreting it for pedagogical purposes, since it is much too general.

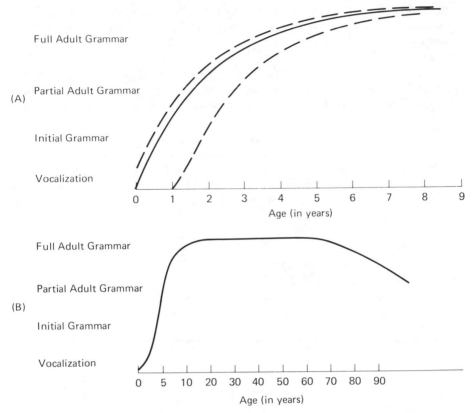

Figure 6-1 *Profiles of verbal development for the first ten years (A) and for ninety years (B).*

The Notion of Norms

A very influential traditional idea is that psychometric norms provide the most appropriate means of language assessment and evaluating intervention. Unfortunately, such norms obscure important information about individual differences, strategies of learning, systems and processes, contextual constraints, communicative intent, verbal functions and speech acts, and alternative codes. The result is that they deal with superficial aspects of language: the *products* of acquisition. Current approaches deal more with underlying *processes*. Normative approaches deal with *what* an individual does; process approaches deal with *how* an individual does it. For example, a psychometric norm might state the age at which a child of a certain sex and socioeconomic status would produce pronouns. A process approach would describe the linguistic and referential conditions under which an individual's pronominal system operates to issue pronouns. The former may indicate that a problem *exists,* but the latter accounts for the *nature* of a problem.

Vocabulary size and mean length of utterance are two examples of the fallacy of using psychometric norms to account for language acquisition. They are also the most widely used in the applied fields. Vocabulary size is only a very gross indication of overall language acquisition (Lorge and Chall 1963). The two most common ways of estimating vocabulary size are inadequate. These are such devices as the *Peabody Picture Vocabulary Test* (Dunn 1959), the *Full-Range Picture Vocabulary Test* (Ammons and Ammons 1948), and the Thorndike and Lorge (1944) word lists. The PPVT deals only with labeling or the comprehension of labels. Nation (1972) has shown that word usage is different from word comprehension as measured by the PPVT. Recent work, particularly by H. Clark (1973a), E. Clark (1973a,b, 1974, 1975), Reich (1976), Bowerman (in press a,b), Smith et al. (1974), and Rosch and Mervis (1975), clearly show that a label is a poor index of underlying thought processes. The more important issue is whether a child has alternative labels for one referent and alternative but stable referents for one label. The same general criticism can be made for word lists such as the Thorndike and Lorge lists. No provision is made for the more important dimensions of labeling behavior, e.g., utility of naming (Brown 1958a), available referents (Olson 1970, 1971), intent (Schlesinger 1971; Bowerman 1973), and various communicative functions (Halliday 1975). Some efforts have been made to provide more appropriate norms on the PPVT for different groups, and more appropriate word lists have been made for studying child language (Carroll, Davies, and Richman 1971). Nevertheless, the primary criticisms remain. Frequency of word occurrence in language is not a significant determiner of word learning. Complexity and available models are also relatively unimportant. The most important determinant is intended meaning in communicative context (Cromer 1976).

Mean length of response or utterance is a good case in point. McCarthy (1954) and Templin (1957) advocated mean length of response (MLR) and mean length of utterance (MLU) as the best single measure of language development. MLR is "the simplest and most objective measure of the degree to which children combine words at various ages" (McCarthy 1930, p. 50, reported by Darley and Moll 1960). No measure "seems to have superseded the mean length of sentence for a reliable, easily determined, objective, quantitative, and easily understood measure of linguistic maturity" (McCarthy 1954, pp. 550–51). However, relatively recent evidence indicates that MLR and MLU are inadequate indices, particularly when calculated for words rather than morphemes and for children over four years of age (Shriner 1969; Cowan et al. 1967; Cazden 1968; Bloom 1970, p. 2). The inadequacy is that necessary information concerning the acquisition of underlying mechanisms and individual variations specific to these mechanisms is not discerned. Moreover, they reflect performance or situational influences better than developmental processes. For example, an MLR administered to disadvantaged children at home or in their neighborhood would be considerably higher than one administered at school or in a test situation. At home they are much more verbal than at school. Several efforts have been made to obtain more developmentally sensitive indices, such as developmental sentence types (Lee 1966), developmental sentences scores (Lee and Canter 1971), complexity scores (Frank and Osser 1970; Minifie, Darley, and Sherman 1963; Miner 1969; Siegel 1962). These indices have the limitation of obscuring individual differences and being product rather than process based.

Brown, Cazden, and Bellugi-Klima (1969) and Brown (1973a,b) showed that the relationship between age and mean utterance length (by morphemes) is very low. Indeed, individual variations were so great that Brown et al. (1969) excluded age as a developmental reference. They reasoned that inasmuch as their inquiry was concerned with the emergence of grammatical mechanisms, evidence should be about how mechanisms operate rather than their products. They opted to use MLU (by morpheme) as a gross match between children. However, it should be remembered that they were studying children under four years of age, a period when MLU appears to be a viable index of development. To appreciate the extent of individual variability, note that of the three subjects, the ages varied considerably even though they were grossly equivalent on languge competence. When MLU was 1.75 morphemes (at the start of the study), the three children were 18, 27, and 27 months old. When MLU was 4.0 morphemes (at termination), the children were 26, 42, and 48 months old. Notice that it took them 8, 15, and 21 months respectively to increase the same amount in mean morpheme length. Undoubtedly there was considerable variation in the specific grammatical structures being acquired, as well as the rate of acquisition.

The Imitation Notion

There has been much emphasis on imitation in the applied fields. This derived from two types of correlational evidence. One is that animals, particularly parrots, were credited with learning language through imitation (Mowrer 1952, 1960). Another is that babies spontaneously imitate sound patterns in their environment. The imitations of parrots can hardly be regarded as language learning. They are fixed patterns that become conditioned to specific stimuli. Verbal behavior, on the other hand, is rule governed and capable of referring to alternative stimuli in novel ways. The most advanced verbal behavior of a nonhuman was produced by the famous chimpanzee named Washoe (Gardner and Gardner 1969; Bronowski and Bellugi 1970; Limber 1977). Washoe's best performance was trivial by human standards. Kellogg (1968) and Premack (1971) have reported similar work with chimpanzees. McNeill (1970) reviewed communicative systems of various nonhumans. He concluded that human language is easily more complicated, versatile, and powerful than nonhuman systems.

Infant verbal imitation is much more complex than has previously been realized (Ramer 1976; Blaisdale and Jensen 1970; Guillaume 1971; Hartup and

Coates 1972; Bloom, Hood, and Lightbown 1974). Moreover, it is relatively limited as a means of language learning. Its importance seems to have been greatly exaggerated by traditional views. It is rule governed. A child will imitate to the extent that his grammar will allow. As McNeill (1966a, p. 53) wrote, "no matter how strong the tendency is for children to imitate speech they receive from their parents, they will not imitate the appropriate feature unless important parts of syntax have already been acquired." Verbal imitation is a reassembly task. A target utterance contains an inherent structure. A child deduces this structure to the extent that his grammar allows. Then he issues a verbal product that corresponds to what he deduces and is capable of producing. Child imitations are not faithful reproductions of available models but systematic reductions. The order of elements is maintained even though deletions occur on predictable aspects of modeled utterances. Imitation is selective. The basic aspects are retained but the unnecessary ones are deleted in accordance with what the child knows and can process. For example, functors are typically deleted whereas contentives are retained. Behavior of this sort, particularly when it is spontaneous as opposed to induced, provides good evidence of what a child knows. Bloom, Hood, and Lightbown (1974) showed that some children spontaneously imitate while others do not, that there were lexical and grammatical differences in imitative and spontaneous speech, that imitated words eventually became spontaneously available, and that imitation was highly selective.

Slobin and Welsh (1971) delineated several kinds of information that can be gleaned from child imitations. They showed that: (1) number of words or morphemes is not a useful index of imitation capacity; (2) stress and pausing are important determinants of what is imitated; (3) repetitions in modeled sentences are ignored; (4) a child will fail to imitate his own spontaneous utterances—utterances that originally were the product of communicative intent and available reference; (5) underlying meaning is preserved but surface structure may be altered; (6) for sentences containing two or more propositions, the last proposition is usually imitated first—a recency effect; (7) processing capacity may be used up so unwarranted redundancy or awkward parallel structures occur; (8) an individual may have certain expectations that prevent him from perceiving an utterance as it is; (9) the second noun phrase may become pronominalized, even if the second noun phrase was deleted in the model sentence; (10) in *who* constructions, the *who* is usually deleted; (11) a child may attempt to imitate an utterance, then make a second attempt in which slight variations occur; (12) advanced constructions were regarded as word lists; (13) young children seem to rely on syntactic strategies (subject-verb-object); and (14) unknown words may be replaced by known words.

Memory constraints can supersede one's knowledge in imitation. That is, even though a child may know the grammatical structure for an utterance, he may still not produce it faithfully because a memory processing overload prevents it. However, contextual support and communicative intent may be sufficient to overcome these processing constraints. Thus, a child may perform better if he spontaneously imitates than if his imitations are induced (Prutting and Connolly 1976). The same principles hold for comprehension and production (Bloom 1974; Ingram 1974a). Young children do much better in comprehension and production when contextural supports in terms of communicative intent and available reference are present.

Piaget (1954, 1962) regards imitation as a clear example of accommodation. He believes that new learning does not occur in imitation. A child imitates to the extent that his existing knowledge allows. McNeill (1966a) made the same point about language learning. Thus, imitation per se is probably not very important in language learning—with the possible exception of imitation as a rehearsal device. However, Bloom, Hood, and Lightbown (1974) found that for some children and some lexical and grammatical domains, imitation constitutes a potent means of acquisition.

Ervin-Tripp (1973) indicates that "input to children is characterized by repetitiveness" (1973, p. 264). Brown and Bellugi (1964) studied a particular kind of repetitiveness: parent-child cyclic imitations. Parents may spontaneously imitate and expand a few child utterances, and the child may spontaneously imitate and reduce selected parent utterances. Occasionally, cyclic interactions occur in which a mother expands her child's utterances, then a child reduces his mother's utterances, followed by mother expansions. These cyclic exchanges may be brief or extend over several rounds. There are several important aspects to them. First, mother expansions are very important, since they are timely by virtue of being appropriate to a child's grammar, presumed intent, and available referents. Second, child reductions are specific to available linguistic and referential models. They conform to his grammatical knowledge and ability to process an utterance. Third, by about the third exchange a child frequently varies his production in the direction of an available adult expansion (Ervin 1966; Brown and Bellugi 1964). These variations are presumed to be the locus of new learning during imitation. Fay (1967) regarded variations in verbal imitation as *mitigated echolalia*. He contended that learning occurs in mitigated echolalia. Bloom (1972) agreed that learning probably occurs with variation. She also wondered why variations usually do not occur immediately after the first expansion. She suggested that perhaps a child needs to repeat an utterance in order to hold it in short-term storage preparatory to long-term storage and manipulation, or that he uses this overt means to scan the structure of the utterance for a locus which can be altered.

Adult expansions of child utterances offer an effective means for facilitating language learning. Studies by Brown and Bellugi (1964), and Shipley, Smith, and Gleitman (1969), testify to the effectiveness of adult expansions. Cazden (1965) had nursery school teachers expand child utterances. She used two other groups. In one, teachers were asked to elaborate on topics the children raised. In the other, teachers were not given any special instructions. At the end of the study, the children in the elaborated group had progressed further than the group in which the teacher had no special instructions. However, neither of the groups had significantly improved over the other. Apparently, one major difference between Cazden's study and natural adult expansions is that natural expansions occur only on occasion, where contrived expansions dominate teachers' responses. Brown (1973a) held that if expansions are selectively and judiciously applied, significant results might be obtained. Imitation seems to contribute to learning when a child *varies* his utterance. Faithful imitation alone may not be productive for children in just one lexical or grammatical domain.

Traditional accounts of language development have placed heavy emphasis on faithful imitation. The evidence indicates that although spontaneous imitation does occur, other, more powerful means are available. Chomsky and Miller (1963) have calculated that it would take many years for children to learn the basic sentences of a language if they had to learn each aspect by imitation or association. But they learn this and much more within two to three years, and from only fleeting contacts and meager samples of their language. Moreover, imitation fails to account for child utterances not derived from adult language. Children say such derivational words as "runned," "goed," and "mines" even though they do not occur in adult language. Finally, imitation fails to account for why certain words drop out of one's vocabulary, never to be used again—word mortality (Bloom 1973).

The principle of imitation pertains to the associationist (or S-R) theories of language learning. These have been proposed and supported by Skinner (1957), Staats (1968), Mowrer (1960), MacCorquedale (1970), Jenkins (1964), Guess, Sailor, Rutherford, and Baer (1968), Guess, Sailor, and Baer (1974), Girardeau and Spradlin (1969), and Deese (1965). Braine's (1963a,b, 1965) theory of contextual generalization probably comes closer than any associationist position in providing for linguistic constraints. His theory has been strongly criticized (Bever, Fodor, and Weksel 1965a,b; Bever 1968), but modifications have made it more palatable by accounting for semantic functions in early utterances (Bowerman 1976). Skinner's views on language were subjected to criticism by Chomsky (1959). Katahan and Koplin (1968) and Wiest (1967) regarded the Skinner-Chomsky controversy as a paradigm clash. The S-R theories dealt only with superficial aspects of verbal behavior. As indicated in Chap. 2, several S-R theorists have abandoned their explanations for psycholinguistic ones. These include Deese, Palermo, Cofer, and Jenkins. ". . . In principle, such S-R analyses of language behavior can never adequately account for the acquisition and maintenance of language" (Palermo 1971). As Deese put it,

> If we were to argue that a sentence is nothing more than a complicated kind of conditioned reponse (as has been suggested; see Mowrer, 1954, for example) or a set of associations, or some more complicated version of these via the principle of mediation (see Osgood, 1968), we would be asserting (1) that each element in a sentence is a reaction to some preceding stimulus, and (2) these reactions are always chained together in a string. There are several ways of showing that these two propositions are false (Chomsky, 1956) (1970, p. 5).

Deese added,

> These operations—which constitute the result of generative theory—cannot be accounted for, derived from, or otherwise interpreted within the traditional psychological points of view about intellectual processes. They are particularly difficult for any theory that reduces cognition to associations between elements (1970, p. 42).

Piaget (1962, 1970) outlined a developmental sequence for imitative behavior: contiguity, mutual imitation, sporadic imitation, and delayed imitation. In contiguity, a child verbalizes when someone or something around him makes a noise. In mutual imitation, a child reimitates a behavior he has just performed that was imitated by someone else. A mother might imitate a word her child had just uttered, whereupon her child will then reimitate his mother. Sporadic imitation occurs for no apparent reason. A child may be playing as his mother is talking to a friend, when to their surprise, the child utters a close approximation of something they said. Delayed imitation occurs with an intervening period of time or activity. Delayed imitation is especially important, since it means a child can hold something in storage, reformulate it, and retrieve it. *Selective imitation* may be a good descriptor of language learning through imitation (Whitehurst and Novak 1973; Whitehurst and Vasta 1973).

Sherman (1971) provided a comprehensive review of verbal imitation and language development. This review is primarily oriented on an S-R (more specifically, behavior modification) viewpoint. Krasner (1958) reviewed a number of studies on behavior modification or conditioning. Flanders (1968) provided a comprehensive review of imitative behaviors, both verbal and nonverbal. Prutting and Connolly (1976) cautioned that elicited imitation is not well understood.

In summary, verbal imitation does play a role in language learning, but not the central role, as had been previously thought. Induction of latent structure is considerably more important. Verbal imitation is limited to one's underlying grammar, which is in turn usually restricted. Apparently, variations in imitation have developmental significance. A child can produce more elaborate utterances through communicative intent and available reference than through imitation.

Determinants of Language Acquisition

Clinicians should realize that there are both biological and environmental determinants of language acquisition (Osser 1970). Figure 6-2 outlines them. Biologically, humans have an innate capacity or predisposition for language learning. There are strong and weak versions of this argument (Cazden 1967). Through physical and physiological maturation, children are increasingly prepared to acquire both the cognitive processes underlying language and the language itself (Lenneberg, 1967). According to Piaget (1962, 1970), the acquisition of cognitive skills is based upon

Figure 6-2 *Biological and environmental determinants of cognitive-linguistic-communicative development.*

Biological Determinants	Environmental Determinants
Manner of learning	Content
Sequence	Rate

biological stages of readiness. For this reason, developmental stages are invariant, though variations of rates (delays) may occur. The biological character of language acquisition accounts for both the *manner* and *sequence* of language learning. As Brown (1973a) contends, sequence is remarkably stable whereas rate is notoriously variable.

Both *content* and *rate* are determined by environmental influences. A child learns the language of his environment. The rate at which he learns his language is the result of a constellation of environmental influences. Intrapersonal constraints can also curtail learning. A warm, accepting, loving, verbal, and responsive environment seems to foster language learning (Cazden 1966a). The following studies have dealt with environmental influences: Hess and Shipman (1965); Bernstein (1970); Lawton (1963, 1968); Plumer (1970); Robinson (1970); Williams (1970); Broen (1972); Snow (1972); Cole and Bruner (1972); Bee et al. (1970); Cole et al. (1971); Davis and Lange (1973); Shatz and Gelman (1973); and Bates (1976a,b). Martin (1975) has an excellent review of this literature. It is also discussed below in *Verbal Models and Dialogue.*

What impels children to acquire language? We do not know why they begin, or, once learning occurs, why they continue. We are all the more puzzled because there appear to be only occasional environmental pressures to learn language. According to Cazden and Brown (1975) and Brown and Hanlon (1970), parents do not assert selective pressure on their children to speak like adults. Parents ignore immature syntax—though they are concerned about function. Environmental pressures may impel a child to learn more about language in order to be more successful in realizing his intended functions. Increased verbal capacities certainly increase explicitness, audience, and efficiency—in sum, instrumental power. Whether a child realizes this and is thereby led to further learning, or whether the realization comes later, there is no question that such benefits accrue in language learning. Both innate capacity and environmental influences play a role.

Induction of Latent Structure—Hypothesis Testing

Innate capacity and environmental influences can be appreciated in terms of the induction of latent structure. Brown and Bellugi (1964) described spontaneous language learning as induction of latent structure. Through meager and fleeting contacts with his language, a child spontaneously induces the nature of language. It is as if the first contact one has with language activates a predisposition for language learning. The induction process is very remarkable. A child grasps an extremely complex system in a relatively short time with what seem to be rather obscure or tangential clues.

This indicates that more than environmental influences are operating. Innate capacity or predisposition must play a role as well. Several arguments have been given for this. Lenneberg (1967), McNeill (1966a, 1970), and Schlesinger (1974) have been the main advocates of the role of innate capacity in language learning. One of their most compelling arguments is that all humans exhibit some form of verbal behavior. This is true for the mentally retarded (Carroll 1963)—excluding the profoundly retarded "crib cases"—and also true of the grunts and noise patterns of those few children who have been subjected to isolation in attics or back rooms by their parents. Such children have grammatical systems for grunts, squeals, and other sounds, although they may not speak the language of their communities. Human verbal behavior easily surpasses that of nonhumans (McNeill 1970; Limber 1977), and is structurally and functionally much more complex.

Physiologically, evidence indicates that humans are uniquely "wired" for verbal behavior (Geschwind 1965a,b; Millikan and Darley 1967). There are at least three major types of this evidence: (a) a high correlation between developmental stages of myelinization in the central nervous system and developmental stages in language acquisition, (b) structural differences between humans and other animals in primary sensory areas, secondary association areas, and tertiary association areas of the cortex, with their connections to other areas of the cortex and the limbic system, and (c) the relative ease of humans in performing intermodality transfer tasks compared to the comparative difficulty (indeed virtual impossibility) for nonhumans. The organization of the human central nervous system is such that verbal behavior is facile, but the organization of central nervous systems in higher primates makes verbal behavior extremely difficult to establish, and even then it exists only at a rudimentary level. The Gardners' chimpanzee Washoe (Gardner and Gardner 1969; Bronowski and Bellugi 1970) learned a vocabulary and a few rudimentary generative rules. Moreover, a chimpanzee can accommodate for its decoder. Most verbal capacities spontaneously available in humans are either so difficult to achieve that they are accomplished only on a rudimentary level or completely beyond the abilities of higher primates. Certainly, bees, parrots, porpoises, and other animals have communication devices (McNeill 1970) but they do not compare with those of humans. Human verbal behavior is a unique capacity. Any account of language aquisition must provide for it.

Once it is agreed that human verbal behavior is quite different from nonhuman verbal behavior, a large part of the argument that innate capacity is basic to language acquisition has been accepted. Additionally, there is evidence that innate capacity plays a role in language acquisition. First, there is the interesting finding that children in vastly different cultures and with different languages learn their respective languages in much the same manner, that is, in a generic sequence by inducing properties about the nature of their language. This holds for Japanese (McNeill 1966a, 1970), Russian (Slobin 1966), American (Brown and Bellugi 1964; Brown 1973a,b; Ervin 1966; Braine 1963a,b), and Finnish (Bowerman 1975) children. Moreover, it holds for low and middle socioeconomic levels. In referring to two-word utterances in the acquisition of various languages, it has been observed that the utterances read like direct translations of one another. There is a great similarity of basic vocabulary and basic meanings conveyed by the word combinations. And to paraphrase Bowerman (1976, pp. 138–39), in samples from almost every language one finds sentences that name constructions dealing with recurrence, disappearance, rejection, denial, location, possession, and relationships among agents, actions, and objects.

Second, the general profiles of language acquisition for children in different parts of the world are remarkably similar (Lenneberg 1967). Children learn their first word at about one year of age. They have learned most of adult syntax by about four. These profiles indicate that an innate maturational capacity is operating. Lenneberg (1967) summarized evidence that correlates maturation with language acquisition. He contended that language acquisition occurs when one is biologically ready. Apparently, a child's needs for language arise from increased cognitive skills and volition. The more he knows, the more he wants to know, and language is one way he does it. Lenneberg felt that it is virtually impossible to stop humans from engaging in linguistic behavior. He held that humans are predestined to be verbal just as fish are predestined to swim. In the biological bases of language learning, this is strongly evident.

Third, language universals provide strong evidence of innate capacity. Apparently, humans throughout the world are endowed with the same basic cognitive mechanisms for language learning and use. Languages throughout the world share certain basic characteristics, called language universals. Greenberg (1963) identified and described many of these, including a subject-predicate system, tenses, a number system, modification systems, and speech as the primary modality.

Finally, there are two characteristics of language learning that cannot be explained by theories of learning. These are the spontaneous employment of generative mechanisms and the extremely fast and easy learning of language. Very young children spontaneously employ hierarchical structure, transformations, recursiveness, pronominalization, and derivations, even though these operations are not apparent in the surface structure of their utterances. This is truly remarkable, and is strong evidence in favor of innate mechanisms. The utterances themselves are the products of very powerful underlying generative mechanisms, yet very young children can differentiate *processes* from *products*. I have already indicated that current theories of learning cannot account for the spontaneous speed and ease of language learning. All these point strongly to innate capacity as the basis for language learning.

On a conceptual level, induction of latent structure appears almost to be a mystical ability. Several accounts of inductive processes are available (Brown 1958a; Brown and Bellugi 1964; Macnamara 1972; Nelson 1973, 1974; Bowerman 1973, 1976; Schlesinger 1971). However, this ability can be appreciated best at the operational level: how a child induces latent structure from meager and fleeting contacts with his language. He does this through hypothesis testing, which describes the *manner* in which he learns while also accounting for why the *rate* of learning is so variable. Thus, an explanation of language acquisition must be flexible and dynamic enough to allow for considerable variability in rate of acquisition while providing for stable sequences. Bowerman (in press, a,b) indicated that theories of word acquisition should be flexible and dynamic. Moreover, such accounts must be consistent with the nature of the mechanisms that are being acquired—which account must not only provide for variability of rate and stability of sequence, but also explain the acquisition of underlying generative capacities and processes rather than simply their products. An account of language acquisition in terms of induction of latent structure through hypothesis testing meets these criteria and even allows for alternative strategies.

Figure 6-3 shows the dimensions of hypothesis testing in language acquisition. A parallel is drawn between hypothesis testing in language acquisition and the dimensions of formal inquiry. The latter appear on the right side.

Because a child spontaneously inquires or puzzles about his language, the source of his hypotheses is thought to lie in his innate capacity. Moreover, he does not inquire about just any aspect of language; he inquires about certain aspects—

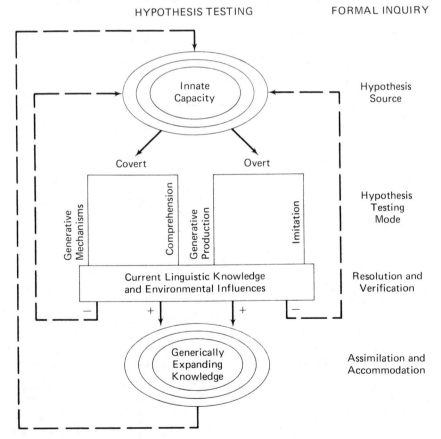

Figure 6-3   *Induction of latent structure—operational hypothesis testing.*

those he is ready to learn at a given time and with respect to particular opportunities for learning. For those individuals who employ an imitation strategy, this probably accounts for the selective nature of spontaneous imitation. His inquiries are systematic in that they deal with general issues that subsequently become more specific. The pattern of general to specific is very pervasive. It appears in concept learning and in the acquisition of the semantic, syntactic, and phonological domains (Brown 1973a,b; Menyuk 1964a,b; McDonald 1964). This is called generic learning, and an underlying hierarchical structure is the best evidence that something has been acquired through it. It will be recalled from previous discussion that hierarchical structure is strongly evident in verbal behavior (McNeill 1966; Brown 1973b; Bruner 1964, 1966; Johnson 1965, 1966).

One of the most fundamental questions in language acquisition is why children are inspired to learn more about language when their early verbal efforts seemingly work so well. McNeill (1966) offered two reasons: (1) memory overload and (2) increased explicitness, thus more communicative efficiency. He argued that as children learn more words they become faced with an increasingly difficult problem: remembering them. The child spontaneously strives to acquire appropriate structures to resolve his memory overload. He apparently does this by establishing classes for words and concepts and an organization for them (Macnamara 1972; Nelson 1973, 1974). An organized set is easier to remember than a list. In both class formation and organizational rules for classes, a child exhibits generic learning. He begins with the most general classes and differentiates subordinate classes. Accordingly, his organizational rules begin with the most general and proceed to the specific. McNeill (1966) provides an excellent discussion of how children learn classes and rules. Menyuk (1971) describes the acquisition of bins and structures in a similar way. Menyuk (1964a,b) also indicated that in addition to generic differentiation, children can also reorganize newly learned structures: "varying degrees of generalization take place throughout the age range from greatest generalization to increasing differentiation to complete differentiation and, possibly, new organization" (Menyuk 1964a, p. 487). Generic learning follows a stable sequence and provides a means for overcoming memory overload.

As for increased explicitness and communicative efficiency, it is a misconception that early child verbal efforts work quite well. Rather, they work well only in certain circumstances. As Brown (1973b) indicated, infants are narrowly adaptive in verbal behavior. They depend on someone who knows their verbal repertoire to interpret intended meanings. Even then, the interpretations may conflict with their intent, since the child's verbalizations lack explicitness. One-word utterances can have several idiosyncratic meanings (Bloom 1970). These words are called *holophrastic* utterances. However, they are actually not holophrastic because early one-word utterances are too unstable to credit alternative meanings (Dore 1975; Bowerman 1976). Moreover, a child's utterances are limited to the "here and now" (Bloom 1973). When faced with a communicative obstacle, they are not very adept at recoding a more appropriate message (Flavell et al. 1968; Schacter et al. 1974;

Clark-Stewart 1973; Shatz and Gelman 1973; Glucksberg, Krauss, and Higgins 1975). Thus, their communicative efficiency leaves much to be desired. As their motivation to be more clearly understood increases, they strive to be more explicit. They learn more about the nature and use of language. Brown (1958a) indicated that the frequency of occurrence of structures in verbal behavior was insufficient to account for acquisition; increased explicitness seemed to be the primary determinant because it provides a means of disambiguating utterances. Both Brown (1958a) and Olson (1970, 1971) indicated that available reference is more important than frequency of occurrence in the determination of an explicit code. Thus, a child spontaneously tests hypotheses about the nature and use of his languauge in order to become more explicit and effective in communication.

Hypothesis testing can be carried out overtly and covertly. Overt testing can be done through imitation and generative production. Covert testing can be through comprehension and generative mechanisms. Resolution and verification of hypotheses can be accomplished through environmental influences and current linguistic knowledge. Hypotheses are resolved through imitation when a child varies his restricted imitative behavior in the direction of an available model. Very little, if any, learning seems to occur during imitation per se. However, imitation with *variation* seems to point out a new locus of learning. In overt generation, a child speculates about the ways his language works, exemplified by such utterances as "goed," "opened," "hitted," "covered," etc. If his listeners accept the utterance, his hypothesis is confirmed. However, if they reject it, his hypotheses will be rejected and modified. Thus, acceptance will occur for "opened" and "covered" but not for "goed" and "hitted." The child will eventually realize that a past tense rule can be generalized to certain verbs but not to all. This realization can also come about through covert hypothesis testing. A child may hear "go" in one circumstance and "went" in another and deduce that "go" is the present tense and "went" in the past. Thus, he resolves hypotheses through comprehension.

Several authorities regard comprehension as the primary means of language learning. As Ervin-Tripp (1973) wrote, "Every speaker's primary role has been first as an understander." Macnamara (1972), Bowerman (1973, 1976), Winograd (1972), Schank (1972), Bever (1970, 1973), Carroll and Freedle (1973), Huttenlocher (1974), and Bransford and Johnson (1972) regard comprehension as fundamental to language learning. There is no direct evidence, but apparently a great deal of learning occurs through covert generative mechanisms. Here one presumably mediates new information about a system or process from knowledge of a few exemplars. Thus, he intuitively learns. He may also contemplate the legitimacy of various aspects of language. Covert generation apparently occurs because children spontaneously learn and produce much more than they have an opportunity to experience.

Clinicians should understand that *positive and negative exemplars* are useful in resolving and verifying overt and covert hypotheses and for discovering various rules. Children love to play verbal games. An actual verbal game of six four-year-old disadvantaged children illustrates the point that negative examplars are instructive in resolving hypotheses. One boy said, "Look at the black street, look at the long street, look at the high street," whereupon the others laughed with joy. He continued with "fat street," "blue street," and was joined by his friends with "yellow street," "polkadotted street," "pink trees," "silly car," etc. They were playing a game that required generating negative examplars for the rules of inanimate noun modifiers. After each attempt to generate a nongrammatical exemplar, the children would pause briefly for a moment of laughter, which verified the existence of a negative exemplar. No laughter or an occasional "no" or "yeah" meant the effort was not a negative exemplar but rather a positive one. After a series of negative exemplars, the children began to chant. The chant contained only the negative exemplars. The positive exemplars were simply dismissed. Notice that this facilitated covert as well as overt hypothesis testing. Overtly, the children had their productions resolved and verified through laughter and chant. Covertly, the ones who waited before they giggled used laughter to resolve and verify their hypothesis. Weir (1962), Menyuk (1969), and Bowerman (1976) report similar overt testing behaviors in young children. Clearly, environmental influences play a role in hypothesis testing, as does innate capacity.

When a hypothesis is verified, the information is incorporated into generically expanding knowledge. However, if it is not, a new or revised hypothesis is generated. Both correct and incorrect hypotheses thus end in the issuance of new hypotheses. *Positive exemplars* seem to extend knowledge by delimiting a domain. *Negative exemplars* substantiate the range of a domain.

An understanding of hypothesis testing helps one appreciate the principle that the rate of learning is variable but the sequence is stable. I have already mentioned that stable sequences reflect generic learning. The variable rate reflects not only environmental stimulation but also that a child is *actively* involved in the issuance and resolution of hypotheses (Blank 1974; Blank and Solomon 1968, 1969; Bloom, Hood, and Lightbown 1974). In the applied fields emphasis is placed on stimulation and enrichment. However, it is now clear that though stimulation and enrichment are necessary, they are insufficient (Bruner 1961). A child may be amply stimulated but only passively involved in the learning process. Such a situation is inefficient, and that is a problem with most traditional English education programs (Mellon 1967). The rate of learning is apparently the product of environmental influences (Cazden 1966a, 1972a).

Principles of Hypothesis Testing

There are basic language learning principles attendant to hypothesis testing: (a) contextual learning, (b) partial learning, (c) operantly determined locus of learning, and (d) operantly determined switching loci of learning.

Natural language learning always occurs in referential and linguistic contexts.

New grammatical classes emerge through differentiation of existing, generically broader classes. New rules emerge from the organizational requirements of previously learned rules. Thus, on a linguistic level, learning has a contextual relationship to previous learning. Moreover, sequence of learning for any given grammatical system proceeds in terms of contextual constraints. Co-occurring linguistic structures are important in language learning and assessment (Muma 1973a,b). Co-occurring events in phonetic contexts are fundamental principles in coarticulation. Contextual constraints are strongly evident in phonology. Studies by Daniloff, Oller, Compton, Ingram, and others indicate that contextual learning is clearly occurring in phonology. The literature on the acquisition of semantic-syntactic systems also shows that contextual learning is occurring. Bloom (1970, 1973), Bloom, Hood, and Lightbown (1974), and Bloom, Lightbown, and Hood (1975) showed that syntactic systems are learned in referential contexts. Klima (1965) and Klima and Bellugi-Klima (1969) documented co-occurring structures in the acquisition of negations and questions. Brown's (1973b) five stages of development deal with co-occurring structures. Brown, Cazden, and Bellugi-Klima (1969) outlined contextual constraints in acquiring semantic-syntactic systems. Contextual learning is evident in concept development (Gagne 1965, 1967; White 1965). As Hunt (1969) argued, a cognitive match must be made between what one is ready to learn and opportunities for learning, which is consistent with Piagetian psychology. The opportunities to learn are embedded in available contexts. Wells (1974) defined *language learning* as a child's effort to match the organization of language with cognitive organization derived from experience.

Efforts to isolate an element from its context invite distortion and misrepresentation. This is a problem Bronfenbrenner (1974) raised concerning the child development literature, and a prevailing problem with traditional efforts to "simplify" the environment in the hope of promoting learning. Cazden (1966b) worried that the strategy of simplifying a child's environment may work to his detriment, because options he might otherwise use have been eliminated. The "simplification" or isolation of things such as speech sound patterns and core vocabulary may actually make the learning process more difficult, since one is asked to learn something that does not occur naturally. A child might indeed learn labels in a core vocabulary; however, the essential learning task is the acquisition of alternative meanings for these labels. This is something that is deducible only through contextual learning. While a child can learn to make certain sound patterns in isolation, he must also learn to make them in a variety of contexts.

Referential contexts are the referents mapped or coded according to one's intent. Language is essentially a mutually shared coding system used to convey intended meanings. An utterance is a code or map that hopefully represents similar concepts in both encoder and decoder. As Bruner (1975a) said, language regulates joint attention and joint action. The skill with which a speaker can employ the most appropriate code(s) for any given circumstance is the degree to which communication will be realized (Muma 1975a). A speaker not only must know the various linguistic, paralinguistic, nonlinguistic, and metareferential coding devices of his culture, but also must have the necessary cognitive basis to perceive available referents and appreciate his listeners' needs for alternative codes. Codes are issued according to available referents (Brown 1958a; Olson 1970, 1971). Thus, utterances themselves do not provide evidence of a child's linguistic capacities. It is necessary to know the context of available referents in order to assess linguistic knowledge (Bloom 1970, 1973, 1974). Even then, various constraints—particularly memory and linguistic context—are operating to cloud the picture.

Much of what is done in the applied fields is contrary to this principle of contextual learning. Referential context was virtually ignored until Bloom (1970, 1973) and Olson (1970, 1971) pointed out its importance. Similarly, communicative intent (Bowerman 1973; Schlesinger 1971) and roletaking in playing the communication game (Flavell et al. 1968; Muma 1975a; Glucksberg, Krauss, and Higgins 1975) have been virtually absent in most applied areas. As McNeill (1965) pointed out, only in language intervention is language learning isolated from context; isolation never occurs in natural language learning. Baer, reported in Bateman (1974), argues that it may be necessary to contrive intervention programs different from normal language learning because individuals who need language intervention apparently have failed to avail themselves of normal opportunties. Regardless of whether Baer has a point, it is clear that most efforts in the applied fields to provide a language development approach to intervention have fallen considerably short because inadequate provision has been made for contextual learning.

Contextual learning is strongly evidenced in the recent literature on semantic development and speech acts. Bowerman (in press a,b), Rosch (1973b), Rosch and Mervis (1975), and Smith et al. (1974) indicate that word learning is intimately tied to initial referential functions rather than perceptual features (E. Clark 1973a,b, 1975) or action patterns (Nelson 1974). Words are interpreted a variety of ways depending upon context (Bransford and McCarrell 1974; Friedman and Seely 1976). Active processing of model utterances is relative to the contexts in which they occur (Bloom, Hood, and Lightbown 1974). Labeling or imitation occur as a function of dynamic events (Nelson 1974; Wieman 1976; Firbas 1964; Hinds 1975), and are more likely to occur in the presence of actual things rather than representational ones (Sigel 1971). This also holds for spontaneous imitation (Abravarel, Levan-Goldschmidt, and Stevenson 1976). Donaldson and McGarrigle (1974) discussed the importance of contextual learning in terms of a three-stage model in semantic development: lexical rules, syntactic rules, and local rules. Lexically, a labeling effort indicates that something is to be labeled. Syntactically, there may be an attempt to combine labels in a somewhat loose way. But local rules are specific to an event or circumstance. The *event* provides a decoder insight into the referential function of an utterance and the encoder initial prototypic knowledge of a label— idiosyncratic, complexive, or unstable semantic.

Contextual learning is intrinsic to the concept of speech acts (Searle 1969; Bruner 1975a,b; Dore 1975). A child becomes aware that speech acts realize various verbal functions (Halliday 1975, 1977a,b). Functions are contextual in nature. The regulation of joint attention and joint action (Bruner 1975a) occurs in dynamic contexts. A child learns language by attempting to match the organization of language to the cognitive organization he has already imposed upon his experiences (Wells 1974).

Just as contextual learning is basic to normal language acquisition, so also is *partial learning*. A child never learns a grammatical system completely on his first effort. He learns it in stages (Brown 1973b; Bloom, Lightbown, and Hood 1975). For example, a child does not learn adult negations from the beginning; a developmental sequence occurs. He learns to negate by the structure "no + S." Thus, he would say, "No, I go," which usually means "I don't want to go," or "I won't go." Then, he inserts a negation into a sentence but fails to integrate it into the auxiliary system, producing, "I no go." Later, he integrates the negation into the auxiliary system by producing, "I will not go," or "I won't go." With respect to the acquisition of different functions of negation, the child's developmental sequence is first to learn nonexistence, then rejection, and then denial (Bloom 1970). If contextual learning occurs with the attendant constraints of co-occurring structures and referents, partial learning must necessarily follow. A child cannot learn a complete system until he encounters enough rich and varied contexts to allow him to deduce the entire system, with its nuances and constraints. I believe that this is what Braine's (1963a,b; 1975) theory of contextual generalization is about.

The next principle is *operantly determined locus of learning*. The locus of learning is the specific grammatical form or function a child is acquiring at any given moment. He may be focusing on the distinction between mass and count nouns, adjective modifiers that semantically match certain noun types, semantic-syntactic properties of verbs, or any other form or function. The selectivity of imitation (Bloom, Hood, and Lightbown 1974) and spontaneous labeling reflect operantly determined loci of learning. Clinicians have little control over the specific grammatical dimensions a child will choose to learn, but do have the opportunity to assess a child's language knowledge in such a way as to reveal the dimension the child is actively learning. Procedures such as co-occurring and restricted structures (Muma 1973a,b), revision model (Blank and Frank 1971; Muma 1971b), combination model (Mellon 1967; Muma 1971b), and careful observation of natural speech acts (Bloom 1970, 1973; Bloom, Hood, and Lightbown 1974; Bloom, Lightbown, and Hood 1975; Brown 1973b) provide this kind of information. Perhaps the best strategy is to base intervention on the assumption that a child evidences active learning. This strategy is a marked contrast to the traditional one, in which clinicians select particular dimensions and provide highly structured activities for learning them.

Operantly determined loci of learning are *operant* because the individual's choices meet internal requirements. A child will attempt to learn a given dimension because it is somewhat consistent with what he had previously learned. He will not attempt to learn a dimension simply because a clinician, teacher, or parent requests him to do so. There must be a match between his readiness to learn and the environmental opportunities to learn (Hunt 1969, p. 42). This argues against programs in which content, sequencing, reinforcement, and pacing are externally derived and controlled by teachers or clinicians (Muma 1977a).

The next principle, *operantly switching loci of learning,* is closely related to the above principles of contextual learning, partial learning, and operantly determined locus of learning. A child determines not only *which* dimension of grammar to learn, but *when* to switch from one to another. The underlying assumption is that a child can choose among several possible grammatical loci. He is conceptually ready to learn at several different loci at any given time. This potential allows him to take advantage of various opportunities available to him.

Two pieces of evidence suggest that children switch their loci of learning. First, detailed studies of the acquisition of grammar indicate that children vary in the particular grammatical system they focus on. One child may focus on nominalizations, then auxiliaries, then adverbials, and so on. Another may focus on these in a different sequence. Moreover, a given child switches from one system to another, then back to a previous system because it was only partially learned. Bloom, Lightbown, and Hood (1975) reported that some children begin learning nominal systems by learning pronominal forms, whereas other children begin by learning explicit nominals. After these children reached the MLU of 2.0, they switched their respective orientations. While grammatical systems follow stable sequences and individuals apparently have prerogatives for switching loci, contextual constraints restrict the degree of freedom in switching. Thus, a child cannot focus entirely on one system, but can learn only a given amount in one system before he must switch to another. This means not only that he is engaged in contextual learning but that grammatical systems are intimately related and indeed overlap or squish (Ross 1974).

Previously, I said that sequence was stable, but now I am implying that there are individual differences in learning grammatical systems. How can this apparent contradiction be reconciled? Studies on various grammatical systems indicate that the sequence of learning *within* systems is highly stable but switching prerogatives apparently exist *between* systems. This, of course, does not mean that systems are independent. On the contrary, it is evident that they contain important nuances that can probably be best appreciated by switching loci in highly integrated systems. The studies by Menyuk (1964a,b) on dampened oscillatory functions in error reduction provide evidence consistent with this interpretation, although not specific to it (see Fig. 6-4).

Second, operantly determined switching of loci reflects contextual learning. As a child learns what he can learn about a locus in a particular context, he has the option to switch within that context to other co-occurring systems. Depending on what he knows and wants to know from available information, he may or may not switch his loci of learning.

The principles of contextual learning, partial learning, operantly determined

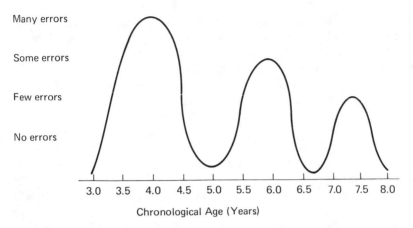

Many errors

Some errors

Few errors

No errors

3.0   3.5   4.0   4.5   5.0   5.5   6.0   6.5   7.0   7.5   8.0

Chronological Age (Years)

Figure 6-4 *Schematic of the dampened oscillatory function for "error" reduction. (Adapted from Menyuk 1963a, 1964a.)*

locus of learning, and operantly determined switching of locus of learning offer an interesting but speculative explanation for the "dampened oscillatory function" in "error" reduction reported by Menyuk (1964a,b). Figure 6-4 shows a schematic of the dampened oscillatory function for "error" reduction. Overt language learning seems to occur in spurts of variable duration (Brown, Cazden, and Bellugi-Klima 1969). The specific intervals on the age scale are not important (Brown 1973b). The essential features are (a) a fluctuation in occurrence of "errors," (b) a replacement of "error" types (not shown in the figure but presented in the original sources), and (c) a decreasing magnitude of successive fluctuations. The replacement of "error" types (distortion and redundancies replace omissions; redundancies replace distortions; adult forms replace redundancies) is evidence of partial learning. A child proceeds through stages of successive approximations to adult structures.

Instances of increased "errors" are apparently occasioned by a venture into new grammatical domains, whereas instances of decreased "errors" result from performance within previous partially acquired domains. When a child switches to a new domain, "errors" increase. When he practices or explores a limited but somewhat mastered domain, "errors" decrease. Reductions in amplitude of successive oscillations presumably reflect newly acquired grammatical knowledge. The evidence of a dampened oscillatory function is based upon the composite performance of many children, but the above interpretation concerned individual prerogatives. Research is needed to substantiate it. Brown's (1973b) discussion of oscillatory omissions of major constituents may reflect a switching in loci of learning, yet may also reflect memory constraints as described by Bloom (1970, 1973) in reductionism.

Obviously, these principles of language learning have considerable implications for what is done in the applied fields. If one wishes to emulate first language learning, the principles of *variation* and *active participation* should be promoted and those of *simplification* and *high structure* should be discouraged. Issues of content, sequence, pacing, and reinforcement are essentially within the province of the child rather than his parents, teachers, or clinician.

The Language Acquisition System (LAS)

Ervin-Tripp (1973) outlined what she called the Language Acquisition System (LAS). LAS is important because it is an attempt to integrate specific cognitive processes such as short-term memory, long-term memory, representation, and mediation-heuristics—in the acquisition of linguistic capacities. Thus, language learning is not simply a matter of learning words and making sentences. The learning process is much more substantial.

The five major features of LAS are hierarchical in nature. Moreover, each feature is not age specific.

1. *Speech perception.* An individual selectively retains features of a speech event (particularly order) in short-term memory.
2. *Assimilation/accommodation.* An individual selectively attends and reorganizes phonological and semantic data for retention in long-term memory.
3. *Interpretation.* An individual interprets the verbal information in terms of semantic properties.
4. *Mediation-heuristics.* The information is chunked into usable units. Thus it may not be necessary to process all phonemic units completely.
5. *Formal feature generation.* An individual identifies the appropriate linguistic mechanisms of a message.

Ervin-Tripp indicated that input conditions change considerably during development. External semantic reference decreases with age while linguistic complexity increases with it. Awareness and availability of various memory capacities also increase with age.

Young children selectively retain features, particularly the order of acoustic input, in short-term memory. The rapid fading of an acoustic signal probably requires short-term storage, allowing a listener to compare what he decodes with what he discerns from ongoing events. Short-term memory is limited in capacity as well as duration, requiring the individual to be selective. Ervin-Tripp suggested that the following have the highest probabilities for retention in short-term memory and thus conversion into long-term memory:

1. *Most recent material.* This is a recency effect.
2. *Initial words.* This is a primacy effect.
3. *Vowel quality of stressed syllables.* This is a seemingly novel aspect in an otherwise continuous acoustic event.
4. *Intonational contour.* This is a dimension superimposed on an acoustic pattern.

5. *Friction and nasality.*
6. *Order.*

Long-term memory depends on short-term storage. Ervin-Tripp outlined the following long-term correlates in language acquisition:

1. Prosodic contrasts and terminal juncture contrasts should be acquired early.
2. Particles, enclitics, and items that are sentence-final should be learned early, before prefixes and other material earlier in sentences.
3. Suffixes should be learned more easily than prepositions.
4. Fixed-position sentence-initial forms should be learned more easily than material in the middle of utterances.
5. Syllabic morphemes should be learned more easily than consonantal morphemes.
6. Friction and nasal morphemes should be understood sooner than stop or glide forms.
7. Relative order of stem and affix should not be altered.
8. Relative order of high-frequency morpheme sequences should not be altered.
9. Where there is a dominant order for classes having structural meaning, when construction is acquired, it will reflect input order.
10. Unstressed syllables may be lost in the storage of words.

Obviously, these principles have considerable implications for clinical assessment and intervention. The notions of digit memory span, mean length of utterance, and synthetic sentence building conflict with modern language learning principles.

Ervin-Tripp (1973, p. 261) also held that contextual learning is essential. Speaking of referential context, she said, "the learner must know the referent for learning to occur." She felt that sentences without referents may be of no value in language learning. Yet it is not uncommon in the applied fields for sentences to be learned outside of referential contexts—indeed outside of communicative contexts. She also contended that reference is much more complex than observable objects, since it entails perceived relationships. She held that diversity is essential for concept and word learning. Parents spontaneously simplify and repeat available codes, thereby maximizing opportunities to deduce coding devices for available references. Broen (1972) reports that parents simplify the communicative process by talking slowly, reduce the length and complexity of utterances, use familiar vocabulary and fluent production, talk about the "here and now," and accept most child variations. Moerk (1974) reported that parents alter their verbal behavior as a function of the verbal skills of their children. The "simplicity" strategy in the applied fields is both contradictory and different from that in normal spontaneous simplification. In the applied fields, simplicity is a matter of reducing available referents so a child will not be distracted from what someone thinks he should be learning. Yet learning things out of context is how essential meanings are distorted.

Slobin's Principles of Language Learning

Slobin (1970) outlined some very provocative principles of language learning. *Operating Principle 1* states that "New forms first express old functions, and new functions are first expressed by old forms" (1970, p. 2). He indicated that this principle is supported by Piagetian psychologists such as Furth (1969), Sinclair-deZwart (1969, 1973a,b), Flavell (1963), Elkind and Flavell (1969), and Inhelder (1969). As Slobin (1970, p. 2) concluded, "It seems as if the first functions of two-word utterances may be only to make more explicit the functions already expressed by one-word utterances." Bloom's (1970) famous account of "Mommy sock" illustrates the point that one utterance can have several functions. In this case, it could be conjunction, attribution, genitive, or subject-object. Bloom (1970) and McNeill and McNeill (1968) showed that a single form for negation could have different functions: nonexistence, rejection, and denial. H. Clark (1973a) showed that old forms for spatial terms can come to be used to express temporal functions. This foretells the ultimate verbal capacity—the ability to realize several referents with one word and several words for one referent.

Operating Principle 2 is that cognitive growth is the pacesetter for linguistic development. Slobin indicated that the rate and order of development of semantic notions are fairly constant across languages. Semantic notions are learned very early and quickly. Some people think that they comprise universals in language acquisition. Slobin derived the following from this principle:

1. Expressive utterances (performatives, demands) precede referential utterances.
2. Expressions of location and direction are acquired earlier than expressions of time.
3. The order of development of the functions of negative utterances is (1) nonexistence (expected referent not present); (2) rejection (referent present but not desired); (3) denial (negation of actual or supposed assertion).
4. In early stages of development, the order of mention of events in an utterance matches the chronological order of their occurrence.
5. In sentence conjunction, coordinating conjunctions are acquired (used correctly) before subordinating and implicating conjunctions.
6. Utterances requiring time perspectives other than the present are late to develop.
7. Hypotheticals, counterfactuals, and conditionals are late to develop.
8. The course of development goes from gross classes to increasingly subdivided classes, and from general to finely delimited contextual constraints on the occurrence of members of classes; i.e., more and more features are added to lexical items and more and more rules are added for handling the co-occurrence restrictions on features. Thus, forms are not completely developed when first used. Various constraints must be learned to realize their appropriate use.

Additional operating principles outlined by Slobin are the following:

OPERATING PRINCIPLE 3: Intonation and intensity of vocalization have expressive significance.

OPERATING PRINCIPLE 4: The flow of speech can be segmented.

OPERATING PRINCIPLE 5: Speech has nonexpressive significance (words make reference).

OPERATING PRINCIPLE 6: Words can be used in combination.

OPERATING PRINCIPLE 7: The meaning of an utterance is more than a combination of the meanings of its elements.

OPERATING PRINCIPLE 8: The order of elements in an utterance is significant.

OPERATING PRINCIPLE 9: Rules applicable to larger classes are developed before rules relating to their subdivisions.

OPERATING PRINCIPLE 10: Rules relating to semantically defined classes take precedence over rules relating to formally defined classes.

OPERATING PRINCIPLE 11: There is a preference for clear acoustic marking of functors.

OPERATING PRINCIPLE 12: There is a tendency to preserve the internal structure of linguistic units.

OPERATING PRINCIPLE 13: Processing space is limited and gradually increases with age.

OPERATING PRINCIPLE 14: Storage capacity increases with age.

OPERATING PRINCIPLE 15: The longer something has been stored and used, the more accessible it is for use in speech production.

These principles were modified and elaborated in Slobin (1973). They have many implications for assessment and intervention. Many of them will be pointed out throughout the balance of the book.

Emergence of Specificity

The principle of specificity is pervasive in language acquisition. It appears in concept development, word learning, acquisition of syntax and morphology, phonological development, and the development of communicative functions, as well as intrapersonal functions. The principle of specificity is that a young child begins with the general and proceeds to the specific. Additionally, a young child occasionally needs to reorganize what he knows. Technically, the process of emerging specificity entails both differentiation and reorganization. An underlying hierarchy is the best evidence of the emergence of specificity.

In concept development, Gagne (1965) and White (1965) demonstrate that learning is fundamentally hierarchical in nature. The various Piagetian stages demonstrate increased differentiation in the movement toward increased mental representation (Uzgiris and Hunt 1975). In remembering that the earlier sensorimotor Piagetian stages are based on action patterns, it should be pointed out that motor development itself proceeds from gross to fine. Word learning is hierarchical in nature. The studies by E. Clark 1973a,b 1974, 1975; H. Clark 1970, 1973a,b; Bartlett 1976; Friedman 1976; Maratsos 1973a; Townsend 1976; Donaldson and McGarrigle 1974, and others show that there is a hierarchical relationship between underlying concepts and word learning. This relationship is dealt with by H. Clark's (1973a) correlation and complexity hypotheses.

The *correlation hypothesis* states that there will always be a close correlation between one's P-space (perceptual space) and L-space (language space). This means that a person can label only what he is developmentally, physiologically, cognitively, and emotionally capable of perceiving. Thus, there is a hierarchical relationship between P-space and L-space. Moreover, within P-space certain aspects emerge before others (H. Clark 1973a; Inhelder and Piaget 1964).

The *complexity hypothesis* is "that the order of acquisition of English spatial terms is constrained by their rules of application" (H. Clark 1973a, p. 29). Spatial terms will be acquired after the underlying notion entailed by the term has been perceptually acquired. The complexity hypothesis is closely related to E. Clark's (1973a) *semantic features hypothesis*. This states that word knowledge occurs through successive accumulation of semantic features one at a time. Specifically, it was posited that an individual first becomes aware of a dimension and learns a label for it. Subsequently, he learns contrastive aspects of it, then words to not only label it, but also segment or mark contrastiveness. Both the complexity hypothesis and the semantic features hypothesis deal with the perceptual knowledge underlying word learning. Both could be considered antecedents to Brown and Hanlon's (1970) *cumulative complexity hypothesis,* which says that everything conceptually entailed in an utterance determines the utterance itself. In addition to conceptual limitations, the labeling function of an utterance is also determined by processing capacities (Slobin 1970; Ervin-Tripp 1973), available referents (Brown, 1958a; Olson, 1970, 1971), intent (Bowerman 1973, 1976; Schlesinger 1971, 1974), and functions entailed in the speech act (Halliday 1975; Bruner 1975a,b; Dore 1975; Searle 1969). Clearly, what a young child says by word or sentence is not what an adult is likely to mean, since meanings have yet to be fully realized. Early meaning is fused to an event by local rules (Donaldson and McGarrigle 1974). Thus, it is inappropriate to accept a young child's utterances as evidence of adult language. The products of one's underlying systems may be deceptive concerning a child's understanding and use of language. It is imperative to keep notes not only of available reference and intent but also of alternative uses of a label or a word.

Bruner (1964, 1966) held that nothing is more evident in language than hierarchical structure. He was referring to hierarchical structure in the cognitive systems that underly language, in word learning, and of course, in syntax and morphology. While hierarchical structure may be but slightly evident in intonations, pauses, and inflections, it is dominant in underlying structure (Yngve 1960; Johnson 1965, 1966; Fodor and Bever 1965; Bever, Lackner and Kirk 1969). Presumably, the perceptual processes of comprehension are organized in a hierarchical fashion so that one can perceive in terms of available categories rather than simply making discriminations. We perceive speech in terms of what we know about speech (Garner 1966).

In development, a child first labels objects, actions, relationships, or events by single words. These are quasi holophrases—one-word utterances that have many functions. Such words are tied to a restricted set of action-based relations for each concept (Nelson 1974). Two-word utterances are simply more explicit versions of one-word utterances. Then, function words such as articles and demonstratives begin to mark aspects of noun and verb phrases. Inflections also begin to appear. The order of elements resembles sentences. Soon a child will do simple combinations and permutations in syntax. Later he will engage in elaborate embedding. Through this sequence, a child acquires increased explicitness in labeling objects, actions, relationships, and events. Through explicitness he obtains increased communicative capacity and instrumental power with language.

In the acquisition of morphological rules, a developmental hierarchy appears. A child first acquires words as undifferentiated labels or complexes (Vygotsky 1962; Bowerman in press, a,b). Subsequently, he discovers that words can be segmented into components. For example, the word *books* can be segmented into *book* $+/s/$. Further, he learns that there are classes of words. Words with certain properties go into one class, those with other properties go into another class, those with still other properties go into still another class. When a property extends across two or more classes, it defines a superordinate category for those classes. As he learns to segment and classify words, he discovers that morphological rules are used for many words of a general class. He may discover that $/s/$ or $/z/$ pluralizes the general class of nouns. But later he will have to reorganize this knowledge because he discovers that the rule works only for a subclass of nouns—regular nouns. Thus, in learning morphological rules, children pass through a three-stage developmental sequence: *vocabulary words* (with or without undifferentiated adult inflections), *overgeneralization of rules,* and *appropriate generalization of rules.* Bever (1970) reported a similar overgeneralization of perceptual strategies.

This three-stage developmental sequence accounts for a common misunderstanding of parents and teachers: it is not uncommon for them to refer a child to a clinic because he is "losing his language" or "regressing to an earlier stage." Many of the children had impressed their parents and teachers by saying advanced words such as "went," "ran," "mine," and "him." But as they grasped the segmentation of words and inflectional rules for word classes, they began to overgeneralize, producing forms distressing for their parents and teachers, such as "wented," "ranned," "mines," and "hims." Actually, these are a *good* sign, because they indicate the child has moved from the vocabulary stage to the over-generalization stage for inflectional rules (Palermo and Eberhart 1968; Cazden 1968).

The auxiliary system reveals developmental sequences. The ones for the present progressive and past participle are similar. The present progressive has a three-stage sequence: V*ing*, *be* + V*ing*, and *be* + tense + V*ing*. An example of V*ing* is "Me *eating.*" The *be* + V*ing* is "Me *be eating.*" And *be* + tense + V*ing* is "Me *am eating.*" As for the past participle, the three-stage sequence is V part, *be* + V part, and *be* + tense + V part. Respective examples are "Me *eaten,*" "Me *have eaten,*" and "Me *had eaten.*" Before a child begins to learn the present progressive and past participle, he modifies unmarked verbs in three ways (Cromer 1976): he begins to use a past tense marker for immediate past events, then produces a semiauxiliary form that glosses auxiliary mechanisms (i.e., "gonna," "wanna," and "hafta"), and finally produces V*ing* constructions as the initial attempt to learn the present progressive. Thus, he begins to modulate the meaning of verbs by auxiliary devices. These provide a means of coding intended meanings on verbs: immediate past, intention or prediction, and present temporary duration. A fourth meaning—imperative—is not handled by the auxiliary. However, a child begins to use "please" at this time, which is an imperative.

Emergence of specificity is evident in phonological development. The early phonetic patterns are those which entail gross sensorimotor movements—the bilabials /p/, /b/, /m/. A developmental sequence follows that ends with phonetic patterns which entail fine sensorimotor movements—/l/ and /r/. McDonald (1964) described the emergence of specificity for phonology in terms of greater specificity in sensorimotor skills.

Emergence of specificity is also evident in the development of communicative and intrapersonal functions. Communicatively, a young child's early verbal behavior is egocentrically oriented. He verbalizes because it is intrinsically motivating. As he learns to code things and events, egocentricity is manifest in a "talk-to" way. It is not until eight or ten years of age (Flavell et al. 1968) that he attends to listener clues in an adult nonegocentric way in order to tell if his message is the most appropriate (Muma 1975a). Surely, early vestiges of listener orientation appear in early childhood (Shatz and Gelman 1973a; Schachter et al. 1974; Clark-Stewart 1973).

As for intrapersonal functions, language becomes internalized (Vygotsky 1962), develops into a mediating agent (Bruner 1964), and serves a representational function. Piaget (1954, 1962, 1963); Flavell (1970); Flavell, Beach, and Chinsky (1966); Flavell et al. (1968); Vygotsky (1962); and Mead (1934) considered egocentric or private speech as a behavior intimately related to thought and language. Kohlberg, Yaeger, and Hjertholm (1968) reviewed these theories and provided additional evidence that "private speech is common among young (4–6-year-old) children, declines thereafter in regular fashion, and is practically absent in older children capable of internalized logical thought" (Kohlberg et al. 1968, p. 731).

Piaget (1954, 1961, 1963) held that thought developed before language and private speech was egocentric speech. Egocentric speech is produced for oneself, without regard to a listener. Piaget argued that as a child develops a communicative intent, his speech is directed toward others. Thus, "egocentric" speech wanes as a child learns to communicate with others. Egocentric speech disappears as social speech appears. Figure 6-5 summarizes these theories.

Vygotsky, on the other hand, regards private speech quite differently. He thinks of it as overt thinking that subsequently becomes internalized as thought. From a social perspective, Vygotsky regards private speech as somewhat over-socialized, in the sense that it displays one's thoughts. These displays are not true social speech because they are apparently not issued with communicative intent. Such utterances also seem to regulate and direct behavior. Kohlberg, Yaeger, and Hjertholm (1968) reported a developmental hierarchy consistent with Vygotsky's and Mead's (1934) views:

Category 1: Word play and repetition
Category 2: Remarks to nonhuman objects
Category 3: Describing own activity
Category 4: Questions answered by the self
Category 5: Self-guiding comments
Category 6: Inaudible mutterings
Category 7: Silent inner speech

For Vygotsky, then, private speech becomes thought or inner speech.

Vygotsky's account of private speech has an additional interesting dimension: it seems to follow a curvilinear function proportional to cognitive difficulty. In young children it usually does not occur when a task is familiar and trivial, but does when the task is difficult. Kohlberg, Yaeger, and Hjertholm (1968) also provide evidence to this effect. Luria (1961) contended that the intrapersonal speech of a young child organizes or regulates his activities. Wozniak (1974) did an extensive review of the literature regarding verbal regulation of motor behavior.

Moreover, it is not uncommon in older children and adults to "lip read" during silent reading of difficult or exciting material. In cerebral palsied children, as well as normals, one frequently sees "cerebral overflow" in the tongue and jaw (movement of the tongue, usually a slow chewing movement) during difficult or studied tasks. Locke's (1970) review of the literature concerning subvocal speech deals with pertinent mechanisms.

Markedness

Markedness is a theoretical way of accounting for the emergence of specificity in language learning. The semantic feature hypothesis (E. Clark 1973b) utilizes the markedness theory. Briefly, it states that an individual becomes aware of a domain and may employ a general label for it, but then becomes aware of its contrastive

Figure 6-5 *Theories of private speech.*

	Piaget	Vygotsky	Mead	Flavell
Age-development course	Straight age decline and replacement by social speech	Curvilinear increase and decline—goes underground as thought	Curvilinear	Cognitive self-guidance curvilinear, expressive uncertain
Relation to cognitive maturity	Negative	Curvilinear	Curvilinear	Unspecified
Functions and functional types of private speech	Functions uncertain	Cognitive self-guidance	Functional hierarchy from self-description to dialogue to self-directing speech	Multiple functions, self-guiding, social substitutive, affect expression
Social orientation of private speech	Egocentric lack of differentiation of self as speaker and other as listener	Parasocial lack of differentiation of self as listener and other as listener	Parasocial dialogue of self as speaker and self as listener	Partly substitution for absent other
Social situations arousing private speech	Situations where self and other undifferentiated with adults	Situations where other can listen like the self-comprehending peers	Situations requiring taking role of an absent other	Alone or socially deprived
Task situations arousing private speech	Unspecified	Task situations with obstacles	Unspecified	Tasks requiring verbal mediation

From Kohlberg, Yaeger, and Hjertholm (1968), in *Child Development*, 39, pp. 691–736. © The Society for Research in Child Development.

aspects and the labels for denoting that contrastiveness. General awareness and undifferentiated labels constitute unmarked awareness and terms, whereas contrastive awareness and differentiated terms constitute marked awareness and terms.

Markedness seems to explain why children treat adult antonyms as synonyms. A child may be aware of a dimension and use either of two polar labels, although usually the positive one. For example, he may say "more" for "less," "big" for "small," "long" for "short." Subsequently, as he becomes aware of contrastiveness, the polar terms will be used selectively. "More" is unmarked because it denotes a dimension, whereas "less" is marked because it denotes not only a dimension but also contrastiveness.

Edwards (1974) has shown that "substitution" patterns in phonology reflect a markedness principle. Substitutions, at least for initial fricatives and glides, are unmarked. Thus, phonetic substitutions reflect the deletion or absence of a marked member or feature. For example, a child will say [tʰɔp] for *stop*, [laid] for *slide*, [ɡɔk] for *clock*, etc. Occasionally a child will delete the unmarked member (Ingram 1976), producing [sɔp] for *stop*, and [liʏ] for *three*.

Markedness occurs within words and phonemes. English has special mechanisms for explicitly indicating it. These include the morphological system, the determiner system (articles, demonstratives, number, etc.), and the functors, especially prepositions. Morphologically, possessiveness, plural, and gender are marked. Thus, *his, books*, and *he/she* are more advanced than *a, book,* or *it,* respectively.

Old Information/New Information

Children attend to and name things that change. This has led to the old information/new information theory of language learning. Hinds (1975) defined *old information* as that which is predictable from context and *new information* as that which is not. In addition to "predictable," I would prefer to include "presumed," to denote one's intent and socio-emotional-perceptual processing of information. Old information is *thematic material* and new information is *rhematic material*. This is the basis for the theme and rheme theory of language development (Firbas 1964; Hinds 1975). The topic and comment theory (Gruber 1967; Wieman 1976) shows that stress patterns in early child language reflect neither normative word orders nor adult sentence patterns (as was traditionally believed), but a hierarchy of semantic functions about new information. The hierarchy is from most to least likely: locatives, possessives, objectives, attributives, verbals, and agentives. However, some stress patterns deviate from this hierarchy. The best description of differential stress is new information in the context of old. As Bruner (1975a) indicated, a speech act regulates joint attention and joint action. This regulation is needed for new events and thus new information. Early utterances are not labels but comments about new information in the context of old information (Cromer 1976).

Labels: Experience, Perception, Events, Intents

Labeling behavior in any form—differentiated infant cries, complexive or idiosyncratic words, intonation patterns, adult words, phrases, or sentences—is a very complex mixing of an individual's past experience, perceptions, ongoing events, communicative intents, available reference, and linguistic capacities. A child attempts to match the cognitive organization derived from his experience to the organization of his language (Wells 1974). In the course of doing this he utilizes available reference, perceptions, new information, and communicative intent. Thus, labels are not just *any* labels, but are presumed to be the most appropriate for a given set of circumstances. New words are not the most frequent, less complex, nor directly modeled. They are efforts to code intended meanings (Cromer 1976).

This is important for clinicians, since it means that labels should not be learned out of communicative context. Further, it means that the particular labels learned must be those an individual needs to learn in a given circumstance. Language learning varies in significant ways from most of the programs advocated in the clinical arena. Clinicians should be wary of simple, easy, "packaged" assessment and intervention programs. They may not be relevant to the actual needs and opportunities of an individual.

I observed a situation in which a four-year-old child spontaneously learned *smother* from his mother. It illustrates the importance of context, new information, action, and perception in language learning. The boy was watching a smoldering cigarette butt in an ashtray. He was about to put his finger on it when his mother saw him. She said, "No, don't touch it. It's hot. It will burn you." Then she placed a paper sack full of old clothes on top of the ashtray. The boy was bewildered. He obviously had not seen that before—paper over something burning. "Mommy, what's that for?" "It will smother the fire, honey. It will make the cigarette go out." His mother left him watching the smoke die down as the cigarette went out. He muttered to himself twice: "Smother. Smother."

Acquisition of Semantic Systems

Semantic systems deal with meaning. Meaning pertains to what one knows in a given circumstance—knowledge pertaining to available codes, referents, and intents. Obviously, the acquisition of semantic systems is inextricably tied to what one knows in general—cognitive systems. Scholars differ as to what they mean by *semantic knowledge*. Bowerman (1976, pp. 108–9) has summarized the major positions:

> Bloom (1973, p. 2), for example, distinguishes sharply between *semantic* knowledge, which she defines as involving the meaning of particular words and of meaning relations between words, and *conceptual* knowledge, or underlying cognitive structures that the child uses to represent to himself the relations among persons, objects, and events in the

world. Like Bloom, Dore (1975) argues against assigning linguistic significance to such nonlinguistic aspects of context as crying, gestures, etc. He recommends maintaining a clear distinction between "knowledge of language and knowledge of the world" to "prevent basing claims about the former on data about the latter" (p. 34). Similar arguments have been made by Bowerman (1974b) about the need to make a clear distinction between the general conceptual knowledge that is reflected in a child's behavior at the time of speech and knowledge of the internal structure (i.e., semantic components) of words.

The matter of distinguishing semantic knowledge from cognitive knowledge is clearly a complex one and cannot be analyzed in detail here. However, the position I would advocate, in line with the sort of arguments made by Bloom (1970, 1973), Dore (1975), Schlesinger (1974) and Bowerman (1974b), is that the term "semantic" be reserved for cognitive knowledge that has demonstrably become linked to aspects of *language* for the child—i.e., that has begun to "make a difference, linguistically," to borrow Schlesinger's useful phrase (1974, p. 144). In other words, a concept that the child grasps at the nonlinguistic level achieves semantic significance only if (1) it has an effect on the way he selects a word to refer to a situation, or chooses an inflection and determines the class of words to which the inflection can be applied, or selects a word order or intonation pattern, or decides whether or not a particular operation can be performed (such as using a noncausative verb in a causative sense, see Bowerman, 1974b), and so on, or, conversely, if (2) it governs the way in which he *understands* a word, inflection, word order, intonation pattern, etc.

Thus, semantics deals with linguistic mechanisms and cognition. Chapter 3 dealt with general cognitive systems—Piagetian stages, perceptual space, development of attending patterns, Bruner stages, cognitive distancing, memory, etc. This section focuses on word learning and concept development. A paragraph in Chap. 4 on linguistic systems contained several quotes indicating that language is predicated on cognitive systems. As Nelson (1973, p. 21) put it, "Categorization of sound patterns and of objects and events in the real world is basic to learning a language." Lenneberg (1967, pp. 332–33) held that cognition, and specifically concept formation, is central to an understanding of meaning: "The abstractness underlying meanings in general . . . may best be understood by considering concept-formation the primary cognitive process, and naming (as well as acquiring a name) the secondary cognitive process." According to Brown (1956, p. 247), first language learning is "a process of cognitive socialization," involving "the coordination of speech categories with categories of the nonlinguistic world." By stating cognitive socialization, Brown recognized the significance of social systems in cognition. This is an issue that has become increasingly important in language learning (Schlesinger 1971; Bowerman 1976; Bates 1976a,b; Dore 1974, 1975; Wells 1974; Bruner 1975a,b).

Categorizations of experience and language are basic cognitive capacities. Bowerman (1976, pp. 105–6) referred to Bruner and Tyler regarding categorization:

According to Bruner, Goodnow and Austin, for example, "virtually all cognitive activity involves and is dependent on the process of categorizing (1956, p. 246). The grouping of discriminably different stimuli into categories on the basis of shared features is an adaptive way of dealing with what would otherwise be an overwhelming array of unique experiences. As Tyler puts it, ". . . life in a world where nothing was the same would be intolerable. It is through . . . classification that the whole rich world of infinite variability shrinks to manipulable size" (1969, p. 7).

It must be emphasized that concept development in natural language learning is quite different from the usual laboratory learning experiments. There, concept learning is studied in terms of a child's ability to identify instances of a concept. Such data actually provide little, if any, evidence on the selection and formation of natural concepts. Nelson (1974, pp. 271–72) decried the superficiality of concept learning in artificial conditions:

> The concept domain is well defined, it is limited, and its components (e.g., colors and forms) are well specified and learned prior to the experimental session. Further, the child is informed that his task is to identify that component or combination of components that the experimenter has selected. He makes a guess and receives feedback from the experimenter, usually on every trial, as to whether or not he is correct. These conditions are not comparable in any particular way to those met in the child's natural word-learning situation, where the referent concept domain is undefined, the number of possible concepts is unlimited, the components are unspecified, and the feedback is unreliable. Paradoxically, while laboratory studies carried out under such apparently more favorable conditions have shown the young child to be a relatively deficient concept former, the child under the apparently more difficult conditions of natural language learning is found to be a highly competent concept former.

A related issue is that most of what is done in both the laboratory and intervention is based on manipulation and training of static attributes, i.e., color, size, shape, number. But natural concept learning derives from complex dynamic events (Nelson 1974). As Piaget (1962, 1970) contends, schema or concept development rises from action patterns rather than static attributes. According to Nelson (1974, p. 281), "Children in the early stages of talking do often comment on changes in the state of objects (e.g., 'open,' 'hurt,' 'broken,' 'all gone') but not on their invariant attributes." It is easy to devise an assessment and intervention program on static attributes, but the program may be superficially relevant to a child's needs.

As Bowerman (1976, pp. 126–27) points out:

> Studies of children's first words have revealed that children tend to ignore names for items that are "just there" and do not do anything, like furniture, trees, and rooms, in favor of names for objects that act or which they can act on, like pets and other animals, cars, shoes, foods, and toys (Nelson, 1973b, 1974; Anglin, 1975). For example, Huttenlocher (1974) discusses a boy who, despite his emerging ability to understand other words, apparently did not learn the referents of "kitchen" and "refrigerator" even after extensive and persistent maternal modeling and demonstration. It seems, then, that children's attention is drawn to objects with potentials for acting or being acted on, and they will tend to learn names for such objects earlier than names for more static objects. However, classifying such objects as equivalent for purposes of word use appears to depend more upon their perceptual qualities than upon their functions.

Spontaneous attention to dynamic attributes is consistent with Piaget's contention of an action pattern basis for early concepts, and provides indirect evidence of the potency of discrepancy learning: dynamic changes beget discrepancies. In referring to studies by Macnamara (1972) and Wells (1974), Bowerman (1976, p. 128) states, "Early labels for *properties* of objects primarily designate changeable and transitory states like 'hot,' 'wet,' and 'dirty' rather than permanent qualities like 'round' or 'red.' "

Object and picture sorting tasks have been used to demonstrate categorization. Clustering tasks and over- and underextensions also index categorizations. Olver and Hornsby (1966, pp. 74–76) identified several general types of groupings that occur in a sorting task: superordinate, complexive, and thematic.

There are two types of superordinate groupings: general and itemized. A *general superordinate* grouping is the use of a common characteristic for all items, e.g., "They're all blue." An *itemized superordinate* grouping is the use of a common characteristic for all items, with each item specifically identified as containing the attribute, e.g., "The ball is blue," "The block is blue," "The shirt is blue," etc.

Five types of *complexives* occur: collections, edge matching, key rings, associations, and multiple groupings. *Collections* are groupings based on complementary or related properties somewhat incidental to the items: "The dog is black," "The deer is brown," "The apple is red," "The banana is yellow." *Edge matching* is grouping adjacent pairs by association. There is no consistency of attributes between successive pairs: "Corn and bananas are yellow, bananas and leaves come from trees, leaves and a baseball mitt have bumps like fingers." *Key rings* occur when one item is regarded as having a feature common to the others: "The picture is painted. The bicycle, wagon, and house are painted." *Associations* occur when two items are linked by an attribute and this attribute is used to link the other items: "The bell and key are steel, the truck is steel, and the roller skates are steel." *Multiple groupings* occur when some of the items are grouped one way and some another. These types of complexives correspond to those reported by Vygotsky (1962).

Thematic groupings occur when the items fit into a story or theme: "The shovel digs the garden. The seeds grow the plants. The plants make potatoes and apples."

Olver and Hornsby (1966, pp. 71–72) also reported that children who were asked to report equivalences for items revealed the following:

Perceptible-intrinsic (adjective or noun): "They are both big." "They have hair."
Perceptible-extrinsic (preposition—time or space): "They are on top."
Functional-intrinsic (use or function—verb): "They come apart."
Functional-extrinsic (use or function—verb): "You can eat them."
Affective (value or internal state): "I like them."
Nominal (label): "It is a hammer."
Fiat equivalence (like or not, without giving the reasons): "They are the same because."

Olver and Hornsby reported that at six years of age perceptible responses were promient, i.e., colors, sizes, shapes, and place. "From age six on there is a steady increase in functionally based equivalence" (Olver and Hornsby 1966, p. 72). "The nine-year-old, for all his functionalism, forms groupings that are neither particularly appropriate nor realistic for adaptive action. . . . Their functional groups are often arbitrary and . . . they ignore the conventional or sensible uses to which objects are put" (Olver and Hornsby 1966, p. 73). Vygotsky (1962) reported a similar developmental progression. A young child sorts in "heaps" or "piles" but subsequently learns adult categories. Nonadult categories, or those unique to children, are called *idiosyncratic* categories. They are the products of their limited experience.

Natural concept development has been portrayed in terms of increased validity, status, and accessibility in Chap. 4. Increased validity pertains to the process whereby one's concepts conform more and more closely to those of others (adults) in his community. Increased status refers to the semantic complexity issue (E. Clark 1973a,b, 1974), and means that concepts obtain increased definition as new attributes are acquired. Accessibility means that concepts become available for use. Flavell (1970) and Mussen, Conger, and Kagan (1969, pp. 429–30) discuss increased validity, status, and accessibility in concept development.

Presumably, concepts have internal hierarchical structures that are related to each other. Heider (1971) and Rosch (1973a,b) employed the strategy of focal or central and peripheral exemplars to substantiate this point. This is clinically useful because it provides a way to get an idea whether an individual knows the core attributes of a given concept (focal exemplars) and whether his knowledge of a concept is sufficiently broad to extend to peripheral examplars as well. Burger and Muma (1977) showed that some aphasics had difficulty with peripheral items but not focal items. The trend was not strong enough to be significant, however. Fluent and nonfluent aphasics were significantly different on cognitive distancing. Fluent aphasics had significantly more difficulty than normals and nonfluent aphasics in sorting pictures rather than objects.

Gibson (1969) proposed a distinctive feature theory of concept development that is similar in principle but different in theoretical detail to that of Maccoby and Bee (1965). These views have been criticized by Johannsen (1967). Referring to Gibson's distinctive feature theory of concept development, Mussen, Conger, and Kagan (1969, p. 289) said, "The increasing differentiation of the child's world— objects, sounds, pictures—is at least in part, a result of learning to respond to the distinctive features of objects, of phonemes . . . and so on."

Gibson substantiated her distinctive feature theory by showing that the acquisition of visual perception for forms follows the sequence: (a) breaks and closes (O versus C), (b) transformation from line to curve (U versus V), (c) rotations (M versus W), (d) reversals (d versus b), and (e) transformations in perspective (spanting or tilting). Children had progressively fewer errors on this continuum for the age range of four to eight years (Gibson 1963, 1969, 1970). It should be pointed out that

Gibson reported substantial individual differences in movement along this continuum. Moreover, the attachment of labels to features served to heighten their distinctiveness, resulting in increased attentiveness and acquisition of concepts. In short, differentiation of stimuli and attachment of labels facilitate conceptual development (Mussen, Conger, and Kagan 1969, pp. 287–95). Saltz, Soller, and Sigel (1972) and Saltz (1971) argued against Gibson's distinctive feature theory. They reasoned that concepts must derive from previous concepts through differentiation and reorganization.

Words or labels seem to facilitate concept development. Brown (1956, p. 278) held that a word acts as a "lure to cognition." Cazden (1972a, p. 229) indicated that a word draws attention to another instance of a concept: "If one has no name for a phenomenon, one may not notice it." As Gagne and Smith purport, "It would appear that requiring verbalization somehow 'forced the Ss to think' " (Gagne and Smith 1962, p. 378). Brown (1958b) elaborated on this process in what he called the *Original Word Game*. A child hears a name or label and hypothesizes about the categorical nature of what is being named. He tests his hypothesis by attempting to name new instances of what he thinks the label is about. His environment—parents, siblings, peers, etc.—confirm or reject his labeling effort. Further discussion of labeling as an activator of cognition appears in Chap. 3.

Vygotsky (1962) contended that the relationships between words and labels are bidirectional in acquisition. In *spontaneous learning,* one spontaneously induces the attributes of concepts; a label serves to consolidate spontaneous inductions. For example, a child may spontaneously be aware that dogs, cats, squirrels, and cows have certain mutual characteristics. The word "animal" may serve to consolidate his awareness. Spontaneous concepts are "saturated with experience from the very beginning" (Cazden 1972a, p. 230). In *scientific learning,* one is given a label, then goes about hypothesis testing to discover alternative meanings for it. "Spontaneous concepts and scientific concepts thus develop in different directions, the former 'upward' from concrete experience and the latter 'downward' from a verbal definition" (Cazden 1972a, p. 230).

It is necessary to realize that words do not have the absolute meanings indicated in a dictionary. They carry both connotative and denotative meaning (see Chap. 4). A word can have a variety of referents, which are similar in certain respects but different in others (Lenneberg 1967). In referring to Lyons (1968, p. 426), Bowerman (1976, p. 114) indicated that "the referential boundaries of words are not always fully determinate." That is, it is not clear to what extent a particular thing is indexed by a word, a phrase, or an utterance. As Olson (1970, p. 265) points out, "Simply being shown an object does not indicate the set of alternatives from which it is differentiated. You might note a few features of the object without knowing if you'd noticed the critical ones on which recognition is to be based." Bowerman (in press, b) cited the concerns of Fillmore, Anglin, and Posner concerning the problems of interpretation of meaning of early words. Perhaps it is better to define meanings of early words in terms of functions rather than presumed attributed features.

The problem of not knowing what is salient for a child in either concept or label learning is a serious one in assessment and intervention. Duchan (1976) held that cognitive bias may predispose certain behavior regardless of verbal labels. The applied fields place an emphasis on vocabulary level and word naming, with little if any regard for alternative labels for the same referents. The static rather than dynamic aspects of available referents are usually subjected to the labeling process. Unfortunately, what is typically done with vocabulary and naming can be regarded only as tangential to normal language learning.

E. Clark (1973b, 1974) held that usage by young children reflects a semantic complexity hypothesis. A child overextends a label because he has not yet learned the set of attributes typically used for the label by his community. Thus, he might say "horsie" in reference to a cow. The term is overextended because it goes beyond the adult conceptual class of "horseness." The same principle holds for underextensions (Nelson 1974). A young child may refuse to call a large short-haired dog by the label "Doggy": "No, that's no doggy. Fluffy is a doggy." The child's refusal occurs because he has not yet deduced mutual attributes between the large short-haired dog and "Fluffy." Thus, "Doggy" is underextended. It should extend across the entire class of dogs, but it is limited to a subclass. E. Clark indicated that overextensions (and presumably underextensions) occur for both ostensive terms and relational terms. *Ostensive terms* are labels for directly perceivable objects, actions, and relationships. *Relational terms* occur with substantive or contentive terms. They are primarily spatial adjectives ("in"), temporal adjectives ("then"), and dimensional adjectives ("big"). Overextensions (and presumably underextensions) occur from about one to two-and-one-half years of age. Bloom's (1973) use of the terms "overinclusion" and "underinclusion" is comparable. Reich (1976) indicated that early word labels are narrow in meaning and that overextensions appear later. Moreover, he indicated that five types of contrast occur between a child's initial label and when it becomes an adult word. They are mismatch, overlap, identity, underextension, and overextension.

The end of the period of over- and underextensions is marked by a large increase in questioning activity, rapid growth of vocabulary, and reduced reliance on a limited set of perceptual attributes for categorization (E. Clark 1974). Bloom (1973) indicated that over- and underinclusions are closely related to a child's awareness of object permanence or constancy. The developmental sequence for object permanence is that things exist, exist apart, recur, and recur without perceiving disappearance. Bloom contended that the developmental pattern for naming is overinclusion, word mortality from twelve to eighteen months of age, and a sudden increase in naming from eighteen to twenty-four months. Naming behavior begins first with substantive words that are dynamic in nature or deal with change, then static forms. Relational terms are learned after substantive ones, although there is overlap. As for word mortality, the meanings of early object names are unstable. As a child becomes aware of object permanence, some of the early words drop from use—word mortality.

Nelson (1974) described word learning in three stages. First, a small set of words is learned. These are selected from the larger set of parent words on the basis of dynamic properties and relations to referents. Second, a child will invent words if he does not encounter a label to fit his purposes. Concepts are generated to which a child will attach his own label if necessary. Third, words become generalized to new instances that are similar but different.

These three stages must be seen in the perspective that a young child is operating under considerable constraints—limited attention, memory, inference, knowledge, and strategies (Nelson 1974). Nelson held that the function of concepts is to produce fewer wholes from the complexity of available experience. She outlined three levels in the concept formation process: concepts, instances, and attributes. The process proceeds from whole to part. From a single instance, one can *synthesize a concept*. Over many and varied experiences he *perceives new instances* of the concept. Upon identifying these he deduces attributes to establish a *functional core* or *prototypic concept* with hierarchically arranged focal, peripheral, or optional attributes. A prototype is very powerful because it allows one to deal with innumerable exemplars, whereas a specific set of exemplars is too restricted to deal with discrepancies. *Concept generation* pertains to the first level. *Concept identification* pertains to the second and third levels. Attaching a name to something in experience is a matter of knowing the label for a prototype and recognizing instances of it. *Concepts* are cognitive organizations of information about objects and events encountered in the world (Nelson 1974). Notice that concepts are internal and psychological in nature. A child's concepts are essentially beyond a parent's, teacher's, or clinician's abilities to perceive and deduce. Indeed, only one of the three levels of concept formation outlined by Nelson (instances) can be perceptually witnessed by someone else. Even then, it is witnessed as a perceptual whole; there is no way other than inference to suppose what is salient to a child in concept learning.

Nelson (1974, p. 274) reported an unpublished paper by Bransford that distinguishes four classes of concepts as they explicitly relate to linguistic categories:

> (a) possible objects (nouns), (b) possible properties of objects (adjectives), (c) possible transformations that objects undergo (verbs), and (d) possible properties of transformations (adverbs). He proposed that the psychological meaning of a concept is a function of the types of relations into which it can enter with other concepts.

Nelson indicated that Bransford made some analogies among perception, thought, and language. Morehead and Morehead (1974) have attempted to show certain parallels between Piagetian psychology and Chomskian theories of language. Greenfield, Nelson, and Saltzman (1972) and Goodson and Greenfield (1975) have shown analogous cognitive and linguistic capacities. There is of course the question of how far one can press such parallels without distortion.

Most researchers of early child language agree that single-word utterances express basic semantic functions and relations (Bloom 1970, 1973; Brown 1973a,b; Schlesinger 1971; Edwards 1974; Chafe 1970; Halliday 1975; Greenfield and Smith 1976). These functions and relations, and those for two-, three-, and four-term utterances, are summarized below (Miller and Yoder 1974).

Substantive functions at the single-word level include

1. Comments or greetings (attaching a linguistic label to a perceived event)
2. Vocatives (call for someone)
3. Agent (person or thing responsible for action)
4. Object (recipient of action)
5. Action (type of action or state)
6. Possession (objects associated with or belonging to someone or something)

Relational functions of single-word utterances include

1. Recurrence (return of something missing)
2. Nonexistence (expect the occurrence of something)
3. Disappearance (comment that something or someone just disappeared)
4. Rejection (deny existence of something present)
5. Cessation (an event stopped)
6. Existence (objects, people, events noticed or discovered)

Thus, a considerable amount of learning occurs at the single-word level. The cognitive basis for language is well underway.

There is a dispute over the developmental sequence of semantic functions and relations. Bloom (1973) indicated that owner's name preceded the use of such names to indicate possession. Rodgon and Rashman (1976) indicated that object naming is much more frequent than owner naming. If the owner was unknown, neither object naming nor owner naming occurred. Bloom indicated that rejection preceded nonexistence, recurrence occurred before animateness, and relational functions occurred earlier, persisted, and occurred more frequently in the first half of the second year than the substantive forms that predominate in the last half of the second year. However, the evidence of Greenfield and Smith (1976) conflicts with Bloom's. Moreover, they point out that if Bloom included person names with other substantives, her data would reveal that substantives appeared first, and predominated over relational terms. Objects are typically encoded whereas agents are deleted (implied). Moreover, objects are more elaborated than agents (Brown, Cazden, and Bellugi-Klima 1969). The old information/new information view probably accounts for the preference for encoding object more than agent.

On the production of somewhat elaborate word combinations, Bloom, Lightbown, and Hood (1975) reported the following developmental sequences:

1. Encoding actions preceded encoding statives or attributives.
2. Nonlocative relations preceded locative relations.
3. Affected-object was most often nominal and agent most often pronominal (notwithstanding individual pronominal/nominal strategies).

4. Dative and instrumental are acquired late because they are matrix verbs entailing at least two functions.
5. Locative state is easier than locative action.
6. The two types of stative events, nonaction statives (existence, nonexistence, recurrence, possessive) precede active statives (location, notice, attributive) because they entail additional functions as the result of action. In a sense, early words are action dependent. They regulate joint attention and joint action (Bruner 1975).

Acquisition of Syntactic Systems

The acquisition of semantic systems rests on a cognitive base. As a child learns to make word combinations, he ventures more and more into the linguistic domain known as syntax. Just as word learning is paced by concept learning, syntactic knowledge depends upon semantic development. Syntactic knowledge entails knowing the various semantic-syntactic devices of one's language—the linguistic coding devices. Once a child acquires single-word utterances and their substantive and relational functions, it then becomes essentially a matter of effective and efficient *codification*. As Bloom (1973, p. 31) said, "children using single-word utterances know little if anything about sentences, but they have begun to know considerably more about the world of objects, events, and relations." Bowerman (1976, p. 142) indicated that "syntactic relations are more abstract than semantic ones because they subsume a number of semantic distinctions that could be made" (see Brown, 1973, pp. 120–23; Bowerman, 1973a,b, 1975b, for further discussion).

Antecedents of sentences are, of course, early two- and three-word utterances. Intonation patterns and successive single-word utterances seem to be precursors of two- and three-word utterances. As for intonation patterns of single-word utterances, Bloom (1973, p. 60) questioned whether their rising and falling contours may not actually correspond to those of adult speech. Wieman (1976) showed that early stress patterns do not reflect stress in adult speech. Bloom discussed the significance of successive single-word utterances: "Successive single-word utterances presented evidence of awareness of the intersection of different aspects of a situation" (1973, p. 53). This is consistent with what Donaldson and McGarrigle (1974) call "local rules." It seems that successive single-word utterances serve one of two purposes: simple naming behavior, and precursors to relating words together. The acquisition of syntactic systems provides efficient and effective means for expressing relationships within a single utterance. Successive single-word utterances are early attempts at coding relationships. Some time later, after a child learns the rudiments of a syntactic system, he joins sentences by the use of "and." As for the naming or labeling function of single-word utterances, McNeill (1970) contended that it is much more than a labeling process. He held that such utterances serve a communicative function in which certain aspects of a situation become overtly segmented. Bruner (1975a) had a similar point when he held that language regulates joint attention and joint action. Bloom (1973, p. 45) acknowledged that a communicative function beyond labeling occurs with successive single-word utterances—some of them have a "primitive discourse relation." Children who use successive single-words possess a sufficiently rich and varied vocabulary and know the substantive and relational functions to make sentences, but not the linguistic coding mechanisms or devices of their language (Bloom 1973).

At the two-, three-, and four-word levels, children combine substantive functions or relational and substantive functions. Thus, at the two-word level the following occur (Miller and Yoder 1974, p. 515):

Semantic relations (combinations of substantive functions)

1.	Agent-action	N + V	Daddy go
2.	Action-object	V + N	Eat cookie
3.	Agent-object	N + N	Daddy shoe
4.	Possessive	N + N	Mommy purse
5.	Locative	N + N	Purse chair
		V + N	Go bed
6.	Attributive	Adj + N	Big doggie
7.	Experience-state		I (me) + want, need . . .
8.	Datives of indirect object		Give Joey
9.	Commitatives		Walk Daddy
10.	Instrumentals		Hit bat

Functional relations (relational and substantive functions)

1.	Existence	Article or demonstrative + substantive word	This doggy
2.	Recurrence	More + substantive word	More milk
3.	Nonexistence	No + substantive word	No mousie
4.	Rejection	No + substantive word	No want
5.	Denial	No + substantive word	No milk

Three-term relations are

1.	Agent-action-object	Adam hit ball
2.	Agent-action-locative	Mommy go store
3.	Action-object-locative	Eat pie table
4.	Noun phrase expansions (usually object-noun-phase)	Sit Daddy chair

Four-term relations are further elaborations of three-term ones.

Bloom, Lightbown, and Hood (1975) provided a developmental sequence for various semantic and functional relations. They pointed out that existence, nonexistence, and recurrence of objects precede those involving verb relations. Within verb relations, actions precede status. Possession and attribution emerged in variable order. Instrumentals, datives, *wh*-questions, locatives, explicit intention, and causality were late in development. Spatial relations precede temporal relations (H. Clark 1973a). Bloom (1973, p. 24) indicated that children's early sentences dealt with existence, nonexistence, recurrence, location, possession, agent-action, action-goal (locative or direct object). These early sentences did not contain attributives, predicate adjectives, size, color, quantity, datives (indirect objects), identity, or disjunction. "Thus, the children were selective in what they chose to talk about."

After a child launches his syntactic career and begins to formulate more complex utterances, an interesting question arises concerning the developmental sequences of the semantic and relational functions he will attempt to load onto a single utterance. Some verbs require only one or two semantic functions; others require more (Perfetti 1972). Chapman and Miller (1975) and Suci and Hamacker (1972) have studied the issue from the standpoint of a limited set of semantic functions and relations. They confirmed Schlesinger's (1974) and Ervin-Tripp's (1973) speculations that early agents are animate and early objects are inanimate, and that early agents are of self rather than others. By this stage, alternative strategies become apparent, so developmental sequences are not as clear as one would hope.

Brown (1973b, p. 173) worried that this semantic and relational functions approach of accounting for the early stage of language development may be "little more than a technique of data reduction." The models proposed by Bloom (1970, 1973), Schlesinger (1971, 1974), Fillmore (1968), and others have given interesting accounts, but Brown (1973a,b) admonished that we should be critical of them in order to fully appreciate their significance to language learning.

Brown (1973a,b) and Brown, Cazden, and Bellugi-Klima (1969) have outlined five stages of early language learning. These are widely used in the literature, and are summarized in Fig. 6-6. They are based upon mean length of utterances, or "linguistic age." This is important because chronological age is notoriously variable—there are wide fluctuations in chronological age for each of the five stages of linguistic age. It should be stressed that while mean length of utterance seems to be a viable means of estimating linguistic development in the early stages, it loses its power during the preschool years. By four years, it reflects situational variables more than developmental ones (Shriner 1969).

Brown's five stages show that language acquisition follows a rather stable sequence. As a child enters into the period of word combinations (Stage I), he is able to express the basic semantic and relational functions of his language. His utterances show a strong order between elements and the elements are predominantly content, with functors noticeably absent. Obligatory morphemes are missing. He is narrowly adaptive in the use of language. In Stage II, many functors and noun and verb inflections become acquired. These provide various ways of modulating meanings. Stages III, IV, and V are merely speculative. Brown (1977) cautioned that the data base for these stages is not yet available or sufficiently studied. In Stage III a child develops the ability to deal with different utterance types: modalities of sentences. In addition to declaratives he becomes able to make negations, imperatives, yes/no questions, and various types of *wh*-questions. The aquisition of these question types is particularly interesting because it requires a rather sophisticated knowledge of constituent equivalence. Earlier, before a child knew of constituent equivalence or the mechanisms for modulation within constituents, he used tag questions. For example, he might say, "He good doggy, right?" or "He good doggy (rising intonation)?" Tag questions are relatively simple compared to *wh*-questions (Brown 1968, 1973b). In Stage IV a child learns the mechanisms of embedding one sentence into another. In Stage V he learns the mechanisms for coordinating sentences and constituents.

Slobin (1970) outlined a slightly different progression: intonation, word order, addition of morphemes to words and sentences, positioning of morphemes in sentences, permutation of morphemes, and sentence embedding. The important difference between Brown's and Slobin's sequences is that the last two stages are reversed. I personally think that embedding is more difficult, and thus later in development, than permutations. Wood (1976, p. 148) outlined a six-stage sequence of the acquisition of syntactic systems (see Fig. 6-7). Moreover, Brown's Stage II involved the beginning of modulation of meaning primarily through the acquisition of derivational and inflectional systems, or morphology. Wood (1976, p. 125) outlined the acquisition of English morphology. This appears in Fig. 6-8.

The acquisition of the determiner system entails learning the mechanisms that delimit nouns exclusive of adjectival mechanisms (adjectives, noun modifiers, relative clauses, etc.). The determiner system includes articles (a, some, the . . .), demonstratives (this, that, these, those . . .), possessives, number (*ten* bats, *three* balls, *six* players), and various pre- and postdeterminers (Thomas 1965, Roberts 1964).

A very interesting thing happens in the development of noun phrases in general and in the determiner system in particular: the object noun phrase develops first and more elaborately than the subject noun phrase (Brown, Cazden, and Bellugi-Klima 1969). As a child learns inflectional rules, they are likely to appear as object inflections before subject inflections. Moreover, when a child learns various embedding mechanisms, particularly nominalization, they are most likely to occur in object noun phrases first. This highlights a marked difference between natural language learning and programs that claim to be based upon language development, many of which advocate developing the subject noun phrase before the object noun phrase.

It should be stressed that this finding is not absolute in natural language learning. Various linguistic and referential conditions can influence the early elaboration of the subject noun phrase. Indeed, Cromer (1974) described two alternative strategies children can adapt in learning adjective modification: subject modification and object modification. The latter seems to be most widely used, undoubtedly due to the ease of dealing with recency effects in sentence processing (Ervin-Tripp 1973; Slobin 1973) and from a topic/comment perspective, a topic is implied by context (old information) whereas a comment requires explication (new information).

Figure 6-6 Brown's five stages of early language development.

Stage	MLU	Primary Description	Characteristics	Examples
				Semantic Functions and Relational Functions
I	1.00–2.00	Basic semantic and relational functions	(a) Linear position-order (b) Contains content words; lacks functors (c) Obligatory functional morphemes (inflections, case endings, articles, prepositions) (d) Narrowly adapted in communication; expects to be understood	1. Nominative — That ball 2. Recurrence — More ball 3. Disappearance or Nonexistence — All gone ball 4. Possessive — Daddy chair 5. Two locatives — Book table, Go store 6. Attributive — Big house 7. Agent-action — Daddy hit 8. Action-object — Hit ball 9. Agent-object — Daddy ball
				Order of acquisition of Morphemes
II	2.0–2.5	Grammatical morphemes and modulation of meaning	(a) Noun and verb inflections (b) Articles (c) Spatial prepositions (d) Copula (e) Auxiliary *be* (f) Order of requisition dependent upon semantic and grammatical complexity (g) Order invariant, rate variable (h) Morphemes modulate meanings of words, nouns, and verbs (i) Combining and ordering relations	1. Present progressive (He *going*) 2. in 3. on 4. Plural (dogs) 5. Past irregular (went) 6. Possessive (Mommy's) 7. Uncontractable copula 8. Articles (*a* dog) 9. Past regular (opened) 10. Third person regular (he eats everyday) 11. Third person irregular (he *has* a puppy) 12. Uncontractable auxiliary 13. Contractable copula (I'm a boy) 14. Contractable auxiliary

Stage	MLU	Constructions		
III	2.5–3.25	Modalities of sentences	(a) Yes/No questions (b) Constituent questions (*wh*-questions) (c) Negatives (d) Imperatives	*wh-questions* 1. Who—subject nominal 2. What—object nominal 3. What—predicate 4. Where—locative adverbial 5. When—time adverbial 6. How—manner adverbial 7. Which—attributive nominal *Negatives* 1. Nonexistence 2. Rejection 3. Denial
IV	3.25–3.75	Embedding one sentence into another	Embedding one sentence function as a constituent in another sentence: (a) Object noun phrase complements (b) Embedding *wh*-questions (c) Relative clauses	1. Simple sentence functions as object noun phrase—I think *I can fly.* 2. *Wh*-question functions as a noun phrase—They went *where the rabbit ran.* 3. Relative clause modifies a noun—The boy *who laughed* is always silly.
V	3.75–4.25	Coordination of simple sentences and propositional relations	(a) Coordination (b) Contrastive coordinators	1. Mary and Bill dance together. 2. Sue swims and hikes. 3. He is big but slow.

"Stages III, IV, and V can only be characterized in a hypothetical way at the present. Roger Brown and many others are still trying to settle the sequences of constructions involving sentence modalities, sentence embedding, and sentence coordinating" (Brown 1977, personal correspondence).

Adapted from Roger Brown, *A First Language* (Cambridge, Mass.: Harvard University Press, 1973). Copyright © 1973 by Harvard University Press.

Figure 6-7 *Six stages in children's syntactic development.*

Stage of Development	Nature of Development	Sample Utterance
1. Sentence-like word	Word combined with nonverbal cues (gestures and inflections)	"Mommy." "Mommy!" "Mommy?"
2. Modification	Modifiers joined to topic words to form declarative, question, negative, and imperative structures	"Pretty baby." (declarative) "Where Daddy?" (question) "No play." (negation) "More milk!" (imperative)
3. Structure	Both subject and predicate included in sentence types	"She's a pretty baby." (declarative) "Where Daddy is?" (question) "I no can play." (negative) "I want more milk!" (imperative)
4. Operational changes	Elements added, embedded, and permutated within sentences	"Read it, my book." (conjunction) "Where is Daddy?" (embedding) "I can't play." (permutation)
5. Categorization	Word classes (nouns, verbs, and prepositions) subdivided	"I would like *some* milk." (use of *some* with mass noun) "Take me to the store." (use of preposition of place.)
6. Complex structures	Complex structural distinctions, as with ask-tell and promise	"Ask what time it is." "He promised to help her."

From Barbara S. Wood, *Children and Communication: Verbal and Nonverbal Language Development,* © 1976, p. 148. By permission of Prentice-Hall, Inc., Englewood Cliffs, New Jersey.

Figure 6-8 *Children's development of morphology.*

Stage	Starting Age
1. First words: parents, objects, and so forth; declarative, imperative, and interrogative functions	12–18 months
2. New words: added through expansion and contraction (vocabulary building)	3–4 years
3. Early bound morphemes a. plurals b. possessive c. verb tense 　(1) present progressive 　(2) simple past 　(3) third-person present 　(4) irregular past 　(5) future	5+ years
4. Compounding a. identity b. salient feature c. related feature d. etymological	4–6+ years
5. Later bound morphemes a. adjective forms 　(1) comparative 　(2) superlative b. deriving c. diminutives d. agentives	6+ years

From Barbara S. Wood, *Children and Communication: Verbal and Nonverbal Language Development,* © 1976, p. 239. By permission of Prentice-Hall, Inc., Englewood Cliffs, New Jersey.

Bloom (1970, 1973) reported another interesting phenomenon in early language learning: *reductionism*. This is interesting from two points of view: it shows that much more is behind what is observed on the product level, and it shows the importance of placing observed events in a larger perspective. Both of these issues are formidable criticisms of quantitative-normative and taxonomic measures in language assessment.

In reductionism, a child reduces a grammatical system that he knows at least on a rudimentary level to something more manageable yet salient. Figure 6-9 illustrates the point. A child might say three things, depending on what he thinks is most salient for a given circumstance: "Mommy eat," "Eat cookie," and "Mommy

Figure 6-9 *Reductionism in a transitive system.*

	Subject NP	*Transitive Verb*	*Object NP*
Utterance A	Mommy	eat	
Utterance B		eat	cookie
Utterance C	Mommy		cookie
	S	V	O

cookie.'' The composite in these utterances is an SVO pattern (a transitive system) but independently, they show SV, VO, and SO patterns, respectively. Taking each one alone, one might conclude that the child needs to learn object noun phrases (SV), subject noun phrases (VO), or transitive verbs (SO). However, taken all together, it becomes clear that the child knows the transitive system at least on a rudimentary level but reduces it, retaining the most salient aspects. Why does he do this to a system he already knows? Apparently certain mental constraints are operating that do not allow him to process a linguistic code fully. The most obvious is a memory processing limitation of some sort. Whatever it may be, his limited performance is not due to a lack of linguistic knowledge. Rather, the evidence is that the linguistic system is within the child's repertoire, but processing capacity forces him to reduce it to its most salient aspects.

Cognitive systems underlie semantic systems (Chap. 3) and cognitive processing constrains early linguistic behavior (Slobin [1973], Olson [1973], and Ervin-Tripp [1973]). Bowerman (1974) outlined several possible types of cognitive-linguistic-communicative problems that may occur because of various cognitive constraints. Perhaps it is helpful to note some parallels in the way cognition and language have been conceptualized, particularly in regard to development. Figure 6-10 shows some of these. However, it must be stressed that one should not try to establish a one-to-one *explanation* of the relationships between thought and language. Efforts to do so have failed, e.g., the Sapir-Whorf hypotheses. Such efforts dismiss a basic relationship between thought and language: an element of language can have several referents and one referent can have several elements. However, there may be a partial isomorphism (Sinclair-deZwart 1973a; Greenfield, Nelson, and Saltzman 1972; Goodson and Greenfield 1975).

Returning to the acquisition of syntactic systems, Macnamara (1972) developed a rationale for the cognitive basis of language learning in infants. He pointed out that thought and affect are not only distinguishable from language but can develop without the benefit of it. Piagetian psychology substantiates this point with respect to thought. Evidence for affect is reported by Kohlberg et al. (1968). In early naming behavior, children name entities before they name attributes and attend to varying states rather than steady states. Macnamara (1972) held that meaning or semantics is inextricably related to syntax. A child uses meaning to unravel syntactic puzzles. Macnamara indicated there is a difference between *discovering* syntactic devices and *stating* them. An individual can intuitively produce

Figure 6-10 *Some parallels in characterizing cognitive and linguistic domains.*

Cognition	Language
"Concepts and systems"	"Categories and rules" (McNeill 1966a)
"Schemata and structure" (Piaget 1970; Kagan 1971)	"Bins and structure" (Menyuk 1971)
"Concepts and hierarchies" (Gagne 1965; White 1965)	"Classes and hierarchies" (Johnson 1966; Yngve 1960)
"Peripheral and core" (Rosch 1973a,b)	"Surface and deep" (Chomsky 1957, 1965a,b)
"Differentiation and restructure" (Saltz 1971; Witkin et al. 1962)	"Differentiation and reorganization" (Brown 1973a,b; Menyuk 1964a,b)

complex utterances and immediately know if a mistake has been made, yet not be able to explain what the mistake is. Macnamara (1972, p. 11) held that language learning is much more complex than what has been traditionally thought: "infants use meaning to learn vocabulary, vocabulary to learn syntax, and syntax to learn phonology." Perhaps a better description is,

> Children initially take the main lexical items in the sentences they hear, determine referents for these items, and then use their knowledge of the referents to decide what the semantic structures intended by the speaker must be. . . . Once the children have determined the semantic structure, their final task is to note the syntactic devices, such as word order, prepositions, number affixes, etc., which correlate with the semantic structures. Such a strategy will yield most of the main syntactic devices in the language. (Macnamara 1972, p. 7)

Macnamara stressed the importance of meaning to "get at" form and a child's spontaneous responsiveness to inherent patterns: "(a) the child cannot discover many syntactic structures without the aid of meaning, and (b) the child is prodigiously skilled at noting the regularities in the language which he hears" (1972, p. 7).

The development of negations and questions can be viewed from two perspectives: form and function. According to Bloom (1970) and McNeill and McNeill (1968), the order of development of negative functions is (1) nonexistence (expected referent not present), (2) rejection (referent present but not desired), and (3) denial (refusal to accept something). Structurally, Klima (1965) and Klima and Bellugi-Klima (1969) reported the following developmental sequence for negations and questions: (1) negations or questions are first marked outside a sentence: "No, I go." "I go, no." "I go, right?"; (2) negations or questions are marked internally but the marker is not integrated with the auxiliary system: "I no go." "I go (rising intonation to mark question)"; (3) negations or questions are integrated into the auxiliary system: "I will not go." "I won't go." "I didn't go." "Will I go?"

Another very important piece of information came from the study of the acquisition of negations and questions: co-occurring structures are influenced by negations and questions. Bloom (1970) reported that when negations appear, deletions of recently acquired structures also occurred. This underscores the importance of co-occurring structures in language learning and probably reflects the security base premise described before.

Acquisition of the Pronominal System

The acquisition of the pronominal system is much more complex than merely learning the pronouns of one's language. A child must come to realize the constituent equivalences of various pronouns as well as the *anaphoric* use of pronouns. Moreover, he must learn the forms of each pronoun as it functions as a subject or object. Constituent equivalences are very important, since they allow one to use a simple grammatical device such as pronouns to stand for a nominal (noun phrase) which may be rather elaborate. For example, one might say, "*He* opened the door." *He* could stand for something rather elaborate such as "the man who had the winning dog in the field trials."

Anaphoric reference means that a linguistic marker such as a pronoun refers to what came before. Thus, *his* and *he* in the following refer to the noun phrase *the boy*: "As the boy was eating *his* ice cream cone, *he* dropped it." Actually, *it* also has an anaphoric reference to *ice cream cone*. Anaphoric reference can be very complicated, particularly if the pronouns are of the same gender. When a pronoun is used several times, a child may lose the appropriate anaphoric reference. Bloom (1970) contended that the first stage of negation entails anaphoric reference. In "No, I go," the "no" denies or rejects what came before.

Figure 4-1 outlines the pronominal system for English. It shows that virtually the entire pronominal system is irregular—each element must be learned by itself. This underscores the difficulty some children have in acquiring the system. Frequently, a child will learn objective pronouns (me, her, him), then generalize to the subject resulting in utterances such as "Me go," "Her eat," and "Him jump."

Complexity

It is very difficult to know what complexity is in language. Psycholinguistic theories were originally thought to offer a way of dealing with complexity. In the early days of transformational generative grammar, Miller (1962, 1965) suggested that complexity could be accounted for by the number of transformational operations. However, the work of Clifton and Odom (1966) dispelled this proposition. Complexity also has been defined in terms of the type of transformation. Double base transformations were thought to be more difficult than single base transformations. Menyuk (1969) showed that some of the earliest sentence elaborations contained double base transformations. Another approach regarded the type of recursiveness. Right recursive sentences were thought to be easier than left recursive ones, and left recursive sentences were thought to be easier than self-embedding ones. The elaborateness of underlying hierarchical structure was also thought to be a means for ascertaining complexity (Yngve 1960; Johnson 1965, 1966). Frank and Osser (1970) reviewed these models of complexity. Unfortunately, they deal only with the syntactic domain. Equal, if not more important, is the semantic domain: how many semantic relations are included in a message. Psychological distancing undoubtedly plays a role in complexity. In short, we are a long way from an adequate theory of complexity. The entire communicative context of available referents, intents, etc. must be considered.

Perhaps the best we can do is simply state that as a child acquires increased command of his language, he becomes more adept in its use, and adeptness entails increased complexity. There is some evidence that complexity operates to constrain performance. The discussion of reductionism suggests that processing load is too great to deal with the entire system. The concept of co-occurring structures is tied up with the issue of complexity. A child will constrain the occurrence of certain structures in the presence of others. I have shown (Muma 1971a) that young children use certain transformations in the context of certain structures, but not others. Menyuk (1969) reported that when several transformations occur, they are at first different types and in different aspects of sentences. Subsequently, they may be the same ones applied repeatedly. Another interesting observation concerns relative clauses. Young children are prone to retain the relative clause marker because it facilitates both comprehension and production. "The girl *who* is over there is very nice" becomes "The girl over there is nice." Deletions are also complex (O'Donnell, Griffin, and Norris 1967). It takes greater linguistic skill to say, "He can," than, "He can swim." The acquisition of "if" reveals two levels of complexity. First, a child will use "if" to express uncertainty (Cromer 1976): "See if Mommy wants it." Then he will use "if" for hypothetical conditionality: "If I pick it up, it may fall."

Learning After Four Years of Age

By four years of age most children know the basic semantic-syntactic rules of their language (Menyuk 1969). They must, however, learn subtle nuances of various linguistic systems and to be adept in language usage. They need to transfer their intuitive knowledge to explicit knowledge to read and write. They must develop a roletaking attitude that gives them an opportunity to develop skills in playing the communication game (Muma 1975a).

Palermo and Molfese (1972) and McNeill (1970) reviewed this literature. Children over four years of age learn exceptions to the *minimum distancing principle* (Rosenbaum 1967). C. Chomsky (1969) demonstrated that children are somewhat late in fully realizing which verbs operate under this principle and which do not. "In sentences which conform to the MDP, the noun phrase which immediately precedes an infinitive complement verb is the subject of that verb. Thus, in 'John wanted Bill to leave,' it is Bill who does the leaving but in 'John promised Bill to leave,' it is John who does the leaving." "Promise" is an exception to the rule.

Roughly between two and four years of age, syntax seems to be conspicuous in perception and comprehension. According to Bever, Mehler, and Valian (1967) and Huttenlocher (1974), children of this age have syntactic strategies in comprehension. By about five years, they begin to adapt semantic strategies (Bever, Mehler, and Valian 1967; McNeill 1970, p. 124; Muma, Adams-Perry, and Gallagher 1974). The shift from a syntactic to a semantic strategy derives from the work on reversibility of transitive sentences (Slobin 1966; Turner and Rommetveit 1967; and many others). "The dog was chasing the cat" can be reversed to give "The cat was being chased by the dog." But, "The cat was chasing the dog" is an entirely different sentence. The passive transformation is a mechanism for topicalizing the object of a sentence. The use of the passive to topicalize is an advanced stage.

In addition to the minimum distancing principle, C. Chomsky (1969) studied children's awareness of pronominal reference for sentences containing certain verb complements. Pronouns that appear in a main clause when the main clause precedes a noun phrase must refer to some other noun phrase. For example, in "*He* knew that Tom was right," *he* cannot be *Tom*. On the other hand, if the sentence were "Tom knew *he* was right," *he* could be *Tom* or someone else.

An interesting phenomenon occurs around seven years of age: the syntagmatic-paradigmatic shift (Brown and Berko 1960; Deese 1965; Entwisle 1966a,b; Entwisle, Forsyth, and Muuss 1964; Ervin 1961, 1963; Emerson and Gekoski 1976; Jenkins et al. 1971, McNeill 1963, 1966b; Jenkins and Palermo 1964; Jenkins 1964, 1966). Given a stimulus word, children under seven will give a syntagmatic response. If the stimulus word is "cookie," a young child might say "is good" or just "mm." However, older children and adults give another word from the same form class as the stimulus: For "Cookie," they are likely to say "cake" or "candy." A syntagmatic response is placing the stimulus word in a syntactic context. A paradigmatic response is giving another word in the same class, i.e., noun-noun, verb-verb, adjective-adjective. Unfortunately, we do not understand the mechanisms that underly the shift of syntagmatic to paradigmatic responses. Francis (1972) conjectured that some type of reorganization in the semantic domain accounts for the shift.

I developed a task intended to give new insight on the shift. It presents regular single syllable pluralized high frequency nouns in systematically varying contexts. The contexts are as follows:

Noun   (animate) _____
Noun (inanimate)_____
_____ Noun (animate)
_____ Noun (inanimate)

Noun   (animate) _____ Noun (animate)
Noun   (animate) _____ Noun (inanimate)
Noun (inanimate) _____ Noun (animate)
Noun (inanimate) _____ Noun (inanimate)
_____ Noun (animate) _____
_____ Noun (inanimate) _____

Subjects were asked to utter a stimulus word and anything they thought went into a given context. My wife conducted the study on children who were clearly younger than the age at which the shift occurs, as well as on children who were older. Her work lead to refinements in the task and the development of the data reduction procedures. I then had a student conduct her master's thesis on this task, using five-year-old, nine-year-old, and adult subjects (Zwycewicz 1975). Zwycewicz reported some interesting findings. Each context was repeated eight times, but in different sequences. The responses to the various contexts were remarkably similar and strong. At the five-year-old level listing behavior was strongly evident. Their responses were almost entirely nouns. At the nine-year-old level the responses were differentiated across the various contexts. At the adult level the responses were not only differentiated but well integrated. Nondifferentiated responses including listing behavior similar to that of the five-year-olds as well as varied responses to each of the contexts over the eight replications. Differentiated responses occurred in different types of responses for each context. Two levels of integration occurred. Nine-year-olds manifested first-level integrations. These existed when a given linguistic system appeared across the eight replications and the same exemplar was used. Second-level integrations existed when a given linguistic system occurred across the eight replications and different exemplars were used.

What about the syntagmatic-paradigmatic shift? First and foremost, major changes in performance occurred before and after the age (seven years) at which the shift occurs. Second, at first glance it would appear that the listing behavior of the five-year-olds is a quite unexpected paradigmatic behavior. However, word association tasks are different. In those, words are placed in isolation. In this task, various contexts are provided. Apparently, young children need a context. If it is not there, they will create it.

Acquisition of Phonological Systems

The phonological system has two major domains: speech perception and speech production. Speech perception entails learning the sound patterns of one's language. It is consistently acquired ahead of production. However, it is misleading to think that there is a one-to-one correspondence between the two. Other variables operate that complicate matters (Bloom and Lahey, 1978).

Most clinicians who have a traditional orientation toward speech development are content with an age-referenced normative profile for the acquisition of

Figure 6-11 *Average age estimates for the acquisition of English sounds (based on Sander 1961*).*

Sounds	Median age of customary usage	Age of 90% of subjects
p, m, h, n, w	1;6	3;0
b	1;6	4;0
k, g, d	2;0	4;0
t, ŋ	2;0	6;0
f, y	2;6	4;0
r, l	3;0	6;0
s, š	3;0	8;0
č, ž	3;6	7;0
ž	4;0	7;0
j	4;0	7;0
v	4;0	8;0
θ	4;6	7;0
ð	5;0	8;0
z	6;0	8;6

*From Ingram, D. *Phonological Disability in Children.* Edward Arnold (Publishers) Ltd. New York: Elsevier, 1976.

phonemes. The Templin (1957), McCarthy (1954), and Poole (1934) norms are examples. Figure 6-11 gives the average age estimates for the acquisition of English phonemes.

Unfortunately, normative approaches of this type obscure individual differences and omit important information about phonological processes. A phoneme approach is segment- and place-specific (location of articulators). Most clinicians are oriented on a phoneme approach. It is context-free. By contrast, a phonotactic approach (Menn 1971; Ingram 1974b) is not segment- or place-specific. It is context-sensitive (see the coarticulation approach in Chap. 4). Ingram (1974b, 1976) has shown why the phonotactic approach is more productive in accounting for acquisition than the phoneme approach. Most clinicians use a phoneme approach. However, they should use a phonotactic one because it offers much greater insight into various aspects of acquisition.

Children must learn three components of the phonological system: (a) segmental features, (b) rules for combining these features, and (c) suprasegmental or prosodic features. *Segments* can be phonemes, phonemic clusters, or morphemes. However, phonologically speaking, *segments* refers to phonemes. *Segmental features* are the various distinctive feature states of each phoneme in phonological context. The rules for combining these features are in the context. Indeed, they extend beyond the phonological domain to syllabic structure and even syntax. Certain phonological variations occur when inflectional rules are needed. Menyuk (1971) has shown that some children who had problems with syntax had faulty phonetic skills. It is not surprising that problems in syntax and morphology appear in speech articulation error patterns, since these systems are interrelated. A prevailing attitude in the applied fields is that speech articulation is not only distinguishable but isolable from other linguistic systems. It is now clear that when speech articulation is isolated from other linguistic systems, distortion occurs and the opportunity for appreciating the relevance of phonetic patterns is lost.

Even though a speech receptor mechanism is apparently activated as early as one month of age, the acquisition of the phonological system is a long-term process. Apparently, infants learn about phonemes as they occur in context with other apsects of verbal behavior. Suprasegmental information provides a way of identifying syllables and morphemes, and syllables provide matrices from which segments (phonemes) can be deduced. The prosodic theory of phonological development states that a child acquires phonemes through the realization of prosodic and syllabic information.

This view was advanced by Waterson (1971). A child first selectively attends to regular, nondeviant, highly salient adult forms, while dismissing minor forms. Second, he perceives an utterance as a whole unit. Third, he generates nuclear forms with a limited set of features. Fourth, improved perception and production results from the use of his repertoire of the most salient or pervasive features. Fifth, individual variations reflect different contacts with one's language.

The acquisition process has been described in terms of distinctive features. This was first suggested by Jakobson (1941). The basic premise is that a child obtains increased sensorimotor control over his vocal mechanism, which gives him an increased ability to produce and perceive the sound patterns in his language. Beginning with the first phonemes /p/, /t/, and /a/, a child has a primary triangle in which the vertical dimensions (compact-diffuse) and the horizontal dimension (grave-acute) of the vocal tract become differentiated (Jakobson and Halle 1956). In the course of development, an invariant sequence of differentiation was presumed to occur. The data have been generally consistent with Jakobson's proposals, but discrepancies have occurred. For example, Crocker (1969) held that the first distinctions were ± vocalic and ± consonantal. Such distinctions would give a young child the ability to differentiate the major phonological classes: vowels, consonants, liquids, and glides. On the other hand, Menyuk (1968) indicated that early developments are evidenced by + nasal, + grave, and + voice.

According to Menyuk (1972, p. 26), the rank order of the feature acquisition of perception is slightly different from that of production. The sequence for perception is nasality, voicing, continuancy, place. The sequence for production is nasality, voicing, stridency, continuancy, place. Menyuk outlined what young children can do when they acquire differential control over these features:

1. Oral versus nasal (p, b versus m).
2. Labial versus nonlabial (m, p, b versus n, t, d).
3. Voiced versus nonvoiced (d, b versus t, p).
4. Fricative versus stop (f or v versus p or b).
5. Lingual versus velar (t, d, n versus k, g).

Menyuk indicated that further development depends on rather skillful manipulation of the tongue:

1. Tongue in a rest position (p, b, m, h, f, v).
2. Tongue tip raised and touching (d, t, n, l, c, j).
3. Back of tongue raised and touching (k, g, y).
4. Thrusting the tongue forward (γ , $\ominus$).
5. Raising tongue without touching palate (r, s, z, š, ž).

When a child acquires tongue-jaw differentiation, he can produce many speech sounds he could not make previously.

The newborn infant is structurally unable to phonate, but possesses a speech receptor mechanism that seems to be activated from birth. Infants are especially sensitive to sound frequencies in the speech range. Moreover, if the sounds are patterns rather than simple tones, they exhibit an orienting response. Clearly, perception foreshadows production. Menyuk (1972, p. 15) summarized both speech production and speech perception during the first year (Fig. 6-12).

In re-evaluating Irwin's extensive data, Bever (1961) studied the rates of change of phonetic types. He identified three periods. In the period from birth to almost four months, a very rapid rate of change in frequency and type of vowel-like sounds occurs. A similar but less rapid rate of consonant-like sounds occurs. At four months the rate of change abruptly drops. At five or six months, a peak in the rate of change for vowel-like sounds occurs. At seven months a corresponding peak occurs for consonant-like sounds. At nine or ten months a very large peak in the rate of change occurs for consonant-like sounds. Finally, at eleven or twelve months very little change occurs.

Apparently, vowels and consonants are learned in different ways. Vowels are considered to be continuous whereas consonants are categories. McNeill (1970, p. 130) reported that the direction of development for consonant-like sounds in the first year is from the back of the mouth to the front, but for vowel-like sounds from the front to the back. Menyuk (1972, p. 17) suggested a different developmental pattern. She contended that vowels begin in the middle and extend both forward and backward to other vowels. This corresponds somewhat to the differentiations in Jakobson and Halle's (1956) primary triangle. She also reported that back consonants occur first and more prominently than front consonants at the five–six month period. She indicated that consonants with + voice, + grave, and/or + continuant were missing. She reasoned that this pattern showed that consonants were produced by a minimum of effort. Thus, Zipf's (1949) law of least effort seems to have credence in phonology.

Ervin-Tripp (1967) summarized the developmental predictions according to Jakobson's theory (1941) and compared available evidence from diary studies. The earliest predicted phonemic systems were a front occlusive /p/, an open vowel /a/, a contrast of labial and dental /t/, a contrast of nasal and oral /m/ and /n/. The diary data indicate that initial syllables are open syllables CV. The initial consonant is a

Figure 6-12 *Speech production and perception during the first year of life.*

Production	Perception

Stage I: Birth.
  Crying: basic pattern
  varied due to state
  of infant, i.e., anger
  or pain.
	Stage I: Birth.
	  Responds to sounds and loca-
	  lizes.

Stage II: 3 weeks.
  Pseudo-cry and no-cry utter-
  ances. Variety of temporal
  and frequency patterns
	Stage II: 2 weeks.
	  Distinguishes between voices
	  and other sounds. Voice of
	  caretaker will
	  stop crying.

Stage III: 4–5 months.
  Babbling and production
  of intonated utterances.
  Utterances become increas-
  ingly more speechlike until
  first year.
	Stage III: 2–4 months.
	  Discrimination between
	  angry and friendly, familiar
	  and unfamiliar, male and
	  female voices, and temporal
	  aspects of signal.

Stage IV: 9–12 months.
  Production of patterned
  speech, i.e., words.
	Stage IV: 5–6 months.
	  Increasing evidence of
	  sensitivity to intonation
	  and rhythm. Discrimination
	  of intonational patterns
	  and possibly segmental
	  features.

At 6–8 years: Correct artic-
  ulation of speech sounds.
	At 2 years: Discrimination
	  between all possible minimal
	  pairs of words.

From Menyuk (1972).

stop; the second is a fricative or nasal. Contrasts between stops and continuants appear very early. The first *place* contrast is between labial and dental. Voicing contrast follows place contrast in acquisition. The second predicted stage was a splitting of the vowel between high and low. Then the vowels split into different levels. Diary studies support these predictions. The third stage is that stops precede fricatives /p/ before /f/. Diary data are consistent with this as well. Fourth, fricatives precede affricates in development. Fifth, the splitting of the front/back vowels first occurs for high vowels. Sixth, rounded (lip rounding) back and unrounded front vowels precede rounded front vowels. Seventh, differentiation is maximized in the front consonants. The diary studies are generally consistent with the Jakobson theory.

Other processes operate in phonological development beyond the differentiation of distinctive features. A major influence is phonetic and syntactic-morphological context. For example, vowel type can influence the production of pre- and postvocalic consonants. Coarticulation literature documents many contextual influences. Morphological contexts vary in degree of specificity. The plural of nouns is expressed as /z/ for words like "boy" and "hand," /s/ for words like "mat" and "muff," and /əz/ for "place." But, the plural for "wolf" is "wol+v+z" and for "child," it is "children." The first of these rules are rather general because they pertain to most nouns, and the last of them is greatly limited—specific to particular words. Menyuk (1971, pp. 86–87) held that levels of specificity for pluralizing nouns show the sequence in the acquisition of the phonological patterns. The more general rules are learned first.

The principle of maximum contrast (Jakobson 1941) accounts for an infant's early utterances. The utterances "mama" and "papa" have the greatest degree of closure and the vowel the greatest degree of opening. Subsequent learning involves progressive differentiations of phonemes of lesser contrast.

Ingram (1976) described the acquisition of phonology in terms of (a) the development of perceptual categorization, (b) the development of a phonetic inventory, and (c) the use of general phonological processes. The development of perceptual categorization is more complex than activating a speech receptor mechanism. First, a child must distinguish between speech and nonspeech. Shvachkin (1973) proposed a developmental sequence in the perception of speech: vowels, presence/absence of consonants, sonorants/stops, palatalized/nonpalatalized consonants, between sonorants, sonorants/continuants, labels/linguals, stops/spirants, pre/postlinguals, voiced/voiceless consonants, between sibilants, and liquids /y/. Garnica (1973) reported similar findings. Both studies indicate that the development of speech perception extends to about eighteen to twenty-four months of age.

Edwards (1974) extended the studies of Shvachkin and Garnica. She found that children as old as three have not yet completed the acquisition of phonemic perception, that phonemic perception develops gradually and in advance of production, and that the order of acquisition is rather stable but not universal. Interestingly enough, she reported that vocalic voicing, alternative morphological forms such as various plurals in English, and frequency of occurrence may interfere with normal acquisition.

The development of a *phonetic inventory* offers interesting new insights for clinicians. Ingram indicates that the period from birth to about ten to twelve months is a time when important developments are taking place that pave the way for production. Volitional control of the vocal mechanism is realized, and intentional and selective imitation acquired. The second major period for phonological development is from approximately twelve to eighteen months of age. In this period, a child acquires his initial fifty words. Its end is marked by a sudden increase of vocabulary and the onset of word combinations. The third major period lasts until around four years of age, by which time a child has acquired most of the phonological system of his language. The fourth and last period is when he learns the remaining difficult speech sounds and acquires complex words. Hitherto, his words were limited primarily to single syllable words and perhaps an occasional two- or three-syllable word.

The first fifty-word period exhibits the following phonological activity: initial syllables are CV or CVCV reduplicated; labial consonants (mostly [p]) are followed by [t] and later [k]; first vowel is [a] followed by [i] and/or [u]. The basic vowel triangle is acquired. Sound acquisition reveals considerable individual variation. Moreover, words are primary determinants of what is learned. Coarticulatory influences are evidenced by what Edwards and Garnica (1973) called "trade-off." The acquisition of a new part of a word may alter the production of another part. Words acquired during this period are outside a child's phonological system. That is, a child has not yet deduced productive phonological rules. This explains the limited regression phenomenon that occurs after a child leaves the initial fifty-word period, reflecting various simplification processes.

"Children do not acquire individual sounds suddenly, but gradually over time" (Ingram 1976, p. 29). It is a gradual process because phonemes are not entities but products of complex interrelated processes. One basic process is the tendency to reduce all words to a basic CV syllable. They can be reduced by deleting final consonants, consonantal cluster reduction, deleting unstressed syllables, syllabic reduplication, and even a special rule for voicing (see Chap. 4). Renfrew (1966), Panagos (1974), Fudge (1969), and Moskowitz (1970) report that the open syllable or CV appears early. Syllabic reduplication is most common during the initial fifty-word period and children vary considerably in using it. In consonant cluster reduction, Greenlee (1974) observed a four-stage sequence: deletion of entire cluster, cluster reduction to one segment, segment substitution within a cluster, then adult cluster. The marked segment of a cluster is usually deleted.

Other phonological processes are reported in Chap. 4. Vowels can influence the preceding consonants. First vowel height, then front-back distinctions affect consonants. The voicing phenomenon reported in Chap. 4 appears after the initial fifty words. Vowels can be changed as a function of following consonants. They can also be affected by preceding consonants. Fronting is a process in which palatals and velars are replaced with alveolars. Fricatives and affricates are frequently stopped. Vowels may be neutralized—reduced to [ə].

In summary, the acquisition of the phonological system is not simply a matter of describing the developmental profile for the phonemes of one's language. The process includes progressive differentiation of distinctive features that make up the phonemes. Moreover, there are some features in child phonology that do not occur in adult variations. These were also described in Chap. 4. The presence of child variations invalidates the use of an adult distinctive feature system, specifically the Chomsky and Halle (1968) feature system, in characterizing child speech. In addition to distinctive features, phonetic context is important. It was found that the more specific the context the longer it took to learn. Similarly, contexts that contained maximally contrasting phonetic movements were learned early, whereas minimally contrasting ones were acquired later. Prosodic features were learned relatively early. Initial speech sound production differs from the speech sound production that is the product of a phonological system. The acquisition of phonological systems entails several simplification processes.

Alternative Language Learning Strategies

Individual differences in language learning are common. This is important for clinical assessment and intervention because the previous reliance on normative measures and highly structured programs is questionable, particularly in regard to relevance. Clinicians need to know about developmental principles and sequences such as those described below.

One productive way of appreciating individual differences is to be aware of alternative language learning strategies. The language development literature has recently described some of these. It should be emphasized that they are not incompatible with developmental sequences. Alternative strategies pertain to options *between* grammatical systems and stable sequences occur *within* them.

Nelson (1973) described two strategies of language learning: expressive or phrase learning, and referential or word learning. Phrase learners become preoccupied with word combinations or new ways of expression. Word learners focus on learning alternative referents. Inasmuch as there is a relatively small number of expressions but an unlimited number of referents, referential learners are much more effective. Bloom (1970, 1973) showed that her children had alternative language learning strategies somewhat similar to those reported by Nelson.

Vygotsky (1962), McNeill (1970), and Brown (1958b) described similar strategies. In scientific strategy, a new word is heard and the person goes about discovering the various meanings for it. The strategy is called ''scientific'' because the person begins hypothesizing about the nature of its meaning. In spontaneous strategy one spontaneously deduces the attributes of various experiences and then hears a word that consolidates them.

Bloom, Lightbown, and Hood (1975) reported two strategies in the early acquisition of nominalizations. Some children begin learning nominalizations by learning nominals (frequently proper names). Others begin by learning pronominal forms. When these children reach the age in which their utterances exceed an average of 2.0 morphemes, they switch their strategies. Cromer (1974) described two strategies in the acquisition of adjective modifiers of nouns. Some individuals first learn adjective modifiers in subject noun phrases; others learn them in object noun phrases.

Bloom, Hood, and Lightbown (1974) found that some children imitate available speech models, and others rarely do. The former imitate until the MLU is about 2.0 morphemes. Imitation is selective: it occurs with grammatical forms and functions that were in the process of acquisition. It does not occur with grammatical systems a child knows well, nor with systems of which he knows nothing. This provides evidence of the locus of learning in a communicative context. Bloom, Hood, and Lightbown suggested that imitation allows one to encode an event with the perceptual support of a relevant message.

Eilers, Oller, and Ellington (1974) reported alternative strategies in learning dimensional adjectives. Some individuals attributed the meaning of the marked member to the unmarked member; others adopted the opposite strategy. It may be that the semantic feature hypothesis proposed by E. Clark (1973) posits only one of the two strategies that naturally occur.

The study of alternative strategies is relatively new to language learning literature. It will no doubt be elaborated in the near future. Clinicians should be alert for developments in this area because it is a promising one for understanding the individual differences found in the clinic.

Communicative Interaction: Dialogue

Early utterances are not made to convey information. They are basically extended action patterns. A child of eighteen months and younger responds to adult speech with action. Moreover, adults respond to the child's vocalizations with actions (Weir 1962). Thus, initiated verbal activities are first action-based (Greenfield and Smith 1976). Through action-based behavior, a child begins to understand various functions of language. The informative function that constitutes the basis of dialogue is late in acquisition compared to the instrumental need to satisfy needs, the regulatory need to exert control over the behavior of others, the interactional need to establish and maintain contact with others, and the personal need to express individuality and self-awareness (Halliday 1975). The acquisition of language functions—indeed, semantic functions—is somewhat independent of language, but dependent on context via perceived events and realized actions. However, at about eighteen months, speech is responded to by speech—rudimentary dialogue. Note that parents ask many *wh-* questions that are not responded to by speech until about eighteen months, when a child begins responding to them with nouns. Also, children of this age will follow a command and vocalize their actions as they do them. At this time, they will indicate attention, respond to an adult with utterances such as "Oh," and initiate a dialogue by asking "What's that?" and then repeating the response.

The shift from one- to two-word utterances involves an interesting aspect of dialogue. The transition can be described in five stages (Scollon 1976):

1. Repetition of a single-word utterance accompanied by adult interaction. This repetition apparently has two functions: phonological practice in which sound patterns are varied, and discourse clarification in which explicitness

is attempted. Discourse clarification pertains to Bruner's (1975a) point that language is used to regulate joint attention and joint action. A child would say "Ma, ma mommy," whereupon the mother will respond with an action related to what she presumes the utterance is about.

2. No repetition; simply a one-word utterance accompanied by adult intervention.
3. Simple repetition of the first word and then the second word, in a two-word utterance: "Ma, mommy ca, come."
4. Two consecutive one-word utterances: "Mommy" "come."
5. Two-word construction: "Mommy come."

Adult intervention is particularly interesting because it gives a child an understanding of the possibilities of his utterance in a given context. Thus, it is a way of learning syntax in the context of available reference and communicative intent.

A major aspect in the development of the ability to carry on a dialogue is the production of a coherent string of utterances. Francis (1969) indicated that early utterance strings correspond to early ways of categorization through edge-matching and key-ring strategies. In an edge-matching string the last word of one utterance is used to initiate the first word of the next: "Mommy gave it Daddy," "Daddy put it on table," "The table was big." In key-ring strategy one word occupies a pivotal relationship with several consecutive utterances: "Daddy coming," "Daddy home," "Daddy outside." Children around four years old frequently string several utterances together connected by a conjunction, containing false starts, pauses, and other hesitation phenomena. They are not cognitively ready to organize efficient utterances because they cannot do reversible operations (Piaget 1954, 1962). They lose track of where they were going. The result is a loosely organized set of utterances. This results in a relatively high number of nonfluencies.

Another important aspect in the development of an ability to carry on adult dialogue is roletaking. Roletaking is an encoder's ability to take on the role of the decoder. The encoder plays the role of the decoder to encode the message of presumed best fit for the message, decoder, intent, and context. Both encoder and decoder need to identify and reconcile obstacles in realizing effective communication (Muma 1975a).

Clarke-Stewart (1973) studied interactions between mothers and their children. White children scored higher than black children on the cognitive, language, and social measures used. They also smiled, vocalized, and moved more, and were less physically attached to their mothers. These differences increased with age. Sex differences also increased with age. Boys became more object oriented and girls became more socially oriented. All of them grew increasingly interested in their environment and had less physical interaction with their mothers. The "optimal" maternal care was described as expression of affect, social stimulation, contingent responsiveness, acceptance, stimulation, and age-sex appropriateness. There is a significant correlation between maternal care and child competence. This was manifested by the mothers' verbal stimulation and the children's language development, mothers' presentation of toys and children's skill with objects, and positive social behavior of mothers and children toward each other.

Shatz and Gelman also studied the communicative skills of four-year-old children. Even though the children manifested "egocentrism" on standardized tests, they adjusted their speech when talking to younger children and to adults. Speaking to younger children, the four-year-olds' speech contained more short, simple, and attentional utterances. Similar adjustments were made for formal and informal conditions. Speech patterns to peers were generally comparable to those of adults. Apparently, four-year-olds "talk down" to younger children. Shatz and Gelman indicate there are probably two reasons for this: they are intuitively aware that younger children cannot deal with sophisticated speech (reflecting a social rather than egocentric motivation), and the two-year-olds may have coerced the four-year-olds into conforming because they were more responsive to speech slightly more advanced than their own (Shipley, Smith, and Gleitman 1969).

Schachter et al. (1974) studied the "everyday" interpersonal speech of pre-school children. They report that the age of three seems pivotal. Before then, speech is used mainly (1) to implement desires, (2) to report on self and things, (3) for "me too" self-referring, and (4) for word naming. Moreover, adult-addressed speech is at its highest level. Such speech was termed "primary socially interdependent speech" because its basic function was to ensure gratification during the interdependent attachment of mother and child. After three, primary speech continues but other speech functions appear that reflect a self-other differentiation. "Secondary sociable speech" is characterized by ego-enhancing boasting and peer-addressed collaborative statements. By four and one half to five and one half years, "tertiary socialized speech" begins to emerge. This is adapted to the needs of a listener. More advanced development for the advantaged as opposed to disadvantaged children occurs, but no racial or ethnic differences were found.

Nelson (1973) showed that maternal patterns were specific to language learning style. Referential language learners had mothers who talked about objects, actions, and events. These mothers used language as a descriptive tool. Expressive language learners had mothers who attended to and talked about social manner. These mothers may have implicitly taught their children that language is primarily a social-expressive tool.

Schachter et al. (1976) found that caretaker speech to children varied as a function of development. They showed a three-stage developmental progression for caretaker speech: alter-ego speech, ego-supportive speech, and ego-socializing speech. *Alter-ego speech* includes indicating desires, providing substitutes for prohibitions, commenting on the child, and word teaching. *Ego-supportive speech* centers on enhancing his ego by assisting him to fulfill his desires, encouraging persistence, and so on. *Ego-socializing speech* pertains to appealing to norms. Thus, caretakers adjust their speech to that of children in similar ways as do mothers (Snow 1972).

Summary

The literature on language learning has challenged several misconceptions. The notion of age norms is no longer acceptable as a way of indexing development. Developmental sequences *within* systems are more appropriate. The recent literature is showing an intimate relationship between cognitive-linguistic-communicative systems and processes in language learning. Moreover, it is revealing individual strategies of language learning.

UNIT III
Assessment and Intervention Principles

7

Assessment Principles

Behavior is relative, conditional, complex, and dynamic. Accordingly, clinical assessment must be relative, contextual, process oriented, and dynamic. Contrary to some views, it should not be categorical, quantitative, or normative. These three traditional notions need to be challenged. Clinical assessment should be about an *individual* as he functions in natural contexts (Bronfenbrenner 1977) or deals with systems and processes directly relevant to natural behavior.

There are no definitive tests in the behavioral sciences because behavior is relative, conditional, complex, and dynamic. Assessment should deal with the patterns of behavior of an *individual* in various cognitive-linguistic-communicative systems. A "systems" approach to assessment offers a way of determining the nature of a problem and devising relevant intervention. At best, assessment is probabilistic. The probability of a powerful and useful assessment is high when it is oriented on the naturally functioning systems of an individual. The probability is low when assessment is focused on the products of systems, group performance through norms, or categorical labels and conclusions. Moreover, "ecologically valid" clinical assessment (Bronfenbrenner 1974) offers directly relevant intervention alternatives.

Traditional Assessment: Notions and Fallacies

THE DEFINITIVE TEST FALLACY

It is not uncommon in the clinical fields to hear that an individual's performance on a test relates to the test or what the test is supposed to be about. However, any experienced clinician knows that test performance is not *necessarily* evidence of what the test is supposed to be about. *Just because a test was given to an individual does not mean he was tested.*

Normal test performance varies with repeated testing, and normal performances vary between individuals even though they may be carefully matched.

Statistically, normal variation is estimated by the "standard error of measurement." It is unrealistic to expect that a definitive test can ever be made, because of the variability of individuals. Moreover, it is likely that clinical behavior is even more variable than normal behavior.

The dynamism of cognitive-linguistic-communicative and motoric systems underscores the definitive test fallacy. Dynamism appears in sensation, perception, categorization, and other aspects of cognition. In sensation, acuity thresholds are in continuous dynamic fluctuation. In perception, one's view of an event continually changes in relation to the opportunities to see it repeated, or in relation to time and intervening experience—perceptual drift. Similarly, categorization varies with respect to time and experience. With natural variations added to clinical variations, it is presumptuous to think that test performance is ever definitive. The probabilities are high that test performance is the product of many complexly related variables, only some of which are inherent in a task.

An additional problem is the performance domain and type of task of a test and what the test is supposed to be about. This is a particular problem in cognition and language, where several "tests" are available that claim one thing but "test" another. Some tests of psycholinguistic ability, vocabulary, and memory capacity need to be reexamined for what is claimed of them and the kind of performance they obtain.

THE SINGLE SAMPLE FALLACY

This is closely related to the definitive test fallacy. Here, a clinician is willing to draw conclusions on the basis of a single performance. A test is administered one time and conclusions are drawn regarding intellectual level, grade placement, personality, job placement, and institutionalization. Single test performance is used to label individuals as mentally retarded, learning disordered, reading disabled, etc. Certainly test performance is not the only criterion, but it undoubtedly weighs heavily. Often, when clinicians are pressed as to why a conclusion was made, test performance is usually given as the answer.

THE OBJECTIVITY NOTION

Clinicians are inclined to rely on test performance because it is presumed to be more objective than clinical observation. While test performance reports may be more objective than observations taken in natural "uncontrolled" situations, clinicians should not forget a much more important issue: relevance. Frequently, relevance is sacrificed for objectivity. As a clinician, I would much rather have observations of an individual's natural behavior—even though I may be more subjective about it—than reduce relative, conditional, complex, and dynamic behavior to "objective" categories. It seems that clinical assessment is sometimes so strongly allied to the scientific idea of objectivity that more important issues are sacrificed. "Objectivity" tends to make machines out of people. I can objectively assess the performance of a machine, but am subjective in assessing people. I intend to be subjective *but disciplined* in clinical assessment.

Indeed, it should be said that a clinician's subjectivity is highly desirable. It provides a way of relating to a *client* that transcends *procedure*. Clinicians should be involved with their clients. As with any relationship, clinicians need to take stock of where they are and what their role is. The best ones like their clients and relate to them as people—subjectively. I have seen a few clinicians so committed to the objectivity notion that they were removed physically, emotionally, and psychologically from their clients. They carried out assessment in mathematical equations to the extent that they calculated presumed abilities to the half-month on a developmental scale—a scale that did not have that capacity.

THE ALL-OR-NONE NOTION

If behavior is relative, conditional, complex, and dynamic, more is omitted in a test than is contained in it. Some clinicians have the belief that an entire behavioral domain is not merely described in test performance but that the test exhausts the domain. This logic is found in many clinical reports. If "normal" performance is obtained, some clinicians are prone to say that a client has normal abilities. But, what if the client does not have normal abilities or the test was not relevant to his needs?

Specific assessment procedures are useful for some clients but not for others. Utility is not determined by the type of case or diagnostic label. It is determined by particular needs of particular individuals in particular settings. I once saw a clinician try an assessment procedure on an aphasic individual. The procedure was not productive. The clinician then said that it was unproductive for aphasia in general. This is all-or-none logic. Subsequently she learned that the procedure was useful for some aphasic individuals but not all.

THE CLINICAL GROUP PARADOX

Clinical groups are at once alike and different both within and between one another. This is a paradox with major assessment and intervention implications. Groups such as the mentally retarded, autistic, deaf, learning disabled, and aphasic are alike in many ways. Setting their particular problems aside, it is possible to find many commonalities between individuals with different kinds of clinical problems. Commonalities are undoubtedly more substantial than differences. They provide a license to use normal systems and processes (not normative categories) as a reference in assessment and intervention. Moreover, commonalities allow clinicians to operate with groups. Thus, stutterers exhibit certain behaviors in common. Cerebral palsied children have certain common behaviors. Much of the literature in the clinical fields is based on the notion of commonalities.

However, it is differences that are the most apparent in clinical groups. They are probably at least as important as, if not more important than, similarities in both assessment and intervention. It is all but impossible to find a clinical group whose members are all alike. For example, no two aphasics have the same cognitive-linguistic-communicative problems. Similarly, retarded children are remarkably different. As Alfred Baumeister (who has probably done more research on mental retardation than anyone else) indicated, the most outstanding characteristic of mental retardation is heterogeneity:

> With respect to our discussions regarding the behavior of retarded people, I should say that, if any generalization is possible, the most salient characteristic is variability or heterogeneity of performance, both within and between individuals. On just about every behavioral measure we have taken, retarded subjects, as a group, are significantly more heterogeneous than normal subjects. Of course, the source of this variability is a matter of speculation, but as an empirical fact, it is beyond dispute (Baumeister 1976, personal correspondence).

There is statistical support for the belief that heterogeneity is characteristic of all clinical groups. Clinical behavior is unusual behavior. It departs from normal behavior. Statistically, the further something is from a normal range, the more aberrant it is. The probabilities are high that the aberrant behaviors of several individuals vary because a variety of factors contribute to extreme scores or aberrant performance (Muma and Lubinski, unpublished manuscript).

Beyond the statistical argument, most experienced clinicians readily acknowledge that individual differences are evident in the clinical fields. They agree not only that individual differences are prominent, but also that the same assessment and intervention procedures do not work—indeed are not appropriate—for all individuals in a clinical group. They know that similarities can be used only in a limited way to narrow things down somewhat, and that as they deal with real individuals in the real world, differences are the primary determinants of productive assessment and intervention.

The similarities approach results in a search for *the* assessment and *the* intervention procedures for a clinical group. The individual differences approach regards assessment and intervention as probabilistic and seeks alternative courses of action derived from individual needs and functions. The similarities position is rather widespread in the clinical fields, as evidenced by the wide use of normative assessment and prepackaged *a priori* intervention programs. Most of what is published in the clinical literature, e.g., mean levels of performance, reflects this attitude. This is a paradox because small group designs or clinical studies of individuals can be more relevant to the development of a clinician's skills. The similarities approach offers the opportunity to identify salient variables. The individual differences position requires that salient variables be translated into appropriate operating principles. This translation of variables into principles is neither easy nor apparent. This problem confronted psychologists in the late 1950s. It ultimately led them away from *status* studies (a search for salient variables) to *process* studies (an attempt to understand natural systems and processes). It focused on individuals as they behave naturally, rather than on group performance in unnatural controlled situations. If psychologists found it necessary to shift to small groups and individuals to understand systems and processes, such a shift is all the more necessary in the clinical arena, where individual differences are so evident.

THE QUANTIFICATION NOTION

If behavior is understood to be relative, conditional, complex, and dynamic, it becomes clear that quantification works against a clinician and a client more than for them. Behavior simply cannot be reduced to numbers without losing essential information.

The clinical fields are inundated with normative assessment procedures. While these have a certain value, they undermine the individual. Individuals are not norms and scales. The most that may be said for quantification procedures is that a problem may or may not exist in terms of the particular normative category on the test or scale. The more important issue—the nature of a problem—is not broached by a quantitative procedure. It is my experience that I can determine if a problem exists by describing its nature in terms of underlying systems and processes. This capability is beyond the purview of quantification procedures. Unlike quantitative measures with their tacit assumption that aberrant behavior is "in the child," a complaint is open-ended. The assessment process may very well end with the conclusion that an aberrant behavior is partly an individual's performance and partly in the eye of the complainant.

Quantification of behavior runs the risk of perpetuating arbitrary categories that have no real value. Even though numbers may abound, they do not mean that the quantified categories are either real or relevant. *Data are not necessarily evidence* (Muma and Lubinski, unpublished manuscript). The fallacy that data equal evidence can be found in the *American Association of Mental Deficiency Adaptive Behavior Scale* (Nihira, Foster, Shellhaas, and Leland 1974), the *Individualized Data Base* (Powell 1973; Sounders 1972), *Standards for Residential Facilities for the Mentally Retarded* (1971), *Standards for Community Agencies* (1973), *Program Analysis of Service Systems* (Wolfensberger and Glenn 1973), and the various preschool scales derived from *Vineland Scale of Mental Maturity* (Doll 1965). In the *AAMD Adaptive Behavior Scale,* adaptiveness was bastardized. Adaptiveness is the ability to deal effectively with the various conditions one encounters. Quantification does not permit adaptiveness to be appraised, yet the *AAMD Adaptive Behavior Scale* claims to measure it. The scale contains an exhaustive list of adaptive domains, for each of which an informant is supposed to indicate the relative frequency of a given behavior for an individual. Patterns of occurrence frequency for selected or composite domains are claimed to indicate the individual's adaptiveness. However, adaptiveness is context specific. Reported frequencies of behavior occurrence miss the basic issue that behavior is adaptive or maladaptive according to the conditions in which one functions. It is not important to know whether a child cries frequently. The more important issue is under what conditions he does cry, since crying is adaptive in some circumstances but not in others. Quantification gives data, but that is not necessarily evidence.

THE QUICK AND EASY ASSESSMENT NOTION

Clinicians frequently want quick, easy assessment procedures. They must deal with large numbers of clients. Administrators force them into playing a numbers game regarding the number and type of clients seen and the effectiveness of intervention. It is imperative that clinicians carefully consider what is lost as well as gained by quick and easy measures.

First, because behavior is relative, conditional, complex, and dynamic, it is doubtful that a quick and easy assessment procedure has any value at all. The result is that data are obtained from performance but may not be relevant to the specific needs of an individual. Second, data from such measures are typically categorical. They do not permit interpretation of underlying systems and processes. Third, they allow a clinician to relinquish his responsibility to appropriately appraise a clinical condition. Clinicians frequently claim that such data are evidence of an individual's need for intervention. I have seen many cases in which a clinician acknowledges that data from a quick and easy measure are irrelevant to an individual's needs, and then proceeds to use the data to determine an intervention program. Fourth, there is a legal side to the issue. Legally, clinicians and administrators are responsible for how an individual is assessed and how the assessment process determines intervention. If clinicians and/or administrators use quick and easy measures of questionable value, they may be playing a numbers game that could lead to serious legal consequences. There is concern that much of what has been reported as improvement in language programs probably reflects the operational quality of teachers or clinicians more than gains in children. Nearly every state has seen litigation over the clinical assessment and intervention of retarded children. Fifth, there is accountability. Do clinicians want to be accountable on the basis of numbers or data, or on the basis of evidence? *Ethically and legally, accountability should be an issue of appropriate evidence, not just readily available data.* Siegel (1975) indicated that accountability is premature in the clinical fields in terms of assessment tests. The current national movement for accountability in test performance is naive and misguided. Accountability should be procedural, certified by peer review, as in medicine, clinical psychology, and the legal profession. To commit educational and clinical fields to data base accountability creates unwarranted demands and leads to capricious solutions.

However, the quick and easy assessment notion should be looked at from the personal level to understand the full impact of its potential for neglecting the responsibility to appropriately assess an individual's needs. If I were going to be assessed in a clinic, I would want the best clinician, who knows the latest procedures, rather than one who would do something quick and easy. The medical profession does not rely on quick, easy measures. Doctors do extensive testing and call on consultants. Surely the clinical fields can do the same. Medical doctors employ a variety of assessment procedures. Why is it in the clinical fields that the same procedures are used for nearly every client? Beyond the necessary information on identification, referral complaint, and case history, clinicians should be more selective as to the assessment procedures they will use. The selection should not be in terms of a "diagnostic label or category" assigned to an individual but in terms of his specific behavior.

Clinicians should realize that assessment can be done in a reasonable time, yet provide relevant intervention alternatives to individuals in need of them. Descriptive procedures are not as time consuming or imposing as has been thought (Crystal, Fletcher, and Garman 1976). But more important, they are relevant to an individual's behavior and show a more appropriate direction for intervention.

THE ASSESSMENT/INTERVENTION FALLACY

A legacy of the medical model is a separation between assessment and intervention. This separation seems to be related to the definitive test fallacy and the quantification fallacy, since behavior is thought to be segmentable and reducible to categories and numbers. Thus, it was held that clinical assessment could be based upon normative categories and frequency baselines of performance. Further, it was held that intervention procedures were deducible from such assessments. Thus, assessment was thought to be separate from intervention. The prescriptive assessment movement is based upon this logic.

The current literature indicates that cognitive-linguistic-communicative systems are inextricably related. While natural behavior segments are identifiable, they cannot be isolated or categorized without distortion. One's behavior is not only what one does in a particular behavioral domain but also how that domain is intimately related to other domains, past and present, intrinsically and extrinsically. Behavior must be placed in context rather than being isolated, categorized, or quantified. Assessment must not be separated from intervention. They are continuous, ongoing, and inextricably related.

Clinicians' Perspectives

Clinicians should be aware of five influences in assessment: underlying theoretical-conceptual orientation, perceptions and judgments, ideologies, strategies, and authoritarianism. The preceding six chapters have dealt with the conceptual or substantive knowledge a clinician should bring to assessment. They should have an intervention model that outlines needed information, enabling them to know where they stand in terms of what they know and need to know.

Clinical perceptions and judgments are complex and dynamic. Goldberg (1968) provided a comprehensive review of studies on clinical judgments. Several interesting principles were reported. First, clinical perceptions drift as a function of time and experience. Clinicians do not perceive and judge the same thing the same way every time. Second, even though a rating scale may be used, the points on the scale mean different things to different people. Unless training sessions are used to establish consensus about what each point means, the use of scales is a highly subjective and variable enterprise. Third, naive judges usually have higher reliabilities than sophisticated judges. Naive judges tend not to use all of a scale; they do not make as many distinctions as sophisticated ones. They tend to show a "regression effect." That is, they tend to use the middle of a scale. On a five point scale, they tend to make judgments in the two, three, and four portions. This makes their judgments stable, thereby establishing a relatively high reliability. Sophisticated judges, on the other hand, see new nuances each time they observe an event, so they tend to vary their judgments, leading to relatively low reliability. Reliability of perception and judgment are two different matters. Fourth, when judgments are made on several domains at once, judges tend to focus on only one or two of them. The result is that clinical judgments for those domains are discriminating, whereas they are glossed for the other domains. The full range of distinctions is used for a few scales while the others experience a regression phenomenon. The dynamics of clinical judgments define clinician perspectives as a major dimension of assessment.

As indicated in Chap. 1, ideologies determine what clinicians do. Clinicians may be well informed, but if they do not value their knowledge they will not use it. Many have been so strongly indoctrinated in the use of normative assessment procedures that they frequently have an ideological resistance to the descriptive procedures of systems and processes. Fortunately, nothing beats experience in changing ideologies. I sometimes ask clinicians who resist descriptive procedures to try both. They usually end up preferring the descriptive one. Once they realize that in the actual clinical situation descriptive procedures are more powerful—and not prohibitively time consuming or difficult—ideological resistances are usually dissipated. Once they realize there are alternative strategies and techniques in assessment, they appreciate the challenges and responsibilities. Awareness of clinical challenges and assessment power seem to be persuasive in altering ideology.

AUTHORITARIAN VERSUS ISSUE ORIENTATIONS

The clinical fields tend to adopt authoritarian attitudes, possibly as another legacy of the early influence of the medical model. They often say that they used a particular test or carried out a particular intervention program because someone said it should be used. Much of what is done is authoritarian in nature. Van Riper (1963, pp. 242–305) reported that an effective way to improve articulation problems is the now widely used, even institutionalized, "phonetic analysis" in which a deviant phoneme is identified and its articulation accounted for by initial, medial, and final positions in words, omissions, substitutions, and distortions in production. The traditional placement procedure was based on the notion that a sound is always produced the same way and should be learned in isolation before going on to syllables, words, phrases, and sentences. Current research in child phonology indicates that these notions should be revised (Ingram 1976; Moskowitz 1970). Speech sounds should not be isolated. Important coarticulatory influences are lost. Initial, medial, and final positions of sounds in words have little to do with phonetic influences. Child variations in phonology are not omissions, substitutions, and distortions of phonemes but weak syllable deletions, consonant cluster reduction, voicing phenomena, reduplication, assimilation, and other phonetic phenomena, most of which transcend the phoneme (Ingram 1976; Renfrew 1966; Panagos 1974; Fudge 1969). Another authoritarian position is that phonemic discrimination is essential to phonetic production. While the concept is probably correct, currently available measures of speech sound discrimination are basically invalid because they do not provide a way of assessing discriminations in child speech. Locke (1976) analyzed published speech discrimination tests to see how child variations were incorporated. He found that the Wepman test (1958) was the best, but unfortunately even it had only two (of forty) items related to child variations. This means that much of what has been done with children in speech discrimination is irrelevant—again data but not evidence. Locke has developed a discrimination measure more appropriate to child speech.

How much of what a clinician does is based on authority and how much is issue oriented? No one really knows. However, we should make every effort to recognize authoritarianism and to be issue rather than authority oriented. Clinicians must be constructively critical and open to new evidence and better procedures. To do less is to be a technician rather than a professional. The claim that something has worked before, therefore why change, is the statement of a technician. Technicians focus on authority. Clinicians focus on issues. Authoritarianism has the long-range effect of politicizing a field. The study of issues has the long-range effect of establishing a discipline.

In the assessment of cognitive-linguistic-communicative systems, some hold that normative assessment is needed to establish a baseline. However, given that that behavior is relative, conditional, complex, and dynamic, the issue is how to sustain these properties while carrying out a viable assessment program. It is imperative to maintain natural contexts and/or obtain patterns of performance for functional systems rather than for normative categories.

Assessment Domains

It is one thing to identify assessment domains but quite a different thing to have access to a domain. There is no such thing as a definitive test in the behavioral sciences. Clinicians should think in terms of descriptive procedures rather than tests (Uzgiris and Hunt 1975). Descriptive procedures map one's repertoire or estimated repertoire by describing how an individual functions with a particular system. Descriptive procedures are not frequency counts of behavior categories, as in behavioral analysis. Rather, they deal with the integration of events as an index of underlying systems. This kind of approach is widely used in small group research. It is especially applicable to clinical assessment. Descriptive procedures appear in the works of Piaget, Inhelder, Sinclair-deZwart, R. Brown, Slobin, Bruner, Bowerman, Bloom, Greenfield, Bellugi-Klima, etc.

Assessment domains include cognitive-linguistic-communicative systems. There is a hierarchy in these systems. If an individual does not evidence a cognitive basis for language, there is cause for question about carrying out an assessment of his linguistic systems. Similarly, an individual who is not yet verbal would have only rudimentary communicative skills. This is not an all-or-nothing hierarchy because their acquistion overlaps. Cognitively, an individual should manifest causality, object permanence, and possibly anticipation and alternative action patterns toward and between things before launching his verbal career.

The assessment domains can be divided roughly into two basic questions, each of which has two primary issues. *What* does an individual know about cognitive-linguistic-communicative systems, and *how* does he use what he knows? Notice the parallel between the what and how issues of the individual's capacity to know and use verbal behavior, and the clinician's what and how issues in an intervention model. While knowledge of systems obviously must precede usage, there appears to be a relationship between the two in that usage seems to be the more important. Knowledge is obtained through usage. This is extremely important in intervention. Approaches aimed at teaching knowledge are less effective than those that use available cognitive-linguistic-communicative skills for some purpose, since these systems are purposeful by nature.

The second basic question is: What forms and functions are available to an individual? Forms are the products of systems. The question then becomes what cognitive-linguistic-communicative systems underlie the forms used by an individual. Functions pertain to the intra (cognitive) and inter (communicative) functions of language. Functions of language have priority over form. This is shown by the fact that children learn semantic functions and relationships before form. Moreover, studies on the recall of sentences indicate that functional relationships are retained longer and retrieved easier than forms. Children's performance is disrupted if they have to deal with form alone, as in a sentence imitation task. However, they do much better with the same forms if communicative intent and available reference are functioning. Assessment and intervention programs that are oriented on forms—increasing vocabulary, sentences, structured programming—are not as effective as those that emphasize functions.

Assessment Strategies

Clinicians should know alternative strategies for assessing verbal behavior (Muma 1973b, in press). The assessment of verbal behavior can be conducted according to four approaches: (1) descriptive/quantitative, (2) knowledge/usage, (3) form/function, and (4) informal/formal.

DESCRIPTIVE/QUANTITATIVE ASSESSMENT APPROACHES

These raise a basic issue in clinical assessment: for what purpose is assessment needed? If assessment is needed to resolve the problem/no problem issue, quantitative approaches, with their attendant norms and scales, can be used. Also, follow-up interviewing, as well as observations regarding a referral or clinical complaint, can be done. However, if the assessment is to determine the nature of a problem and provide relevant intervention alternatives, quantitative approaches are inappropriate; descriptive approaches should be used. The determination of the nature of a problem and relevant intervention alternatives is undoubtedly the most important reason for clinical assessment.

Resolution of the problem/no problem issue need not be carried out quantitatively. Follow-up of a clinical referral can resolve whether or not an individual has a problem. The quantification approach is vulnerable to several traditionalist notions and fallacies. If behavior is aberrant as against a norm, clinicians conclude that a problem exists; if it is within normative limits, presumably no problem exists.

However, the quantitative strategy is not so simplistic, especially in clinical assessment where individual differences are considerable and the standard error of measurement is undoubtedly inflated. The large variations of performance of individuals in clinical groups require that repeated samples of behavior be taken (a practice that rarely happens in clinical assessment) in order to resolve the problem/ no problem issue.

Given the inflated standard error of measurement problem in clinical assessment, there is considerable question as to whether a single sample normative assessment has sufficient power to resolve the problem/no problem issue. Statistically, a clinician is faced with what are known as Type I and Type II errors. These are especially common in dealing with large variances and extreme scores. In a Type I error one concludes that something (a clinical problem) exists when in fact it does not. In a Type II error one concludes that something (a clinical problem) does not exist when in fact it does (McNemar 1965, p. 65). Statistically, normative procedures lack the power to deal with the problem/no problem issue.

In addition to a statistical limitation, quantitative assessment procedures have other limitations. These include (a) the specific segment of a domain that is quantified, (b) the assumption that the quantified behavior is intrinsic to an individual, and (c) a lack of intervention implications. When behavior is reduced to numbers, distortion and misrepresentation occur. Psychometric norms deal only with categories. There is no assurance that a particular category is relevant to an individual's clinical needs. Without knowing the relevancy to an individual's needs, validity is a continuing question. Quantitative procedures deal with products of underlying intra- and interpersonal systems. Products are less important in clinical assessment than the patterns of performance that reflect underlying systems. These not only describe the nature of the individual's problem but provide relevant intervention alternatives. Quantitative procedures assume that quantified behavior is intrinsic to an individual. Alas, that may not be so. Behavior reflects complex intra- and interpersonal influences that cannot be parceled out with quantitative procedures. These procedures also lack intervention implications. At best, they suggest that the category of behavior presumed to be aberrant should be corrected by intervention. Typically, intervention is merely an exercise in activities for the segment or category of behavior. Underlying systems are ignored in favor of product oriented intervention.

With all of these shortcomings, it is astonishing that quantitative procedures are so widely used and that so much faith has been invested in them. It is noteworthy that none of the major scholars in the cognitive-linguistic-communicative field use quantitative appraisal. Brown's (1973a,b) mean length of utterance (MLU) comes as close as anything else to a quantitative procedure, but MLU is not an assessment index. It is a device for matching individuals in terms of "linguistic age," not chronological or mental age, and its value is limited to children under approximately four years of age. But in general, quantitative procedures are of dubious value in clinical assessment. They have serious limitations in dealing with the problem/no problem issue and neither deal with the nature of a problem in terms of underlying systems nor provide directly relevant intervention alternatives. Quantitative procedures provide *data to play the numbers game* but not useful *evidence to play the clinical assessment game*.

DESCRIPTIVE PROCEDURES

Descriptive procedures are addressed to underlying systems rather than products. They overcome most of the limitations of quantitative procedures. Patterns of behavior rather than levels of performance describe how an individual functions with various systems. Since patterns of behavior are individual patterns, the data obtained are relevant to that individual, and provide appropriate alternatives in intervention. Descriptive procedures are more powerful than quantitative ones. They deal with an individual's functional command over various systems and thereby provide evidence directly relevant to intervention.

KNOWLEDGE/USAGE ASSESSMENT APPROACHES

Clinicians should make a distinction between knowledge and usage in clinical assessment. Some clinicians will accept any performance (or even lack of performance) as evidence of knowledge of language. But limited performance is not the same thing as limited knowledge. Bloom (1973) showed that young children reduce verbal systems when they cannot deal with the entire system. Reductionism in a linguistic system does not mean that a child lacks knowledge of the linguistic system. He may know it on a rudimentary level but memory processing constraints result in reduction. Slobin (1973), Olson (1973), and Ervin-Tripp (1973) showed several ways in which memory processing constraints operate. Similarly, limited performance on a sentence imitation task is not necessarily evidence of limited knowledge of linguistic systems (Slobin and Welch 1971). Limited sentence imitation could also reflect an absence of communicative intent and available reference in the use of linguistic forms.

An implicit purpose of clinical assessment is to measure what one knows and how he uses it. Since knowledge and usage are often equated, it may be useful to comment on their relationship. First, they are often confounded. It is difficult to know when assessment deals primarily with one or the other. For example, product oriented assessment procedures probably reflect usage, and process and system oriented procedures probably reflect knowledge. Second, evidence about knowledge is always derived from comprehension and production. There are two types of knowledge: knowledge of cognitive-linguistic-communicative systems and knowledge of their appropriate use. Third, assessment procedures reflect a continuum in the degree to which they seem to index knowledge and usage. Fourth, situational constraints can obscure evidence of cognitive-linguistic-communicative knowledge. If performance is sampled in only one context, limited to an *a priori* sample size such as fifty or a hundred utterances, or constrained to one type of verbal behavior, the probabilities are high that situational constraints are being assessed rather than verbal knowledge. Palmer (reported in Kagan 1969) indicated that the intelligence test performance of disadvantaged children probably does not assess intelligence as much as it does the biases of the test situation. Sroufe (1970) made the same point. Stewart (1968) indicated that the performance of disadvantaged children in language assessment reflects their reticence to talk rather than limited knowledge. Fifth, procedural issues about the nature of a task, segmentation, and *a priori* categories may obscure evidence of language knowledge. In short, clinicians should not always conclude that available data are necessarily evidence of knowledge or usage.

FORM AND FUNCTION ASSESSMENT APPROACHES

The assessment of form is somewhat different from that of function. Assessment of form pertains to such things as mean length of utterances, vocabulary size, syntactic structures, transformational operations, or utterance complexity. Berko's (1958) test of English morphology and various sentence recall tasks deals with the assessment of structure or form. Lee's (1966, 1974) and Lee and Canter's (1971) developmental sentence types and scores deal with form. Muma's (1973b) co-occurring and restricted structures procedure deals with form but has a special provision for function. Co-occurring systems are salient to the functional use of a target system. A child will not extend himself in the use of a system unless he can have a certain amount of control over co-occurring systems. The assessment of form deals primarily with the knowledge and use of syntactic and phonological systems.

Form is secondary to function (Bruner 1975; Dore 1975; Halliday 1975; Bates 1976a,b; Greenfield and Smith 1976). It is more important to assess a repertoire of verbal functions than vocabulary size and syntactic structures. Clinicians should note an individual's purposes for being verbal before dealing with the form of his utterances. It is more important to know what he is trying to do with his language than to analyze the words he said. However, after an individual exhibits a repertoire of alternative functions, the assessment process should shift to the form and effi- ciency of coding communicative intent. Bloom (1970, 1973) outlined the impor- tance of the communicative context as a way of knowing what an utterance is about. Her work paved the way for an appraisal of language in which function has priority over form. Schlesinger (1971) and Bowerman (1973) held that communicative intent is the primary determinant of what is said in a given context. Brown (1958b) indicated that things are labeled according to the most appropriate label in a given context. Olson (1970, 1971) held that available reference is the primary determinant of what is said. Recent studies on early stress patterns and labels in infancy (Green- field and Smith 1976; Weinman 1976) indicate that new information/old informa- tion or topic/comment (Gruber 1967) are primary determinants of utterances. Alter- native functions of speech acts have been posited by Bruner (1975), Dore (1974, 1975), Halliday (1975), Searle (1969), and Austin (1962). Thus, communicative context, communicative intent, appropriateness of label, available reference, speech acts, and old information/new information are the essential substantive domains of functional assessment. A functional analysis should also take into account the semantic and relational functions of utterances (Halliday 1975; Dore 1975; Bruner 1975). As Brown (1973a,b) indicated, in Stage I, semantic and relational functions should be acquired by an individual before he launches his linguistic-syntactic career. The establishment of verbal functions reflects Slobin's insight that new functions first appear with old forms and new forms first appear with old functions. Clinical assessment should appraise functions before forms.

Much of clinical assessment is an appraisal of form, usually with psychometric norms. However, a number of individuals have shifted to an assessment of func- tions. This has taken three major directions: underlying cognitive systems, specific semantic and relational functions, and communicative processes. Some clinicians have turned to Piagetian psychology to assess the underlying cognitive functions that may be expressed in language (Morehead and Morehead 1974; Chappell and Johnson 1976; Miller 1976; Moerk 1975). In addition to the excellent framework Piagetian psychology provides, I have found several other frameworks useful in clinical assessment (Muma, in press). Leonard (1973, 1975a,b), Ruder and Smith (1974), and Miller and Yoder (1974) have found that appraisal of specific semantic and relational functions is very useful in clinical assessment. McCaffrey (1976, 1977), Muma (1975a), Longhurst (1974), Longhurst and Siegel (1973), Longhurst and Reichle (1975), and Longhurst and Berry (1975) have found that an evaluation of communicative systems is indispensable for assessing verbal functions.

FORMAL AND INFORMAL ASSESSMENT APPROACHES

A formal assessment procedure is one in which an individual is asked to perform a specific task in which specific behaviors are sought. It is oriented on behavioral domains and categories selected and task-established before encountering the individual in assessment. Since they are established before the assessment process begins, they are *a priori* approaches determined beforehand. Most clinical assessment efforts are of this kind.

Several assumptions underlie formal assessment. First, the domains and categories of verbal behavior are considered relevant to *any* individual's behavior. The problem here is, while domains and categories are undoubtedly important to any individual's ability to function normally, they may not be relevant to a *particular* individual's problems with *particular* verbal systems. Assessment can deal with domains and categories irrelevant to an individual's actual needs. *A priori* approaches run a risk of concluding that no problem exists when in fact one does exist.

On the empirical level, relevance is usually handled either by scaling difficulty as in the ITPA, or by establishing developmental norms as in the PPVT and developmental sentence scores (Lee 1974). Are scaled or developmental norms truly relevant to one's underlying grammatical system? The substitution of norms for individual relevance is questionable because of the shift from individual to group criteria. Group needs are composites. If they are assumed to be useful in assessing individual needs, especially in terms of normative categories, it is assumed that everyone in the group learns language the same way. The evidence from the language learning literature does not support this. Bloom (1970), Nelson (1974), Bloom, Hood, and Lightbown (1974), Bloom, Lightbown, and Hood (1975), Bowerman (in press, a,b), Vygotsky (1962), and Cromer (1974) have shown that language learning is not the same for all children. Rather, language learning strategies vary from child to child. Individual strategies raise serious questions about the value of normative tests and formal assessment. It is noteworthy that the major authorities in child language use neither normative tests nor formal assessment procedures. Their objective is to account for individual strategies according to systems and processes. This is especially important in clinical assessment, where individual differences are so outstanding.

Second, formal approaches are based on the assumption that the rate and sequence of language acquisition can be quantified and used as an assessment index. While verbal behavior can be quantified and/or scaled to reflect developmental trends, there is a major problem concerning the legitimacy of such a procedure. Language acquisition is variable in rate but stable in sequence (Brown, Cazden, and Bellugi-Klima 1969). "Sequence" refers to developmental changes on specific cognitive-linguistic-communicative systems. Individual prerogatives allow for variations in sequence *between* systems. Variations in rate but stable sequences mean that developmental norms obscure major issues in language acquisition. Norms tend to stabilize rate. Indeed, I have seen a "developmental" scale comprehensive to the point that it dealt with a large array of behaviors and had behavioral changes calculated down to a tenth of a month. This is preposterous. No assessment tool in the behavioral sciences has this kind of power. Rates of development are too varied. Clinicians should not be duped into thinking that because developmental milestones occur they can be "calculated" to one-tenth of a month—even six-month intervals. Such precision is not real.

Third, formal approaches are removed from context. Tasks are highly specific. Behavior is evaluated under specific conditions and is limited to certain aspects. Thus, it is atypical rather than representative. Representativeness is a major issue in clinical assessment. The more representative behavior is, the greater are the opportunities to understand it. Formal and *a priori* approaches should be relegated to a supplementary role.

Informal assessment approaches are those in which an effort is made to assess behavior in natural or near natural contexts, under the assumption that it is representative. They have the capability of dealing with individual differences in a productive way because the behavior is representative and the verbal domains are not reduced to *a priori* categories. Unlike formal approaches, the individual determines the dimensions of cognitive-linguistic-communicative behavior available for assessment. These are limited by the nature of situations, but not by the forms and functions of formal tasks and *a priori* scales. The assumption is that assessment will correspond to typical behavior, and evidence and conclusions should be representative and relevant. This evidence can be directly translated into an intervention program predicated on functionally relevant real-life activities. Informal assessment has its greatest power when behavior is placed on descriptive terms: how various cognitive-linguistic-communicative systems operate.

Informal assessment requires that a clinician have a basic knowledge of cognitive-linguistic-communicative systems. It requires that behavior be representative. These place considerable responsibilities on clinicians to make clinical assessment representative as opposed to a numbers game. Clinicians have several ways of assessing cognitive-linguistic-communicative systems, some of which are more appropriate and powerful than others.

Client's Behavior: Perceived and Inferred

There are two basic issues in clinical assessment: Does a client have a problem? What is the nature of the problem? The second issue should be treated so assessment provides directly relevant alternatives in intervention. Thus, the two basic issues are problem/no problem and nature of a problem.

Much of clinical assessment pertains only to the problem/no problem issue. Relatively little is done about the nature of a problem. In view of the limitations of normative procedures, assessment in resolving the problem/no problem issue is open to question. As for the nature of a problem issue, there are two major aspects: intrinsic and extrinsic. A problem may be the result of an individual's intrinsic capacities and limitations or of influences external to the individual. The problem/ no problem issue also has intrinsic and extrinsic aspects. Perhaps the best way to deal with the issue is by follow-up interviewing and observation. These ascertain not only whether a problem exists but whether it is intrinsic to the individual or extrinsic to him. Normative assessment deals only with the intrinsic behavior of individuals. The intrinsic and extrinsic aspects of a problem are best dealt with by a description of the intra- and/or interpersonal systems and processes that pertain to the problem. Figure 7-1 outlines the problem/no problem issue and nature of a problem issue in intrinsic and extrinsic aspects.

Figure 7-1 *Intrinsic and extrinsic aspects of the problem/no problem and nature of the problem issues in clinical assessment.*

No Problem/Problem		Nature of a problem	Directly relevant intervention alternatives
Intrinsic aspects	Extrinsic aspects	Intrinsic aspects	Extrinsic aspects
Quantitative procedures	Descriptive follow-up of referral complaint	Descriptions of intrapersonal cognitive-linguistic-communicative systems	Descriptions of interpersonal cognitive-linguistic-communicative systems
Descriptive follow-up of complaint			

In clinical assessment individual differences are of the utmost importance. Descriptive procedures are especially useful because they deal not only with the intrinsic and extrinsic issues of a problem but also with individual differences. They provide directly relevant alternatives for intervention.

Summary

Current clinical assessment approaches should be critically reexamined with an eye to the definitive test fallacy, the single sample fallacy, the objectivity notion, the all-or-none notion, the clinical group paradox, the quantification notion, the quick and easy assessment notion, and the assessment/intervention fallacy. The issue of accountability must be carefully reviewed, for it is at present committed to a numbers game with the long-range effect of making technicians rather than clinicians and authoritarian organizations rather than professional ones. Clinicians should know about their underlying theoretical-conceptual orientation, the dynamics of their clinical perceptions and judgments, their ideologies and reliance on authority. Unfortunately, the clinical fields tend to be person or authority oriented rather than issue oriented. The assessment process should deal with cognitive-linguistic-communicative systems, and with behavior in terms of relativity, conditionality, complexity, and dynamism. It should be descriptive rather than normative, categorical, and simple. Clinicians should know alternative assessment strategies. They should realize that clinical assessment has two major issues: problem/no problem, and nature of a problem. The latter requires that the assessment process deal with individual differences and be ecologically based. The nature of a problem is the most substantial issue in assessing and appraising progress—the issue of accountability.

8

Intervention
Principles

The primary function of assessment is to account for the nature of a problem in order to provide relevant intervention alternatives. Assessment is continuous throughout intervention. Assessment and intervention are not only inextricably related, but ongoing.

State of the Art

Most of what is done in intervention is arbitrary, capricious, and authoritarian. We are very naive about what to do. There is good reason to be this way. We are only beginning to understand the nature and complexities of cognitive-linguistic-communicative systems. Theories of intervention are practically nonexistent. The positions at present are little more than authoritarianism. Although highly structured intervention programs are available, the probability is high that they may be of little relevance to individual needs. They may serve as a mechanism for relinquishing the clinician's responsibilities in intervention. As I indicated in Chap. 1, Chomsky and Cazden warned that what is done in intervention may be contradictory to what an individual needs. Chomsky felt that the learning situation should not be constrained by what an interventionist thinks it should be. The special needs of an individual's intellect are not yet explicitly known. "What little we know about human intelligence would at least suggest something quite different: that by diminishing the range and complexity of materials presented to the inquiring mind, by setting behavior in fixed patterns, these methods may harm and distort the normal development of creative abilities" (Chomsky, pp. 66–67, cited in Cazden 1972a, p. 28). "Maybe the child is such a powerful consumer that the nature of the environment matters little as long as certain ingredients are present; maybe teaching specific primitive responses will even ultimately retard the development of more advanced processes" (Cazden 1972a, p. 28).

Given the state of the art of intervention (and at the risk of being authoritarian), I propose that the best we can do is *describe (not quantify) an individual's command (knowledge and use) of cognitive-linguistic-communicative systems as he functions naturally or near naturally, then exploit his behavior.* This intervention principle is central to this chapter, indeed to the book.

Given the state of the art in clinical assessment and intervention, knowledge of cognitive-linguistic-communicative systems, the importance of individual differences in clinical conditions, the failings of normative assessment, and the questionable value of highly structured, *a priori,* authoritarian intervention programs, it behooves clinicians to seriously consider intervention as exploitation of an individual's command of cognitive-linguistic-communicative systems as he functions naturally.

Basic Dimensions: Natural and Contrived

Clinicians should be aware of the basic dimensions of intervention, and the similarities and the differences between natural learning and contrived learning. Clinicians who know about these basic dimensions soon realize that many intervention programs that claim to be based upon normal language development fall considerably short of their claim. Many of them ignore basic dimensions or constrain the dimensions in highly structured programs to such an extent that children are made to deal with contrived, irrelevant things. These are the kinds of programs that worried Chomsky and Cazden. An intervention effort based on one or a few basic dimensions may be ineffective not because of the particular dimension(s) but because covarying dimensions may nullify or obviate desired effects. It is imperative that basic dimensions not be isolated or too explicitly structured.

These basic dimensions are *content, pacing, sequencing, reinforcement and motivation,* and *context.* There are important differences between natural learning and intervention for each of these. The probability is high that the less tampering is done with basic dimensions, the greater the power that will be obtained in intervention. Exploitation of an individual's own behavior in natural contexts is a low level of tampering, whereas conforming an individual to highly structured programs is major tampering. This is not to say that highly structured intervention should always be discouraged. There are occasions when I revert to using it, but I am aware of a loss of power—not so much in the activity itself but in the objective of getting desirable results in usable forms for natural purposes.

CONTENT

In normal language learning, content is determined by the natural contexts in which one functions. An individual learns the language and dialect of his community, and to use it as his community does. When he moves, he learns the language of his new community. In this process a child spontaneously extracts information from communicative contexts and ongoing communicative functions (Schlesinger 1971;

Bowerman 1973; Macnamara 1972; Bruner 1975; Dore 1975; Halliday 1975). What is learned—content—is what is used in one's environment. Content in natural language learning is language and dialect with a high utility value.

On the other hand, content in intervention is usually not the same thing. Rather, it is what a teacher or clinician thinks an individual should learn. Individuals who speak nonstandard English have been subjected to programs in which their natural speech was to have been "corrected." I have seen clinicians devote content to "increasing vocabulary size" and "sentence building," "correcting" nonstandard English, and similar intervention activities. Unfortunately, they do not compare to content in normal language learning in natural contexts. These intervention efforts are patently different and probably too far removed to have any important relationship to needed content. Such content emphasizes structure and is nearly void of the most important content area, verbal functions. This is not to say that children may not learn in these activities; they may. The serious question is how relevant the content is to what they *need* to learn. I can count the number of cars passing a certain street sign but I doubt if that knowledge will be very useful in learning how to repair cars. Similarly, children might increase the number of labels they can attach to a set of pictures, but the more important function—appropriate labeling for a variety of referents—has not been accomplished.

The determination of *relevant* content can be deduced better from a client as he functions naturally as opposed to asserting *a priori* content on him. Exploitation of natural contexts increases the probability that content is relevant and thus appropriate.

PACING

In normal first language learning, the rate of learning is notoriously variable (Brown 1973a,b). Spurts of learning seem to occur. Overtly, a child has periods of various duration in which he shows increased knowledge and use of various forms and functions. Covertly, the intervals between these spurts probably contain differentiations and reorganizations. Rates of learning for cognitive-linguistic-communicative systems are not only highly variable *within* a child but normal children vary considerably in the rate of learning. These natural variations mean that age is not a good indicator of development (Brown 1973a,b). The various developmental profiles commonly used in clinical assessment usually do not have accuracy within one- or two-year spreads. They are only gross indices.

In intervention, pacing is usually determined by a clinician or is prescribed by a program. Clinicians have individuals practice something until it is nearly or completely learned. When the clinician is satisfied, the individual goes on to another content area. Some packaged programs instruct clinicians and individuals to shift to another content level after 80 to 100 percent correct performance. Automated programs automatically switch or branch to new content after a specific number of trials on a given topic.

Who knows the "proper" number of trials for a particular individual? The literature on natural learning indicates that this number is determined by an individual's internal readiness to learn (Hunt 1969) and opportunities to be actively involved in learning (Bruner 1961). Frequency of occurrence is not important in learning or using a label (Brown 1958a; Brown and Hanlon 1970). What is important is the extent to which a label *functions* in denoting shared distinctiveness (Dollard and Miller 1950), or as Bruner (1975) put it, regulates joint attention and joint action. Repeat trials may actually be harmful rather than beneficial. Variations of experience are essential to learning, but repetitions imposed from outside may be deleterious. Lack of variation is probably the primary cause of *overlearning*—a problem in which an individual learns something so well it is seen as an entity rather than an example of a principle or concept. Thus, further learning and generalization are obstructed.

Kagan's (1965, 1971) theory on the development of attending patterns points out the importance of variation in cognition. Brown and Bellugi (1964) reported a cyclic interaction between mother and child in which a child sometimes repeats a reduced version of his mother's utterance. The repetitions may go two or three times before the child varies the utterance (Ervin 1966). Bloom (1972) contended that a child may need two or three repetitions to get focused on the code as it functions in communicative context. Some children may not repeat, but others will (Bloom, Hood, and Lightbown 1974). A child may spontaneously repeat some things but not others. The need for repetition and variation is determined by the child as he functions in natural contexts. It would be presumptuous to require him to repeat things. Natural repetition is selective, perhaps reflecting new information in the context of old, much in the same way as early stress variations (Wieman 1976). Bloom, Hood, and Lightbown (1974) showed that spontaneous imitation occurs in structures that children are in the process of learning. Presumably, selectively imitated structures become salient in certain linguistic and referential contexts.

SEQUENCING

Natural sequencing is highly stable (Brown 1973a,b). It is different from the sequences in most intervention and assessment programs, even those that claim to be based upon language development. Natural sequencing refers to stages in the emergence of systems. Typically these are neither linear, quantitative, nor reflected in "developmental" scales. They are hierarchical, differentiating and reorganizing previous stages. There are qualitative differences from one stage to the next that can best be described rather than quantified. Piagetian psychology outlines rather elaborate developmental sequences. Brown's five tentative stages in early language learning are descriptive in nature.

Interestingly enough, linguistic and cognitive systems have their own developmental sequences, but sequences *between* systems are highly variable. Thus, children go through the same sequences in learning negations, interrogatives, relative clauses, inflectional rules, etc., but will vary in learning negations before questions or relative clauses, etc. *Between* systems, considerable variability in sequencing occurs, but *within* them the sequences seem to be highly stable. The opposite case is found in many intervention programs. Most if not all structured programs establish stable sequences between systems but rarely are sequences provided within them. Moreover, at least one widely used intervention sequence contradicts a predominant sentence processing strategy in early language learning. In intervention, sentences are usually "built" by beginning with the subject, adding the verb, and finally the object. However, research by Brown, Cazden, and Bellugi-Klima (1969) and Limber (1977) indicates that young children prefer to learn verb-object prior to and more elaborately than subject-verb, since verb-object is easier for recency processing effects and entails new information about a topic.

Sequencing in an intervention program, particularly an *a priori* program, makes it difficult to learn, since it does not correspond to the sequences needed by a child. *A priori* sequences infringe on the power of intervention by forcing individuals to learn sequences inappropriate for them and to abandon sequences that they would normally follow.

REINFORCEMENT AND MOTIVATION

Natural reinforcement is inherent in an act. If an individual is motivated to say something and if what he says in a certain context leads to what he expects, the act and the result are reinforcing. When a baby says, "Mama," and his mother does whatever the baby intends, he is reinforced for his utterance. Behavior itself is naturally reinforcing when it results in expected outcomes. Extrinsic reinforcers seldom occur.

However, a major dimension of intervention is presumed reinforcement. Indeed, in some intervention programs, reinforcement is central. Clinicians become concerned about types and schedules of reinforcers. Extrinsic reinforcement is thought to follow a continuum from such tangible reinforcers as candy, money, and tokens to social reinforcers such as the clinician's smile or "Good!" Tokens and money are considered delayed reinforcers because the actual reward is acquired by cashing in the tokens. Different reinforcement schedules lead to different rates of acquisition. Continuous reinforcement is not as potent as fixed or variable ratio schedules. Continuous reinforcement is an award for each correct act (sometimes each effort). In a fixed ratio schedule, some (such as every other) correct acts are reinforced. In a variable ratio schedule the same portion of correct acts are rewarded but the sequence is varied. An intermittent schedule is the most powerful of all. Reinforcement is unpredictable. This is somewhat similar to natural reinforcement since extrinsic reinforcement happens only occasionally. However, in natural reinforcement different things are reinforced and the act itself is the reinforcer when it is deemed reinforcing (Kagan 1967). It may be that concern about reinforcers is misguided, since the individual judges what is reinforcing. The tokens, coins, and other extrinsic reinforcers may be little more than another numbers game for clinicians, with little if any value to individuals needing intervention.

CONTEXTS

Natural learning always occurs in real contexts. Moreover, individuals actively participate in these contexts, perceiving, representing, and encoding and decoding communicative intents on topic and comment, available reference, and linguistic systems. However, clinicians maintain an old medical notion that intervention is treatment. Individuals are removed from cognitive-linguistic-communicative contexts to be given therapy. Clinicians should realize that the more an individual is removed from natural functions in natural contexts, the more power is lost in intervention. Language intervention should occur in natural contexts in natural ways about natural things. Under those circumstances the probability is high that what will happen is not only directly relevant but will generalize to other natural events. Such intervention is ecologically valid.

Clinicians should consider the extent to which intervention corresponds to normal learning. Issues of content, pacing, sequencing, reinforcement and motivation, and natural contexts are basic to any intervention effort. Clinicians may need to intentionally depart from normal language learning. Baer (reported in Bateman 1974) held that it may be necessary to depart from normal language learning because individuals in a clinic have failed to use normal opportunities. Whether clinicians attempt to emulate normal language learning or not, it behooves them to know what they are doing in regard to basic intervention dimensions and alternatives available to them.

The following is a brief review of some widely used clinical intervention orientations. This review is made with particular reference to behavioristic and mentalistic orientations (discussed below) and the major dimensions of intervention. Rees (1973b) reviewed six widely used bases for language intervention: structural complexity, mean length of utterance, developmental sequence, cognitive underpinnings, perceptual strategy, and dialect. She held that structural complexity and mean length of utterance are nonproductive for assessment and intervention. The former is not well understood and the latter is a performance rather than cognitive index. Compositely, they are both structural. Structural orientations are generally not very productive. Developmental sequence is productive because it provides useful information about the emergence of systems. However, Rees overlooked one important aspect to the productivity of developmental sequences: some clinical conditions may not reflect a "delay" or arrested learning process but may indeed be deviant. Cromer (1974) raised the same basic issue regarding retarded individuals. Morehead and Ingram (1973) substantiated that some clinical language problems may indeed have deviations.

In regard to cognitive bases for language, Rees indicated that the various models (Piagetian, regulatory, mediational, etc.) constituted "incompatible" views.

On the contrary, I would hold that the cognitive models only appear to be incompatible because they deal with different cognitive processes, because Rees's considerations were not placed in a comprehensive perspective of the cognitive underpinnings of verbal behavior, and she did not consider the distinction between cognitive and communicative functions of language. "Perceptual strategy" pertains to developmental stages in the comprehension of language; dialect pertains to language differences. The Rees paper did not have a systematic discussion of the basic decisions in language training as they deal with content, sequence, pacing, reinforcement, motivation, and context. Each of the areas she dealt with considered one of the major dimensions but no overall framework was given.

Holland (1975) attempted to define language intervention as a "communication microcosm." In the section called "Learning Childrenese" she defined one-word utterances as holophrases, thereby establishing the clinical utility of a core lexicon. Unfortunately, the holophrase concept had been seriously questioned (Brown 1973a,b; Dore 1975) on the grounds that children do not have alternative meanings for a single word; they seem to have complexive meanings (Vygotsky 1962; Bowerman in press,a,b). This means that the core lexicon delineated by Holland is topologically appealing but should not be *a priori* determined. A core lexicon should be derived from high-utility dynamic information in an individual's natural environment. Moreover, it should be derived from his communicative intents. Holland's notion of "organicity" emphasized the importance of assessment and intervention and corresponds to what Bronfenbrenner (1974) calls "ecologically valid." The "here and now" is relevant to early stages of language learning (Bloom 1970, 1973), when a child encodes available references that later he will move away from. Holland placed a much-needed emphasis on dealing with language as a vehicle in the communicative process, as opposed to a clinical product. She indicated that verbal behavior is active, dynamic, interpersonal, reinforcing through function, and multi-code (linguistic, nonlinguistic, etc.).

The core lexicon was claimed to be maximally exploitable, generalizable, and to have a maximum potential for unassisted growth and use. Each item was selected because (1) it presumably provided short, quick transitions from one- to two-word utterances, (2) it was claimed to be appropriate for psycholinguistic thereapy models, and (3) it could be combined to produce five phrases, each of which has two semantic functions. The last criterion was probably made to reflect Slobin's (1970) principle that new forms first express old functions. Holland's article is primarily about content.

MacDonald and Blott (1974) developed the *Environmental Language Intervention Strategy* (ELIS). It emphasizes the semantic functions of language. Their program is described in terms of content, imitation, and context interpreted in terms of rules, generalization, and context. Content is the semantic functions of two-word utterances first realized in imitation and later spontaneously in conversation and play. The communicative context is a way of interpreting communicative intent both linguistically and nonlinguistically. The program is very attractive for dealing with individuals in the one- and two-word stage. The incorporation of the imitation process might be regarded as optional in view of the study by Bloom, Hood, and Lightbown (1974), which shows there are individual strategies in the use of imitation in language learning. Leonard's (1973, 1975,a,b) approach is similar to MacDonald and Blott in content and modeling activities. Leonard stresses semantic functions and relations in early intervention.

Miller and Yoder (1974) and Ruder and Smith (1974) have developed excellent rationales for language intervention. Their programs are similar to those of Leonard and MacDonald and Blott. I (Muma 1975b) have reviewed the Miller and Yoder and Ruder and Smith approaches. Both of them attempt to bring together behavioristic and mentalistic orientations with the idea that behaviorism provides procedures whereas mentalism provides content, particularly information on acquisition processes. Both approaches emphasize the shift in language intervention away from a syntax approach to a semantic one. Miller and Yoder indicate that a program should be child rather than clinician oriented. This is an important statement because clinicians tend to determine content, sequence, pacing, and reinforcement, *before* meeting a child. The *a priori* preschool programs tend to foster clinician oriented approaches (Cazden 1972b; Bartlett 1972). Miller and Yoder set the following intervention criteria:

1. Realistic set of communication exit behaviors
2. Normal cognitive-linguistic development determines sequences
3. Intervention based on ongoing interpersonal interactions
4. Provision for active participation
5. Systematic manipulations

These are augmented by the desire to deal with natural settings; a variety of communicative modes, devices, and functions; and the wish to maintain the functional integrity of verbal skills rather than isolate them. Intervention should be flexible, dealing with individual differences. Mental retardation reflects a slowing of acquisition. Content should deal with both structure and function but early acquisition should emphasize function. Sequence should be determined by frequency of occurrence and order of acquisition. The Piagetian framework provides a good cognitive orientation to early and prelinguistic development. Communicative functions are deducible from ongoing experience and encoding can be inferred from such experience. Relational functions are learned before semantic functions. Slobin's principle that new forms are learned with old functions and new functions learned with old forms is translatable to intervention. Finally, comprehension is more advanced than production.

I feel this approach is well developed, but I have two reservations. First, they hold that mental retardation reflects a slowing process. The literature only partially supports this position (Cromer 1974). Retardation may be a slowing or an arresting process, or an aberration. Second, the position that relational functions precede semantic functions is not well supported by the data, notwithstanding Bloom's (1970, 1973) work.

Ruder and Smith (1974) developed a similar rationale, though it differs in the following respects: (1) more emphasis is placed on structure by orienting the program on agent-action-object utterances and transformational operations and modifications, (2) imitation is incorporated as an initial intervention activity, and (3) modeling and expansions of structure are employed. They describe assessment in terms of informal, formal, and ongoing approaches. They indicate that a formal assessment strategy has limited clinical value because its implications are not apparent.

Cazden (1972b) and Bartlett (1972) have reviewed a number of language intervention programs for early childhood education. The Blank and Solomon (1968, 1969) and Blank and Frank (1971) programs are the most promising, since they are process oriented.

Intervention Agents

The traditional therapy model has the role of the clinician as dispenser of therapy or treatment. However, this function is one of the least important ones. I have been a clinician for about twenty years. Over those years, I have had the greatest success when I work with a variety of intervention agents. The best clinician I have ever seen was a three-and-one-half-year-old girl playing with a four-year-old boy. The boy's mother and I watched, analyzed, commented, and planned for the activities. Clinicians should take advantage of a variety of intervention agents. They need not feel compelled always to "treat" an individual. We can often accomplish more by working through parents, peers, siblings, and even pets. Parents are so important and helpful that I place a great deal of emphasis on parental involvement.

Most parents at the outset do not know what to do. For that matter, neither do I, because it is necessary to study a child before attempting to change his behavior in a productive way. We observe children doing a variety of things with different people. As we focus on certain behavior, various alternatives are tried (several times) until something productive happens. Parents and clinicians must work together to discover the most productive approaches. Usually, parents become so involved that toward the end the process reverts to them. Subsequent visits are made, but in the long run they become viable intervention agents not simply doing exercises but productively carrying out, analyzing, and modifying interventive approaches. This is not a paraprofessional strategy to increase the manpower of a clinician. It is the result of intervention when the intervention process takes its natural course.

Clinical Conditions

Individuals needing clinical assessment and intervention vary considerably. There are major differences *among* clinical groups, such as the mentally retarded, learning-disabled, "delayed language," reading-disabled, deaf, cerebral palsied, aphasic, articulation disordered, and autistic. Considerable variation is also found *within* clinical groups. Since variability is so evident, it is necessary to focus assessment and intervention on individual needs and the conditions of those needs. The best way to deal with individual needs is by describing his command of various systems as he functions naturally or nearly naturally. It is apparent that traditional clinical groups are not very useful in separating assessment and intervention procedures and techniques. Holland (1975) made a similar observation. Retarded children vary considerably in their aberrations of cognitive-linguistic-communicative systems. It is inappropriate to assess or treat all retarded children alike. The same is true for individuals with learning disabilities, aphasia, autism, delayed language, and so on. Clinical categorization and labeling have been carried to such an extreme that similarities have been exaggerated and obscure substantial individual differences. Once an individual is categorized and labeled as having a given clinical condition, assessment and intervention usually follow *a priori* prescribed paths.

Rather than categorize and label clinical conditions, it is more appropriate to focus on individual differences in specific cognitive-linguistic-communicative systems. The clinician should be interested in whether an individual has an iconic as opposed to symbolic processing mode, regardless of whether he was classified as retarded, autistic, deaf, etc. He needs to know where the individual functions in the Piagetian stages. Linguistically, he needs to know which semantic functions and relations an individual knows and uses regardless of the clinical group he is in. He needs to know whether the client is operating with a projective or Euclidean spatial awareness. He needs to know which concepts are limited to focal attributes and which extend to peripheral attributes, which indicate overextension or underextension in labeling, etc. Communicatively, he needs to know if the individual has a roletaking attitude and how he deals with anaphoric and deitic reference. Requisite knowledge of cognitive-linguistic-communicative systems and ways of intervening is the same for all clinical groups. The clinical fields tend to stress contrasts, but once assessment and intervention begin, clinical group differences are subordinated.

The *clinical groups position* tends to emphasize similarities within groups and differences between them. The result is an orientation on and a search for *the* assessment and *the* intervention procedures. This position deals with categorization and labeling. On the other hand, the *individual differences position* tends to deemphasize similarities within and differences between groups. It is oriented on active, dynamic, complex, and integrated systems in which assessment and intervention alternatives are related to the individual's needs and consist of different sets of alternatives for each one. This position deals with descriptions of the ongoing, naturally functioning systems available to the individual.

Behaviorism and Mentalism

There are two major philosophies of intervention: behaviorism and mentalism. Clinicians should know about them, since they not only dominate the applied fields but contrast in their underlying assumptions and execution. Undoubtedly, behaviorism is the more common in American education and clinical work. However, there has been a shift toward mentalism in recent years because of the interest in Piagetian psychology and the influence of psycho-sociolinguistics.

Behaviorism and mentalism were first articulated by Locke and Rousseau, in the seventeenth and eighteenth centuries, respectively. The basic assumption of behaviorism is that the child is molded by his experiences. As a passive recipient of environmental influences, he is presumed to be at the mercy of external influences. Accordingly, the primary intervention strategy is stimulation. Content, pacing, sequencing, reinforcement, and context are presumed to be in the control of the interventionist. Learning is to be dispensed at the discretion of teachers and clinicians, who are viewed as repositories of knowledge to be imparted by directives, instruction, drill, and exercises. Learning is presumed to be overt and observable. It is thought to be reinforced by rewards. Because it is observable, it is measurable through tests and frequency counts. This philosophy is usually carried out in an instructional or lecture format in which the teacher tells children what, when, where, how, and why something is to be learned. The learning process is invested in the teacher or clinician.

Behaviorism dominates traditional American education and clinical work, so it is rather easy to observe it in action. It has been formalized in the behavior modification movement (Skinner 1957; Krasner 1958, 1976; Staats 1969; Guess, Sailor, and Baer 1974); and somewhat by modeling theory (Bandura 1971).

Programs that contain *a priori* material, are highly structured, or deal with explicit categories and reinforcement reflect behavioristic attitudes. This philosophy has been called the "jug-and-mug" approach. A teacher selectively "pours" knowledge into the head of a child. Individual needs are subordinated to group needs and general assumptions about learning. This occurs through normative levels of performance and presumed explicitness in the learning process.

I once observed a striking example of behaviorism. I was watching an aide in an institution for the retarded "teach" colors to eight children from eight to ten years old. She began with the first child, asking him to name the colors she pointed to. The boy did not name them but pointed to them. She went to the next child, who gave less precise responses. Meanwhile, the aide broke the continuity of the task on two occasions by directing the second child to sit up and "pay attention." During this time, the girl fourth in line was spontaneously naming each of the colors. When the aide asked this girl to name the colors, the girl exhibited the same behavior as previous children. The aide tried to prod her into naming the colors, but the girl did not do it. The aide then turned to me and said, "See, she doesn't know her colors."

This aide was operating under a behavioristic notion of intervention. The behavior she was looking for did not appear when, where, and how she wanted it. She concluded that it did not exist.

In contrast to behaviorism, the basic assumption of mentalism is that a child is an active learner rather than a passive one. Children actively take information from experience. Stimulation is necessary but insufficient by itself. Environmental influences are influential but must be selectively utilized when a child is cognitively-emotionally ready. Active processing means that issues of content, pacing, sequencing, reinforcement, and context are at the child's discretion rather than the clinician's. This makes clinicians facilitators rather than directors of learning. Facilitators try to deduce where a child is in learning and the most optimal conditions for his learning. Then they try to facilitate the learning process by providing rich and varied experiences relevant to what, when, where, how, and why the child learns. Mentalism is a child rather than clinician oriented approach.

Mentalism appears in Piagetian assessment and intervention programs and the true Montessori program (Hunt 1968; Elkind 1967a; Rambusch 1962). It is important that it be a *true* Montessori program. I have visited a number of "Montessori" schools and found programs that bore little resemblance to Montessori principles. I even found some that were heavily influenced by behaviorism.

In language intervention with preschool children, the philosophy of Blank and her colleagues is consistent with mentalism (Blank and Soloman 1968, 1969; Blank and Frank 1971).

In recent years there has been a significant shift toward mentalism. For example, Krasner (1976), an eminent behaviorist, recently lamented the death of behavior modification. This shift seems to have been brought about by several factors. First and foremost has been the resurgence of Piagetian psychology. This has shaken the American empirical tradition, with its reliance on group data and norms, experimental paradigms, levels of performance, etc. It has redirected concern for ecologically valid evidence (Bronfenbrenner 1977; Proshansky 1976; Brooks and Baumeister 1977), individual differences and variations (Gagne 1967; Kagan and Kogan 1970; Underwood 1975), and alternative styles of learning and performance.

Second, studies on active versus passive learning have shown that active participation is much more potent. Studies on concept development involving discrepancy learning have shown that both covert and overt procedures operate as children process experience (Kagan and Lewis 1965). Studies on memory storage and retrieval strategies have shown that active processes are operating (Jenkins 1973, 1974). Indeed, perception is an active process (Garner 1966). In language learning, active processes operate in the induction of latent structure (Brown and Bellugi 1964), differentiation and reorganization of rules (Menyuk 1964a; Klima and Bellugi-Klima 1969; Cazden 1968; Saltz, Soller, and Sigel 1972; H. Clark 1973a, E. Clark 1973a,b, 1974), and extraction of information from communicative contexts and intents (Schlesinger 1971; Bowerman 1973, 1974). Chunking experiences involve active perceptual and conceptual operations (Simon 1974). Classificatory skills can be mediated by actively labeling or demonstrating functions of items. The Piagetian sensorimotor stages entail active processing. They are necessary precursors to concrete and formal operations, notwithstanding the perceptual underpinnings also needed (H. Clark 1970, 1973a). Symbolic or representational operations entail active processes. As Bruner (1964, p. 4) said,

> In effect language provides a means, not only for representing experience, but also for transforming it. . . . Once the child has succeeded in internalizing language as a cogni-

tive instrument, it becomes possible for him to represent and systematically transform the regularities of experience with far greater flexibility and power than before.

Third, the success of "Sesame Street" and "The Electric Company" shows the importance of active learning. Both programs are designed according to the mentalistic philosophy. They have been highly successful in getting and maintaining attention and fostering learning in preschool and early school aged disadvantaged children. These children have been virtually written off by behavioristic educators. Fourth, active learning makes learning relative rather than absolute. Learning occurs according to not only available conditions but also how an individual avails himself of his opportunities. Concepts are continually differentiated and reorganized rather than learned as a one-shot affair. According to Flavell (1970), concepts acquire increased validity, status, and accessibility in the course of development. Memory is not constant but dynamic and varies with experience (Jenkins 1973, 1974). Memory capacities vary as a function of previous knowledge, chunking strategies, type of memory process, means of coding, storage, and retrieval. In sum, the reasons for the shift from behaviorism to mentalism are compelling.

Intervention Strategies

Clinicians should be aware of the six major language intervention strategies. These give clinicians important options for devising intervention. The first four deal with the acquisition of grammatical systems. The last two are concerned with the use of verbal systems.

FIRST LANGUAGE LEARNING

The aim of this strategy is to reconstitute normal first language learning processes. This is done by emulating various aspects of first language learning. The underlying assumption is that if natural learning processes can be reestablished, spontaneous learning will occur.

There are several limitations to this strategy. First, in most instances it is undertaken after "critical" or optimal periods of language learning have passed. Lenneberg (1967) indicated that the most critical period of language learning is from birth to about four years. It may be that a first language learning strategy is most effective (if effective at all) during the optimal learning period. Second, individuals who need intervention have already failed to avail themselves of normal language learning opportunities (Baer, cited in Bateman 1974). If the failure was due to arrested learning, a first language learning strategy may be warranted. However, if the failure was due to an inability to learn in normal ways, the strategy would be inappropriate. Unfortunately, there are no definitive assessment procedures to substantiate these assumptions and establish the validity of the strategy for a given individual. Third, very little is known about first language learning. That is why it is generally carried out in a piecemeal manner. Content, pacing, sequencing, reinforcement, and context are typically separated, isolated, and controlled. These dimensions are inextricably related. A serious limitation of most first language learning strategies is the distortion that results from isolating dimensions, dealing with issues out of communicative context, structuring, explication of content and reinforcement, etc. This strategy is in large measure based on intuition that is verified or refuted through trial and error in the exploitation of an individual's behavior in accordance with known principles of language acquisition. Intervention is at best probabilistic. As first language learning becomes better understood, the likelihood of more effective and efficient strategies increases. Clearly, it is useful for individuals with arrested or delayed language development. It is appropriate for retarded individuals with arrested or delayed learning (Cromer 1974), as well as preschool children. To the extent that the verbal behavior of an individual manifests a delayed or arrested component, this strategy would be appropriate.

Operationally, the interventionist provides a variety of communicatively appropriate experiences in which various target activities are incorporated. First language learning is encouraged by replicating developmental sequences or by operationally carrying out Slobin's (1970) observation that new functions first appear with old forms and new forms with old functions. This type of model is advocated by Miller and Yoder (1974), Ruder and Smith (1974), Leonard (1973), Waryas (1973), Cazden (1972a,b), Blank and Solomon (1968, 1969), Sigel (1971), Lavatelli (1970, 1971, 1974), and Furth and Wach (1974).

SECOND LANGUAGE LEARNING

This strategy entails learning a language or dialect other than the first one. An individual who speaks nonstandard English may wish to learn Standard English in order to "make it" in school (and presumably in a middle class society). The underlying assumption is not only that an individual knows and uses the language of his community but that this language is a viable communicative system.

Before the influence of generative grammars, correct grammar (Standard English) was a continuing concern of teachers and clinicians. It was assumed that certain languages or dialects were more advanced than others. A corollary assumption was that language belies thought—a one-to-one relationship existed between thought and language. It was felt that language and thought are isometrically related. These assumptions have been extended to imply causative relationships. The Sapir-Whorf hypotheses on linguistic determinism and relativity (Dale 1972) were based on the notion that language determines thought. All these assumptions lack empirical support. Indeed, evidence on the nature of language indicates that they are untenable. Yet much of traditional education has been based on these assumptions.

Languages and dialects vary in the ways they code intents and conceptual distinctions, but such variations are not evidence of superiority (Lyons 1970). Nothing in a language or dialect supports the contention that one grammar is better or more highly developed than another. Ideas about the superiority of languages or dialects are issues of prestige rather than linguistic or psycholinguistic ones. Prestige derives from utility and functional value. A dialect has a high prestige in a community when it is widely used, but low prestige in a community in which it is used sparingly. It is inappropriate to say that one should "correct" his dialect if he does not speak Standard English. The real issue is that a speaker use whatever dialects are appropriate for his daily functions. As the parents of some disdvantaged school children once put it, if children need to learn Standard English in school to make it through, they should learn Standard English. But when they go home, they better talk the way we do (Cazden, Bryant, and Tillman 1972). This is a highly desirable attitude because it reflects a desire to use the most effective dialect for the situation.

A second language learning strategy should be based on such an attitude. Both student and clinician should draw parallels between the language one knows well and the second language (Feigenbaum 1970). Moreover, it is imperative that no penalty be made for speaking a nonstandard dialect while learning a standard one. Teachers and clinicians should use both dialects in their daily activities so students will appreciate that both are legitimately valued. This approach will help learning in both dialects and will reduce if not eliminate the resistances that occur when a clinician attempts to teach a given dialect (Labov 1966, 1970a,b). The goal is to have speakers adept in both dialects. This is a considerable change from traditional educational practice. The educational system is now bending to meet the needs of students. Standard and nonstandard forms are not only taught but encouraged. A special issue of *Language Speech and Hearing Services in Schools* (No. 4, 1972), and the Special Anthology Issue of *The Florida FL Reporter* (1969), were devoted to the second language learning strategy. Ervin-Tripp (1971) questioned the legitimacy of the strategy on the grounds that it is directed toward linguistic structures rather than functions.

Obviously, the strategy applies to individuals who have mastered at least one language or dialect and wish to learn a second. It is necessary that they *choose* to learn a second language or dialect rather than have it imposed on them. Otherwise, resistance may be too strong to warrant the effort (Labov 1966, 1970b).

Interestingly enough, evidence on the acquisition of two or more languages in natural language learning indicates that different languages facilitate rather than interfere with learning as had been previously thought. Facilitation has been shown for American-Spanish children (Mazeika 1971) and French-English and English-French children (Macnamara 1967; Macnamara and Kushir 1971).

Students who speak dialects that differ from their teachers have a special problem in school, particularly if much of their education is carried out in a lecture or instructional format. These students must not only learn the material but also translate it from their teachers' dialects to their own. This problem occurs in foreign language learning and when English-speaking Americans go abroad to teach, or attempt to teach Native American students. However, it is a subtle but no less serious problem in the inner city and rural communities, and one that has important long-term implications for both students and society. Failure in the educational system by minority students has been regarded as one of the causes of the social upheavals that rocked the nation in the early 1960s. Beyond the threat of trouble, there is the ethical obligation to make education appropriate to the needs of everyone.

INTERMODALITY TRANSFER

This strategy deals with transferring information about language from one modality (usually speech or listening) to another (usually writing or reading). The assumption is that the same fundamental grammatical systems and processes work for all modalities. For example, interrogatives, negations, pronouns, and anaphoric reference operate the same way for all modalities. If one is adept in one modality and wishes to be adept in another, perhaps the best way to go about it is through intermodality transfer. To be sure, each modality has unique characteristics, and certain special linguistic variants must be learned. However, the differences are relatively minor compared to underlying mutual systems and processes.

This strategy is most often used to develop reading skills (Goodman 1968, 1970; Smith 1971; Geyer 1971; Thorndike 1971; Athey 1970; Chall 1969; Gibson 1970; Entwisle 1971; Blank and Bridges 1964, 1966, 1967; and Kavanagh and Mattingly 1972), and writing skills (Mellon 1967; Moffett 1968). It has been found that when a student develops good speaking and listening skills he more readily learns the mechanics of reading and comprehension. Accordingly, many reading programs provide opportunities to develop speech skills. This is one reason why "Show and Tell" is so important in the preschool and early school years. Moreover, a good reading and writing program will be based on the development of oral skills.

Operationally, a student writes stories for other students to read. Or, a teacher or student writes dictated stories. It is important that dialectic variations of oral speech be retained. They are much easier to relate to (Baratz 1970) than Standard English. Some schools have had class projects in which booklets were produced in student dialects one semester, then translated into Standard English the next. This kind of reading and composition seems to be very productive.

One of the primary reasons for the high level of failure and dropout in American education has been poor reading. If teachers and clinicians start a program where the student is (his dialect), the probability of success will be increased significantly.

Intermodality transfer is equally useful for children with learning disabilities and poor reading skills. We recently used this strategy with a twelve-year-old girl. Her word attack skills and reading retention were very poor. We spent a considerable amount of time talking about school, friends, activities—anything that interested her. After she was spontaneous and reasonably adept in elaborating and altering her stories, we began asking her to dictate stories to her clinician. She then read her stories back. Words that she could not read were extracted after relevant phonetic word attack skills were demonstrated. It is important to know that there was no systematic set of word attack skills. These skills were determined by each word as it appeared. After the story was read, she reread the extracted words with surprising success—to the point of retaining appropriate word attack skills. Moreover, the week following, she reread her stories with relatively few errors and significantly improved word attack skills. This, of course, was only a beginning, but it was a worthwhile one. Her teacher and parents were very impressed with the progress she had made.

LANGUAGE REHABILITATION

Some individuals seem to have unique difficulties with language and/or underlying cognitive processes, along with the attendant communicative processes. Individuals with aphasia, learning disabilities, and/or autism have these difficulties. Though a first language learning strategy may help, it is likely that it is not the most productive strategy with such problems. As Baer (cited in Bateman 1974) put it, they failed this strategy when they had the natural opportunity.

West (1971) showed that in aphasia, it is productive to focus on memory processing. She devised an intervention program that systematically manipulates certain memory operations. Wepman (1972, 1976) has also indicated that aphasia theory should be oriented on cognitive systems. Recent developments have shifted away from an exclusively linguistic orientation (Holland 1969). It is conceivable that such a program, in principle if not in fact, would be appropriate for individuals with learning disabilities or autism. Martin (Martin and Rigrodsky 1974; Martin et al. 1975) has described differentiated phonological patterns for different types of aphasia. The literature on autism indicates that language and cognitive processes are significant if not central to this condition (Baltaxe and Simmons 1975; Prizant 1975). Swinney and Taylor (1971) have shown that some aphasics have short-term memory problems. The literature on retardation (excluding the notion of cultural familial retardation) indicates that memory processes may be significantly disrupted (Kellas, Ashcraft, and Johnson 1973; Blank and Bridges 1966). It is conceivable that learning disabilities would indicate a variety of cognitive dysfunctions that warrant a variety of intervention strategies. However, the learning disabilities literature is muddled by a number of mundane and pedestrian notions about learning dysfunctions, e.g., memory span (which does not index any important memory process), modality differences (rather than similarities of underlying systems), vocabulary size, etc. There is a considerable literature on learning processes and memory functions in psychology that could—indeed must—be accommodated by the field of learning disabilities. Fundamental principles have been ignored while peripheral notions are given much attention. Intervention strategies for this group probably vary significantly from the strategies presented above.

SYSTEMATIC EXTENSION OF AVAILABLE VERBAL REPERTOIRE

This strategy is basically a composite of behavior modification and modeling procedures. There are two views of the role behavior modification plays in altering verbal behavior, reflecting the behaviorist and mentalist philosophies. The former view is that behavior modification techniques induce verbal learning. The latter is that behavior modification techniques do not induce the learning of grammatical rules but systematically condition one to selectively use what he already knows. Mentalists hold this view even in the face of studies in behavior modification that claim to have taught rules (Guess, Sailor, and Baer 1974).

A basic tenet is that everything must be specified in order to be learned. However, such authorities as Jenkins (1973, 1974), Deese (1970), and Nelson (1974) have indicated that explicit views of verbal behavior result in superficial, tangential explanations.

The behavior modification strategy is widely used. Most teachers and clinicians are familiar with its rudiments. An attempt is made to determine one's repertoire for a given target (use of nouns, adjectives, verbs, etc.), then antecedent events, target behaviors, and reinforcement are systematically varied until behavior becomes shaped in a desired way. Sometimes a period of "reversal learning" is instituted, presumably to prove that the behavior is under stimulus control. The mentalist view is that reversal learning substantiates the idea that behavior modification deals with performance variation rather than learning. In clinical work, the publications by McReynolds (1970) and Girardeau and Spradlin (1969) are representative.

Perhaps the major limitation of behavior modification is the lack of generalization or carryover. Generalization to covarying verbal systems (as in the multiple baseline procedure) may occur. However, behavioral changes are typically specific to the behaviors reinforced (Guess, Sailor, and Baer 1974). This is desirable because the behavior of interest has been altered in a desired way. But it is undesirable because the behavior is so strongly tied to the reinforcement program that it rarely generalizes to other contexts. The underlying assumption is that any given behavior can come under stimulus-response control. Moreover, it is assumed that any behavior can be explicitly specified without unnecessary distortion. In verbal behavior, both of these assumptions are untenable.

Nevertheless, behavior modification is one of the most effective strategies in dealing with nonverbal children. Clinical reports of its effectiveness with nonverbal autistic and retarded children are impressive. Such children have been taught limited verbal, expressive, and receptive skills that were apparently difficult to learn by any other means. Once minimal labeling is obtained, behavior modification seems to be less effective than other strategies.

Modeling procedures are similar in principle to behavior modification. An individual, hopefully a peer, provides a model attitude or behavior the student is expected to emulate. The degree to which he identifies with a model is the degree to which he will try to emulate it. Accordingly, a primary issue in modeling procedures is the mechanism and opportunities for identification.

Modeling appears to be very useful in natural language learning. Conceivably, it could be exploited in language intervention. The works by Bandura (1971) refer to the nature and potency of modeling. Leonard (1973, 1975a,b) has applied modeling procedures to language intervention.

It should be stressed that the role of imitation in language learning must not be regarded as synonymous with modeling. Psycho-sociolinguists have taken a new and interesting view of imitation in verbal learning (Bloom 1974; Bloom, Hood, and Lightbown 1974; Ruder and Smith 1974). These views differ significantly from traditional views. For instance, in spontaneous imitation, a parent and child occasionally have cyclic exchanges in which after about three reciprocations the child varies his utterance. Bloom (1972) regarded the first efforts as attempts by the child to orient himself to the code and mental operations that go with it. The locus and nature of the variations are probably more important than faithful modeling (Brown and Bellugi 1964; Ervin 1966; Fay 1967).

Vicarious learning (Zimmerman and Bell 1972; Zimmerman and Rosenthal 1974) is based on modeling. A child participates in (or merely observes) an activity in which other children provide models. The child can learn from seeing others. He does not have to sit passively as he watches them. Indeed, vicarious learning may be stronger when he is engaged in the activity. Thus, it may be desirable to have a few children draw a picture. Each child does his own. During the activity, a clinician could comment on each picture, thereby defining salient aspects in a peer modeling activity. This kind of procedure has been used to successfully alter impulsiveness.

Eckerman, Whatley, and Kutz (1977) studied several behaviors related to the presence or activity of a peer. Figure 8-1 outlines the behaviors studied. Studies of this sort have shown that peer influences are considerable. Clinically, peer modeling has been very useful, especially when disciplined parallel talking accompanies spontaneous peer interactions.

Figure 8-1 *Behaviors related to the presence or activity of the peer.*

Category	Definition
Watch	Continuous visual regard of the peer or his activities for at least 3 seconds.
Distant social response	One or more of the following six behaviors occurs.
Vocalize	A vocal sound or series of sounds, that may or may not be distinguishable as words, emitted while watching the peer.
Smile	Pleasant facial expression distinguished by a curved mouth with corners upturned, while watching the peer.
Laugh	An explosive sound of joy or amusement, while watching the peer.
Fuss	A fretting, whining, complaining sound emitted while watching the peer.

Figure 8-1 *(continued)*

Category	Definition
Cry	Loud continuous wailing while watching the peer.
Gesture	Wave at a peer as in greeting or departure; clap hands while watching the peer.
Physical contact	Touch and/or strike occurs.
Touch	Placing a hand upon the peer in a nonforceful manner, including patting, hugging, rubbing.
Strike	Forceful physical contact with the peer by either hand or foot, including hitting, pushing, or kicking.
Same play materials	Contact of the same toy as the peer or its duplicate for at least 3 continuous seconds without any direct involvement in the activities of the peer.
Direct involvement in peer's play	One or more of the following eight behaviors occurs.
Imitate	Duplication of the peer's activity, preceded by visual regard of the peer's activities. The peer's activity usually involves a toy or some other aspect of the inanimate environment, but it might consist of a distinctive motor response such as jumping.
Show a toy	Hold out a toy toward the peer, but out of his reach, while looking at and/or vocalizing to the peer.
Offer a toy	Hold out a toy toward the peer within his reaching distance, while looking at and/or vocalizing to the peer.
Accept a toy	Take a toy offered by the peer.
Take over a toy	Contact a toy released by the peer not more than 3 seconds previously.
Take a toy	Take an unoffered toy from the possession of the peer without a struggle.
Struggle over a toy	Both children attempt to gain sole possession of the same toy, including pulling, pushing, whining, etc.
Coordinate play	Act together with the peer to perform a common task, such as building a tower of blocks; or each child repeatedly takes turns performing an activity with attention to the other's activity, as when one child builds a tower of blocks, stands back and laughs as the other kicks it down.

SPONTANEOUS EXPLORATION AND VARIATION OF AVAILABLE VERBAL REPERTOIRE

In this strategy, an individual strives to discover the nature and power of his verbal capacities. This is done through a series of exploratory operations on the range and variations of his verbal capacities. The underlying assumption is that as he discovers the range and variation of his verbal capacities, his verbal repertoire extends. Another assumption is that it is not enough simply to know various verbal systems; one must become adept in knowing how to use them in a variety of combinations and variations for a variety of purposes. Moreover, it is assumed that one is selective in the use of verbal behavior. This selectivity pertains to the perception of the appropriateness of code and referent (Muma 1975a; Olson 1970, 1971; Brown 1958a).

Most intervention strategies are directed at increasing knowledge of verbal behavior. However, an issue of equal if not more importance may be increasing adeptness in the use of what one does know. The more recent literature suggests that strategies on language usage may be more important than strategies on language learning.

I have developed a game, somewhat like Monopoly, that encourages players to explore a variety of syntactic options in sentence generation. It is called *MAKE-CHANGE—a game of sentence sense*. There are easy and difficult versions of it (Muma 1977b). Many sentence variations can be made with the difficult version. Children like it and it provides opportunities to explore syntactic alternatives. Mellon (1967) and Moffett (1968) have developed procedures for spontaneously exploring verbal repertoire. Blank and Frank (1971) developed a story retelling technique that encourages children to recode messages. This is a fundamental grammatical skill, an awareness that referents can be coded by alternate messages and that messages can have alternate referents. A corollary is that in communication one must recode messages in order to overcome communication obstacles (Muma 1975a). Speakers oriented to an elaborative code accept the need to recode messages for overcoming obstacles, whereas those oriented to a restricted code are less inclined to recode (Bernstein 1970).

Clinicians need not—indeed must not—rely on a single language intervention strategy. They can selectively employ (1) first language learning, (2) second language learning, (3) intermodality transfer, (4) language rehabilitation, (5) systematic extension of available repertoire, and (6) spontaneous exploration and variation of available repertoire. It behooves them to employ these strategies selectively according to the specific needs of clients. As Bowerman (1974) indicated, there are many kinds of problems in verbal behavior, ranging from underlying cognitive processes to linguistic and communicative processes. Clinicians must be aware of the underlying assumptions, limitations, and strengths of each strategy in order to be effective and efficient (Muma 1977a).

"Sesame Street"

"Sesame Street," and its companion program for older children, "The Electric Company," are highly successful and have incorporated basic principles of child development. Some of these principles conflict with traditional notions about early childhood education. "Sesame Street" should be considered a model for what can be done in implementing principles of child development and overcoming traditional notions of childhood education. Even though a teacher or clinician may not have the television equipment, techniques, and resources to fully emulate "Sesame Street," he can extract principles applicable to regular classroom or clinical situations.

In the mid-1960s the War on Poverty established many programs. "Sesame Street" was one of several intended to deal with various aspects of poverty. Others include Head Start, Parent-Child Centers, Follow Through, Legal Aid, and food stamps. "Sesame Street" was conceived of as a program that would develop readiness skills of preschool poverty children. The logic was that middle class children begin school with a considerable advantage. Participation in preschool has socialized them to a school setting and school activities. Moreover, most middle class children begin school knowing how to write their name, the alphabet, count to ten, and name colors. It was initially believed that disadvantaged children should come to school with comparable skills. Head Start was established to make disadvantaged children comparable to middle class children in these skills. However, there were two major problems in its early days: the curriculum was not well developed, and it dealt only with a small percentage of disadvantaged children. Then it was reasoned that inasmuch as every poverty family generally had a television set, television offers the greatest potential for reaching the largest segment of disadvantaged children. As for the curriculum, the foremost authorities on child development composed the advisory committee, chaired by Gerald Lesser of Harvard University. These authorities were active in conceptualizing and directing the nature of the program. They were not constrained by traditional notions of early education (Lesser 1976; Meichenbaum 1971).

One basic principle had to do with getting and maintaining attention. Traditional educators had been frustrated by the so-called short attention span of disadvantaged children. Some even said such children are unteachable. Others held that the first thing to do was to develop attention span. However, "Sesame Street" dispelled these notions. The problem of attention was not in the children but the educational process. "Sesame Street" has had remarkable success in getting and maintaining attention. Studies of different types of viewers by the Children's Television Workshop indicate that nearly all fall into one of two groups: glued-on viewers and dual listeners. The so-called glued-on viewers seem to be mesmerized by the program. They are totally enthralled by it. Even momentary disruptions in the classroom seem to have no effect in distracting them. Dual listeners can continue in an activity while also watching "Sesame Street." It seems that some children need to be involved in dual activity, particularly if it has a motor component. Interestingly enough, the studies of glued-on and dual listeners indicate that both types get about as much out of the program, which contradicts the traditional notion that children should do only one thing at a time.

The success of "Sesame Street" in getting and maintaining attention can be attributed to three major principles: discrepancy learning, active learning, and identification. These principles can be implemented by any teacher or clinician. Discrepancy learning rests on the principle of variation. As indicated in Chap. 3, discrepancies get and maintain attention. For example, a child may be taught the concept of "four units." If he is asked to count to four he may learn the steps for getting to four but may not learn "fourness" as the concept useful in mathematical skills. In "Sesame Street," "fourness" as a concept is presented not as a counting skill by itself but with a variety of exemplars: four bats, four rabbits, four chairs, four ducks, etc. Thus, it is an open-ended concept for quantity involving a variety of things. Moreover, "fourness" is shared equally by these things. In discrepancy learning, an individual has a concept of something and encounters instances of the concept as variants of what he knew previously. This variation gets and maintains attention. The rapid exemplars on "Sesame Street" provide a child with a stream of discrepancies from which he will extract ones of special interest. He need not learn from all of them. A large number of them are given so as to entice a large audience. What may be discrepant for one child may not be for another. The more variations, the greater the probability that each viewer will encounter discrepancies between what he knows and available exemplars. Repetitions are not very productive but variations are.

The rapid presentation of a large number of exemplars activates another mechanism quite different from traditional education. I call it "open learning." A child cannot possibly remember all the exemplars, so he realizes there is more to the concept than what he learned in a given presentation. This induces him to look for further exemplars on his own. The concept is open-ended. Indeed, the "Sesame Street" format presents a concept for a few minutes only, then returns to some, but not all, of the exemplars. This is a useful principle for teachers and clinicians prone to teach until a child gets all exemplars correct. Teaching for complete correctness tends to lead the child to the faulty conclusions that all he needs to know is what was taught. He is seduced into restricting his categories and learning. This is a common problem in the clinical fields and contributes to a lack of generalization.

The second major principle is active learning. Many traditional or behavioristically oriented clinicians do not appreciate this aspect of the program because it contrasts with how they see their own role. Active learning is a mentalist principle. The "Sesame Street" format is not instructional. Children are given the chance to consider alternatives and puzzle over events. Problems are defined externally. Big Bird may look at a large block and a small block and verbalize "largeness" or "bigness" but not solve the problem before the context is shifted to something else. A few minutes later, the program returns to Big Bird still puzzling aloud but with other exemplars or participants. In the interval, the viewers have actively assisted Big Bird. They have not forgotten his quandary. When the program switches back to Big Bird, they smile, laugh, giggle, and nudge their neighbors because they were actively puzzling themselves. Smiling is a good overt indicator of information processing (Zelazo 1971, 1972; Sroufe and Waters 1976). The program provides active processing in more direct ways. Occasionally, a character will talk directly to the viewers. The children nod their heads, raise their hands, or speak out.

Another mechanism for active learning is follow-up activities in the classroom. Teachers are given "Sesame Street" lesson plans in advance so they can prepare activities that expand the context of the program.

Notice that there is no direct evaluation of each activity. This reflects individualized learning. To be sure, "Sesame Street" is continually being evaluated; each program is researched in terms of content and audience participation. But each child is not evaluated in each content area, simply because children vary as to what they learn each day. This freedom to extract from each program what the child wants to learn when and how he wants to reflects the active learning principle. Evaluations are made over long periods (several months) rather than on specific activities. The data are impressive (Ball and Bogartz 1970). They indicate that individuals who watch "Sesame Street" do significantly better than those who do not. Moreover, the more an individual watches "Sesame Street" the better he does on various evaluations.

The third major principle is identification. The idea behind it is that the more a child identifies with the program the more likely it is that he will become involved in the learning process. Accordingly, there is a concerted effort to have children, especially minority children, identify with it. Sesame Street is an inner city street. Concepts are taught in street play—a setting that inner city children can identify with. The show generally begins and ends on the street but there are departures to other places, plus such novel characters as Cookie Monster and Big Bird. Different ethnic and cultural groups are represented. Moreover, each individual speaks his own dialect and dresses his natural way. "Sesame Street" is an educational program tailored to meet the diverse needs of a polycultural society. Much of its success can be attributed to this fact alone. Children are not coerced to conform to the educational program. Rather, the program conforms to the needs of the children.

In recent years, there has been a shift of emphasis in "Sesame Street." Initially, it dealt with academics, a product orientation. The current program emphasizes socialization and the enjoyment of learning. This is a process orientation. Also, some programs are directed toward parents and teachers. For example, occasionally a child teaches an adult or solves a problem in which an adult blundered. This serves to challenge the traditional adage that the teacher is the only source of learning. The most successful program is Bill Cosby reciting the alphabet. He does not just name the letters, he enjoys doing it. He varies the names and plays with the letters and sounds. Cosby epitomizes what "Sesame Street" is about: learning can be fun.

Summary

Clinicians should become acquainted with the state of the art in language intervention. Most of what is done is based on authoritarianism. Programs that claim to be about language development violate major principles of language acquisition. As a rule intervention programs that establish content, sequencing, pacing, or reinforcement before meeting the individual violate language learning opportunities in significant ways. There are important differences between what is done in intervention and what happens in natural learning.

Clinicians should take advantage of various intervention agents—peers, siblings, parents, teachers, etc. Peers and parents are especially good. Parents should take increasingly responsible roles in the intervention process. The clinical conditions such as autism, "delayed language," retardation, articulation disorders, deafness, and so on are overworked clinical categories. While these conditions are all unique in some respects, they are not in others. An assessment-intervention program based on systems and processes is much the same across clinical boundaries.

Clinicians should know when they have a behaviorist or mentalist orientation, so they become aware of their biases and the alternatives to these biases. They should know about first language learning, second language learning, intermodality transfer, systematic extension of available verbal repertoire, and spontaneous exploration and variation of available repertoire.

"Sesame Street" offers clinicians useful intervention principles. If anything, "Sesame Street" demonstrates that learning can be fun.

UNIT **IV**
Specific Assessment-Intervention Procedures

9

Assessment-Intervention: Cognitive Systems

Clinical assessment and intervention should deal with cognitive, linguistic, and communicative systems rather than products of these systems. Behavior patterns are *indices* of underlying systems. Any systems approach must take into account the influence of co-occurring systems on target systems. Co-occurrence is especially important in dealing with linguistic systems. Finally, clinical assessment and intervention should be undertaken in natural contexts and conditions relevant to an individual's natural behavior.

The relatively recent literature in developmental psychology reports some clinically useful areas in cognitive research. This chapter presents some of them. Each is described briefly, followed by assessment procedures and intervention implications. Individual patterns of performance are sought as a way of mapping an individual's command of a system. Intervention approaches are derived from these patterns of performance. This assessment-intervention approach is based on the principle that the most powerful assessment describes the patterns of an individual's behavior (as opposed to evaluation through psychometric norms) and exploits these through the various alternatives revealed by them. Assessment and intervention processes are thus inextricably related and directly relevant to the individual.

Before dealing with specific systems, however, clinicians should know about the correlation between minor physical anomalies and minimal brain dysfunction. Waldrop et al. (1968) and Halverson and Victor (1974) have shown that individuals who have a cluster of minor physical anomalies (possibly four or more) may also have minimal brain dysfunctions. They report a significant positive correlation between minor physical anomalies and subtle problems with various cognitive systems. However, while many individuals with minor physical anomalies have subtle cognitive problems, others do not. Clinicians should undertake a thorough cognitive assessment of individuals who have several minor physical anomalies.

Piagetian Stages

Piagetian psychology offers a very productive assessment framework, particularly in appraising an individual's stage of development in early language learning. The sensorimotor stage is particularly important in establishing a cognitive base for language learning. Four indices are vital as developmental markers during this period: causality, object permanence, anticipation, and deferred imitation. A child's knowledge of causality and object permanence should be determined before crediting him with any labeling activity (Bloom 1970, 1973). However, Bowerman (in press, a,b) disputes Bloom's position. Bower (1971) and Bower and Wishart (1972) showed that object permanence occurs many weeks before the first label. Perhaps object permanence is not as critical as action patterns.

Early "naming" may not be representational labeling but extended action patterns toward things (Bruner 1975; Greenfield and Smith 1976). The cognitive skills of children with language problems have been assessed according to Piagetian stages (Uzgiris and Hunt 1975; Lavatelli 1971, 1974; Edwards 1974; Miller 1976; Chappell and Johnson 1976). Lavatelli has formulated a curriculum as well.

Causality can be determined in several ways. A clinician could toss a beanbag to one side of a child when he is not looking. If the child localizes the sound and seeks the causative agent (who tossed the bag) it can be inferred that he is aware of causality. A single trial is insufficient, however. Several are needed to establish a *pattern* of intention. Further, several activities are needed to demonstrate that an individual's awareness of causality includes alternative agents. When an infant hands a wind-up toy to his parents to make it go, he demonstrates an awareness of causality.

"Out of sight, out of mind" describes the individual who does not know *object permanence*. A clinician can shake some keys in front of a child to gain his attention. When the child seems to be interested, the clinician should drop them in front of the child, then cover them with something. A child with object permanence will look for the keys under the cover. Again, a single trial is insufficient; several trials with different objects are needed. The hidden item can be layered, or nested in containers within containers. Nesting is a higher level of difficulty.

Anticipation is another cognitive skill appearing in the sensorimotor period. It is important because it indicates an individual's ability to represent past experience and to use these representations in the service of present experiences. The child is no longer fused directly to present experience. It also means he is in a position to generalize from one experience to others without necessarily engaging in the experiences directly. A child who has played with a ball may activate action patterns toward a new ball in anticipation of playing with it. If he raises his arms and hands to catch the ball, he has had experiences with this activity and has represented them. On the other hand, an absence of anticipation over several tests indicates that he is not yet representing experience and still needs direct stimulation.

Deferred imitation is a cognitive skill appearing toward the end of the sensorimotor period that is important to language development. Piaget outlined a developmental sequence for imitative behavior. It begins with contiguous acts, then sporadic imitation, and finally, deferred imitation. Contiguous acts are those simultaneous with an act of someone else. The child's acts are not only simultaneous but have common characteristics, even though they are not imitations. A mother may sing to her child whereupon the child may coo. A mother may do something such as fold diapers and the baby kicks and flails his arms. Sporadic imitation is unpredictable. A baby may say "Mama" after his mother says it, but may not do it again. Sporadic imitation is not usually faithful imitation, but approximation. Both contiguous acts and sporadic imitation are immediate. Deferred imitation is not. It relies on the child's ability to represent and reestablish an event out of context. It indicates an ability to be removed from direct experience and to operate with representations of past experience.

Causality, object permanence, anticipation, and deferred imitation are major aspects of the sensorimotor stage of development, and seem to be minimum requirements for language learning. The Uzgiris and Hunt (1975) assessment program describes elaborate procedures for this period.

Intervention approaches differ considerably for individuals who exhibit these four skills and those who do not. Individuals who have them can be encouraged to label and classify objects, actions, and relationships. Emphasis should be on coding semantic and relational functions in language (see chap. 10). Individuals who do not have them can be encouraged to participate in activities with varied action patterns toward objects and things. The assumption is that as a child develops a variety of action patterns he will learn new attributes of things that in turn lead to labeling behavior (Flavell 1970).

One of the major problems with children who have not learned cognitive skills in the late sensorimotor period is cyclic behaviors. These result in an inordinate orientation on a limited set of attributes. They are especially noticeable with retarded and autistic children. It is desirable to break up cyclic behavior by varying action patterns toward things, by the use of behavior modification procedures (Baumeister and Rollins 1976; Forehand and Baumeister 1976), or by distracting or removing the child from the activity where cyclic behavior occurs. The more a child engages in rocking, head banging, and echolalia, the more difficult it is to work productively with him. Gesture games (follow-the-leader), gesture songs, and peer modeling in small groups work well in overcoming cyclic behavior. They not only disrupt cyclic activity but are sequential and purposeful. Such children should not be expected to do exactly as their leaders, because exact performance is too demanding. Approximations to a model are sought.

Several cognitive systems and processes reported in developmental psychology are useful in clinical assessment and intervention. Some of these have been consolidated in an assessment-intervention package called MAP (Muma Assessment Program, Muma, in press). MAP provides a way of mapping performance patterns to describe an individual's command of cognitive, linguistic, and communicative systems. MAP deals with the following systems: perceptual salience, iconic/symbolic processing, rule/nonrule learning, primacy-recency memory functions, technology of reckoning, cognitive tempo, part/whole and alternatives thinking styles, differentiation of body parts, cognitive distancing, and categorization/mediation.

Perceptual Salience

Odum (1972), Odum and Corbin (1973), Odum and Guzman (1970, 1972), and Caron (1969) have identified a phenomenon called perceptual salience. This is an inordinate focus on a perceptual domain: color, size, shape, position, and possibly number. A child becomes preoccupied with one of these domains. This phenomenon is strongly evident during the preschool years and somewhat evident in the early school years.

I have had children in the clinic who exhibited abnormal perceptual salience. Two interesting things occurred with them. First, perceptual salience overrode their performance on other cognitive tasks, particularly those regarding rule/nonrule governed learning and iconic/symbolic learning. Second, perceptual salience fluctuated on a daily basis. One day a child might be strongly influenced by color but on the next not show this influence.

Since perceptual salience is such a strong phenomenon, identifying it is simple. It can be done by watching a child play or by asking him to point to two forms that go together on a card containing three forms. This should be done with several cards that systematically vary perceptual attributes over the series. If the child is oriented on a perceptual variable, the clinician should organize intervention on the same variable, to exploit the child's behavior. When the child begins to function with that particular perceptual variable, extend to other perceptual variables, ultimately dealing with a variety of perceptual attributes of things, and finally, action patterns for these things. For example, a child may be preoccupied with color. Intervention could begin by having him find things around him that are colored—red things, blue things, etc. This activity could be extended to other domains by identifying other perceptual attributes of the "red things," "blue things," etc. A clinician can give a variety of labels ("red things bigger than an apple") and the child could show a variety of action patterns toward these things. Intervention thus begins with a perceptual salience domain that is operating for the child. It then extends to other domains and classifications through action patterns and labels.

Iconic/Symbolic Processing

Bruner (1964) and Bruner et al. (1966) have shown a three-stage developmental sequence in cognitive processing. The first is motoric processing. An infant will mouth, finger, touch, pat, or physically manipulate things about him. The second is iconic or image processing. This is an attention to perceptual variables, such as color, size, shape, position, and number. Iconic processing is different from perceptual salience in that the former is of several variables whereas the latter is of a single variable. Moreover, the former is a long-term mode whereas the latter fluctuates daily. The third stage is the symbolic or representational stage. This is an orientation on the *functional* classes of things. Cups and glasses are in the functional class of containers. Perceptually, an item may be big, brown, and rectangular, but functionally it may be a box, a cube, a weight, a support, or many other things. While the perceptual attributes of things remain constant, functions vary considerably, depending upon how one uses them. Symbolic thought is an orientation on various functional categories of things.

Motoric, iconic, and symbolic processing modes are predominant rather than exclusive. Infants are predominantly motoric processors. Children from about two to about five to seven are predominantly iconic processors. Thereafter, normal individals are symbolic processors. This three-stage model may be useful in appreciating the behavior of groups such as the mentally retarded, learning-disabled, autistic, and aphasic. Garrison (1966) indicated that this is a useful model for appreciating mental retardation. I have observed several retarded and autistic individuals who have a strong motoric orientation. They are easy to identify through their physical manipulation of things in play.

Iconic and symbolic processing are more difficult to identify since their cognitive processing is not so easily discerned. Bruner and his colleagues ask children to choose two of three pictures. Patterns of their choices revealed iconic and symbolic orientations. Vespucci (1975) studied ninety-six five-year-old children who selected two of three pictures. She found forty who were predominantly iconic processors, forty who were predominantly symbolic processors, with the remaining having mixed iconic and symbolic patterns. The criterion for a predominant pattern was eleven of fourteen trials. Kelly (1976) showed that more four-year-olds were iconic than symbolic processors. My MAP tasks contain eighteen trials with a two-to-one (color, shape/function) bias toward iconic choices. If an individual makes twelve or more functional responses, he is said to have a strong pattern, twelve or more iconic responses for color *or* shape (or eighteen or more of color *and* shape combined) constitute strong patterns (see Fig. 3-4).

Clinicians should organize intervention according to the predominant cognitive processing shown by the individual. Intervention for a motoric processor should involve motoric activities. The individual should have the opportunity to be physically active in a variety of ways. Gesture games are desirable. A variety of action patterns involving things should be fostered. Intervention for iconic processors should be based on perceptual variables, and should extend across a wide range of them. It should also include a variety of action patterns toward things identified by perceptual attributes. After a rich and varied repertoire of perceptual attributes and action patterns is established, clinicians may provide labels for these things.

Rule/Nonrule Governed Learning

Some individuals are good at organizing experience and shifting orientations; others are not. The abilities to categorize and organize experience efficiently and to be flexible in thinking are rule governed behaviors. Studies by H. Kendler and T. Kendler (1959, 1970a,b, 1971) have shown young children shift from a nonrule governed orientation to a rule governed one. This shift occurs during the preschool period.

The Kendlers used a two-choice discrimination task to identify when a child begins to rely on rules in problem solving. The child is shown a card that contains two items varying in size (large and small) and color (red and blue). The child is told, "Try to guess the picture I'm thinking of. Point to the picture you think is the one I'm thinking of." After a choice is made, the person is told whether he chose the correct picture. Then another card is shown. The procedure continues until an individual has a number of positive responses to warrant the conclusion that he knows the variable (red or blue; large or small) that marks a correct choice. Eight or more consecutive "yeses" are sufficient.

The Kendlers employed three conditions in this procedure: initial set, reversal shift, and nonreversal shift. The *initial set* is the number of cards it takes an individual to learn whichever variable and criteria are initially used. It continues until eight consecutive "yeses" are obtained. The total number of cards needed to get eight consecutive "yeses" is the initial set. Then, without telling the individual or interrupting the presentation, the clinician changes the criteria from blue to red but maintains the variable color. This is a *reversal shift*. The task is how many trials it will take the child to learn the new condition. After eight new consecutive "yeses," the condition is again changed without telling the child. This time the variable is changed from color to size, and a new criterion is used, either large or small. This condition is called a *nonreversal shift*.

Rule governed and nonrule governed learners function quite differently on these tasks. According to the Kendler studies, rule governed learners take about eight to twelve or fifteen trials to get eight consecutive "yeses" on the initial set and reversal shift conditions. They generally take fifteen to twenty trials for the nonreversal shift condition. The reason for the increase is that they resist abandoning a rule that worked on the initial set and reversal shift. By contrast, nonrule governed learners need more trials to obtain the eight consecutive "yeses." They need about thirty to fifty—sometimes two hundred—to learn the three sets. Usually nonrule governed learners take fewer trials on the nonreversal shift than on the others.

The intervention implications for rule governed and nonrule governed learners are not easy to determine. It seems that intervention for rule governed learners would best be in terms of alternative problem solving strategies, whereas intervention for nonrule governed learners would focus on classification skills and variations of action patterns and alternative labeling of things, actions, and relationships.

Additionally, mediational mechanisms should be identified and exploited. The section on classification and mediation below amplifies these intervention suggestions.

Primacy/Recency Memory Functions

Primacy/recency memory functions reflect a serial learning curve. These occur when a series of independent items are given and there are too many to remember, creating a memory overload condition. A recency function refers to items most recently placed in memory. These are the last on the list and are in short-term storage. When the list ends, the individual usually dumps the items most recently placed in memory.

A primacy function refers to the initial items in the list. These have been converted from short-term into long-term memory via rehearsal strategies. After dumping recency items, an individual will dump items at the initial end of a string.

Primacy/recency functions are widely reported in the literature on memory. Most introductory books on memory describe them (Norman 1969; Neisser 1967; Ellis 1972; Flavell 1977). The key to them is that the items must be relatively independent in a memory overload task. This is significant in clinical assessment because primacy/recency functions should not occur with items that are related to each other. Thus, individuals who exhibit primacy/recency functions for inherently structured material are not using the structure to remember the material. Symbolic (as opposed to iconic) memory operates on the rehearsal strategies ordinarily determined by the inherent structure of the material. Thus, a list of items could be organized into classes. It could contain animate nouns, inanimate nouns, transitive verbs, intransitive verbs, and adjectives. The recall of such a list could be in clusters of words from the same class (even though the original list separated items of the same class from each other). A clustering response indicates that an individual uses the inherent categories of the items to remember them rather than trying to remember them independently (Rossi and Wittrock 1967, 1971). Clustering can be used to identify knowledge and functional use of various categories. A sentence contains a high level of structure. If an individual exhibits a primacy/recency function with sentences, it indicates that he does not know or is insufficiently adept in using the inherent structure of the sentences. Thus, primacy/recency functions can be used to determine whether an individual is aware of and utilizes inherent structure in material.

Primacy/recency functions can be observed in natural spontaneous speech as well as in a serial learning task. Slobin (1973), Olson (1973), and Ervin-Tripp (1973) have described a variety of recency functions in early language learning. Brown, Cazden, and Bellugi-Klima (1969) reported that children learn and elaborate on object noun phrases before subject noun phrases because of a recency function in memory processing. Bloom (1973) reported that children reduce linguistic systems because of a memory processing overload.

Clinicians who attempt to work with memory span are about forty years behind the literature on memory (Blankenship 1938). Miller's (1956) famous article on memory capacity, seven units plus or minus two, has been grossly misrepresented in the clinical fields. Miller was referring to *psychological* units or chunks rather than extrinsic units. Simon (1974) and Jenkins (1973, 1974) indicate that symbolic memory is very dynamic, reflecting a variety of chunking mechanisms and conditions. Clinicians should also be aware of differences between iconic and symbolic memory. Iconic memory is not as efficient as symbolic memory. An individual who relies more on iconic memory will have considerable difficulty in learning. Kellas, Ashcraft, and Johnson (1973) have shown that some retarded children have difficulty with symbolic memory. West (1971) demonstrated that some aphasic individuals have difficulty converting short-term storage into long-term storage.

The intervention implications for individuals who exhibit primacy/recency functions on inherently structured material and/or an inordinate reliance on iconic memory are twofold. One is to direct intervention or rehearsal strategies along the lines of West's (1971) work. A variety of rehearsal strategies could be employed to help them deduce inherent structure and use symbolic memory. The second is to vary the material itself so the individual will experience a variety of structures, some of which he can do better than with others. Sentences vary tremendously in underlying structures. Self-embedding sentences are much more difficult than left recursive sentences, and those are more difficult than right recursive ones. Transformed sentences are more difficult than nontransformed ones. Transforms loaded on one constituent are more difficult than transforms spread across them. Sentences with many semantic functions are more difficult than those with few (Perfetti 1972). Sentences containing linguistic structures known to an individual are easier than those containing new structures in new co-occurring contexts. Primacy/recency functions indicate that an individual is dealing with material he is not ready to deal with. Intervention should focus on helping an individual deal with such material by providing either rehearsal strategies or more appropriate material.

Technology of Reckoning

The technology of reckoning is Bruner's (1964, 1966) phrase. It refers to an individual's ability to deal or reckon with various experiences. Infants can identify single attributes of objects and perhaps actions and relationships. Somewhat later they can deal with two, three, or more attributes of a single object, action, or relationship. Then, they can deal with two, three, or more objects, actions, and relationships according to one, two, three, or more attributes. By about six to eight years of age, children can integrate attributes, thereby allowing them to efficiently reckon with transformed or changed states in things. This continuum gives them an increasing ability to efficiently reckon with new experiences by deducing their attributes and organizing them so the experiences can be interrelated and generalization of learning take place.

The technology of reckoning is a highly speculative construct. Much learning about objects, actions, and relationships is beyond what can be demonstrated. Moreover, natural concept learning is apparently different for static variables, in contrast to dynamic ones. Nelson (1973, 1974), Wieman (1976), Bowerman (1976), and others have shown that labeling behavior begins with dynamic variables. Young children are more apt to label something that is changing than something that is constant. If objects change, they will name nouns. If actions change, they will name verbs. If attributes change, they will name adjectives. If locations change, they will name prepositions and adverbs of place. Children do not follow developmental norms by learning nouns, then verbs, then adjectives. They follow the principle that new information/old information (or variation and change) get attention and dynamic attributes are deduced and eventually integrated. Static attributes exhibit a developmental lag in this process, but also provide a means of ascertaining where an individual is in his ability to reckon with experience.

Procedurally, an individual is asked to identify single attributes, attribute clusters of things, and attribute clusters of different things. The integration level is marked by his ability to deal with covarying properties of things as they are transformed in various conservation tasks. There is no direct way of determining an individual's ability to deal with dynamic attributes. Probably the best way to deal with them is to study the individual's naming behavior and ascertain the dynamic attributes he is likely to label. Instances of overextension and underextension (Bloom 1973) may provide patterns of dynamic attributes in labeling.

Intervention should be based on an individual's ability to deal with dynamic and static attributes of objects, actions, and relationships. It should not deal with arbitrary objects, actions, and relationships. Rather, objects, actions, and relationships should be those which an individual naturally encounters and has shown preferences for in attention and labeling. Moreover, they should vary in ways natural to the individual's environment.

Cognitive Tempo

Psychologists have shifted their attitude on intellectual functioning from an attempt to measure performance on intelligence and achievement tests to an identification of cognitive style. It is more important to understand *how* an individual functions in obtaining a score than *what* the score is. Teachers and clinicians who understand how an individual functions have more ability to deal with him than if they have a measurement level.

A great deal of research has been done on cognition in the last two decades. More than one hundred studies have been done on what Kagan and his colleagues call cognitive tempo. This refers to the rate of processing. Reflective thinkers consider various alternatives before committing themselves to a response. They are somewhat slow but highly accurate. Impulsive thinkers are fast but inaccurate. Cognitive tempo excludes fast accurate and slow inaccurate thinkers (Kagan and Messer 1975). The former are sufficiently familiar with alternatives before they encounter a task, and thus come to it with preprocessed information. Slow inaccurate processors are actually not processing information but perseverating.

The best way to identify impulsivity and reflectivity is to employ novel tasks or novel toys. Cognitive tempo is identifiable either formally through patterns of performance on a task designed for the purpose or informally by observing the number of toy changes per unit of time in play. Reflective thinkers spend more time playing with a novel toy than impulsive ones, who have many toy changes. In a cognitive tempo task, individuals are asked to find a drawing identical to a target drawing from among four alternatives. Reflective thinkers take more time and are more accurate in this than impulsive ones.

Research shows that reflective thinkers are better readers and better with mathematic skills than impulsive ones. Interestingly, schools tend to emphasize impulsiveness—the first ones done get to go to recess, etc. Studies on the cognitive style of teachers report an interesting influence on children: reflective teachers tend to make impulsive children more reflective, but impulsive teachers do not make reflective children more impulsive (Yando and Kagan 1968, 1970).

From the intervention point of view, clinicians should take cognitive tempo into account. They need not be concerned about reflective thinkers because these are already considering alternatives and selectively operating with the most appropriate ones. However, they should attempt to modify impulsivity so such children can more profitably learn from their experiences. There are several ways to encourage reflectivity: modeling, explicit alternatives, consequences, and delayed response. In the delayed response approach, a task is given in which a child must wait for a short period before participating. During this delay, the child has an opportunity to survey the task for alternatives. The consequences approach refers to carrying out a task according to a first impulse; then the task is done again from a different starting point. An individual can see that an impulsive choice brings different results than a reflective choice and that the latter choice may be better. The explicit alternatives approach is one in which the clinician attempts to identify alternate ways of doing a task. Then, an individual is asked to choose the way he wishes to do it. The modeling approach is one where an individual can observe someone else doing the same task. Another child may draw a picture, make a paper flower, play in the sandbox. A clinician could add to peer modeling by talking about the alternatives a peer chooses in the activity. Still another approach for dealing with impulsivity is the "means and end" or "stage and goal" approach. Here, a child is selectively reminded of how far along he is and what the goal is. It is helpful to have a completed product in front of him. As he works toward the product, the clinician verbalizes what he is doing and what he needs to do, or selectively points out what other children have done and the variations they have taken. It is important to realize that these procedures do not work on a one-trial basis. Over a period of time and after many activities, impulsive children change their style to a more reflective performance.

I had a preschool child who had a severe speech articulation problem and was impulsive in play. His therapy program was bidirectional in that articulation and cognitive tempo were emphasized. Over a semester, both areas improved significantly. Interestingly, improvement of articulation followed that of tempo and tempo began to markedly change about halfway into the semester.

Part/Whole and Alternatives

The psychological literature reports other kinds of thought processes besides cognitive tempo. Guilford (1967) described convergent and divergent thinking skills. Convergent thinking is part/whole thinking in which an individual strives to put things together. Divergent thinking is "openmindedness" in which one thinks of new or novel uses of things. A screwdriver can be a hammer, a lever, a chisel, a knife, an icepick, etc. Another way of looking at cognitive style is in terms of synthetic and analytic thinking styles (Kagan et al. 1964). Synthetic thinking is part-whole thinking. Analytic thinking is an ability to deduce alternatives and components. It is desirable that an individual have various thinking skills to selectively employ the skill most appropriate to a given circumstance. If he relies too strongly on one or a few thinking styles, he will not be very adept in dealing with the variety of circumstances he will later encounter.

One procedure that has been used to identify cognitive style is to have an individual choose two of three items on each of a number of cards, then see if a pattern or a mixed pattern occurs. The alternatives on the cards have a distribution pattern in which two pairs have a part/whole relationship (flower-bee, flower-butterfly) and one pair has alternatives (bee-butterfly). An individual who operates predominantly with a synthetic thinking style will consistently choose part/whole relationships. One who operates primarily with an analytic thinking style will consistently choose alternatives. And one who uses both styles should exhibit choices that reflect the two-to-one bias for part/whole and alternative choices.

The intervention implication is that individuals who exhibit a strong pattern of either part/whole or alternative choices should be encouraged to use other styles. They could be asked to carry out a task; then when it is finished be asked to do it again but in a different way. Part/whole thinkers tend to want things complete or correct. Perhaps they should have some experience with ambiguous or open-ended tasks that do not have a single solution but many. Individuals with strong alternative thinking patterns often have difficulty "getting started" or maintaining a task to completion. Frequently, it is helpful to provide them a finished product and occasionally point out where they are and where they are going. Peer modeling also seems to be effective with this approach.

Body Parts

Witkin et al. (1962) defined differentiation and integration as fundamental processes. As an infant differentiates himself from his environment, he learns about other influences and responses to things about him. As he differentiates his various body parts, he acquires the potential for doing and perceiving different things in different ways. As various differentiation processes occur throughout life, he is given opportunities to learn more about himself and his world. Differentiation occurs not only in the physical world but in the conceptual world as well. Concepts are continually being differentiated and reorganized.

Awareness of body parts and the alternative functions of body parts represent not only a differentiation-integration process but an important developmental period. Awareness of body parts and functions indicates a time when an individual frees himself from the undifferentiated whole that is psychologically fused to his environment and subject to environmental stimulation. Awareness of body parts and functions liberates him so he can act on and move about his environment. Moreover, he can influence the behavior of others, starting with his parents.

Identification of body parts is an early aspect. The integration of body parts in behavior is a somewhat advanced level. Willful use of body parts in a number of alternative functions is an even more advanced level.

Assessment-intervention should deal with the identification and range of alternative functions of body parts as evidence of an early but important aspect of differentiation. Gesture games and songs are useful for this. Action patterns also lead to differentiation and integration: "Point to your mouth," "Show me all the things you can do with your mouth—smile, eat, talk, sing, laugh, cry, pout, frown, drink, suck, smack lips, kiss, etc."

Some individuals can identify their own body parts and demonstrate their functions, but have more difficulty doing this with others. Girls who play "house" have more opportunities to establish a repertoire of alternative functions for body parts than boys who play "guns." This sex difference in play may partially account for why girls are frequently more advanced than boys in some cognitive skills.

After a child demonstrates body part identification, naming, and alternative functions on himself, have him do the same with a doll or draw a picture of himself, his mother, his father, or someone else. Notice how body parts are defined and the relationships between them in each drawing. The studies by Witkin et al. (1962) give details of the developmental aspects of these drawings.

Cognitive Distance

The idea of cognitive distancing was introduced by Piaget (1962). As an individual becomes cognitively more able to represent experience, he becomes increasingly removed from direct stimulation in dealing with it. Cognitively speaking, he becomes increasingly removed from direct stimulation and more reliant on symbolic or representational thought.

Cognitive distancing was operationally defined in terms of three levels: objects, pictorials, and words (Sigel, 1971). Objects give an individual the opportunity to have action patterns toward things. Through action patterns he has direct involvement with experience. Involvement with objects constitutes a low level of cognitive distancing. Pictorials give prototypic information about things, but opportunities for action patterns are absent. They are a higher level of cognitive distancing than objects. Words are labels for concepts or prototypic classes. Words by themselves do not give attributes of things; rather, they indicate the distinctiveness of attributes (Dollard and Miller 1950; Brown 1958a,b; Cazden 1972a). Words refer to or stand for attributes. They are cognitively more distant than pictorials and objects. Research by Hollenberg (1970) on the potential interference of iconic knowledge on concept development may pertain to cognitive distancing.

The assessment and intervention implications are clear. If an individual does not do well with words, the clinician should shift to pictorials. If he has difficulty with pictorials, the clinician should shift to objects. Conversely, individuals who do well with objects should shift to pictorials and then to words.

Burger and Muma (1977) have shown that cognitive distancing appeared in aphasic and in elderly nonaphasic individuals who performed better with objects than with pictures of the same objects. Cognitive distancing may be a factor in the degenerative processes of aging. I have had firsthand clinical experience with learning-disabled children, mentally retarded children, and autistic children with cognitive distancing. One experience with an autistic child stands out. She was playing with things in a toy house, but her play was inappropriate for the representational items. Then I had her play in a real house with a real kitchen. Her play markedly improved in appropriateness. This was an instance of cognitive distance with objects. The toy house was only a representation of a real house.

Categorization/Mediation

"We talk about what we know." This phrase summarizes the importance of categorization in verbal behavior. As Lenneberg (1967, pp. 332–33) put it,

> The abstractness underlying meaning in general . . . may best be understood by considering concept-formation the primary cognitive process, and naming (as well as acquiring a name) the secondary cognitive process.

According to Brown (1956, p. 247) first language is

> a process of cognitive socialization, involving . . . the coordination of speech categories with categories of the nonlinguistic world.

"Categorization of sound patterns and of objects and events in the real world is basic to learning a language" (Nelson 1973, p. 21). Thus, one's underlying concepts are fundamental to what is said and understood in verbal behavior. It is necessary to orient clinical assessment and intervention on the individual's categorization skills.

The clinical fields have relied on vocabulary tests to assess concepts and word knowledge. This reliance is unfortunate because such tests do not assess specific word knowledge. They quantify performance in a normative procedure. Moreover, the words on these tests have little if any relevance to the particular concepts and words an individual needs for his daily functions. These tests are based on the principle of one-word–one-referent. The more important principles of one-word–many-referents and one-referent–many-words are ignored. The result is that these tests play a kind of vacuous numbers game.

Clinicians should map out the concepts an individual knows from a pool of high utility concepts directly relevant to the individual as he naturally functions. This means that clinicians should describe the stage of acquisition of each concept domain as well as the alternative labels for the domains available to the individual. The quantification approach—the numbers game—is of little value in a descriptive approach.

Clinicians should describe an individual's knowledge of concepts and attendant alternative labels in four ways: (1) prototypic knowledge as exemplified by knowledge of focal exemplars, (2) extended knowledge of concepts as exemplified by knowledge of peripheral exemplars, (3) mediational mechanisms that facilitate concept learning and the acquisition of alternative labels as evidenced by underextensions and overextensions (E. Clark 1973a, 1974b), and (4) specific alternative labels, and functions of these labels.

Nelson (1973, 1974) has an excellent discussion on the acquisition of prototypic knowledge of concepts and attendant labeling. The distinction between focal and peripheral exemplars as manifestations of prototypic and extended knowledge of concepts was developed by Heider (1971) and Rosch (1973). (Rosch is Heider's married name.) Focal exemplars of a concept are those that best represent the concept. They contain attributes that delimit the concept. For example, "apple" is a focal exemplar of fruit because it has attributes that constitute "fruitness." Peripheral exemplars, on the other hand, are those that have some attributes of a concept but not the essential ones. Thus, there is some reluctance to include peripheral exemplars in a concept. For example, a walnut is a peripheral exemplar of "fruitness." It is important that concepts overlap so things can be categorized in different ways. This is the dynamism of classification. Such dynamism provides an efficient means of learning and generalizing from one experience to another.

In assessment, an individual is given a number of items that are focal or peripheral exemplars of two, three, or more categories, and asked to put the items in piles that go together. Clinicians should observe the categories an individual selects—focal exemplars only, focal and peripheral exemplars, or categories not evidenced by either focal or peripheral exemplars. Clincians could conclude that an individual has prototypic knowledge of a concept if he puts focal exemplars together, and that his concepts extend to other concepts if he includes peripheral exemplars.

Concepts that do not evidence either focal or focal and peripheral exemplars are not yet acquired in the adult sense. The next assessment question is which mediators facilitate concept learning for a particular individual. The two types are mediating mechanisms and mediating agents. The former include action patterns or functions, labeling, class name, and exemplars. An individual who does not exhibit adult categories in terms of focal or focal and peripheral exemplars should be asked to demonstrate the function of items. Then ask him to sort the items into piles. If function is a mediator for him, he will utilize focal or focal and peripheral exemplars. If it is not, no change will occur in his performance. Piaget (1954, 1962) held that things that have the same action patterns will be classified alike. Thus, using action patterns can mediate categories. Another strategy is to ask the individual to name or talk about each item. Then, he should attempt to classify the items. Labeling or talking about each item may mediate the classes. An individual could be given a class name such as "fruit," "vegetables," or "candy," whereupon the individual will use the class name to categorize them. Specific exemplars can also be used to mediate categories. A focal or peripheral exemplar can be extracted from a pile of items, whereupon the individual can select other exemplars to go with it. The clinician would try to ascertain the mediators most productive for the individual over a range of concepts.

The individual himself may demonstrate functions, label items, give a class name, or select focal or peripheral exemplars in an attempt to mediate categories. However, other mediating agents may also be effective. A clinician could do these functions. A peer, sibling, or parent could do them also. Peer modeling has worked especially well with some children. A goal of the clinician is to identify not only the mediating mechanisms most productive for the individual, but also the most effective mediating agents.

Categorization skills should deal with concepts of a high utility to the individual. They should be about things at home, school, on the playground, downtown, or anywhere an individual functions. The concepts should be about objects, actions, relationships, and attributes. The categorization process should represent varying levels of cognitive distance, and must always be regarded as open-ended. The individual must never get the idea that he knows all about a concept. He should realize that his experiences with it are only with exemplars. He can always find more exemplars.

In addition to an individual's knowledge of concepts, extension of concepts, and mediational mechanisms and agents, clinicians should ascertain his ability to selectively employ alternative labels for exemplars. These alternative labels should reflect alternative functions of things. Labeling the behavior of young children is misleading. Labeling follows the new information/old information principle

(Wieman 1976; Nelson 1973, 1974), in which things that change get named. However, the names or labels used are not necessarily evidence of what an individual knows (Bowerman, in press,a,b). Child labels are not necessarily adult labels. A child may use a label but not have the differentiated attributes of the concept an adult does. This leads to some unusual naming behavior in childhood, called underextension and overextension (E. Clark 1973a, 1974b, Reich 1976), and underinclusion and overinclusion (Bloom 1973). Overextension is the use of a word beyond adult usage. "Doggy" for a horse is an overextension. Underextension is a child's objections to a label when the label is acceptable in adult usage. A child may object to someone calling his dog an animal: "Fluffy is a doggy. He's not an animal." The early acquisition and use of relational terms indicates that a child's use of labels is not a good index of adult knowledge of the terms. For example, a young child may say, "More Mommy," as he sees his mother pour juice into a glass. But, he means less. His mother continues to pour and the child continues to say, "More Mommy," in frustration. The child has yet to learn contrasts for the particular relational terms. Flavell (1970) has shown that while a term may be used, the underlying meanings or concepts go through stages of increased status, validity, and accessibility in becoming adultlike. A word is not a concept. Indeed it may be misleading in early language learning to accept one label as evidence that the label is an adult label indexing many referents, or that any referent can be named in a variety of ways.

In assessment and intervention, clinicians should keep a running account of the words an individual uses and the range of alternative functions of those words. Also, clinicians should keep track of the individual's ability to give different labels to the same things. One of the most important clues to a limited knowledge of underlying concepts is underextension and overextension. Clinicians must identify referents and labels when they occur. This not only identifies a partially learned concept but directs the clinician to the concepts to deal with it in intervention, and to the attributes of the concept that should be varied with other exemplars. For example, if a child calls a horse, "Doggy," the clinician should give the child experiences with dogs and horses emphasizing the differences underlying the attributes.

Intervention in labeling should be based on the principle that one word has many referents and one referent has many labels. The traditional notion of picture-naming is too superficial—one label, one picture. An improvement would be to talk about each picture. Clinicians should adopt the strategy that as a word is used by a child, he is asked to find several examples of the word. Clinicians should not interrupt the child to find alternative referents for words or alternative words for each referent. Disruptions in the communicative process should be avoided. Clinicians could have special times for such activities. Also, they should vary available references to see if the individual will vary his accordingly.

Figure 9-1 outlines concept/label learning in regard to focal/peripheral exemplars, mediators, and cognitive distancing. This outline pertains to ostensive and relational terms, and to objects, actions, and relationships.

OBJECTS, ACTIONS, RELATIONSHIPS, ATTRIBUTES

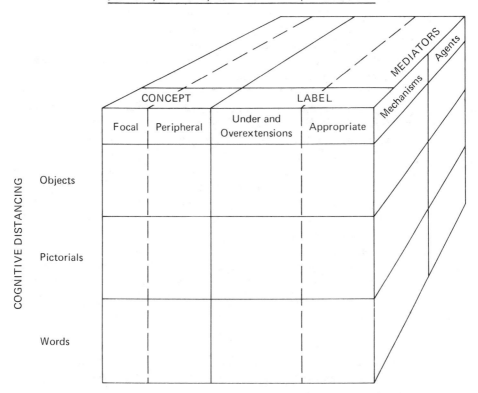

Figure 9-1 *Schematic of concept-label learning in regard to mediators and cognitive distancing.*

Summary

Since language is cognitive and predicated on underlying cognitive capacities, assessment-intervention of an individual's language must deal with cognitive systems. Piagetian psychology, especially the sensorimotor period, provides a useful framework for assessing prelinguistic cognitive capacities. Perceptual salience may account for an inordinate orientation on specific perceptual variables and for the distinctive behaviors of some clinical groups, i.e., autism, learning disabilities, mental retardation, etc. The Bruner model of motoric, iconic, and symbolic processing indicates that intervention should be oriented on the type of processing an individual relies on. Rule/nonrule governed learning assessment-intervention suggests that a nonrule governed learner needs some assistance in categorization and organization of categories. Primacy/recency memory functions provide a useful means of assessment. Recency functions appear in the spontaneous speech of young children and individuals with aphasia, mental retardation, and autism. These functions in either spontaneous speech or prepared material provide a way of assessing the degree to which individuals know or use inherent structure of linguistic material. The technology of reckoning refers to an individual's ability to reckon with single attributes, clusters of attributes, and integrated attributes.

Cognitive tempo pertains to an individual's style of thinking, either impulsive or reflective. In intervention, an impulsive thinker becomes more reflective by peer modeling, examining alternative consequences, delaying decisions, and so on. Another way of dealing with cognitive style is part/whole and alternatives thinking. The body parts of oneself and others constitute an early cognitive stage of the differentiation between the self and the world of experiences. Individuals who have difficulty with this area probably have rather limited concepts. Intervention should be addressed to concept formation through the use of action patterns.

Labeling is based on categorization and the mediation of categories. It is necessary for an individual to categorize objects, actions, relationships, and events in ways that correspond somewhat to the categories of others. Thus, one's labels for categories can be understood by others. If the labels refer to mutual, underlying thoughts, both encoder and decoder have the potential to communicate. The assessment of categorization and mediation skills deal with three major issues about high-utility concepts: (a) concepts the individual knows on a rudimentary level—classification of focal exemplars, (b) concepts he knows that extend to other concepts—classification of peripheral exemplars, and (c) mediators and mediating agents that facilitate his classifications. Intervention is directed toward improved classification skills for those categories an individual has difficulty with, and the utilization of those mediating agents that facilitate his learning.

10

Assessment-Intervention: Linguistic Systems

The keys to appropriate assessment-intervention of linguistic systems are individual differences, process orientations, and contextual influences. Developmental scales and other normative measures are of questionable value. They obscure individual differences, deal with categories and products, and essentially omit contextual influences. An appropriate assessment-intervention program must deal with the particular cognitive-linguistic-communicative systems each individual has at his command. Moreover, it must take into account the particular contextual influences on his command of these systems. Patterns of performance taken from natural behavior are needed. Normative tests and developmental profiles provide only marginally useful information because they force an individual to conform to a group, reduce linguistic systems to categories and numbers, and delete contextual influences. Normative tests and developmental profiles are essentially irrelevant to an assessment-intervention program for individuals.

Descriptive procedures, on the other hand, are appropriate. They are directly relevant to individual differences, to the identification of processes, and to contextual influences. Moreover, they provide directly relevant intervention alternatives. All of the major researchers in child language use descriptive procedures; none use normative tests. These include Brown, Slobin, Bloom, Bowerman, McNeill, Nelson, Bellugi-Klima, Cazden, and in the cognitive domain, Piaget. Moreover, they stress the importance of individual differences and contextual influences.

Bronfenbrenner (1974) argued that natural contextual influences are so important that much of the child development literature, i.e., developmental profiles, group or normative tests, and so on, is ecologically invalid. The research and literature in the clinical fields are even more vulnerable to this criticism because individual differences are so outstanding in clinical groups. Kagan (1967) and Deese (1969) have argued that behavior is relative, not absolute. Tests and developmental profiles are not as definitive or powerful as they may appear. Contextual influences reflect relativity but normative tests and developmental profiles do not.

Clinicians have a choice whether they will play a numbers game and use quantitative measures or deal with an individual according to his needs and how he functions naturally. It may be easier to play the numbers game, but a profession cannot afford to have a large portion of its members playing a numbers game without the profession itself becoming technician oriented and political-authoritarian instead of clinician oriented and disciplined. Ultimately, a technician and political-authoritarian profession will loose public trust and support. The fields of mental retardation, learning disabilities, special education, and speech pathology seem to vacillate between a technician orientation with numbers games and a clinician orientation with descriptive patterns for each individual. This is more than a personal opinion. Class action suits across the country stem from situations where individuals are labeled retarded by intelligence test performance. Technician attitudes in special education and speech pathology have led to narrow views of speech in which speech is separated from language and language from cognition. Moreover, technicians have attempted to make something of modality differences when in fact modality similarities are much more substantial in a systems approach. The whole accountability issue has fostered technician oriented clinical fields. State and federal funding has come to depend upon ''accountability.'' Most clinicians respond to accountability by playing a numbers game by using normative tests and ''developmental profiles.'' Funding agencies like to play numbers games, but unfortunately, normative tests and developmental profiles obscure the most important information in clinical assessment: individual differences, processes, and contextual influences. A much more appropriate and powerful way to deal with is through descriptive procedures. The accountability issue needs to be reexamined. It is premature and misleading (Siegel 1975). Accountability should be dealt with as in the medical profession: peer review.

The Nonverbal Child

The primary goals for a nonverbal child are: (1) to establish a desire to communicate, (2) to identify and increase the number of vocalizations, (3) to vary the vocalizations or establish a repertoire of alternative vocalizations and functions, and (4) to elicit purposeful naming behavior at the one- and two-word levels. An assessment-intervention program for a nonverbal child might be approached from five major points of view: behavior modification, modeling, Piagetian psychology, socio-emotional security base, and realizing the instrumental power of speech acts.

The behavior modification approach can be used to systematically increase vocalizations and decrease behaviors that interfere with vocalizations. Observations of a child are made to establish baselines of performance for target areas, i.e., number of vocalizations, amount of play with noisemaking toys, attentiveness to noise sources or speaking activities, etc. Conditions that lead to vocalizations are systematically varied to identify the contingencies that effect an individual's vocalizations. These are systematically manipulated, especially in regard to reinforcements for increasing vocalizations. Behavior modification approaches have been particularly successful in making nonverbal children[1] verbal.

Modeling procedures have also worked well. Nonverbal children are given an opportunity to play with a variety of toys, some of which make noises. The children are encouraged to make the noises that the toys represent—trucks, babies, dogs, etc. In a more formal approach, a nonverbal child may observe another child making various noises during play. Eventually, the nonverbal child will attempt to make similar noises. A cinician should play with the toys the same way a child plays with them, including making the same kinds of sounds. After awhile, a clinician should vary the sound and action patterns inducing a child to do the same. As a child varies action patterns and verbalizes, he learns more about things. He realizes the power of labeling through the peer, sibling, parent, teacher, and clinician responses to his environment. This kind of activity could be regarded as a precursor to the principle that one referent has many labels. Modeling can be fostered by peer and sibling interaction. Modeling action patterns towards objects, actions, and relationships affords a way of concept formation that Piaget described in the sensorimotor period (1954, 1962).

In a Piagetian approach to a nonverbal child, the child is encouraged to have a variety of action patterns toward things about him. Variations of action patterns provide opportunities to learn new attributes of things. The more attributes the child knows and the more variations he encounters, the more he is likely to attempt to name them (Mussen, Conger, and Kagan 1969; Flavell 1970). As various actions are taken toward something such as a toy truck, the probabilities are high that a variety of labels will also occur. This in turn means that an individual may encounter words he encountered before that have similar action patterns. This is an opportunity to learn the principle that one referent has many words and one word many referents. A variety of action patterns toward things offers a motor analogy to the verbal principle that things can have a variety of labels. If a nonverbal child is in the sensorimotor stage (or is a motoric processor in the Bruner sense) he may need a repertoire of actions before he begins labeling. Gesture games and songs would also be useful for this purpose.

I wish to offer a caution regarding repetitive or cyclic action patterns. Prolonged repetitive action patterns are detrimental to learning, because a child has an inordinate orientation on a constant set of attributes, to the exclusion of others. Variation is what is important. If a child gets into prolonged cyclic motor patterns, the clinician should distract him or change the situation to get him out of the cycle. The sensorimotor period is especially important for a nonverbal child. In addition to action patterns, it may be necessary to focus on cognitive skills (see Chap. 9).

Many nonverbal children are simply reticent. Stewart (1968) reported that many nonverbal disadvantaged children are reticent in school, but at home are

---

[1]Any time a clinician is dealing with a nonverbal child a hearing evaluation must be done and a mental and neurological examination carried out.

highly verbal. Sroufe (1970) made the same point. Apparently, when there are significant contrasts between a child's natural environment and a special circumstance such as a test or schoolroom, the probability increases that the child will be reticent. Cazden (1966a) held that when ethnic and socioeconomic differences between child and adult contrast significantly, the child will be reticent. It follows that dialect differences between child and teacher, especially when the teacher (or clinician) attempts to "correct" the child, will lead to reticence. If reports about a nonverbal child indicate that he is verbal in other circumstances, the clinician should orient the intervention process to a situation where the child can be relaxed.

I once had a nonverbal girl from a middle class white family. Her teacher was frustrated because the girl had been in class for six weeks without saying a thing to anyone—not even during recess. Her teacher and I spoke to the parents, who reported that she and her siblings were very verbal at home. The therapy sessions were changed to playing house with two peers. We got two large refrigerator cartons which we (the girl, two peers, and I) painted to look like houses. Over a period of a few weeks, the girl was talking—a little at first but by the end of the year she was highly verbal.

Clinicians should know a basic principle of child socio-emotional development that accounts for some reticent and unrepresentative behavior in clinical assessment. It is the principle of a *security base* (Bowlby 1969; Antonucci 1976; Ainsworth 1969). Children operate within a security base as defined by them. If forced to operate outside that base, they will be reticent, hostile, or atypical in various ways. Two major mechanisms that violate an individual's security base are separation anxiety and stranger anxiety. A clinician may precipitate separation anxiety and stranger anxiety by taking a child away from his parents into a room with a stranger (the clinician).

I recommend keeping the child and parent together during assessment and intervention. A parent can sit in a chair and observe, and I can comment about things or ask brief questions. Moreover, parents can be progressively incorporated into the intervention process. During the initial session, when my presence may induce stranger anxiety, I have adopted the following procedure: I place several toys on the floor within a few feet of the mother's chair. The mother and I talk about her impressions of the child's play, interests, typical day, etc. During this time, the child is usually in physical contact with his mother, often on her lap. He will make several visual checks of me. If I do not give him any particular attention, he will slip out of his mother's lap and pick up a toy. Usually he brings the toy back to the security base of his mother and plays with it while also making more visual checks of me. As his visual checks of me cease and he becomes involved in play, I get on the floor, maintaining approximately the same distance, and begin playing with a toy in much the same way he does. I may look at him once in awhile, but my play at this point mirrors his. After a few minutes, I will knock my blocks toward him, drive my toy truck toward him, walk my doll toward him, etc. In some way my activity comes closer to him. I purposely miss him while making some kind of physical contact such as brushing him as I pass by. Then I turn around, come back, and play briefly. I may do this several times. I will also give him something to hold that I will use later. I will not ask him for it, but just take it with a matter-of-fact, "Thank you." These kinds of interactions get him oriented toward my activity. When he is watching me more than playing by himself, I will sometimes tease him by putting my body between him and my activity. This usually makes him lean over or move to watch me play. When he does that, I have been accepted into his security base and play will then be relatively representative of his regular play. This procedure works most of the time and takes only twenty to thirty minutes.

Verbal behavior is instrumental behavior. Words serve as instruments to get things done for someone. I can say, "Pass the chicken." When someone passes it, my utterance has served an instrumental function. Differential crying of an infant is instrumental because it leads to different acts by his mother. A very important aspect of intervention for nonverbal children is to develop a child's awareness of the instrumental power of vocalization-verbalizations. Clinicians should be careful observers of a child's behavior. Whenever a child produces a vocalization or verbalization, the clinician should give the child attention, and if its purpose can be deduced, the clinician should respond appropriately. After a variety of responsive reactions by his clinician, teachers, and parents, a nonverbal child should realize that his vocal or verbal acts have instrumental power. Following this, the child will increase the frequency of his utterances and the range of their circumstances and functions. At this point, variations should be encouraged. This leads to differential utterances, which can be vocal as well as verbal. Vocally, differential crying, babbling, and echolalia may occur. Verbally, words are differentiated sound patterns with differentiated meanings. Differentiated utterances require differentiated circumstances and response patterns. Clinicians should be sure to have different responses for different utterances. As a nonverbal child exhibits a variety of utterances and spontaneously increases their number, the clinician should selectively misunderstand some of them, inducing increased explicitness with alternative codes for his communicative intents.

One- and Two-Word Utterances

Assessment-intervention for children who have essentially one- and two-word utterances is based on underlying cognitive skills. Chapter 9 deals with these skills—the Piagetian sensorimotor stage, Bruner motoric-iconic-symbolic cognitive processing stages, categorization-mediation, etc. Moreover, some assessment-intervention suggestions for nonverbal children are also useful for a child with two-word utterances, such as modeling, instrumental functions of utterances, etc.

Assessment-intervention efforts for this type of child should be centered on the principle that one word has many referents and one referent has many words (or labels). Efforts should focus on the principle that early naming behavior is about new information in the context of old and dynamic as opposed to static attributes of objects, actions, and relationships. The principle of cognitive distancing should be used. Given these principles, it follows that intervention should be in natural or near natural contexts rather than special treatment in a special room. Children can play house, cowboys-and-Indians, or anything they wish. During the course of play, things should be named different ways and different things be given the same name. Things should be changed, especially through the child's manipulation. A clinician should parallel talk (label) things, actions, relationships, attributes, and emotional states in the course of play. The clinician should not be a passive bystander labeling events. He or she should be actively involved and enjoying the activity, and should allow the child to play in his way on his terms. Usually it is helpful to have two or three children playing together. Too often clinicians feel compelled to teach during play. They convert the play period to an instructional quiz game that loses the integrity and purpose of play. Such clinicians spend large amounts of time asking a child, "What's this?" Children do not have to display learning in the "What's this?–What's that?" behavioristic manner. Parallel talking by a clinician may be more effective because labels are provided in the course of play and the integrity or continuity of the activity is maintained. Over a long period (such as several weeks or months) evidence can be obtained about what a person has learned.

I have used parallel talking successfully with nonverbal children, as well as with verbal children learning new forms and new functions of language. With Joey, a nonverbal child, I selectively named objects. I chose objects because Joey had a few labels that were mostly names of things. As Joey played with others (me, peers, siblings, parents), I named things, i.e., "doggy," "horsie," "Lassie," "Mama," "tuk" (truck), "do" (coat), etc. At first, I used the same labels he used. But, I changed each one to an adult label after he had used it with a few different referents or after he spontaneously imitated me (Bloom, Hood, Lightbown 1974). If Joey said, "duk" or "dut" for truck; I would use the same word and play with the truck so he had a referent for his label. Or, if he was playing with a truck, I would say "duk" and show an interest in his truck. After he had either heard or said "duk" a few times (particularly if he spontaneously imitated me), I produced the adult form. I would never stop the activity to teach the word, "truck."

Notice what this parallel talking activity offers for language learning. First, it begins with the level of learning of a child, cognitively by virtue of the action patterns he initiates and grammatically in terms of the specific word forms he tries and the phonological patterns he can utter. Second, parallel talking is timely. It deals with actual references and events. Third, it deals with a child's communicative intent when he attempts to label something. Fourth, labels can be used when a child indicates different functions for things. The clinician can say "truck" as the child reaches for a truck, pushes it, loads it, makes truck noises, etc. The child will come to realize that a label has several referents. Then, the clinician should respond to the activity in terms of the *purpose* of a child's utterances. If the child says "duk" while reaching for a truck, the clinician should say "duk" immediately and help him get the truck. *Nothing works better in language learning than a speech act that works as intended.* As Joey begins to label actions, the parallel talking shifts to actions.

With more advanced individuals, parallel talking is the same, in the sense that it is used with an ongoing activity and in response to spontaneous imitation. The only difference is a substantive one: more advanced individuals are trying to learn elaborate semantic-syntactic systems. Thus, parallel talking is oriented to the particular systems an individual is trying to learn and the particular linguistic and referential contexts of his learning. Billy was trying to learn the adjectival system in object noun phrases with inanimate nouns. This target system, with its co-occurring linguistic systems, was deduced from studying patterns of spontaneous speech. Parallel talking was then oriented on alternative adjectival modifications of inanimate nouns. A clinician said, "big chair," "yellow hat," "straw hat," "noseguard," and so on in the course of the activity.

Clinicians can use Roger Brown's (1973b) five stages as an assessment framework. Stage one deals with semantic functions and relations of one- and two-word utterances. The primary concern about early utterances is their range of semantic functions. The actual words spoken are not as important as the kind of events being coded in language. Clinicians should note if single-word utterances are used for the following functions: comments or greetings; vocatives (call for someone); identify agent, action, or object; possession; recurrence; nonexistence; disappearance; rejection; cessation; and existence.

Under Slobin's principle, one word can serve several functions. A child can invent a word and use the word to fill in grammatical constituents until adult linguistic forms are learned. Invented words serve many functions, and can gloss over entire systems. Bloom (1970, 1973) reported that the invented word "wida" functioned in several ways. As the child learned other words in the language that served these functions, "wida" dropped out. Thus, clinicians should describe the various functions of one- and two-word utterances as a way of assessing the range of functions a child is trying to code in language. They should describe the various word forms used for each function.

Bloom (1973) described a period of successive one-word utterances as a transition period from one-word to two-word utterances. Successive one-word utterances are precursors of word combinations. A child might make a one-word greeting, a one-word identification of agent, or a one-word identification of action. Shortly thereafter, he will combine them in a single utterance. The greeting gets the attention of the listener and provides some assurance that the communicative process is under way. Preschool children will sometimes string a series of utterances together with "and" or "and ah," apparently to keep the communicative process going.

Initial two-word utterances are very similar to one-word utterances in that the same functions are coded (Slobin 1973). However, after an individual has made many two- and perhaps three- or four-word utterances, he will add new functions—locative, attributive, experiencer-state, dative, communicative, instrumental, etc. Notice that additional functions lead to increased explicitness.

Some children prefer to focus on the dynamic property of labeling. They are word or referential learners (Nelson 1974), and emphasize alternative referents for words and alternative words for referents. They go around naming everything in sight seeking confirmation for their names. Others adopt a different strategy of language learning, and are phrase or expressive learners (Nelson 1974). These enjoy making new word combinations to explore syntactic mechanisms. Clinicians should identify which strategy an individual is following to be able to use it in intervention. A child will use both strategies but one will be emphasized. Intervention for word learners should deal with action patterns and alternative referents with alternative words. Intervention for phrase learners should focus on syntactic mechanisms.

Two-Word Utterances and Beyond

When an individual begins to make word combinations, assessment-intervention should shift from emphasizing semantic functions to an emphasis on semantic-syntactic systems and the contextual influences and constraints of these systems. It is necessary to sample an individual's verbal behavior in several (a minimum of three) contexts in order to account for the linguistic systems at his disposal. Moreover, it is necessary to note available referents and presumed communicative intent. This information is important because the actual utterances are unreliable indices of the child's language (Bloom 1973; Bowerman, in press,a,b). Clinicians should not assume adult knowledge is in child utterances.

Just as clinicians need evidence about available reference and presumed communicative intent, they must look at patterns of verbal behavior across a number of utterances taken from a variety of communicative conditions. A single utterance is insufficient. A few instances may be suggestive. But a pattern of many instances reveals how a system is functioning. It is inappropriate to say in advance that a certain sample size is needed. The more important issue is that a particular system appears in sufficient quantity and detail to deduce the pattern of the system in the context of other systems and to describe it and identify co-occurring influences.

Brown's (1973a,b) five stages provide a useful framework for analyzing two-word utterances and beyond (see Fig. 6-6). Stage One deals with semantic and relational functions of one-word utterances. Clinicians should describe the extent to which the functions of one-word utterances also appear in two-word ones. They should also describe new functions. Stage Two deals with what Brown calls "modulations of meaning." Various linguistic mechanisms modulate meanings—inflectional rules, determiner system, etc. Clinicians should identify and describe the linguistic mechanisms an individual tries to use to do this. Stage Three deals with the sentence types and the mechanisms that make sentence types—yes/no questions, *wh*-questions, negations, imperatives, etc. They should identify and describe these systems in terms of how the child tries to use them. Stages Four and Five deal with elaborations and modifications of utterances. Clinicians should identify and describe the various transformational operations at the child's disposal. These descriptions should be of developmental sequences for each system and its co-occurring influences, and of phrase structure equivalences and transformational operations.

Clinicians have two ways of describing linguistic systems in detail. One is from induced recall of spontaneous utterances and the other is a perusal of spontaneous speech samples. Until recently, sentence recall tasks were considered a useful way of identifying the linguistic systems an individual knows or does not know. The various responses on sentence recall indeed provide useful information on an individual's language learning (Slobin and Welch 1971). However, Prutting and Connolly (1976) warned that induced recall might not be important. Apparently there are fundamental problems with sentence recall tasks. First, they predetermine co-occurring structures for a target system before meeting the child. A child's co-occurring systems, which are unique to the individual, undoubtedly vary considerably from those of published sentence recall tasks. Even though published sentence recall tasks may be comprehensive in surveying syntactic systems, they lack relevance for the child's individual systems.

Second, they are referentially removed from the coding process. Third, they eliminate communicative intent. If the assessment process is reduced to linguistic domains, these two limitations would occur. The best way to use induced sentence recall to assess linguistic knowledge is to derive target sentences from a child's spontaneous speech, preserving relevant co-occurrences. This is done by analyzing spontaneous speech samples and identifying specific systems for assessment. Then, specific utterances containing a target system can be used in a sentence recall task. Such utterances could also be used to devise slightly altered sentences for recall.

A perusal of spontaneous speech samples gives clinicians the ability to identify target systems for a descriptive analysis and for identifying co-occurring systems. The procedure is this: Analyze each utterance in a large language sample (over several circumstances), usually 200–300 utterances. Make notes about the basic sentence types, transformational operations, alternatives or equivalencies within systems, and restricted structures (linguistic systems that evidence child stages). Note which systems a child knows well, which he knows partially, or which are missing. It is difficult to know if missing systems are absent because the child does not know them or because there was no occasion to use them. Note the linguistic conditions—co-occurring structures—of each target system. Look for instances in which a child: (a) says an utterance, then says it again (usually with a slight variation), (b) utters spontaneous imitations of available models, (c) makes false starts and revisions, and (d) exhibits overextensions and underextensions of labels.

These four kinds of events provide specific information about the particular aspects of learning an individual may be attempting, the linguistic conditions of learning (co-occurrences), and the referential conditions of learning.

Let me illustrate how a descriptive assessment procedure works in describing an individual's command of a target system, and the influences of co-occurring systems on this system. Billy was a five-year-old boy who had a learning disability that was manifested in cognitive and linguistic systems. Spontaneous speech samples were taken in play sessions, in speech therapy, in kindergarten play time, and at home. Perusal of his language samples indicated that he had several syntactic systems that were "delayed or aberrant" in development. The pronominal system was of special interest because Billy placed an inordinate reliance on it and evidenced some interesting variations both structurally and functionally with pronominals, and because the co-occurring systems were sufficiently plentiful for deriving patterns of the command of his pronominal system. Resuming the numbers used in Chap. 4, utterances (71) through (83) illustrate Billy's inordinate reliance on the pronominal system. This reflects co-occurring difficulties with noun phrases.

(71) Him got some some marbles
(72) Him got a mitt, a new mitt, a new baseball mitt
(73) Me have one; me have a bike; me have a two two-wheeler
(74) Me have it
(75) Him gonna win; he gonna win
(76) Me give him a bat
(77) Her Mommy seen it
(78) Her, the lady say I can
(79) Her, my my teacher say it OK
(80) The man, he was nice
(81) My sis sister she, she watch TV
(82) My Daddy Daddy, he work all day
(83) The turtle it was big; it was big

Notice that all subject noun phrases contained personal pronouns. In some subject noun phrases, Billy attempted to use the proper noun system or the determiner plus noun system, but in each case he buttressed his efforts with pronouns. Also, notice that the pronominal forms in the subject noun phrases were in the objective form (him, me, her) rather than the subjective form (he, I, she), probably indicating that the first acquisition of these pronominals was in object noun phrases, which in turn may indicate a recency processing function in acquisition (Slobin 1973; Olson 1973; Ervin-Tripp 1973; Brown, Cazden, and Bellugi-Klima 1969). Notice the instances in which Billy said a noun phrase, then either expanded it or changed it to another form. Several patterns emerged regarding co-occurring systems. It was evident that Billy was in the process of learning a variety of nominals (noun phrases). His reliance on pronouns and co-occurrences (and his false starts) provided descriptive patterns that not only indicated difficulty with various nominals and an inordinate reliance on pronouns, but revealed co-occurring influences. This kind of information is not deducible from published tests. More important, it is directly relevant to an individual's command of linguistic systems. The intervention implication is to provide opportunities for the child to vary and explore the linguistic systems he is currently learning in the context of the systems he is using.

The concept of co-occurrence appears in most of these utterances, but consider only (71) and (72) for a moment. In (71) the object noun phrase is "some some marbles" which is a repeated determiner (nondefinite article) and an inanimate noun. In (72) the object noun phrase is "a mitt, a new mitt, a new baseball mitt," which is a determiner (nondefinite article) and an inanimate noun that is initially unmodified, then modified by a prenoun adjective and finally by a second prenoun adjective which modifies the previous one. In (71) it appears that he is trying to deal with the determiner system, specifically nondefinite articles, and in (72) that he is trying to learn adjectival modifiers. I should mention that the adjectival effort in (72) is rather remarkable for him. I have analyzed more than 200 of his utterances. Billy has considerable difficulty with the determiner system. Further utterances would substantiate or refute these impressions. Co-occurrences for these loci are somewhat similar in both (71) and (72). Notice that both occur in object noun phrases and involve inanimate nouns. Also, notice that the subject noun phrases are personal pronouns in the objective form and the auxiliary, and verbs are evidenced by a gloss verbal "get." Thus, it can tentatively be said that Billy attempts the determiner system in the following co-occurring linguistic conditions: object noun phrase with an inanimate noun, subject noun phrase with a personal pronoun in the objective form, and the gloss verb, "got." His attempts to deal with adjectives exhibit similar co-occurrences. If these are sustained in subsequent utterances, they would define the linguistic conditions with which the determiner and adjectival systems should be dealt in intervention. Thus, co-occurrence defines how the acquisition of specific linguistic systems enters into an individual grammar: in linguistic context.

Glossing is a process in syntactic acquisition in which a verbal form represents several forms. Previously, I indicated that children will invent words if they do not know one yet wish to code something. Invented words drop out as a child learns the appropriate ones. Glossing is a similar process. Children will use one or a few words to stand for many words. As the specific words are learned, the "all-purpose" words become limited in their function. Verbs and auxiliaries are frequently glossed by "got"/"get"; "have ta," and "wanna." When these first appear in child language it is difficult to know their auxiliary or verbal function: "Me gotta go." "Me gotta doggy." "Me gotta watch it." These are different functions of "gotta." The only way a clinician can discern the intent is by mapping out the various uses the child has for this form. Common gloss forms for nominals are "one," "some," and "it."

Clinicians should realize that although a descriptive assessment procedure of co-occurring systems is time consuming and requires some linguistic knowledge on their part, it is neither prohibitively time consuming nor too difficult. Indeed, the patterns in these few sentences should be substantiated by more utterances, but the point is that descriptive patterns of co-occurrences are discernible from small samples. Larger samples are needed because some patterns are so infrequent that they may be misleading. By including co-occurring systems in the description of a target system, analysis need be done only for a small number of target systems, since the information overlaps. Clinicians need not be distressed if they lack linguistic knowledge. I have conducted many workshops with such clinicians. They can find useful patterns in language samples even though they may not be able to name the linguistic labels for the patterns.

Sampling, data reduction, translation, and analysis can be done on a tentative basis for a child in half a day. Although further substantiation is needed, such a preliminary analysis will provide a clinician much more information, and information directly relevant to the individual, than the amount of information acquired in a comparable amount of time with formal standardized tests. Indeed, the clinician trained in descriptive assessment procedures can produce more than one who uses normative tests. Given the same amount of time with the client, the clinician using a descriptive approach will provide more evidence, and it will be more directly relevant to how the child functions.

Operational Framework: Linguistic Analysis

It is sometimes helpful to have an operational framework for carrying out a linguistic analysis. The following is a step-by-step procedure.

STEP 1: OBTAIN APPROPRIATE LANGUAGE SAMPLE(S)

The goal is to obtain sufficiently long and varied utterances to be *representative* of the client's natural verbal behavior. It is impossible to say in advance how large the sample must be. The size is determined by the kind of structures and the extent to which the utterances are sufficiently detailed patterns of performance to map out systems of interest. For example, a clinician may want to study an individual's command of negations. It is necessary to sample his speech until a number of negations occur that permit describing a pattern of usage. This may require fifty or 500 utterances.

Representativeness requires that the speech samples be taken from several typical situations. I feel that at least three different situations are needed. Frequently these include the child with a peer, a sibling, a parent, and a clinician. They are usually child-initiated play. Sometimes the samples are obtained at his home, school, and playground in addition to the clinic.

Videotape recording is the best recording method because it not only allows a way of rechecking what was said, but also provides a way of noting available reference and communicative intent. Audio recording can be done, but simply writing the utterances seems to be better. A clinician has to decide in advance which domain will be the primary focus—phonological, morphological, syntactic, semantic functions and relations, alternative encoding devices, communicative play—because it is all but impossible to keep notes of all of these areas.

Clinicians must be especially careful in transcribing and segmenting speech samples. Naive clinicians tend to alter child utterances in transcription, thereby inserting unwanted biases. They delete word, phrase, and sentence fragments that provide useful clues about loci of learning. They must be careful not to segment the sample in such a way that relevant information is lost.

STEP 2: SEMANTIC FUNCTIONS AND RELATIONS

The first step in analysis is to map out the various functions or purposes the individual attempts to encode or decode. This is especially important in dealing with one- and two-word utterances. Clinicians should describe nominal, verbal, adverbial, and adjectival functions, and utterance modes such as questions, imperatives, declaratives, and negatives. Within each of these areas are various subfunctions. Subfunctions of nominals include agent, object, dative (indirect object), explicit (proper) nouns, pronouns, animate/inanimate nouns, and ego/nonego nominals. Verb functions include actions, relationships, states, animateness/inanimateness, tense, and modality. Adverbial functions include place, time, manner, conditionality, cause, duration, and so on. Adjectival functions include dynamic attributes, static attributes, number, possessiveness, relativity, etc. Many of the various functions have explicit linguistic markings or devices that can be ascertained in the syntactic analysis.

STEP 3: SYNTAX

It is necessary to give a description of each sentence or sentence fragment. This description should be in terms of sentence type, transformation operations, and specific constituents. For example, utterances (71), (74), and (77) would have the following descriptions:

(71)	NP_1	*aux*	*verbal*	NP_2		*N*
	personal pronoun (object)	(?)	(got)	det (NA) repeated	det (NA)	inanimate plural

Sentence type: VT
Transformations: None

(74)	NP_1	*aux*	*verbal*	NP_2
	personal pronoun (object)	present	Vh	Pronoun

Sentence type: Vh
Transformations: None

(77)   *NP*₁   *aux*   *verbal*   *NP*₂

Det   N   past   VT   pronoun
pos   animate
Sentence type: VT
Transformations: None

Clinicians should be especially alert for spontaneous imitations, consecutive utterances that are slight variations of each other, false starts and revisions, and overextensions and underextensions. The last pertain more to underlying concept formation whereas the others reflect syntactic knowledge, memory processing, and conceptual underpinnings such as cognitive distancing and classification. These are of special significance in assessment and intervention because they indicate varying co-occurrences of loci of learning.

Next, a clinician should analyze syntactic equivalencies and their linguistic contexts. What are the different types of nominals and what are the contexts of their appearance? Can an individual use the following nominals as agents or objects: proper nouns, pronouns, indefinite nouns, determiner and animate noun, determiner and inanimate noun, factive nominal, for-to nominal, gerund, etc.? What are the different kinds of adjectivals? Adverbials? Verbals? What morphological rules does he have?

STEP 4: PHONOLOGY

Which phonemes does an individual have difficulty producing? For each of these phonemes, it is necessary to map out coarticulatory influences. This is done by describing the phonetic contexts in which a target phoneme occurs. In looking over these contexts, it is possible to deduce which phonetic parameters give the individual difficulties and which do not. For example, a child may produce an [s] well in "soup," "sock," "supper," "street," but not in "stop," "goose," and "ice." Thus, a clinician might conclude that he produces a better [s] in a prevocalic position than a postvocalic one. However, a prevocalic [s] in a consonantal cluster before a high front vowel is better than with a low front vowel.

Next, a clinician should analyze the child's phonetic production in terms of phonotactic rules such as voicing, duplication, cluster reduction, diminutive, weak syllable deletion, and syllabic reduction (CV syllables). On a more advanced level, phonetic variation can be analyzed according to a more elaborate syllabic structure (see Chap. 5).

STEP 5: COMMUNICATION GAME

If an individual seems to know various linguistic systems, the assessment process could shift to his command of these systems in communication. Clinicians could set up circumstances in which the individual encodes certain events. After he does this, the available referents could be changed to see how adept he is in appropriately recoding a message. Clinicians should map out alternative coding devices used by the individual and the appropriateness of their use. They should establish a communicative situation, in which they could describe how an individual plays the communication game in recognizing and overcoming obstacles. Representative activities are described in Chap. 11.

Ten Syntactic Techniques

The first five of the ten techniques that follow are child-initiated. The second five are clinician-initiated. They can be used singly or in combination. It is probably desirable to use various combinations rather than to rely on a single model. These techniques are merely suggestive. Clinicians are encouraged to use a variety of others. The techniques developed by Blank (Blank and Solomon 1968, 1969; Blank and Frank 1971) are highly recommended.

CORRECTION MODEL

In this model a clinician identifies aberrant behavior and tries to correct it, usually by showing the individual his error and correcting him. Mellon (1967) did an extensive review of this model because it has been widely used in American education. It is a behavioristic notion. His conclusion was that it was not very effective. Cazden et al. (1970, p. 4) held that it was not very potent: ''All analyses of corrections between parents and children whose language is developing well show that neither correction of immature forms nor reinforcement of mature forms occurs with sufficient frequency to be a potent force.'' Brown and Bellugi (1964) also indicate that corrections are unnatural and infrequent in the acquisition of syntax. However, corrections are rather common from parents for semantic or referential errors. If teachers or clinicians do much correcting of syntactic errors, the children will become reticent. However, they will usually accept corrections of referential errors.

The correction model is illustrated by the following:

Syntactic Correction
    Child: Doggy runned.
Clinician: No, not Doggy runned. The doggy ran.
Referential Correction
    Child: He ate supper.
Clinician: No. She ate supper. *She* is a girl.

EXPANSION MODEL

Brown and Bellugi (1964) reported that in normal parent-child interactions, parental verbal responses to children learning language are occasionally syntactic expansions of child utterances. These are timely, because they are based on the child's grammar at a particular point in time, because they pertain to a child's intent to communicate in a particular circumstance, and because they pertain to available references in the circumstance. Moreover, Brown and Bellugi reported that sometimes a child will reduce parent utterances. These reductions are not just word deletions that shorten utterances. The deletions are at certain points in the utterances that correspond with the child's grammar. Thus, the deletions reflect a child's knowledge of a linguistic model. Occasionally both parents and child have cyclic interchanges in which a parent expands the child's utterances and the child reduces the parent's utterances. This cyclic interchange may continue for a few exchanges, in which both parent and child verbalize back and forth, one expanding and one reducing. Apparently expansions are an important language-learning activity.

Cazden (1965) studied expansions by having teachers of preschool disadvantaged children expand the utterances of these children. After six months, the expansion group exhibited more gain in various measures of language learning than the control group. However, the gain was not significant. Brown (1973a) reasoned that significant gains were not obtained because the expansion model was used too much and not interspersed with other response patterns. He held that the expansion process seems to offer too many opportunities for learning and that the failure to obtain significant results may be a fault in the application of expansions rather than the model itself.

The expansion model is illustrated in this exchange.

   Child: Doggy bark.
Clinician: The doggy is barking.

Notice there is no attempt to tell the child, "Do it this way." An alternative model is provided. A child may or may not use the model and he may or may not engage in cyclic interchanges. Ervin (1966) indicated that after two or three cyclic interchanges the child will vary his utterance. The variation is considered a locus of learning for a given utterance in a given communicative context. Clinicians should take note of child utterances, parent expansions, child variations, and available references. Together they make the circumstances with which a child extends himself in learning something new about his language.

SIMPLE EXPATIATION MODEL

Cazden (1965) had a different group of teachers respond to child utterances with simple sentences. She found that the children in this group made more significant progress than either those in the expansion or control group. McNeill (1966a) analyzed the data. He found that the teachers had not merely used simple sentences but had enlarged or extended a child's topic. Extending the topic is apparently more productive than expanding the syntactic model. McNeill called this model "expatiation" which means to enlarge or broaden. It indicates that functions may have priority over forms in language intervention. The priority of functions over form was also manifested in the correction model. Correction of form is poorly tolerated by language learners, but correction of reference is accepted. The expatiation model is illustrated as follows:

Child: Doggy bark.
Clinician: The doggy's hurt. Puppies whine sometimes. Sometimes they bark.

COMPLEX EXPATIATION MODEL

Complex expatiation is a syntactic variant of simple expatiation. As with simple expatiation, a child's utterance is the locus of communication. Semantic aspects are elaborated in complicated syntactic structures. The complex expatiation model is illustrated as follows:

Child: Doggy bark.
Clinician: The black doggy is named Spotty. Of all the dogs I know, he barks most.

ALTERNATIVES MODEL

The alternatives model is only one of several that Blank and Solomon (1968) devised for developing abstract thinking. This model deals with the role of language in the development of logic. The clinician inquires directly or indirectly about the underlying logic of a particular utterance. Such questions serve to make a speaker aware of the instrumental power of utterances through realizing alternative interpretations and motivations. Moreover, the questions provide a way of making underlying assumptions explicit. Obviously, this model must be used judiciously because it disrupts the continuity of communication. It should not be confused with the replacement model presented in the section on clinician initiation. It is illustrated as follows:

Child: Doggy bark.
Clinician: Yes. Why do doggies bark? Is it a big doggy or a puppy?

COMPLETION MODEL

The completion model is the first of five clinician-initiated models. Bandura and Harris (1966) had children and adults make sentences with various words and phrases. They were interested in whether or not children utilized syntactic models employed by the adults. The data indicated that they do. Moreover, studies by Snow (1972), Clarke-Stewart (1973), Shatz and Gelman (1973), and Schachter et al. (1974) indicate that older children and adults "talk down" to young children so that the models available to the child correspond somewhat to the child's level. Leonard (1973, 1975a,b) has incorporated this principle in language intervention.

The completion model is one in which an incomplete sentence is given. Children are supposed to analyze what is needed and supply the appropriate words. Thus, this model has to do with an individual's ability to deduce constituent requirements and equivalencies. The sentences the clinician gives to the child to complete should be derived from the descriptive analysis of the target and co-occurring systems the child is already dealing with. A clinician could omit the structures he wants the child to deal with. The child could complete a sentence with any structure equivalent to the deleted slot. Moreover, he should complete it in a variety of ways so he will realize constituent equivalencies and eventually deal with structures germane to the particular sentence. It is important that the child complete the sentences with elaborate phrases rather than simple one-word completions. One-word completions give simple realizations of constituent equivalencies, but elaborate completions (wild, silly sentences) provide abundant opportunities for discovering equivalencies and alternatives. The completion model is illustrated as follows:

Clinician: Doggy _____ .
    Child: Doggy ran home.
Clinician: The doggy is _____ .
    Child: The doggy is black. The doggy is barking.
Clinician: The _____ is old.
    Child: The doggy is old.

REPLACEMENT MODEL

Gunter (1960) discussed the appropriateness of using proportional drill in altering children's syntax. In principle, the drill deals with various dimensions of a sentence except those for the missing constituent. The object is to complete the sentence on the basis of constituent analysis and contingencies of grammar. Thus, proportional drill is like the completion model. However, it appears to be more powerful as a replacement model because there are more alternatives that can be taken. By using a replacement rather than a completion model, an individual can choose the particular syntax that meets his needs.

The clinician says a sentence to a child and instructs the child to take something out and replace it with something else. The sentence has been devised with grammatical systems the individual is dealing with. Clinicians should encourage a variety of replacements to foster language exploration of equivalencies.

Clinician: The doggy is barking.
    Child: My doggy is barking.
    Child: My doggy named Spotty is barking.

ALTERNATIVE REPLACEMENT MODEL

Among several behavior modification studies dealing with verbal behavior, Krasner (1958) reported a study by Toffel (1955) that dealt with an alternative replacement model. The principle of the model is that alternatives can be made in syntactic linkage. Exemplars of one form class can be alternatively replaced with alternative exemplars of another form class, provided that the various exemplars share semantic attributes that constrain syntactic operations.

Operationally, a clinician outlines several alternatives from one form class (pronouns: I, he, she, they; animate nouns: frog, goat, horse; human nouns: boy, girl, man, woman, lady, etc.). Then the clinician outlines several alternatives from another class that could be syntactically linked to the first (transitive verbs: open, carry, hit; intransitive verbs: fall, jump, run, sleep, etc.). A child is asked to make alternative replacements with the various exemplars in the two classes. A child should recognize which alternatives are legitimate and which are not. He should also realize when certain conventions are needed. For example, "I sleep" is similar to "He sleeps," but the /s/ on "sleeps" is an added linguistic convention. On the other hand, while "the tree" or "the rock" may be semantically-syntactically equivalent for some predicates to "he," the semantic constraints do not permit "sleep."

After a child has done a fair amount of replacements and the alternatives extend beyond single words, a clinician could change the activity to include negative exemplars—things that violate the rules. These serve to define the domain of a rule. Children in spontaneous language learning use negative exemplars.

The alternative replacement model is frequently used by behavior modificationists because it is oriented on class learning, explicitness, criteria of complete or near complete learning, and "reversal learning." Behavior modificationists assume that this kind of model offers a way of accounting for semantic-syntactic knowledge. The pivot-open grammars of the 1960s were based upon a similar premise, that privileges of occurrence of form classes are needed in language learning. The most elaborate argument for pivot grammars was developed by McNeill (1966a). A similar argument was developed by Braine (1963a,b, 1965) for contextual generalization. Brown (1973a) has indicated that such approaches deal with rather superficial aspects of language learning. McNeill (1970) has shifted away from a pivot-open or distributional analysis of early language learning. Braine (reported in Bowerman, 1976) has redefined his theory from a syntactic to a semantic one.

COMBINATION MODEL

Mellon (1967) presented a series of sentences to junior high school children and asked them to combine the sentences in any way they wanted. The children worked in small groups, competed with their peers, and did not discuss parts of speech. They produced a large number and variety of sentences. The activity gave them the chance to explore their language by making new combinations of things. These children were compared with children in two other groups. One was taught traditional English and the other was taught English literature. After six months, the children in the sentence combining activity were writing competitively with junior and senior high school students whereas the other two groups were still at the junior high school level.

The combination model is illustrated as follows:

Clinician: The dog is barking. The dog is old. The dog is in the street.
Child: The old dog that is barking is in the street.

REVISION MODEL

O'Donnell (1967) prepared a series of one-paragraph stories loaded with certain linguistic systems. Students were instructed to revise the stories. This activity was useful diagnostically because the clinician could determine the systems an individual could work with in the context of other systems. From the intervention standpoint, this provided a way of playing, manipulating, and exploring selected linguistic systems. Subsequent model paragraphs could include additional linguistic systems that reflect what a child learned on previous model paragraphs.

The revision model is as follows:

Clinician: The dog is black. His name is Spotty. The dog eats popcorn.
Child: Spotty, the black dog, likes popcorn.

Figure 10-1 summarizes these techniques. First, they deal with different aspects of verbal behavior. Second, the selection of a technique is based on the linguistic need to deal with a particular domain—they are not determined by a clinical condition such as mental retardation, deafness, "delayed language," etc. Third, most of them can be done with both oral and written language. Fourth, they should be used in combination rather than singly. Fifth, an individual should feel free to modify them in any way he wishes. Sixth, negative or false examplars provide a useful way of learning and can be incorporated into most of these techniques. Seventh, individuals should think of silly and elaborate responses for the techniques, because that provides opportunities to explore alternatives in their language. Finally, the linguistic materials employed should be derived from each child's speech rather than from a clinician's notebook of *a priori* activities.

Make-Change (A Game of Sentence Sense)

One of the best ways to learn syntax is to spontaneously play with and explore alternatives in sentence making. Make-Change (Muma 1977b) is a game developed for the purpose of providing an activity in which individuals spontaneously play

Figure 10-1 *A summary of the ten techniques according to salient features.*

	Model	*Syntax*	*Semantics*	*Language Functions*
Child-initiated	Correction	Errors identified and corrected by completion	Errors of reference identified and corrected	
	Expansion	Utterance retained but syntactically completed according to child's current sentence structure and available referents		
	Expatiation (simple)		Semantic aspects featured while syntax is not	Utterance the locus of communication
	Expatiation (complex)		Semantic aspects featured but diffused in complicated syntactic structures	Utterance the locus of communication
	Alternatives			Logical assumptions underlying utterance
Teacher-initiated	Completion	Constituent analysis and equivalence	Grammatical-conceptual classes	
	Replacement	Constituent analysis and equivalence	Grammatical-conceptual classes	
	Alternative-replacement	Constituent analysis and alternatives. Morphology: semantic markers	Grammatical-conceptual classes	
	Revision	Exploring alternatives	Generalizing and reorganizing concepts	
	Combination	Exploring alternatives	Generalizing and reorganizing	

with and explore alternatives in sentence making. The game has two stages. Players make sentences according to various symbolic patterns that lead to sentences. There are a number of decisions in making each sentence. After a sentence is made, it must be changed at least once. Several changes can be made on any one sentence. Several decisions are made for each sentence change. Thus, players have a number of decisions for both the make and change steps of sentence production.

After a sentence has been made or changed, a player's opponents must agree that it makes sense. Moreover, opponents can sabotage each other's sentences. Sabotaging also requires syntactic analysis. After a player makes and changes an agreed number of sentences (one to three), the game is over. The players count the point values of sentences to see who won. There is an easy version and a difficult version of the game. The easy version does not have the grammatical range the difficult one has. The difficult version is much more fun to play.

Make-Change has been used with late elementary school children, children with learning disabilities, children with reading problems, and adult education classes. Students from elementary to adult levels enjoy the game, and their teachers report that it has led to improved language arts.

Summary

Clinicians should employ assessment-intervention procedures that preserve information about individual differences, systems and processes, and contextual influences. These must deal with relativity, conditionality, complexity, and dynamism of behavior. Descriptive procedures have this potential but normative-quantitative procedures lack them (Muma, in press).

The nonverbal child can be successfully dealt with by the following approaches: behavior modification, modeling, Piagetian psychology, socioemotional security base, and the realization of the instrumental power of speech acts. The assessment-intervention of individuals at the one- and two-word levels entails various cognitive capacities described in Chap. 9. Linguistically, descriptive procedures emphasize language functons and the principle that one word has many referents and one referent has many words. Carefully planned parallel talking in the context of action patterns is highly successful. Brown's (1973b) five stages provide a useful framework for determining where a child is in his language acquisition.

The analysis of syntax entails identifying the developmental stage of acquisition of structure-systems and the linguistic contexts or conditions (co-occurrences) as each system enters an individual's grammar. Descriptive procedures are used to assess spontaneous utterances. Special attention is given to linguistic systems in spontaneous imitation, consecutive utterances that vary slightly, revisions or false starts, overextensions and underextensions, and generalizations. Phonologically, phonemes are considered in terms of phonetic features, coarticulatory influences, and phonotactic rules. Phonotactically, deviant speech sound production can be accounted for in terms of the following processes: voicing, diminutive, reduplication, cluster reduction, weak syllable deletion, fronting, open syllable structure, and alternative syllabic structures. Intervention should be oriented on these processes and influences.

Ten syntactic techniques were presented. Five were child-initiated and five were clinician-initiated. Those that dealt with functions of language were usually more successful than structure oriented approaches. It was suggested that clinicians should not select just any structures for these techniques. The structures and the co-occurrences used in the techniques should be derived from a child's speech.

Make-Change (a game of sentence sense) is a game in which players can spontaneously play with and explore their language. Moreover, players can sabotage their opponents' sentences. As players make decisions about making and changing sentences, they learn about their language.

11

Assessment-
Intervention:
Communicative Systems

Both cognitive and communicative functions are more important than form, because verbal behavior is used in the service of cognitive and communicative functions. Early language learning exhibits a priority for cognitive development and for communicative functions (semantic and relational). After the basic syntactic mechanisms are learned there is an emphasis on learning to become adept in the use of these mechanisms and on learning to use listener feedback in realizing effective communication. Intervention programs that reflect verbal functions are consistently more effective than those aimed at learning form, such as sentence making, vocabulary building, etc.

Verbal function approaches are more effective than structure or form approaches because (1) they reflect the principle that form operates in the service of function, (2) they deal with communicative intent, (3) they deal with available reference, and (4) communicative systems are intact and operational, in the sense that linguistic and referential contexts are real and functional. The Blank and Solomon (1968, 1969) approach is a function oriented program. The Blank and Frank (1971) story-retelling procedure exemplifies this kind of program, as do the expatiation condition in Cazden's (1965) study, the approaches developed by McCaffrey (1976, 1977) and Moffett (1968), the various studies about roletaking by Flavell et al. (1968), Glucksberg and Krauss (1967), Glucksberg, Krauss, and Higgins (1975), and the communicative game *Dump and Play* (Muma 1975a; Shewan 1975; Longhurst and Reichle 1975), provide a useful assessment-intervention framework for dealing with communicative systems.

The assessment-intervention process should deal with an individual's (a) ability to code messages according to available referents (actual and presumed) for his communicative intent, (b) adeptness in coding not only relevant but efficient messages, (c) repertoire in using and appreciating a range of alternative linguistic, nonlinguistic, paralinguistic, metareferential, and contextual coding devices, and (d) ability to play the communication game. In short, it should deal with how an individual functions with communicative systems.

Evidence of this is obtained by having him participate in several communicative activities and describe his performance. Intervention is then a matter of changing the activities. They can be natural situations with peers, siblings, parents, teachers, strangers, etc. And when there is a need to observe or manipulate certain aspects of the communicative process, various contrived activities can be used.

McCaffrey Guidelines

McCaffrey (1976, 1977) outlined ten principles that should be considered in conceptualizing and implementing a communication based curriculum. These principles, derived from his research at Harvard, are consistent with issues raised by the Bullock Report (1975), a survey of language arts programs in England. I have paraphrased the principles below:

1. *Organic.* The communicative process must be intact in intervention. Even though communication may be artificially segmented into components, intervention should not be on each component level. Intervention should deal with various components as they are naturally integrated in a functional communicative system, thereby maintaining organic integrity.
2. *Human.* Because language is a uniquely human form of social interaction, language intervention should be with individuals actively engaged with others. Human involvement affords opportunities to learn various functions of human communication.
3. *Modeling.* As an individual witnesses others' use of language in the same contexts in which he intends to communicate, he is provided timely and probably appropriate models.
4. *Practice.* The more an individual uses language in purposeful ways, the more adept he becomes with language. This is not imitative practice or drill, but using language in a variety of ways for a variety of communicative functions. Language is like any other cognitive system such as perception and memory; the more it is used in purposeful ways, the more it becomes available for use. Motoric systems also evidence this use-function effect. Highly verbal children are usually good readers who excel in other academic and social areas.
5. *Integrating "talking" and "listening."* Intervention should provide opportunities in which an individual functions as both an encoder and a decoder in actual communicative exchanges where these functions naturally shift between participants.
6. *Match-up.* The intervention materials and activities must match the needs of each participant. This usually means that activities should be sufficiently flexible so that adjustments can be made to match the needs of participants more closely.
7. *Feedback.* Feedback is spontaneously available in natural communication. As an individual becomes aware of the effect of his messages on others, he

learns to alter his utterances to obtain more desirable effects. Feedback can be explicit (someone may say, ''I don't understand'') or it may be deduced from the actions of others.

8. *Acceptance.* A major premise is that each utterance in a natural communicative context is made for a purpose. The principles above will operate to modify utterances. Accordingly, utterances should be accepted rather than monitored by a clinician.

9. *Principles, processes, ideas.* An intervention program should be oriented on principles, processes, and ideas rather than on specific products. Rather than parts of speech and basic sentence frames, intervention should be about functions of language in a variety of natural contexts. Rather than teach colors per se, intervention should teach colors as static attributes of a variety of things.

10. *Child-task orientation.* One major goal of intervention is to help a child become an independent learner. One means of achieving this is to create learning situations that are flexible and child oriented. Children who work with other children in problem solving tasks come to rely on themselves and their peers. Moreover, they realize that there are many solutions or approaches and that they can generate them.

McCaffrey informally added that natural communicative processes are heuristic. One activity leads to another. Anyone who has watched children play knows it is heuristic. They play something for a time, then go on to something else. Generally, one play leads to another. A physical activity may have been so strenuous that the next activity is quiet. Group activity may lead to individual activity. Seeing watermelons on a truck may lead to sneaking into a watermelon patch.

Gaming Procedures for the Communication Game

THE BARRIER GAME

In recent years, several procedures have been devised to deal with the communication game. The studies by Glucksberg and Krauss (1967) and Flavell et al. (1968) have shown that gaming procedures are useful in assessment and intervention. They have developed the Barrier Game. In this game, one child is an encoder and the other a decoder. The children have two sets of the same materials. The materials are novel items or pictorials. A barrier is placed between them so they cannot see each other's materials but can see each other's faces. The materials are made in such a way that each item has common and also distinctive properties with the other. The encoder is shown a model arrangement of the item or actions. Certain sequential, action, or spatial relationships are made. The encoder must make a message that will make the decoder duplicate the model. The barrier makes them rely on verbal codes.

This game is excellent in that it provides a way of observing how an individual communicates intent and available reference. It also contains the ten tasks outlined by McCaffrey. Encoder and decoder can switch roles, use modeling and feedback, match up codes for a decoder's needs, accept alternative codes, proceed according to common ideas, use decoder cues to encode better messages, etc.

Clinicians should observe the kinds of messages the encoder uses for his available references. What were the ways he coded his message? How efficient and appropriate were they? What devices did he employ—linguistic, nonlinguistic, paralinguistic? When a communicative obstacle occurred, how did he deal with it?

Clinicians should similarly watch the performance of the decoder. They should observe the degree to which he comprehends the messages, and his pattern of inappropriate responses. Also, how does he notify the encoder of difficulties he has? How appropriate is he in identifying and dealing with communicative obstacles?

Finally, when the encoder is satisfied that he has done his job and the decoder satisfied about his performance, let them see each other's materials. The clinician should then observe the degree to which both participants realize the discrepancies between the model and the product, as well as the degree to which they recognize and accept their roles in causing the discrepancies.

The encoder and decoder can then change functions. An encoder can have several decoders, one at a time. A decoder can have several encoders. Over several games, the clinician can discern the communicative patterns of the individuals. By selective manipulation of the encoder-decoder roles and the materials, the clinician can change some of the patterns.

This game has been widely studied in recent years (Glucksberg, Krauss, and Higgins 1975; Gleason 1972). Longhurst has done several studies on the communication skills of retarded individuals with this activity (Longhurst 1974; Longhurst and Reichle 1975; Longhurst and Berry 1975; Longhurst and Siegel 1973).

THE OVER-THE-SHOULDER GAME

McCaffrey (1976, 1977) has a variation of the barrier game in which the encoder stands behind the decoder and talks over his shoulder about what to do next. This lets the encoder see what effect his messages have. Also, obstacles were easily visible from the performance of the decoder. Considerable responsibility is thus placed on the encoder not only to code messages of presumed best fit but also to use decoder performance to revise messages. This game would be very useful in encouraging a roletaking or decentered attitude in the communication process. It is also recommended for impulsive encoders. It is not recommended for those who need better listener skills since the responsibility of the decoder in identifying and reading communicative obstacles is substantially reduced.

THE "WHO" GAME

Encoders can give a variety of clues to several listeners in "Who am I?" questions. An encoder may want his listeners to guess that he is a farmer, a policeman, etc., by giving them clues. The various guesses provide feedback to the encoder. Decoders get the same information. At the end, when the identity is known, there is usually considerable discussion on how relevant the clues were. Both encoder and decoder benefit from this kind of discussion. They learn new attributes of things, revise knowledge of things, and evaluate the best ways to code information in language. Other versions of this game include "Where am I?" "How am I?" "When am I?" "What am I?" and "Why am I?"

THE ADD-ON GAME

There are several versions of this game: "Gossip," "Party-line," "Telephone," and "What next?" Basically, one person begins with a short one- or two-sentence statement which is whispered from person to person. After everyone has had a turn, the final sentence is compared to the first one. Usually there is some distortion. If the players trace back, they can sometimes narrow down who made the changes.

The "What next?" game is a slight variation. A topic, picture, or object is the focus of the game. One person begins by making a statement about the item or topic—where it came from, etc. The next repeats what the previous one said, but adds something. By observing an individual in this game, the clinician can identify the aspects of the story the individual has trouble with.

ALTERNATIVES

The clinician has an individual name anything he wishes. Other players must think of something they can say about it. Synonyms are desirable. Generic terms are better than attributes. Elaborate phrases and sentences are better than single words, since they require the integration of attributes. Novel or unusual names of things are best. Gestures and sound patterns are low-level representations. Players could be given scores for their various responses.

Ingenious clinicians can think of other kinds of communicative games. It is important to build in as many of McCaffrey's ten points as possible. One game that is somewhat limited in communicative skills but good for realizing derivational mechanisms is what I call "Funny words." Children try to think of funny new words for old ones. A child will say "dog" to the group. The others try to think of a funny derivation, e.g., "dog*er*," "dog*ness*," "dog*ly*," "*un*dog," "*non*dog*ly*," etc. Occasionally, the play is stopped for a brief discussion about what is "nondogly." Even though the game produces nonexistent words, it is a way of discovering derivational mechanisms. This game can extend to changes of words in a sentence: "The *un*blue man*ly* eat*ness* some gum*er*."

Parent-Child Development: A Comprehensive Curriculum

A language intervention program should be integrated into an entire curriculum. Parent participation is important. As research director of the Parent-Child Developmental Center in Birmingham, Alabama, I developed a rationale and program model (Muma 1971c), and curriculum with Barbara Dawson (Dawson and Muma 1971). Language development was one of the major areas of the curriculum. Others included motor development, cognitive development, socioemotional development, physical development, health, and parent-child interaction.

Since there is considerable interest in infant and preschool programs for the handicapped and for disadvantaged families, the rationale, program model, and curriculum outline are given here. There are Parent-Child Development Centers (PCDC) in Birmingham, New Orleans, and Houston, and several Parent-Child Centers (PCC) throughout the country. The PCDC centers were originally established as research programs and the PCC centers as service programs. However, after several years the research efforts of the PCDC became suspect and most of the national consultants withdrew from participation. The Birmingham program in particular deviated from the model and curriculum under study. The following description is of the rationale, model, and curriculum before erosion set in.

The program was developed in the following sequence: basic assumptions, basic objectives, program model, strategies and vehicles of implementation, program execution, and program effects. It was assumed that poverty conditions were varied and that the reasons individuals were disadvantaged varied. Thus, the program should be broad in scope and flexible to deal with a variety of individual needs. It was assumed that while poverty is a handicap the individuals themselves were normal. Thus, the program should focus on ways of overcoming poverty conditions rather than "deficiencies" in individuals. It was assumed that before an individual can deal effectively with his poverty he must be healthy. The program therefore provided a nutritional program, complemented by a medical and dental program. It was assumed that the participants (both infants and parents) had the ability to learn but may have lacked desire and appropriate opportunity. The program therefore provided educational activities for both infants and parents (Dribin 1971). Education of parents centered on child care and homemaking. Adult education courses were also offered. It was assumed that a potent mechanism for establishing motivation to learn and cope effectively with poverty conditions is peer interaction. The program was devised to foster peer interaction and movement in the program (taking various responsibilities) was by peer decision. Moreover, training on child development and mothering was based on peer comparisons. It was assumed that parent-child relationships were an important motivational context. Parents want to be good parents. They want to feel that they are giving their children the best opportunities to make it in society. The program emphasized developing parental skills. It was assumed that one of the major problems of the disadvantaged is lack of control over environment and future. Thus, participants themselves determined to a great extent the nature of the program. Moreover, participation was voluntary. It is interesting to note that the program had 100 families participating, there was a waiting list of families wanting to join, attendance was very high (over 90 percent), and only three or four families a year withdrew from the program. Finally, it was assumed that active participation was essential. Participants were actively involved. In addition to active participation, a variety of stimulation was needed because of the variety of learning needs. Therefore, a variety of experiences was provided.

The PCDC objectives were:

1. Parents would become more effective intervention agents with their children.
2. Infants would develop in ways commensurate with their more advantaged peers in health and motivation, cognition, language, and motorically and socioemotionally.

The program model is best described as a three-stage peer (parents) model. The model and program are more fully described by Dribin (1971), and an educational television program was produced on it by the Westinghouse Corporation in 1971. Its three stages are: Participating Observer, Model Mother I, and Model Mother II. The program dealt with infants and their mothers (fathers were included in the educational, recreational, and other activities). When an infant became three months old, he and his mother entered the program. Mothers began by participating in a series of observational activities in which they watched other mothers doing activities (multiple mothering concept) and a variety of infants in activities (multiple child development concept). The observations were always with another new mother and a Model Mother I (MM-I) so they could discuss what they saw. The observations were with actual parents and children as well as with videotape recordings of their peers doing activities. MM-I mothers were responsible for the discussion and dealt with the intended topic. They were also responsible for directing the new mothers in selecting topics for observation. Model Mother IIs were responsible for programming activities for small groups of children. They worked with different age groups over the course of a year. A mother would typically be a participating observer one year, an MM-I one year, and an MM-II one year. However, the other mothers in the program decided when a mother would change responsibilities. Additionally, a toy library was established so mothers could take toys home to their children. The mothers had to explain the various ways a toy could be used before checking it out, and gave feedback about how their children were playing with the toy. The toys were age-"graded" at six-month intervals. Most toys were kept but some of the larger ones were returned and repaired. Parents also kept a cumulative notebook

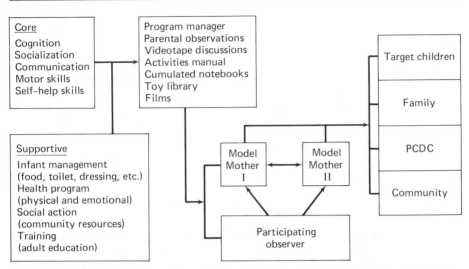

Figure 11-1 *Model for the Birmingham, Alabama, PCDC for training disadvantaged parents to become more effective intervention agents with their children.*

about the program activities they had seen. Films on child development were shown. Adult education classes were given in obtaining a high school equivalency certificate; additionally other useful skills were taught, e.g., dressmaking, cooking, baking, shopping skills, house decoration, etc. Figure 11-1 outlines content, implementation, levels of assumed responsibilities, and intervention domain for the PCDC program.

Summary

After an individual acquires basic linguistic structures, the next issue is how adept he is in their use. Communicative conditions can be set up to assess or intervene by manipulating available reference, encoder functions, and decoder functions. Clinicians can use games to describe the ways an individual encodes and decodes in particular circumstances. An individual should receive direct feedback on his encoding and decoding efforts.

Clinicians are frequently asked to contribute to a comprehensive program for infants and preschool handicapped children. The Parent-Child Development Center (PCDC) is one kind of program. The PCDC model and curriculum were particularly useful in conceptualizing and implementing a program that received national attention.

12

Epilog

Clinicians need a language intervention model that describes the *what* and *how* issues in terms that help them know where they are and what they need to advance their clinical skills. The intervention model in Chap. 1 describes conceptual and assessment issues as *what* issues: what clinicians need to know about verbal learning and verbal behavior, and what they need to know about clinical assessment. It describes *how* issues as intervention issues.

Clinicians need to have basic concepts about cognitive systems, semantic-syntactic-phonological systems, communicative systems, and language development. As these concepts were discussed throughout the book, clinical implications were made. Thus, assessment-intervention material appears throughout the book. This helps focus clinicians on basic concepts before attempting assessment-intervention. Assessment implications have been included with the material presented so the theoretical discussion is not isolated from the applied.

It is vital that clinicians adopt a "systems approach" rather than a normative one. Verbal behavior is complex, dynamic, relative, and conditional rather than simple, static, categorical, and absolute. The complexities require clinicians to integrate information and to look for patterns as evidence of underlying processes. Dynamism forces clinicians to appreciate change. Relativity makes them consider stages and sequences (Kohlberg 1969). Conditionality requires them to take into account contextual influences. Accordingly, they should adopt descriptive assessment and intervention procedures rather than quantitative ones. Descriptive procedures are recommended because they (1) provide a means for dealing with systems, (2) account for behavior on relative and conditional terms, (3) provide a way of understanding the nature of a clinical condition rather than merely categorize and label it, (4) give directly relevant alternatives in intervention founded on ecologically based information, and (5) provide for individual differences and alternative strategies. *Individual differences are central to any clinical endeavor.*

Assessment-intervention is probabilistic, not absolute. Clinicians should attempt to describe how a particular individual functions with particular cognitive-linguistic-communicative systems. Intervention is deducible neither from the literature nor from the assessment process. The best that can be done is to exploit an individual's behavior in a way consistent with what is known about the acquisition of various systems. The intervention effort should be based upon the systems an individual uses or attempts to use.

Clinicians must deal with cognitive, linguistic, and communicative systems. They should realize the importance of keeping these systems intact and maintaining communicative contexts. They should be aware of the importance of verbal functions. And they should realize the reduction in clinical power when intervention takes content, sequence, pacing, reinforcement, and motivation away from the individual.

Clinicians in Canada (particularly Montreal), England, and recently Sweden, have adopted comprehensive and rigorous training programs. These clinicians are frequently better trained than their American counterparts. However, American clinical training is becoming more and more substantial. Training programs in the last few years have begun to offer a full-fledged curriculum in language assessment-intervention. The old notion of one or two courses is inadequate. That yields technicians who look for *the* assessment test or *the* intervention program, and the numbers games these bring. Many of the training programs now have a four-course sequence intimately tied to clinical experience. A typical one is:

(1) Introductory linguistics—the nature of language
(2) Language development
(3) Language assessment
(4) Language intervention

Clinicians are acquiring a groundwork in child development, Piagetian psychology, and cognition. They are taking courses in speech articulation disorders, cleft palate speech, aphasia, autism, stuttering, cerebral palsy, reading disorders, voice disorders, speech and hearing science, and basic audiology. With this kind of training, they are qualified to deal with a variety of clinical problems involving cognitive-linguistic-communicative systems.

Appendix *A*
Relevant Publications

Journals

American Journal of Mental Deficiency. Peabody College, P.O. Box 503, Nashville, TN 37203.

Asha. American Speech and Hearing Association, 10801 Rockville Pike, Rockville, Md. 20852.

Child Development. University of Chicago Press, 5801 Ellis Avenue, Chicago, IL 60637.

Cognitive Psychology. Academic Press, 111 Fifth Avenue, New York, NY 10003.

Developmental Psychology. American Psychological Association, 1200 Seventeenth Street, N.W., Washington, DC 20036.

Exceptional Children. Council for Exceptional Children, 1920 Association Drive, Reston, VA 22091.

Harvard Educational Review. Longfellow Hall, 13 Appian Way, Cambridge, MA 02138.

Human Communication. Corbett Hall, School of Rehabilitation Medicine, University of Alberta, Edmonton, Alberta, Canada T6G 2G4.

Human Development. Albert J. Phiebig, Inc., P.O. Box 352, White Plains, NY 10602.

Journal of Child Language. Cambridge University Press, 32 East 57th Street, New York, NY 10022.

Journal of Child Psychology and Psychiatry. Association for Child Psychology and Psychiatry, Department of Psychological Medicine, The Hospital for Sick Children, Great Ormond Street, London, WCIN 3JH, England.

Journal of Communication Disorders. American Elsevier Publishing Co., 52 Vanderbilt Ave., New York, NY 10017.

Journal of Experimental Child Psychology. Academic Press, 111 Fifth Avenue, New York, NY 10003.

Journal of Learning Disabilities. Professional Press, Room 1410, 5 North Wabash Avenue, Chicago, IL 60602.

Journal of Psycholinguistic Research. Plenum Publishing Corporation, 227 West 17th Street, New York, NY 10011.

Journal of Speech and Hearing Disorders. American Speech and Hearing Association, 10801 Rockville Pike, Rockville, Md. 20852.

Journal of Speech and Hearing Research. American Speech and Hearing Association, 10801 Rockville Pike, Rockville, Md. 20852.

Journal of Special Education. 3515 Woodhaven Road, Philadelphia, PA 19154.

Journal of Verbal Learning and Verbal Behavior. Academic Press, 111 Fifth Avenue, New York, NY 10003.

Language and Speech. Robert Draper, Ltd., Kerbihan House, 85 Udney Park Road, Teddington, Middlesex, England.

Language, Speech, and Hearing Services in Schools. American Speech and Hearing Association, 10801 Rockville Pike, Rockville, Md. 20852.

Mental Retardation. American Association of Mental Retardation, AAMD Publications Sales Office, Boyd Printing Company, 49 Sheridan Avenue, Albany, NY 12210.

Merrill-Palmer Quarterly: Behavior and Development. The Merrill-Palmer Institute, 71 East Ferry Avenue, Detroit, MI 48202.

Monographs of the Society for Research in Child Development. University of Chicago Press, 5801 Ellis Avenue, Chicago, IL 60637.

Special Education. 12 Park Crescent, London, WIN 4EQ, England.

Books

COGNITION

ELKIND, D. and FLAVELL, J. (eds.) *Studies in Cognitive Development.* New York: Oxford University Press (1969).

ELLIS, H. *Fundamentals of Human Learning and Cognition.* Dubuque, Iowa: William C. Brown Company (1972).

FLAVELL, J. *Cognitive Development.* Englewood Cliffs, N.J.: Prentice-Hall (1977).

GINSBERG, H. and OPPER, S. *Piaget's Theory of Intellectual Development.* Englewood Cliffs, N.J.: Prentice-Hall (1969).

NEISSER, U. *Cognitive Psychology.* New York: Appleton-Century-Crofts (1967).

NORMAN, D. *Memory and Attention: An Introduction to Human Information Processing.* New York: Wiley (1969).

GRAMMAR

BOLINGER, D. *Aspects of Language.* New York: Harcourt Brace Jovanovich (1975).

JACOBS, R. and ROSENBAUM, P. *English Transformational Grammar.* Waltham, Mass.: Xerox College Publishing (1968).

LILES, B. *An Introduction to Linguistics.* Englewood Cliffs, N.J.: Prentice-Hall (1975).

COMMUNICATION

FLAVELL, J., et al. *The Development of Role-taking and Communication Skills in Children.* New York: Wiley (1968).

PSYCHOLINGUISTICS

CAZDEN, C. *Child Language and Education.* New York: Holt, Rinehart and Winston (1972).

CHOMSKY, N. *Language and Mind.* New York: Harcourt Brace Jovanovich (1968).

CLARK, H., and CLARK, E. *Psychology and Language.* New York: Harcourt Brace Jovanovich (1977).

DALE, P. *Language Development: Structure and Function.* (2nd ed.) New York: Holt, Rinehart and Winston (1976).

DEESE, J. *Psycholinguistics*. Boston: Allyn & Bacon (1970).
DEVESTA, F. *Language Learning and Cognitive Processes*. Monterey, Calif.: Brooks/Cole (1974).
HOPPER, R. and NAREMORE, R. *Children's Speech*. New York: Harper & Row (1973).
SLOBIN, D. *Psycholinguistics*. Glenview, Ill.: Scott, Foresman (1971).
WOOD, B. *Children and Communication*. Englewood Cliffs, N.J.: Prentice-Hall (1976).

SOCIOLINGUISTICS

FISHMAN, J. *Sociolinguistics: A Brief Introduction*. Rowley, Mass.: Newbury House Publishers (1972).

READING

SMITH, F. *Understanding Reading*. New York: Holt, Rinehart and Winston (1971).

PHONOLOGY (CLINICAL)

INGRAM, D. *Phonological Disability in Children*. New York: Elsevier (1976).

SYNTAX (CLINICAL)

CRYSTAL, D., FLETCHER, P., and GARMAN, M. *The Grammatical Analysis of Language Disability*. New York: Elsevier (1976).

PSYCHOLINGUISTICS (CLINICAL)

MOREHEAD, D. and MOREHEAD, A. *Normal and Deficient Child Language*. Baltimore: University Park Press (1976).
SCHIEFELBUSCH, R. and LLOYD, L. (eds) *Language Perspectives: Acquisition, Retardation, and Intervention*. Baltimore: University Park Press (1974).
RUDER, K. and SMITH, M. (eds.) *Developmental Intervention*. Baltimore: University Park Press (in press).

LANGUAGE IN EARLY EDUCATION

CAZDEN, C. (ed.) *Language in Early Childhood Education*. Washington, D.C.: National Association for the Education of Young Children (1972).
LAVATELLI, C. (ed.) *Language Training in Early Childhood Education*. Urbana: University of Illinois Press (1971).

DEVELOPMENT

BLOOM, L. *Language Development: Form and Function in Emerging Grammars*. Cambridge, Mass.: MIT Press (1970).
BLOOM, L. *One Word at a Time*. The Hague: Mouton (1973).
BLOOM, L. and LAHEY, M. *Language Development and Language Disorders*. New York: Wiley (1978).

BROWN, R. *A First Language: The Early Stages*. Cambridge, Mass.: Harvard University Press (1973).

GREENFIELD, P. and SMITH, J. *Communication and the Beginnings of Language: The Development of Semantic Structure in One-Word Speech and Beyond*. New York: Academic Press (1976).

LENNEBERG, E. and LENNEBERG, E. (eds.) *Foundations of Language Development*. Vols. I and II. New York: Academic Press (1975).

LEONARD, L. *Meaning in Child Language*. New York: Grune & Stratton (1976).

McNEILL, D. *The Acquisition of Language: The Study of Developmental Psycholinguistics*. New York: Harper & Row (1970).

MOERK, E. *Semantic and Pragmatic Aspects of Early Language Development*. Baltimore: University Park Press (1977).

MINIFIE, F. and LLOYD, L. (eds.) *Communicative and Cognitive Abilities—Early Behavioral Assessment*. Baltimore: University Park Press (1977).

RODGON, M. *Single-word Usage, Cognitive Development and the Beginnings of Combinatorial Speech: A Study of Ten English-speaking Children*. New York: Cambridge University Press (1976).

SNOW, C., and FERGUSON, C. (eds.). *Talking to Children: Language Input and Acquisition*. New York: Cambridge University Press (1977).

WATERSON, N., and SNOW, C. (eds.). *Development of Communication: Social and Pragmatic Factors in Language Acquisition*. New York: Wiley (in press).

Appendix B

Introductory Grammar: Semantic-Syntactic Domains

I. Semantic Functions and Relations

The following is a table of semantic functions and relations for two-word utterances according to MacDonald and Blott (1974). Similar presentations derived from Ramer (1976), Leonard (1973, 1975a,b), and Miller and Yoder (1974) appear in the text in Fig. 4-1 and in the section on semantics in Chap. 6.

Semantic-Grammatical Rules		*Brown's Early Sentence Types*	
Rule	*Examples*	*Sentence*	*Examples*
1. Agent + Action	Daddy throw cargo	Agent + Action	Eve read
2. Action + Object	Throw ball See sock Want more	Action + Object	Pat book
3. Agent + Object	Daddy ball Mommy soup (as when daddy is throwing ball or Mommy is eating soup)	Agent + Object	Mommy sock
4. X + Locative a. Entity + Locative b. Action + Locative	Ball chair Ball there Throw me Throw here	Locative (Noun + Noun) Locative (Verb + Noun)	Sweater chair Walk street
5. Negation + X a. Nonexistence	no ball no more ball (as when child finds no ball when he expects one)	Nonexistence	allgone rattle

Semantic-Grammatical Rules		Brown's Early Sentence Types	
Rule	*Examples*	*Sentence*	*Examples*
b. Rejection	no ball (as when child is given but doesn't want the ball)	—	—
c. Denial	no ball (as when child denies the assertion that an apple is a ball)	—	—
6. Modifier + Head			
a. Attribution	Pretty boat Big boy	Attribution (Adj + Noun)	Big train
b. Possession	Daddy chair My car	Possession (Noun + Noun)	Mommy lunch
c. Recurrence	More book More read	Recurrence (More + Noun)	More milk
7. Introducer + X	See boy Hi dolly It doggie	Notice Nomination	Hi belt That book
8. X + Dative	Throw me	No correspondence (may be included in Brown's locative V + N sentence type)	

II. Phrase Structure Rules

A. NOUN PHRASE (NP)

$$NP \rightarrow \begin{bmatrix} \text{Proper Noun} \\ \text{Indefinite Pronoun} \\ \text{Personal Pronoun} \\ \text{Determiner + Noun} \end{bmatrix}$$

Proper noun: Mommy, Daddy, Jimmy, Spotty, Mr. Jones, etc.

$$\begin{matrix} \text{Indefinite} \\ \text{Pronoun} \end{matrix} \rightarrow \begin{bmatrix} \text{some —} & \text{— one} \\ \text{any —} & \text{— thing} \\ \text{no —} & \text{— body} \\ \text{every —} \end{bmatrix}$$

Personal Pronoun → I, he, she, it, they, us, we, etc.

Determiner → predeterminer + $\begin{bmatrix} \text{demonstrative} \\ \text{article} \\ \text{number} \\ \text{possessive} \end{bmatrix}$ + postdeterminer

Predeterminer (optimal) → some of, many of, etc.
Demonstrative → this, that, these, those, etc.
Article → definite, nondefinite
Definite → the
Nondefinite → a, some, ø
Number → two, ten, 100, 217, etc.
Possessive → pos
Postdeterminer (optimal) → ordinal numbers
Noun → common (count), mass (noncount)
Mass → truth, sand, sawdust, etc.
Common → animate, inanimate
Animate → cow, dog, boy, snake, etc.
Inanimate → house, car, tree, road, etc.

B. AUXILIARY

Aux → C + (M) + (aspect)
C → tense
Tense → past, present
M (modal) → can, may, shall, will, must
Aspect → (have + part) + (be + ing)

Examples of a progressively expanded auxiliary system on the sentence I go:

NP	Tense	Modal	Aspect	VI	Result
I	present	———	———	go	I *go*
I	past	———	———	go	I *went*
I	present	can	———	go	I *can* go
I	past	can	———	go	I *could* go
I	present	———	be + ing	go	I *am* going
I	past	———	be + ing	go	I *was* going
I	present	———	have + part	go	I *have gone*
I	past	———	have + part	go	I *had gone*
I	present	———	(have + part) + (be + ing)	go	I *have been* going
I	past	———	(have + part) + (be + ing)	go	I *had been* going
I	present	can	be + ing	go	I *can be* going
I	past	can	be + ing	go	I *could be* going
I	past	can	have + part	go	I *could have gone*
I	past	can	(have + part) + (be + ing)	go	I *could have been* going

C. VERB PHRASE (WITHOUT THE AUXILIARY SYSTEM)

VP → aux + verbal

Verbal →
$$\begin{bmatrix} BE + & NP \\ BE + & Adj \\ BE + & Adv\text{-}p \\ VI \\ VT + & NP \\ Vh + & NP \\ Vs + & adj \\ Vb + & adj \\ & NP \end{bmatrix}$$

Adj → Adjectival
Adv-p → Adverb of place: on the table, by the car, here, etc.
BE → am, is, are, etc.
VI → intransitive verbs (action verbs): walk, smile, fall, etc.
VT → transitive verbs (action relationship verbs): eat, carry, open, etc.
Vh → possessive verbs: have, cost, weigh, etc.
Vs → appearance verbs: seem, appear, look, etc.
Vb → become verbs: become, remain, etc.

Verbs can be classified in different ways (Bowerman, 1976): state, action, and relationship verbs; recipient of action, initiator of action; animate actions, inanimate actions, circumstantial action; ego action, nonego action; etc.

D. ADVERBIALS

Adverbs have many functions in adult speech. Clinicians are usually concerned only with a limited number of them in early language learning, e.g., place, time, manner, duration, conditionality, and cause.

III. Transformations

The following table illustrates common transformational operations of English.

Single	Double	Name	Example
1	—	1. Elliptical	He does. (modal, do, be)
1	—	2. Imperative	Study this carefully.
1	—	3. Noun-del	We saw that _____ yesterday.
—	1	4. Relative	The man *who answered* was Jones.
1	1	5. Del	The man *on the street* was Jones.
1	1	6. Del-ing	People *owning property* should pay taxes.
2	1	7. Adj	An *excellent* spot was selected.
2	1	8. N modifier	The *dancing* girl was pretty.
2	1	9. N + N	A *school* teacher applied for the job.
—	1	10. Pos	*Her* book is old.

Single	Double	Name	Example
—	1	11. Pos-prep	The House *of Commons* is old.
—	1	12. Comparative	The *taller* boy is Bill.
—	1	13. Superlative	The *biggest* share is yours.
—	1	14. That + S	*That he was guilty* was obvious.
—	1	15. S nominal	The dog ate the meat *thinking it was good.*
—	1	16. Wh + S	*What we should do* was obvious.
—	1	17. For-to	*For him to object* was foolish.
—	1	18. To + V	*To object* was foolish.
—	1	19. Ving	*Objecting* would be fatal.
—	1	20. Pos-ing	His *objecting* could be advantageous.
—	1	21. Pos-V	His *refusal* could be embarrassing.
—	1	22. Conjunction	Boys *and* girls were in the class.
1	—	23. Contr	They did*n't* care.
1	—	24. Yes/No-Question	Are you sure it is here?
2(1)	—	25. Do	*Do* you study often?
1	—	26. Negative	We will *not* go.
2(3)	—	27. Wh-Question	*What* do you study at night?
1	—	28. Passive	The book *was* read *by* many people.
1	—	29. Passive-del	The book *was* read.
1	—	30. 10-del	I offered John my help.
1	—	31. VT	Give the book *to Mary*.
—	1	32. Comp V	We heard him *call*.
—	1	33. Comp Inf.	We persuaded him *to play*.
—	1	34. Comp Ving	We found him *searching*.
—	1	35. Comp Adv-p	They went *to the movie*.
—	1	36. Comp NP	They elected him *chairman*.
—	1	37. Comp Adj	They consider him *necessary*.
—	1	38. Multiple Adv	He went *to the movie yesterday with us*.
1	—	39. Adv shift	*Formerly* we studied at noon.
—	1	40. SM	*Therefore,* we cannot study now.
1	—	41. Inversion	*Beyond the hills* lies a new land.
1	—	42. There	*There* was a mouse in the cupboard.
1	—	43. It	*It* is necesary to wait.
—	1	44. Sub Adv	We were ready *when they called*.
—	1	45. Reflexive	I hurt *myself*.

From Muma (1971a).

IV. Morphology

According to Brown's (1973b) Aquisition Order (exclusive of *in* and *on*)

1. *Present progressive (be + Ving)*: I *am* walk*ing*
2. *Plural*: regular: boys; irregular: men
3. *Past irregular*: I *went*.
4. *Possessive*: regular: boy's; irregular: mine
5. *Uncontractible copula*: I *am* a boy
6. *Articles*: a, some, the

7. *Past regular*: I open*ed* it
8. *Third person regular*: Mommy carrie*s* the box.
9. *Third person irregular*: Mommy has it.
10. *Uncontractible auxiliary*: I *am* walk*ing*
11. *Contractible copula*: I'*m* a boy.
12. *Contractible auxiliary*: I'*m* walk*ing*

V. Special Clues for Identifying an Individual's Loci of Learning Semantic-Syntactic Systems

A. CO-OCCURRENCE

Co-occurrence is a way of providing evidence of the emergence of specific systems by identifying and delineating the linguistic contexts for the acquisition of any target system. *Vertical co-occurrences* give evidence of the acquisition of a particular system. Clinicians should study many utterances to fully understand how a specific system is functionally available to an individual. An examination of pronominals can reveal the range of pronominal forms and functions, both linguistic and anaphoric. This information can be related to evidence on acquisition stages and sequences, and to alternative strategies of learning. *Horizontal co-occurrences* provide evidence about the linguistic contexts (form and/or function) for the acquisition of a target system. Clinicians should identify which other systems coexist in an utterance containing a target system. Co-occurring systems within sentences can define (to some extent) the linguistic conditions in which a target system appears. For example, a pronoun may initially occur in object noun phrases when a transitive verb involving an animate function appears, when the subject noun phrase is a proper noun, when the auxiliary is unmarked, or when an adverb of place is used. Such co-occurrences are unique to each individual's linguistic contexts of language learning.

B. SPONTANEOUS IMITATION

Spontaneously imitated utterances are generally about something linguistically or referentially new. Clinicians should take careful notes of spontaneous imitation. They should be especially alert that deviations from available models can be evidence of a system that is not yet linguistically mastered. They should note the available references. As the linguistic analysis is undertaken, they should give high priority to systems and co-occurrences that appeared in spontaneous utterances. These pertain to loci of learning because spontaneous imitations are highly selective (Bloom, Hood, and Lightbown 1974).

C. CONSECUTIVE SIMILAR UTTERANCES

Children sometimes utter two or three consecutive statements that are slight variations of each other: ''Mommy eat cookie.'' ''Mommy eat a cookie.'' ''Mommy eat a gingerman cookie.'' These are very useful for identifying a locus of learning of particular systems in particular contexts. Above, the child is having difficulty with prenoun modifiers and determiners of inanimate nouns in the object noun phrase.

D. OVEREXTENDED AND UNDEREXTENDED LABELS

When children overextend or underextend labels, clinicians should take careful note of the particular labels and the available references. This will help identify which label the child is in the process of learning and the extent to which it conforms to an adult label. Available reference provides a description of the conceptual domain that should be varied and exploited to develop more appropriate categorization skills.

E. INVENTED WORDS AND GLOSSING

Children invent words for linguistic purposes, and have words that gloss over systems. Clinicians should identify invented and glossed words as evidence of linguistic domains a child is ready to learn.

Appendix C

Phonetic Features and Phonotactic Processes

I. Phonetic Features

Phonetic features are defined as follows:

Closure: degree of closure of a primary target movement.
    Open: relatively slight degree of closure, modulates air-sound stream. +
open: relatively slight degree of closure to modulate air-sound stream;
pertains to all vowels and /h/. − open: any degree of closure more than
that which modulates air-sound stream.
    Approximation: relative degree of closure, alters but not greatly obstructs
air-sound stream. + approximation: degree of closure that alters but does
not obstruct air-sound stream; must be greater than a closure that merely
modulates air-sound stream; pertains to degree of closure for liquids and
glides. − approximation: any degree of closure either less than or greater
than that prescribed by + approximation.
    Obstruction: relative degree of closure, obstructs air-sound stream to the
point that turbulence is produced, resulting in emission of high frequency
noise; pertains to fricative consonants. − obstruction: insufficient closure
to cause turbulence in air-sound stream or complete closure to impound
air-sound stream.
    Occlusion: degree of closure needed to impound air-sound stream. +
occlusion: closure to extent that air-sound stream is impounded; pertains
to stop consonants. − occlusion: any closure insufficient to impound
air-sound stream.
Place: location of a primary target movement.
    Vertical: relative vertical location of primary target movement to hard
palate: (1) vertical = close or high; (2) vertical = midway or mid; (3)
vertical = far or low.
    Horizontal: relative horizontal location of primary target movement to
anatomical features of vocal mechanism.

Bilabial: primary target posture obtained by bilabial movement. + bilabial: bilabial occlusion. − bilabial: no bilabial occlusion.

Labiodental: primary target posture obtained by labio-dental movement. + labiodental: labio-dental obstruction. − labio-dental: no labio-dental obstruction.

Lingua-dental: primary target posture obtained by lingua-dental movement. + lingua-dental: lingua-dental obstruction. − lingua-dental: no lingua-dental obstruction.

Lingua-alveolar: primary target posture obtained by lingua-alveolar movement. + lingua-alveolar: lingua-alveolar obstruction or occlusion. − lingua-alveolar: no lingua-alveolar obstruction or occlusion.

Lingua-palatal: primary target posture obtained by anterior lingua-palatal movement: (1) lingua-palatal = anterior lingua-palatal obstruction; (2) lingua-palatal = open or approximal lingual movement in horizontal region of anterior portion of hard palate; (3) lingua-palatal = no lingua-palatal movement.

Lingua-mid-palatal: primary target posture obtained by lingua-palatal movement in horizontal region of posterior portion of hard palate. + lingua-mid-palatal: open or approximal lingual posture in horizontal region of posterior portion of hard palate. − lingua-mid-palatal: no lingua-mid palatal posture.

Velar: primary target posture obtained by lingual movement in horizontal region of velum or soft palate. + velar: primary posture in horizontal region of velum or soft palate. − velar: no primary posture in region of velum or soft palate.

Glottal: primary target posture made at glottis. + glottal: primary target posture made at glottis. − glottal: primary target posture not at glottis.

Manner: particular nature of phoneme other than closure and place features.

Voiced: vocal fold function: (1) voice = laryngeal phonation; (2) voice = aspiration; (3) voice = no laryngeal phonation.

Oral: primary cavity of air-sound stream transmission. + oral: oral cavity; − oral: nasal cavity as secondary aperture.

Continuant: fixed articulatory posture in which either oral or nasal cavity is open. + continuant: steady state articulatory posture; − continuant: nonsteady-state articulatory posture.

Duration: relative duration of phonetic movement. + duration: long duration, slow onset, target maintained, rapid offset; − duration: short duration, targets approximated; transitions relatively brief, relatively long offset.

Movement: movement of articulators throughout sound production. + movement: movement continuous; − movement: movement halted in target posture.

Fusion: blend of two target postures; stop-continuant juncture. + fusion: blend of two target postures; − fusion: single target posture.

Lateral: lateral air movement around tongue blade. + lateral: lateral air-sound stream movement over tongue blade; − lateral: lack of lateral air-sound stream flow.

Labialization: secondary closure by lip rounding: (1) labialized = lip rounding; (2) labialized = neutral lip contour; (3) labialized = labial spread.

The early work on distinctive feature theory (Jakobson, Fant, and Halle 1963; Halle 1957) posited the biuniqueness theory, which established criteria for specificity of features. This theory stated that features must be explicit enough to indicate plus or minus states. However, some features such as labialization, nasality, and voicing have degrees rather than absolute states.

II. Phonotactic Processes

1. *Diminutive:* add high front vowel to end of proper noun, e.g., Mommy, Daddy, Spotty.
2. *Voicing:* voice initial consonant, unvoice final consonant.
   toad → [dot]
   cookie → [doti]
3. *Consonant cluster reduction:* features of clusters absent resulting in reduced cluster.
   stop → [top]
   first → [fʌrs]
4. *Weak syllable deletion:*
   elephant → [ʌfant]
   telephone → [ʌfon]
   tomato → [mato]
5. *Assimilation:* one phonetic activity replaces another; forward assimilation or coarticulation when forthcoming phonetic activity replaces earlier phonetic activity; backward coarticulation when earlier phonetic activity replaces forthcoming activity.
   Forward coarticulation: coat → [tot]
   Backward coarticulation: soup → [sos]
6. *Reduplication:* syllable repetition: Mama, Dada, Tootoo, Choo-choo, Bye-bye.
7. *Fronting:* anterior tongue movement replacing other expected phonetic activity.
   top → [thop]
   soap → [thop], [top]

8. *Simplification:* closed syllables simplified by deleting final consonants, resulting in open syllables: CVC → CV.
boat → [bo]
dog → [da]

Appendix D

Developmental Sequences and Strategies

I. Cognitive Sequences

1. *Piagetian stages: sensorimotor:* causality, anticipation, object permanence, delayed imitation, alternative means
2. *Perception:*
   a) Topological   a) Space
   b) Projective   b) Time
   c) Euclidean
3. *Attending:*
   a) All-or-none
   b) Discrepancy—variation
   c) Density
4. *Bruner stages:*
   a) Enactive—motoric
   b) Iconic—perceptual
   c) Symbolic—functional
5. *Distancing:*
   a) Object—actual
   b) Object—representational
   c) Pictorial
   d) Word
6. *Differentiation:*
   a) Ego—self   a) Animate
   b) Nonego—self b) Inanimate
   c) Body parts—self
   d) Body parts—others
7. *Memory:*
   a) Iconic   a) Recency
   b) Symbolic b) Primacy—recency

8. *Verbal regulation:*
   a) Verbal activation but no inhibition
   b) Verbal activation and inhibition
   c) Verbal activation and direction or modification
9. *Technology of reckoning:*
   a) Single attributes   a) Dynamic attributes
   b) Attribute clusters   b) Static attributes
   c) Separate clusters
   d) Integrated attributes
10. *Dimensional salience* (daily fluctuations):
    a) Strong and attribute specific
    b) Weak and diffused
11. *Set shifts:*
    a) Nonrule governed   a) Progressively easier:
                                    Initial set, reversal
                                    shift, nonreversal shift
    b) Rule governed   b) Initial set and reversal
                                    shift relatively easier
                                    than nonreversal shift
12. *Tempo:*
    a) Impulsive
    b) Reflective
13. *Alternative mediators and agents:*
    a) Mediators: Action patterns or functions, category name, specific
       labels, focal/peripheral exemplar
    b) Agents: Individual himself, peer, sibling, parent, teacher, clinician

II. Semantic Sequences

1. *Semantic functions and relations:* developmental sequence not yet established
2. *Labels:*
   a) Complexes (idiosyncratic, situational)
   b) Categories
   a) Idiosyncratic categories and labels
   b) Increased validity, status, accessibility
3. *Semantic feature hypothesis:*
   a) Conceptual underpinnings
   b) Space → time
   c) Overextensions and underextensions → appropriate generalizations
   d) Unmarked → marked or contrastive

   4. *Categorization—mediation:*
      a) Core concepts—focal exemplars
      b) Extended or overlapping concepts—peripheral exemplars
      c) Mediators
   5. *Paradigmatic shift:*
      a) Syntagmatic responses (contextual)
      b) Paradigmatic responses (categorized)
      c) Differentiated systems
      d) Differentiated exemplars
   6. *Relational terms:*
      a) In
      b) On
      c) Under
   7. *Dimensional attributes:*
      a) Dynamic attributes
      b) Static attributes
         1) Form
         2) Color
         3) Size
   8. *Anaphoric reference:*
      a) Single referent, immediate context: *He* is here.
      b) Two or more referents to the same thing: Bill walked fast because *he* was late for *his* class and because *he* had to speak.
      c) Competing referents: Mary waited for *him* but *she* decided to go before *he* got there.

III. Syntactic Sequences

   1. *Early utterances*
      a) Action patterns/dynamic events
      b) One-word utterances: extended action
      c) One-word utterances: new information, complexive
      d) One-word utterances: multifunctions
      e) Different words: same referent; different referents: same word
      f) Consecutive one-word utterances
      g) Two-word utterances
      h) Consecutive multiword utterances
   2. *Shift from one- to two-word utterances*
      a) Repetition of single-word utterance accompanied by adult intervention
      b) No repetition but one-word utterance with adult intervention
      c) Single repetition of the first word and the second word in a two-word utterance

    d) Two consecutive one-word utterances
    e) Two-word constructions

3. *Brown stages* (general and hypothetical for stage III, IV, and V)
    a) Semantic functions and relations
    b) Modulations of meaning
    c) Utterance types and modes
    d) Modification
    e) Embedding

4. *Inflection rules*
    a) Vocabulary
    b) Overgeneralization
    c) Appropriate generalization

5. *Morphemes (mean order of acquisition for Brown's fourteen morphemes)*
    a) Present progressive
    b) In
    c) On
    d) Past irregular
    e) Possessive
    f) Uncontractible copula
    g) Articles
    h) Past regular
    i) Third person regular
    j) Third person irregular
    k) Uncontractible auxiliary
    l) Contractible copula
    m) Contractible auxiliary

6. *Present progressive*
    a) V ing   I eat*ing*
    b) be + V ing   I *be* eat*ing*
    c) tense + be + V ing   I *am* eat*ing*

7. *Past participle*
    a) V part   I eat*en*
    b) have + V part   I *have* eat*en* yesterday
    c) tense + have + V part   I *had* eat*en*

8. *Negation* (structural)
    a) N + S; S + N   No, I go; I go, No
    b) (N)S   I no go
    c) NS   I did not go

9. *Negation* (function)
    a) Nonexistence
    b) Rejection
    c) Denial

10. *Questions*
    a) Tag questions: S + Q   I go, right?

      b) Yes/no questions   Can I go?

      c) *Wh*-question—nominals   Who goes?

      d) Other *Wh*-questions   Why do I go?

11. *Relative clause*
    a) Relative clause marker: The boy who is by the tree is tall.
    b) Relative clause marker deleted: The boy by the tree is tall.

12. *Conjunction*
    a) And
    b) Or
    c) But

IV. Communicative Sequences

1. *Early functions*
   a) Instrumental
   b) Regulatory
   c) Interactional
   d) Personal
   e) Heuristic
   f) Imaginative
   g) Informative

2. *Context bound/unbound*
   a) Mutual action
   b) Child speech → adult action
   c) Adult speech → child action
   d) Commands, requests → verbalized actions
   e) Speech → speech

3. *Repetition*
   a) Phonological practice
   b) Discourse clarification

4. *Socialization*
   a) Egocentrism and external thinking
   b) Socialization and internal thinking

   a) Primary socially interdependent speech
   b) Secondary sociable speech
   c) Tertiary socialized speech

   a) Alter-ego speech to child
   b) Ego-supportive speech to child
   c) Ego-socializing speech to child

a) Egocentrism
b) Roletaking
c) Communication game: Dump-and-Play

V. Alternative Strategies

1. *Intonational labels*
   Nonconventional primitive
   speech acts

   Word labels
   Conventional primitive
   speech acts

2. *Sentence builders*
   One-word utterances become
   two-word utterances—
   increased length and complexity

   Sentence analyzers
   Early word strings are
   subsequently analyzed by
   synthesizing new combinations

3. *Imitators*
   Individuals who spontaneously
   imitate 15 percent or more
   of their utterances

   Nonimitators
   Individuals who spontaneously
   imitate less than 15 percent of their
   utterances

4. *Spontaneous word learning*
   Semantic features of a word
   spontaneously realized because
   of previously deduced attributes
   in natural experiences; label
   serves to consolidate previous
   learning

   Scientific word learning
   A word is given, thereby
   precipitating an hypothesis-
   testing attitude about
   alternative meanings of the
   word; individual sets out
   learning about the word

5. *Negative contrasts*
   In learning contrastive terms,
   the negative term is learned
   first, e.g., "short" learned
   before "long," "little" before
   "big," "thin" before "thick"

   Positive contrasts
   In learning contrastive
   terms, the positive term
   is learned first

6. *Pronominal*
   Reliance on pronominals for
   noun phrases

   Nominative
   Reliance on explicit nominals:
   first proper nouns, then
   determiner and nouns

7. *Subject noun phrase*
   Nominals in the subject noun
   phrase learned
   and elaborated first

   Object noun phrase
   Nominals in object noun
   phrases learned
   and elaborated first

8. *Adjectives—subject NP*
   Adjectives (and other noun
   modifers) appear first in the
   subject noun phrase

   Adjectives—object NP
   Adjectives (and other noun
   modifiers) appear first in
   the object noun phrase

9. *Referential learner*
Individual is oriented
on the principle that one word
has many referents and one
referent has many words

Expressive learner
Individual is oriented
on the principle that different
combinations of words can be
made

10. *Referential models*
Language models (usually
parents and siblings) interact
with a language learner
oriented on the principle
that one word has many
referents and one referent
has many words

Expressive models
Language models interact with
a language learner with a limited
set of utterances for a range
of functions, but range of
functions itself is greatly
limited

11. *Elaborated codes*
A predominant verbal style in
which communicative intent is
coded explicitly, individualized,
tailored to perceived available
reference, and readily altered to
overcome communicative
obstacles

Restricted codes
A predominant verbal style in
which communicative intent
is coded by implied or communal
devices with a limited audience

12. *Reflective thinking*
Cognitive tempo in which
an individual considers
available alternatives and
is highly accurate

Impulsive thinking
Cognitive tempo in which
an individual does not consider
all available alternatives and is
highly inaccurate

13. *Analytic thinking*
Thinking in which one deduces
components

Synthetic thinking
Thinking in which one integrates
or "puts together" components to
construct a "whole"

14. *Divergent thinking*
Thinking in which one realizes
novel aspects such as unusual
functions of things

Convergent thinking
Thinking in which one realizes
integrative aspects of things

References

ABRAHAMS, R., and GAY, G. 1972. Talking Black in the classroom. In *Language and cultural diversity in American education,* eds. R. Abrahams and R. Troika. Englewood Cliffs, N.J.: Prentice-Hall.

ABRAVANEL, E., LEVAN-GOLDSCHMIDT, E., and STEVENSON, M. 1976. Action imitation: The early phase of infancy. *Child Development* 47:1032–44.

ADLER, S. 1975. *The nonverbal child.* 2d ed. Springfield, Ill.: Charles C Thomas.

AINSWORTH, M. 1969. Object relations, dependency and attachment: a theoretical view of the infant-mother relationship. *Child Development* 40:969–1025.

ALVY, K. 1973. The development of listener adapted communications in grade-school children from different social-class backgrounds. *Genetic Psychology Monographs* 87:33–104.

AMMONS, R., and AMMONS, H. 1948. *The full-range picture vocabulary test.* New Orleans: R. B. Ammons.

ANDERSON, S., and MESSICK, S. 1974. Social competency in young children. *Developmental Psychology* 10:282–93.

ANGLIN, J., ed. 1973. *Beyond the information given: Studies in the psychology of knowing by Jerome S. Brunner.* New York: W. W. Norton Co.

ANTONUCCI, T., ed. 1976. Attachment: A life-span concept. *Human Development* 19 (no. 3): 135–42.

ATHEY, I. 1970. Theories of language development and their relation to reading. Presented at the National Reading Conference.

ATHEY, I., and RUBADEAU, D., eds. 1970. *Educational implications of Piaget's theory.* Waltham, Mass.: Ginn-Blaisdell.

ATKINSON, R., and SHIFFRIN, R. 1971. The control of short-term memory. *Scientific American* 225:82–90.

AULT, R. 1973. Problem-solving strategies of reflective, impulsive, fast-accurate, and slow-inaccurate children. *Child Development* 44:259–66.

AUNGST, L., and FRICK, J. 1964. Auditory discrimination ability and consistency of articulation or /r/. *J. Speech and Hearing Disorders* 29:76–85.

AUSTIN, J. 1962. *How to do things with words.* New York: Oxford University Press.

BAIRD, R., and BEE, H. 1969. Modification of conceptual style preference by differential reinforcement. *Child Development* 40:903–10.

BALL, S., and BOGATZ, G. 1970. *The first year of* Sesame Street. Princeton, N.J.: Educational Testing Service.

BALTAXE, C., and SIMMONS, J. 1975. Language in childhood psychosis: A review. *J. Speech Hearing Disorders* 40:434–38.

BANDURA, A. 1971. Analysis of modeling processes. In *Psychological modeling: Conflicting theories,* ed. A. Bandura, pp. 1–62. New York: Aldine-Atherton.

BANDURA, A., and HARRIS, M. 1966. Modification of syntactic style. *J. Experimental Child Psychology* 4:341–52.

BARATZ, J. 1968. Language in the economically disadvantaged child: A perspective. *Asha* 10:143–46.

BARATZ, J. 1969a. A bi-dialectal task for determining language proficiency in economically disadvantaged Negro children. *Child Development* 40:889–901.

BARATZ, J. 1969b. Language and cognitive assessments of Negro children: assumptions and research needs. *Asha* 11:87–92.

BARATZ, J. 1970. Teaching reading in an urban Negro school system. In *Language and Poverty: Perspectives on a Theme,* ed. R. Williams. Chicago: Markham Publishing Co.

BARTLETT, E. 1972. Selecting preschool language programs. In *Language in early childhood education,* ed. C. Cazden. Washington, D.C.: National Assoc. Education of Young Children.

BARTLETT, E. 1976. Sizing things up: The acquisition of the meaning of dimensional adjectives. *J. Child Language* 3:205–19.

BATEMAN, B. 1974. Discussion summary: Language intervention for the mentally retarded. In *Language perspectives: Acquisition, retardation, and intervention,* eds. R. Schiefelbusch and L. Lloyd. Baltimore: University Park Press.

BATEMAN, D. and ZIDONIS, F. 1966. *The effect of a study of transformational grammar on the writing of ninth and tenth graders.* National Council of Teachers of English, Research Report No. 9.

BATES, E. 1976a. *Language and context: the acquisition of pragmatics.* New York: Academic Press.

BATES, E. 1976b. Pragmatics and sociolinguistics in child language. In *Normal and deficient child language,* eds. D. Morehead and A. Morehead. Baltimore: University Park Press.

BATES, E., CAMAIONI, L., and VOLTERRA, V. 1975. The acquisition of performatives prior to speech. *Merrill-Palmer Quarterly* 21:205–06.

BAUMEISTER, A. 1976. Personal correspondence.

BAUMEISTER, A., and MUMA, J. 1975. On defining mental retardation. *J. Special Education* 9:293–306.

BAUMEISTER, A., and ROLLINGS, J. 1976. Self-injurious behavior. In *International review of research in mental retardation,* vol. 8. New York: Academic Press.

BEARISON, D., and CASSEL, T. 1975. Cognitive decentration and social codes: communicative effectiveness in young children from differing family contexts. *Child Development* 11:29–36.

BECKWITH, L., and THOMPSON, S. 1976. Recognition of verbal labels of pictured objects and events by 17- to 30-month old infants. *J. Speech Hearing Research* 19:690–99.

BEE, H., VAN EGEREN, L., PYTKOWICZ, A., NYMAN, B., and LECKIS, M. 1970. Social class differences in maternal teaching strategies and speech patterns. *Developmental Psychology* 40:146–49.

BEM, S. 1975. Sex-role adaptability: one consequence of psychological androgyny. *J. Personality and Social Psychology* 31:634–43.

BERKO, J. 1958. The child's learning of English morphology. *Word* 14:150–77.

BERNSTEIN, B. 1970. A sociolinguistic approach to socialization: with some reference to educability. In *Language and poverty: Perspectives on a theme,* ed. F. Williams. Chicago: Markham Publishing Co.

BEVER, T. 1961. Pre-linguistic behavior. Unpublished honors thesis, Department of Linguistics, Harvard University.

BEVER, T. 1968. Associations to stimulus-response theories of language. In *Verbal behavior and general behavior theory,* eds. T. Dixon and D. Horton. Englewood Cliffs, N.J.: Prentice-Hall.

BEVER, T. 1970. The cognitive basis for linguistic structures. In *Cognition and the development of language*, ed. S. Hayes. New York: Wiley.

BEVER, T. 1973. Perceptions, thought, and language. In *Language, comprehension, and the acquisition of knowledge*, eds. J. Carroll and R. Freedle. Washington D.C.: Winston.

BEVER, T., FODOR, J., and WEKSEL, W. 1965a. Is linguistics empirical? *Psychological Review* 72:493–500.

BEVER, T., FODOR, J., and WEKSEL, W. 1965b. Theoretical notes on the acquisition of syntax: A critique of "contextual generalization." *Psychological Review* 72:467–82.

BEVER, T., LOCKNER, J., and KIRK, R. 1969. The underlying structures of sentences are the primary units of immediate speech processing. *Perception and Psychophysics* 5:225–34.

BEVER, T., MEHLER, J., and VALIAN, V. 1967. Linguistic capacity of very young children. Lecture at Graduate School of Education, Harvard University.

BIRCH, H., and LEFFORD, A. 1964. Two strategies for studying perception in "brain-damaged" children. In *Brain damage in children: Biological and social aspects*, ed. J. Birch. Baltimore: Williams and Wilkins.

BIRDWHISTELL, R. 1970. *Kinesics and context*. Philadelphia: University of Pennsylvania Press.

BLAISDELL, R., and JENSEN, P. 1970. Stress and word position as determinants of imitation in first-language learners. *J. Speech Hearing Research* 13:193–202.

BLANK, M. 1974. Cognitive functions of language in the preschool years. *Developmental Psychology* 10:229–45.

BLANK, M., and BRIDGES, W. 1964. Cross-modal transfer in nursery school children. *J. Comparative and Physiological Psychology* 58:277–82.

BLANK, M. and BRIDGES, W. 1966. Deficiencies in verbal labeling in retarded readers. *American J. Orthopsychiatry* 36:840–47.

BLANK, M., and BRIDGES, W. 1967. Perceptual abilities and conceptual deficiencies in retarded readers. In *Psychopathology of mental development*, ed. J. Zubin. New York: Grune & Stratton.

BLANK, M., and FRANK, S. 1971. Story recall in kindergarten children: effect of method of presentation on psycholinguisic performance. *Child Development* 42:299–312.

BLANK, M., and SOLOMON, F. 1968. A tutorial language program to develop abstract thinking in socially disadvantaged preschool children. *Child Development* 39:379–390.

BLANK, M., and SOLOMON, F. 1969. How shall the disadvantaged child be taught? *Child Development* 40:47–61.

BLANKENSHIP, A. 1938. Memory span: a review of the literature. *Psychological Bulletin* 35:1–25.

BLOOM, L. 1970. *Language development: form and function in emerging grammars*. Cambridge, Mass.: MIT Press.

BLOOM, L. 1972. Cognitive and linguistic aspects of early language development; short course. *American Speech Hearing Association Convention*.

BLOOM, L. 1973. *One word at a time: the use of single-word utterances before syntax*. The Hague: Mouton.

BLOOM, L. 1974. Talking, understanding, and thinking. In *Language perspectives: acquisition, retardation, and intervention*, eds. R. Schiefelbusch and L. Lloyd. Baltimore: University Park Press.

BLOOM, L. 1975. Language development. In *Review of child development research*. No. 4, ed. F. Horowitz. Chicago: University of Chicago Press.

BLOOM, L., HOOD, L., and LIGHTBOWN, P. 1974. Imitation in language development: if, when, and why. *Cognitive Psychology* 6:380–420.

BLOOM, L., LIGHTBOWN, P., and HOOD, L. 1975. Structure and variation in child language. *Monographs of the Society for Research in Child Development* 40, serial no. 160.

BOLINGER, D. 1965. The atomization of meaning. *Language* 41:555–73.

BOLINGER, D. 1975. *Aspects of Language*. New York: Harcourt Brace Jovanovich.

BONDARKO, L. 1969. The syllable structure of speech and distinctive features of phonemes. *Phonetics* 20:1–40.

BOOMER, D. 1965. Hesitation and grammatical encoding. *Language and Speech* 8:148–58.

BOUSFIELD, W. 1953. The occurrence of clustering in the recall of randomly arranged associates. *J. General Psychology* 49:229–40.

BOUSFIELD, W., ESTERSON, J., and WHITMARSH, G. 1958. A study of developmental changes in conceptual and perceptual associative clustering. *J. Genetic Psychology* 92:95–102.

BOWER, T. 1966. The visual world of infants. *Scientific American* 215:80–92.

BOWER, T. 1971. The object in the world of the infant. *Scientific American* 225:30–38.

BOWER, T., and WISHART, J. 1972. The effects of motor skill on object permanence. *Cognition* 1:165–72.

BOWERMAN, M. 1973. Structural relationships in children's utterances: syntactic or semantic? In *Cognitive development and the acquisition of language,* ed. T. Moore. New York: Academic Press.

BOWERMAN, M. 1974. Discussion summary: Development of concepts underlying language. In Schiefelbusch, R., and Lloyd, L. (eds.), *Language perspectives: Acquisition, retardation, and intervention.* Baltimore: University Park Press.

BOWERMAN, M. 1975. Cross-linguistic similarities at two stages of syntactic development. In *Foundations of language development,* eds. E. Lenneberg and E. Lenneberg. New York: Academic Press.

BOWERMAN, M. 1976. Semantic factors in the acquisition of rules for word use and sentence construction. In *Normal and deficient child language,* eds. D. Morehead and R. Morehead. Baltimore: University Park Press.

BOWERMAN, M. (In press, a). The acquisition of word meaning: An investigation of some current conflicts. In *Development of communication: social and pragmatic factors in language acquisition,* eds. N. Waterson and C. Snow. New York: Wiley.

BOWERMAN, M. (In press, b). Words and sentences: uniformity, individual variation, and shifts over time in patterns of acquisition. In *Communicative and cognitive abilities—early behavioral assessment,* eds. F. Minifie and L. Lloyd. Baltimore: University Park Press.

BOWLBY, J. 1969. *Attachment and loss, Vol. I: Attachment.* New York: Basic Books.

BRAINE, M. 1963a. The ontogeny of English phrase structure: the first phrase. *Language* 39:1–13.

BRAINE, M. 1963b. On learning the grammatical order of words. *Psychological Review* 70:323–48.

BRAINE, M. 1965. On the basis of phrase structure: A reply to Bever, Fodor, and Weksel. *Psychological Review* 72:483–92.

BRANSFORD, J., and JOHNSON, M. 1972. Contextual prerequisites for understanding: some investigations of comprehension and recall. *J. Verbal Learning Verbal Behavior* 11:717–26.

BRANSFORD, J., and McCARRELL, N. 1974. A sketch of a cognitive approach to comprehension: some thoughts about understanding what it means to comprehend. In *Cognition and the symbolic processes,* eds. W. Weimer and D. Palermo. Hillsdale, N.J.: Lawrence Erlbaum Associates Publishers.

BRIER, N., and JACOBS, P. 1972. Reversal shifting: its stability and relations to intelligence at two developmental levels. *Child Development* 43:1230–41.

BRIGGS, C., and WEINBERG, R. 1973. Effects of reinforcement in training children's conceptual tempo. *Journal of Educational Psychology* 65:383–94.

BROEN, P. 1972. The verbal environment of the language-learning child. *ASHA Monographs,* No. 17.

BRONFENBRENNER, U. 1974. Developmental research, public policy, and the ecology of child-hood. *Child Development* 45:1–5.

BRONFENBRENNER, U. 1977. Toward an experimental ecology of human development. *American Psychologist* 32:513–31.

BRONOWSKI, J., and BELLUGI, U. 1970. Language, name, and concept. *Science* 168:669–73.

BROOKS, P., and BAUMEISTER, A. 1977. A plea for consideration of ecological validity in the experimental psychology of mental retardation: a guest editorial. *American Journal of Mental Deficiency* 81:407–16.

BROWN, R. 1956. Language and categories. Appendix in J. Bruner, J. Goodner, and G. Austin. *A study of thinking*. New York: Wiley.

BROWN, R. 1958a. How shall a thing be called? *Psychological Review* 65:18–21.

BROWN, R. 1958b. *Words and things*. New York: The Free Press.

BROWN, R. 1965. *Social psychology*. New York: Free Press.

BROWN, R. 1968. The Development of Wh- questions in child speech. *J. Verbal Learning Verbal Behavior* 7:279–90.

BROWN, R., ed. 1971. *Psycholinguistics*. Riverside, N.J.: The Free Press.

BROWN, R. 1973a. Development of the first language in the human species. *American Psychologist* 28:97–106.

BROWN, R. 1973b. *A first language: the early stages*. Cambridge, Mass.: Harvard University Press.

BROWN, R., and BELLUGI, U. 1964. Three processes in the child's acquisition of syntax. *Harvard Educ. Review* 34:133–51.

BROWN, R., and BERKO, J. 1960. Word association and the acquisition of grammar. *Child Development* 31:1–14.

BROWN, R., CAZDEN, C., and BELLUGI-KLIMA, U. 1969. The child's grammar from I to III. In *Minnesota symposia on child psychology,* vol. 2, ed. J. Hill. Minneapolis: University of Minnesota Press.

BROWN, R., and HANLON, C. 1970. Deprivational complexity and order of acquisition in child speech. In *Cognition and the development of language;* ed. J. Hayes. New York: Wiley.

BROWN, R., and McNEILL, D. 1966. The "tip of the tongue" phenomenon. *J. Verbal Learning Verbal Behavior* 5:325–37.

BRUNEAU, T. 1973. Communicative silence. *J. Communication* 23:17–46.

BRUNER, J. 1957. On perceptual readiness. *Psychological Review* 64:123–52.

BRUNER, J. 1961. The act of discovery. *Harvard Educational Review* 31:21–32.

BRUNER, J. 1964. The course of cognitive growth. *American Psychologist* 19:1–15.

BRUNER, J. 1968. *Processes of cognitive growth: infancy*. Worcester, Mass.: Clark University.

BRUNER, J. 1973. Organization of early skilled action. *Child Development* 44:1–11.

BRUNER, J. 1975a. The ontogenesis of speech acts. *Journal Child Language* 2:1–19.

BRUNER, J. 1975b. From communication to language—a psychological perspective. *Cognition* 3:255–88.

BRUNER, J., GOODNOW, J., and AUSTIN, G. 1956. *A study of thinking*. New York: Science Editions, Inc.

BRUNER, J., and KENNEY, H. 1966. The development of the concepts of order and proportion in children. In J. Bruner, R. Olver, P. Greenfield, *Studies in cognitive growth*. New York: Wiley.

BRUNER, J., OLVER, R., GREENFIELD, P., et al. 1966. *Studies in cognitive growth*. New York: Wiley.

BULLOCK, SIR A. 1975. *A language for life*. London: Her Majesty's Stationery Office.

BURGER, R., and MUMA, J. 1977. Mediated categorization behavior in two representational modes: fluent aphasics, afluent aphasics, and normals. *Journal Child Language* (in press).

BURLING, R. 1973. *English in black and white.* New York: Holt, Rinehart and Winston.

BURT, C. 1949. The structure of the mind: a review of the results of factor analysis. *British Journal of Educational Psychology* 19:100–11,176–99.

BUSH, E., and DWECK, C. 1975. Reflections on conceptual tempo: relationships between cognitive style and performance as a function of task characteristics. *Developmental Psychology* 11:567–74.

CARMICHAEL, L., HOGAN, H., and WALTER, A. 1932. An experimental study of the effect of language on the reproduction of visually preceived form. *Journal of Experimental Psychology* 15:73–86.

CARON, A. 1969. Discrimination shifts in three year olds as a function of dimensional salience. *Developmental Psychology* 1:333–39.

CARROLL, J. 1956. *Language, thought and reality: selected writings of Benjamin Lee Whorf.* Cambridge, Mass.: MIT Press.

CARROLL, J. 1963. Psycholinguistics in the study of mental retardation. In *Research in speech and hearing for mentally retarded children,* eds. R. Schiefelbusch and J. Smith. Report of a conference at the University of Kansas.

CARROLL, J. 1964. *Language and thought.* Englewood Cliffs, N.J.: Prentice-Hall.

CARROLL, J. 1968. Review of the nature of human intelligence. *American Educational Research Journal* 5:249–56.

CARROLL, J., DAVIES, P. and RICHMAN, B. 1971. *The American Heritage word frequency book.* Boston: Houghton Mifflin.

CARROLL, J., and FREEDLE, R., eds. 1973. *Language, comprehension, and the acquisition of knowledge.* Washington, D.C.: Winston.

CATTELL, R. 1963. Theory of fluid and crystallized intelligence: a critical experiment. *Journal of Educational Psychology* 54:1–22.

CAZDEN, C. 1965. Environmental assistance to the child's acquisition of grammar. Unpublished doctoral dissertation, Harvard University.

CAZDEN, C. 1966a. Subcultural differences in child language: an interdisciplinary review. *Merrill-Palmer Quarterly of Behavior and Development* 12:185–219.

CAZDEN, C. 1966b. Some implications of research on language development for preschool education. Paper presented for the Social Science Research Council Conference on Preschool Education, Chicago.

CAZDEN, C. 1967. On individual differences in language competence and performance. *J. Special Education,* 1:135–50.

CAZDEN, C. 1968. The acquisition of noun and verb inflections. *Child Development* 39:433–48.

CAZDEN, C. 1971. The psycnology of language. In *Handbook of speech, hearing, and language disorders,* ed. L. Travis. New York: Appleton-Century-Crofts.

CAZDEN, C. 1972a. *Child language and education.* New York: Holt, Rinehart and Winston.

CAZDEN, C. 1972b. *Language in early childhood education.* Washington, D.C.: National Association for the Education of Young Children.

CAZDEN, C., BARATZ, J., LABOV, W., WILLIAM, F., and PALMER, F. 1970. Language development in day-care programs. Chapter commissioned by Office of Economic Opportunity for a "State of the Art" document on day-care.

CAZDEN, C., and BROWN, R. 1975. The early development of the mother tongue. In *Foundations of language development,* eds. E. Lenneberg and E. Lennenberg. New York: Academic Press.

CAZDEN, C., BRYANT, B., and TILLMAN, M. 1972. Making it and going home: the attitudes of black people toward language acquisition. In *Language in Early Childhood Education,* ed. C. Cazden. Washington, D. C.: National Association for the Education of Young Children.

CHAFE, W. 1970. *Meaning and the structure of language.* Chicago: University of Chicago Press.

CHALL, J. 1969. *Learning to read: the great debate.* New York: McGraw-Hill.

CHAPEY, R., RIGRODSKY, S., and MORRISON, E. 1976. Divergent semantic behavior in aphasia. *J. Speech Hearing Research* 19:664–77.

CHAPMAN, R., and MILLER, J. 1975. Word order in early two and three word utterances: does production precede comprehension? *Journal Speech Hearing Research* 18:355–71.

CHAPPELL, G., and JOHNSON, G. 1976. Evaluation of cognitive behavior in the young nonverbal child. *Language, Speech, Hearing Services in Schools* 7:17–27.

CHERRY, E. 1965. Children's comprehension of teacher and peer speech. *Child Development* 36:467–80.

CHOMSKY, C. 1969. *The acquisition of syntax in children from 5 to 10.* Cambridge, Mass.: MIT Press.

CHOMSKY, N. 1956. Three models for the description of language. *I.R.E. transactions on information theory.* Vol. IT-2. Reprinted in R. Luce, R. Bush, and E. Galanter (eds.), *Readings in Mathematical Psychology,* Vol. II. New York: Wiley, 1965.

CHOMSKY, N. 1957. *Syntactic structures.* The Hague: Mouton.

CHOMSKY, N. 1959. A review of B. F. Skinner's *Verbal Behavior. Language* 35:26–58.

CHOMSKY, N. 1961. Some methodological remarks on generative grammar. *Word* 17:219–39.

CHOMSKY, N. 1965a. Current issues in linguistic theory. In *The structure of language,* eds. J. Fodor and J. Katz. Englewood Cliffs, N.J.: Prentice-Hall, Inc.

CHOMSKY, N. 1965b. A transformational approach to syntax. In *The structure of language,* eds. J. Fodor and J. Katz. Englewood Cliffs: Prentice-Hall.

CHOMSKY, N. 1965c. *Aspects of the theory of syntax.* Cambridge: MIT Press.

CHOMSKY, N. 1968. *Language and mind.* New York: Harcourt Brace Jovanovich.

CHOMSKY, N., and HALLE, M. 1968. *The sound patterns of English.* New York: Harper & Row.

CHOMSKY, N., and MILLER, G. 1963. Introduction to the formal analysis of natural languages. In *Handbook of mathematical psychology, vol, 2.* eds. R. Luce, R. Bush, and E. Galanter. New York: Wiley.

CHURCH, J. 1971. In the discussion "Limitation of the term 'language.' " In *Language acquisition: models and methods,* eds. R. Huxley and E. Ingram. New York: Academic Press.

CICIRELLI, V., et al. 1969. *The impact of Headstart,* vols. I and II. Bladensburg, Md.: Westinghouse Learning Corp.

CLARK, E. 1973a. Non-linguistic strategies and the acquisition of word meanings. *Cognition: International J. Cognitive Psychology* 2:161–82.

CLARK, E. 1973b. What's in a word? On the child's acquisition of semantics in his first language. In *Cognitive development and the acquisition of language,* ed. T. Moore. New York: Academic Press.

CLARK, E. 1974. Some aspects of the conceptual basis for first language acquisition. In *Language perspectives: acquisition, retardation, and intervention,* eds. R. Schiefelbusch and L. Lloyd. Baltimore: University Park Press.

CLARK, E. 1975. Knowledge, context, and strategy in the acquisition of meaning. In *Developmental psycholinguistics' theory and applications,* ed. D. Dato. Washington, D.C.: Georgetown University Press.

CLARK, H. 1970. The primitive nature of children's relational concepts. In *Cognition and the development of language,* ed. J. Hayes. New York: Wiley.

CLARK, H. 1973a. Space, time, semantics and the child. In *Cognitive development and the acquisition of language,* ed. T. Moore. New York: Academic Press.

CLARK, H. 1973b. The language-as-fixed-effect-fallacy: A critique of language statistics in psychological research. *Journal of Verbal Learning and Verbal Behavior* 12:335–59.

CLARK, H., and CLARK, E. 1977. *Psychology and language.* New York: Harcourt Brace Jovanovich.

CLARK, R., and DELIA, J. 1976. The development of functional persuasive skills in childhood and early adolescence. *Child Development* 47:1008–14.

CLARKE-STEWART, K. 1973. Interactions between mothers and their young children: characteristics and consequences. *Society for Research in Child Development. Monograph* no. 153.

CLIFTON, C., and ODOM, P. 1966. Similarity relations among certain English sentence constructions. *Psychological Monograph* 80: no. 613.

CLIFTON, R., GRAHAM, F., and HATTON, H. 1968. Newborn heart-rate response and response habilitation as a function of stimulus deviation. *J. Experimental Child Psychology* 6:265–78.

CLIFTON, R., and MEYERS, W. 1969. The heart-rate response of four-month-old infants to auditory stimuli. *J. Experimental Child Psychology 7:122–35.*

COLE, M., and BRUNER, J. 1972. Cultural differences and influences about psychological processes. *American Psychologist* 27:867–76.

COLE, M., GAY, J., GLICK, J., and SHARP, D. 1971. *The cultural context of learning and thinking.* New York: Basic Books.

COMPTON, A. 1970. Generative studies of children's phonological disorders. *J. Speech Hearing Disorders* 35:315–39.

CORSINI, D., PICK, A., and FLAVELL, J. 1968. Production deficiency of nonverbal mediators in young chidren. *Child Development* 39:53–8.

COURTWRIGHT, J., and COURTWRIGHT, I. 1976. Imitative modeling as a theoretical base for instructing language-disordered children. *J. Speech Hearing Research* 19:651–54.

COWAN, P., WEBER, J., HODDINOTT, B., and KLEIN, T. 1967. Mean length of a spoken response as a function of stimulus, experimenter, and subject. *Child Development* 38:191–203.

CRAIK, F., and LOCKHART, R. 1972. Levels of processing; A framework for memory research. *J. Verbal Learning Verbal Behavior* 11:671–84.

CROCKER, J. 1969. A phonological model of children's articulation competence. *J. Speech Hearing Disorders* 34:203–13.

CROMER, R. 1970. 'Children are nice to understand.' Surface structure clues for the recovery of deep structure. *British J. of Psychology* 61:397–408.

CROMER, R. 1974. Receptive language in the mentally retarded: processes and diagnostic distinctions. In *Language perspectives: acquisition, retardation, and intervention,* eds. R. Schiefelbusch and L. Lloyd. Baltimore: University Park Press.

CROMER, R. 1976. The cognitive hypothesis of language acquisition and its implications for child language deficiency. In *Normal and deficient child language,* eds. D. Morehead and A. Morehead. Baltimore: University Park Press.

CROWDER, R. 1972. Visual and auditory memory. In *Language by ear and by eye,* eds. J. Kavanagh and I. Mattingly. Cambridge, Mass.: MIT Press.

CRYSTAL, D., FLETCHER, P., and GARMAN, M. 1976. *The grammatical analysis of language disability.* New York: Elsevier.

CURTIS, J. 1964. The case for dynamic analysis in acoustic phonetics. In McDonald, E., *Articulation Testing and Treatment: A Sensory-Motor Approach.* Pittsburg: Stanwix House, Inc.

DALE, E., and O'ROURKE, J. 1976. *The living word vocabulary.* New York: Field Enterprises Educational Corp.

DALE, P. 1976. *Language development: structure and function,* 2d. ed. New York: Holt, Rinehart and Winston.

DAMARIN, F., and CATTELL, R. 1968. Personality factors in early childhood and their relation to intellience. *Monographs of the Society for Research in Child Development* 33, serial no. 122.

DANILOFF, R., and HAMMARBERG, R. 1973. On defining coarticulation, *Journal Phonetics* 1:239–48.

DANILOFF, R., and MOLL, K. 1968. Coarticulation of lip rounding. *J. Speech Hearing Research* 11:707–21.

DARLEY, F., and MOLL, K. 1960. Reliability of language measures and size of language sample. *J. Speech Hearing Research* 3:166–73.

DARLEY, F., and WINITZ, H. 1961. Age of first word: review of research. *J. Speech Hearing Disorders* 26:271–90.

DAVIS, A. J., and LANGE, G. 1973. Parent-child communication and the development of categorization styles in preschool children. *Child Development* 44:624–29.

DAWSON, B., and MUMA, J. 1971. *Parent-Child Develop Center curriculum.* Birmingham, Alabama.

DE AJURIAGUERRA, J., and TISSOT, R. 1975. Some aspects of language in various forms of senile dementia (comparisons with language in childhood). In *Foundations of language development,* vol. 1, ed. E. Lenneberg and E. Lenneberg. New York: Academic Press.

DE CECCO, J. 1967. *The psychology of language, thought and instruction.* New York: Holt, Rinehart and Winston.

DEESE, J. 1965. *The structure of associations in language and thought.* Baltimore: Johns Hopkins Press.

DEESE, J. 1969. Behavior and fact. *American Psychologist* 24:515–22.

DEESE, J. 1970. *Psycholinguistics.* Boston: Allyn & Bacon.

DENNY, D. 1972. Modeling effects upon conceptual style and cognitive tempo. *Child Development* 43:105–19.

DIETZE, D. 1955. The facilitating effect of words on discrimination and generalization. *J. Experimental Psychology* 50:255–60.

DIVESTA, F. 1966. A normative study of 220 concepts rated on the semantic differential by children in grades 2–7. *J. Genetic Psychology* 109:209–99.

DOLL, E. 1965. *Vineland social maturity scale.* Circle Pines, Minn.: American Guidance Service.

DOLLARD, J., and MILLER, N. 1950. *Personality and Psychotherapy.* New York: McGraw-Hill.

DONALDSON, M., and BALFOUR, G. 1968. Less is more: A study of language comprehension in children. *British J. of Psychology* 59:461–62.

DONALDSON, M., and MC GARRIGLE, J. 1974. Some clues to the nature of semantic development. *J. Child Language* 1:185–94.

DONALDSON, M. and WALES, R.J. 1970. On the acquisition of some relational terms. In J.R. Hayes (ed.), *Cognition and the Development of Language.* New York: Wiley.

DORE, J. 1974. A pragmatic description of early development. *J. Psycholinguistic Research* 3:343–50.

DORE, J. 1975. Holophrases, speech acts, and language universals. *J. Child Language* 2:21–40.

DRIBIN, E. 1971. Parent Child Center—mother and child: learning how to learn together. *Opportunity.* Washington, D.C.: Office of Economic Opportunity. March-April:16–19.

DUCHAN, J. 1976. Personal correspondence.

DUCHAN, J., and ERICKSON, J. 1976. Normal and retarded children's understanding of semantic relations in different verbal contexts. *J. Speech Hearing Research* 19:767–76.

DUNCAN, S. 1969. Nonverbal communication. *Psychological Bulletin* 72:118–37.

DUNN, L. 1959. *Peabody picture vocabulary test.* Circle Pines, Minn.: American Guidance Service.

ECKERMAN, C., WHATLEY, J., and KUTZ, S. 1975. Growth of social play with peers during the second year of life. *Developmental Psychology* 11:42–49.

EDWARDS, D. 1974. Sensory-motor intelligence and semantic relations in early child grammar. *Cognition* 2:395–434.

EDWARDS, M. 1974. Perception and production in child phonology: The testing of four hypotheses. *J. Child Language* 1:205–19.

EGELAND, B. 1974. Training impulsive children in the use of more efficient scanning techniques. *Child Development* 45:165–71.

EILERS, R., OLLER, D., and ELLINGTON, J. 1974. The acquisition of word-meaning for dimensional adjectives: the long and short of it. *J. Child Language* 1:195–204.

EIMAS, P., SIGUELAND, E., JUSCZYK, P., and VIGORITO, J. 1971. Speech perception in infants. *Science* 171:303–6.

EISENBERG, R. 1970. The organization of auditory behavior. *J. Speech Hearing Research* 13:453–71.

EISENSON, J. 1954. *Examining for aphasia.* New York: The Psychological Corp.

ELKIND, D. 1967a. Piaget and Montessori. *Harvard Educational Review* 37:535–45.

ELKIND, D. 1967b. Piaget's conservation problems. *Child Development* 38:15–27.

ELKIND, D., and FLAVELL, J., eds. 1969. *Studies in cognitive development: essays in honor of Jean Piaget.* New York: Oxford University Press.

ELLIS, H. 1972. *Fundamentals of human learning and cognition.* Dubuque, Iowa: Wm. C. Brown Co.

ELLIS, N. 1970. Memory processes in retardation and normals. In *International Review of Research in Mental Retardation,* vol. 4, ed. N. Ellis. New York: Academic Press.

EMERSON, H., and GEKOSKI, W. 1976. Interactive and categorical grouping strategies and the syntagmatic-paradigmatic shift. *Child Development* 47:1116–21.

EMERSON, L. 1931. The effect of body orientation upon the young child's memory for position of objects. *Child Development* 2:125–42.

ENGLER, L., HANNAH, E., and LONGHURST, T. 1973. Linguistic analysis of speech samples: a practical guide for clinicians. *J. Speech Hearing Disorders* 38:192–204.

ENTWISLE, D. 1966a. Developmental sociolinguistics: a comparative study in four subcultural settings. *Sociometry* 29:67–84.

ENTWISLE, D. 1966b. *Word association of young children.* Baltimore: Johns Hopkins Press.

ENTWISLE, D. 1966c. Form class and children's word associations. *J. Verbal Learning Verbal Behavior* 5:558–65.

ENTWISLE, D. 1968. Developmental sociolinguistics: inner city children. *American J. Sociology* 74:37–49.

ENTWISLE, D. 1971. Language socialization and reading. Paper presented at the *Conference on Developmental Psycholinguistics,* Linguistic Society of America.

ENTWISLE, D., FORSYTH, D., and MUUSS, R. 1964. The syntactic-paradigmatic shift in children's word associations. *J. Verbal Learning Verbal Behavior* 3:19–29.

ERVIN, S. 1961. Changes with age in the verbal determinants of word-association. *American J. Psychology* 74:361–72.

ERVIN, S. 1963. Correlates of associative frequency. *J. Verbal Learning Verbal Behavior* 1:422–31.

ERVIN, S. 1966. Imitation and structural change in children's language. In *New directions in the study of language.* Cambridge, Mass.: MIT Press.

ERVIN-TRIPP, S. 1967. Theoretical considerations and possible subsidiary studies. In *A field manual for cross-cultural studies of the acquisition of communicative competence,* ed. D. Slobin. Berkeley: University of California Press.

ERVIN-TRIPP, S. 1971. Social backgrounds and verbal skills. In *Language acquisition: models and methods,* eds. R. Huxley and E. Ingram. New York: Academic Press.

ERVIN-TRIPP, S. 1973. Some strategies for the first two years. In *Cognitive development and the acquisition of language,* ed. T. Moore. New York: Academic Press.

EVANS, R. 1973. *Jean Piaget—the man and his ideas.* New York: Dutton.

FARNHARM-DIGGORY, S. 1967. Symbol and synthesis in experimental "reading." *Child Development* 38:221–31.

FAY, W. 1967. Mitigated echolalia of children. *J. Speech Hearing Research* 10:305–10.

FEIGENBAUM, I. 1970. Using nonstandard to teach standard: contrast and comparison. In *Teaching standard English in the inner city,* eds. R. Fasold and R. Shuy. Washington, D.C.: Center for Applied Linguistics.

FERGUSON, C., and GARNICA, O. 1970. Theories of phonological development. In *Foundations of Language Development,* eds. E. Lenneberg and E. Lenneberg. New York: Academic Press.

FERGUSON, C., PEIZER, D., and WEEKS, T. 1973. A model-and-replica phonological grammar of a child's first words. *Lingua* 31:35–65.

FERGUSON, C., and SLOBIN, D. (eds.). 1973. *Studies of Child Language Development.* New York: Holt, Rinehart and Winston.

FERREIRO, E., and SINCLAIR, J. 1971. Temporal relations in language. *International Journal of Psychology* 6:39–47.

FESTINGER, L. 1957. *A theory of cognitive dissonance.* New York: Harper & Row.

FILLENBAUM, S. 1966. Memory for gist: some relevant variables. *Language and Speech* 9:217–27.

FILLENBAUM, S., and JONES, L. 1965. Grammatical contingencies in word association. *J. Verbal Learning Verbal Behavior* 4:248–55.

FILLMORE, C. 1968. The case for case. In *Universals in linguistic theory,* eds. E. Bach and R. Harms. New York: Holt, Rinehart and Winston.

FIRBAS, J. 1964. On defining the theme in functional sentence analysis. *Travaux Linguistiques de Prague* 1.

FISHMAN, J. 1970. *Sociolinguistics.* Rowley, Mass.: Newbury House.

FLANDERS, J. 1968. A review of research on imitative behavior. *Psychological Bulletin* 69:316–37.

FLAVELL, J. 1963. *The developmental psychology of Jean Piaget.* Princeton, N.J.: Van Nostrand.

FLAVELL, J. 1970. Concept development. In *Handbook of child psychology,* ed. L. Mussen. New York: Wiley.

FLAVELL, J. 1977. *Cognitive development.* Englewood Cliffs, N.J.: Prentice-Hall.

FLAVELL, J. et al. 1968. *The development of role-taking and communication skills in children.* New York: Wiley.

FLAVELL, J., BEACH, D., and CHINSKY, J. 1966. Spontaneous verbal rehearsal in a memory task as a function of age. *Child Development* 37:283–99.

FLERX, V., FIDLER, D., and ROGERS, R. 1976. Sex role stereotypes: developmental aspects and early intervention. *Child Development* 47:998–1007.

FODOR, J., and BEVER, T. 1965. The psychological reality of linguistic segments. *J. Verbal Learning Verbal Behavior* 4:414–20.

FOREHARD, R., and BAUMEISTER, A. 1976. Deceleration of aberrant behavior among retarded individuals. *Progress in Behavior Modification,* vol. 2. New York: Academic Press.

FORSTER, K. 1966a. Left-to-right processes in the construction of sentences. *J. Verbal Learning Verbal Behavior* 5:285–91.

FRANCIS, H. 1969. Structure in the speech of a 2½-year-old. *British J. Educational Psychology* 39:291–302.

FRANCIS, H. 1972. Toward an explanation of the syntagmatic-paradigmatic shift. *Child Development* 43:949–58.

FRANK, F. 1966. Perception and language in conservation. In *Studies in Cognitive Growth,* eds. J. Bruner et al. New York: Wiley.

FRANK, S., and OSSER, H. 1970. A psycholinguistic model of syntactic complexity. *Language and Speech* 13:38–53.

FRANKLIN, M. 1973. Nonverbal representation in young children: a cognitive perspective. *Young Child* 29:33–53.

FRASER, C., BELLUGI, U., and BROWN, R. 1963. Control of grammar in imitation, comprehension, and production. *J. Verbal Learning Verbal Behavior* 2:121–35.

FREEDMAN, P., and CARPENTER, R. 1976. Semantic relations used by normal and language-impaired children at Stage I. *J. Speech Hearing Research* 19:784–95.

FRIEDMAN, W., and SEELY, P. 1976. The child's acquisition of spatial and temporal word meanings. *Child Development* 47:1103–8.

FROMKIN, V. 1966. Neuro-muscular specification of linguistic units. *Language and Speech* 9:170–99.

FRY, C. 1969. Training children to communicate to listeners who have varying listener requirements. *J. Genetic Psychology* 114:153–66.

FUDGE, E. 1969. Syllables. *J. of Linguistics* 5:253–87.

FURTH, H. 1969. *Piaget and Knowledge*. Englewood Cliffs, N.J.: Prentice-Hall.

FURTH, H.G., and WACH, H. 1974. *Thinking goes to school. Piaget's theory in practice*. New York: Oxford University Press.

FURTH, H., and YOUNISS, J. 1976. Formal operations and language: A comparison of deaf and hearing adolescents. In D. Morehead and A. Morehead (eds.), *Normal and Deficient Child Language*. Baltimore: University Park Press.

GAGNE, R. 1965. *The conditions of learning*. New York: Holt, Rinehart and Winston.

GAGNE, R., ed. 1967. *Learning and individual differences*. Columbus, Ohio: Charles E. Merrill.

GAGNE, R., and SMITH, E. 1962. A study of the effects of verbalization on problem solving. *J. Experimental Psychology* 63:12–18.

GAINES, R. 1970. Children's selective attention to stimuli: stage or set? *Child Development* 41:979–91.

GALLAGHER, J., BAUMEISTER, A., and PATTERSON, G. 1970. Word association norms for institutionalized retarded, noninstitutionalized retarded and normal children. *Research Bulletin*. Psychology Department, University of Alabama.

GALLAGHER, T., and SHRINER, T. 1971. The relationship between syntactic theories and psychological complexity. Manuscript, University of Illinois.

GARDNER, A., and GARDNER, B. 1969. Teaching sign language to a chimpanzee. *Science* 165:664–72.

GARMIZA, C., and ANISFELD, M. 1976. Factors reducing the efficiency of referent-communication in children. *Merrill-Palmer Quarterly* 22:125–36.

GARNER, W. 1966. To perceive is to know. *American Psychologist* 21:11–19.

GARNICA, O. 1973. The development of phonemic speech perception. In *Cognitive development and the acquisition of language*, ed. T. Moore. New York: Academic Press.

GARRISON, M., ed. 1966. Cognitive models and development in mental retardation. *American Journal Mental Deficiency*. Monograph Supplement, vol. 70, no. 4.

GESCHWIND, N. 1965a. Disconnexion syndromes in animals and man. *Brain* 88:237–94.

GESCHWIND, N. 1965b. Disconnexion syndromes in animals and man. *Brain* 88:585–644.

GEYER, J. 1971. Comprehensive and partial models related to the reading process. In *The literature of research in reading with emphasis on models*, ed. R. Davis. New Brunswick, N.J.: Rutgers University.

GIBSON, E. 1963. Development of perception: discrimination of depth compared with discrimination of graphic symbols. *Basic cognitive processes in children*. Monograph of the Society for Research in Child Development.

GIBSON, E. 1969. *Principles of perceptual learning and development*. New York: Appleton-Century-Crofts.

GIBSON, E. 1970. The ontogeny of reading. *Am. Psychologist* 25:136–43.

GIBSON, E., and GIBSON, J. 1955. Perceptual learning: differentiation or enrichment? *Psychological Review* 62:32–41.

GINSBURG, H., and OPPER, S. 1969. *Piaget's theory of intellectual development: an introduction*. Englewood Cliffs, N.J.: Prentice-Hall.

GIRARDEAU, F., and SPRADLIN, J., eds. 1969. Functional analysis approach to speech and language. *Am. Speech and Hearing Association*, Monographs.

GLEASON, J. 1972. An experimental approach to improving children's communicative ability. In *Language in early childhood education,* ed. C. Cazden. Washington, D.C.: National Association for the Education of Young Children.

GLUCKSBERG, S. 1966. *Symbolic processes.* Dubuque, Iowa: Wm. C. Brown Company.

GLUCKSBERG, S., and KRAUSS, R. 1967. What do people say after they have learned how to talk? Studies of the development of referential communication. *Merrill-Palmer Quarterly Behavior and Development* 13:309–16.

GLUCKSBERG, S., KRAUSS, R., and HIGGINS, E. 1975. The development of referential communication skills. In *Review of Child Development Research,* ed. F. Horowitz. Chicago: University of Chicago Press.

GOLDBERG, L. 1968. Simple models or simple processes? Some research on clinical judgments. *Am. Psychologist* 23:483–96.

GOLDMAN, A. 1962. A comparative developmental approach to schizophrenia. *Psychological Bulletin* 59:57–69.

GOLINKOFF, R. 1975. Semantic development in infants: the concepts of agent and recipient. *Merrill-Palmer Quarterly* 21:181–94.

GOODMAN, K., ed. 1968. *The psycholinguistic nature of the reading process.* Detroit: Wayne State University Press.

GOODMAN, K. 1970. Reading: a psycholinguistic guessing game. In *Theoretical models and processes of reading,* eds. H. Singer and R. Ruddell. Newark, Del.: International Reading Association.

GOODSON, B., and GREENFIELD, P. 1975. The search for structural principles in children's play: a parallel with linguistic development. *Child Development* 46:734–46.

GOSS, A. Verbal mediating responses and concept formation. *Psychological Review* 68:248–74.

GREEN, D. and SWETS, J. 1966. *Signal detection theory and psychophysics.* New York: Wiley.

GREENBERG, J. 1963. Some universals of grammar with particular reference to the order of meaningful elements. In *Universals of language,* ed. J. Greenberg. Cambridge, Mass.: MIT Press.

GREENFIELD, P., MAY, A., and BRUNER, J. 1972. *Early words: language and action in the life of a child.* New York: Wiley.

GREENFIELD, P., NELSON, K., and SALTZMAN, E. 1972. The development of rule-bound strategies for manipulating seriated cups: a parallel between action and grammar. *Cognitive Psychology* 3:291–310.

GREENFIELD, P., and SMITH, J. 1976. *Communication and the beginnings of language: the development \of semantic structure in one-word speech and beyond.* New York: Academic Press.

GREENLEE, M. 1974. Interacting processes in the child's acquisition of stop-liquid clusters. *Papers and reports on child language development* 7:85–100.

GROSSMAN, H., WARREN, S., BEGAB, M., EYMAN, R., NIHARA, K., and O'CONNOR, G. 1973. Manual on terminology and classification in mental retardation (1973 revision). *American Association on Mental Deficiency,* Special Publication Series No. 2.

GRUBER, J. 1967. Topicalization in child language. *Foundations of language* 3:37–65.

GUESS, D., SAILOR, W., and BAER, D. 1974. To teach language to retarded children. In *Language perspectives: acquisition, retardation, and intervention,* eds. R. Schiefelbusch and L. Lloyd. Baltimore: University Park Press.

GUESS, D., SAILOR, W., RUTHERFORD, G., and BAER, D. 1968. An experimental analysis of linguistic development: the productive use of the plural morpheme. *J. Applied Behavior Analysis* 1:297–306.

GUILFORD, J. 1967. *The nature of human intelligence.* New York: McGraw-Hill.

GUILLAUME, P. 1971. *Imitation in children.* Chicago: University of Chicago Press.

GUNTER, R. 1960. Proportional drill as a technique for teaching grammar. *Language Learning* X:123–34.

GUSINOV, J., and PRICE, L. 1972. Modification of form and color responding in young children as a function of differential reinforcement and verbalization. *J. Experimental Child Psychology* 13:145–53.

HALLE, M. 1957. In defense of the number two. In *Studies presented to J. Whatmough,* ed. Pulgram.

HALLE, M. 1965a. Phonology in generative grammar. In: Fodor, J., and Katz, J., eds. 1965a. *The structure of language.* Englewood Cliffs, N.J.: Prentice-Hall.

HALLE, M. 1965b. On the bases of phonology. In *The structure of language,* eds. J. Fodor and J. Katz. Englewood Cliffs, N.J.: Prentice-Hall.

HALLIDAY, M. 1975. Learning how to mean. In *Foundations of language development: a multidisciplinary approach,* eds. E. Lenneberg and E. Lenneberg. New York: Academic Press.

HALLIDAY, M. 1977a. *Learning how to mean.* New York: Elsevier.

HALLIDAY, M. 1977b. *Explorations in the functions of language.* New York: Elsevier.

HALVERSON, C., and VICTOR, J. 1974. Minor physical anomalies and problem behavior in elementary school children. *Society for Research in Child Development.* Regional Meeting, Chapel Hill, N.C.

HAMMOND, K., and SUMMERS, D. 1972. Cognitive control. *Psychological Review* 79:58–67.

HARRIS, Z. 1965. Co-occurrence and transformation in linguistic structure. In *The structure of language: reading in the philosophy of language,* eds. J. Fodor and J. Katz. Englewood Cliffs: Prentice-Hall.

HARTUP, W., and COATES, B. 1972. Imitation: argument for a developmental approach. In *Recent trends in social learning theory,* ed. R.D. Parke. New York: Academic Press.

HARVARD SCHOOL OF EDUCATION. 1971. Challenging the myths: the schools, the blacks, and the poor. Cambridge, Mass.: *Harvard Educational Review.*

HASS, W., and WEPMAN, J. 1969. Surface structure, deep structure, and transformations: a model for syntactic development. *J. Speech Hearing Disorders* 34:303–11.

HEIDER, E. 1971. "Focal" color areas and the development of color names. *Developmental Psychology* 4:447–55.

HENKE, W. 1967. Preliminaries to speech synthesis based upon an articulatory model. 1967 Conference Speech Communication Processes, Cambridge Research lab. 170–77.

HESS, R., and SHIPMAN, V. 1965. Early experience and the socialization of cognitive modes in children. *Child Development* 34:869–86.

HINDS, J. 1975. Passives, pronouns, and themes and rhemes. *Glossa* 9:79–106.

HOBBS, N., ed. 1974a. *The futures of children: categories, labels, and their consequences.* San Francisco: Jossey-Bass.

HOBBS, N., ed. 1974b. *Issues in the classification of children: a sourcebook on categories, labels, and their consequences.* San Francisco: Jossey-Bass.

HOCKETT, C. 1960. The origin of speech. *Scientific American* 203:88–95.

HOLLAND, A. 1969. Some current trends in aphasia rehabilitation. *Asha* 11:3–7.

HOLLAND, A. 1975. Language therapy for children: some thoughts on context and content. *J. Speech Hearing Disorders* 40:514–23.

HOLLENBERG, C. 1970. Functions of visual imagery in the learning and concept formation of children. *Child Development* 41:1003–15.

HUNT, J. McVICKER. 1968. Revisiting Montessori. Reprinted in: Forst, J., ed. *Early childhood education rediscovered.* New York: Holt, Rinehart and Winston.

HUNT, J. McVICKER. 1969. *The challenge of incompetence and poverty.* Urbana: University of Illinois Press.

HUNT, K. 1964. *Differences in grammatical structures written at three grade levels, the structures to be analyzed by transformational methods.* Report to the U.S. Office of Education, Cooperative Research Project No. 1998, Tallahassee, Fla.

HUTT, C. 1972. *Males and females.* Baltimore: Penguin.

HUTTENLOCHER, J. 1974. The origins of language comprehension. In *Theories in cognitive psychology: the Loyola symposium,* ed. R. Solso. New York: Wiley.

HYMES, D. 1964. *Introduction: toward ethnography of communication.* Washington, D.C.: American Anthropological Association.

HYMES, D. 1967. Models of the interaction of languages and social setting. *J. Social Issues* 23:8–28.

HYMES, D. 1971. Competence and performance in linguistic theory. In *Language acquisition: models and methods,* eds. R. Huxley and E. Ingram. New York: Academic Press.

HYMES, D. 1972a. Models of the interaction of language and social life. In *Directions in sociolinguistics,* eds. J. Gumperz and D. Hymes. New York: Holt, Rinehart and Winston.

HYMES, D. 1972b. Introduction. In *Functions of language in the classrooms,* eds. C. Cazden, V. John, and D. Hymes. New York: Teachers College, Columbia University.

INGRAM, D. 1971a. Transitivity in child language. *Language* 47:888–910.

INGRAM, D. 1971b. Toward a theory of person deixis. *Papers in linguistics* 4:37–54.

INGRAM, D. 1974a. The relationship between comprehension and production. In *Language perspectives: acquisition, retardation, and intervention,* eds. R. Schiefelbusch and L. Lloyd. Baltimore: University Park Press.

INGRAM, D. 1974b. Phonological rules in young children. *Journal Child Language* 1:49–64.

INGRAM, D. 1976. *Phonological disability in children.* New York: Elsevier.

INHELDER, B. 1969. Memory and intelligence in the child. In *Studies in cognitive development,* eds. D. Elkind and J. Flavell. New York: Oxford University Press.

INHELDER, B., BOVET, M., SINCLAIR, H., and SMOCK, C. 1966. On cognitive development. *American Psychologist* 21:160–64.

INHELDER, B., and Piaget, J. 1964. *The early growth of logic in the child.* New York: Norton.

ISSACS, N. 1960. *A brief introduction to Piaget.* New York: Agathon Press.

JACOBS, R., and ROSENBAUM, P. 1968. *English transformational grammar.* Walton, Mass.: Xerox College Publishers.

JAKOBSON, R. 1968. *Child language, aphasia, and phonological universals.* The Hague: Mouton. Translation of 1941.

JAKOBSON, R. 1971. *Studies on child language and aphasia.* The Hague: Mouton.

JAKOBSON, R., FANT, C., and HALLE, M. 1963. *Preliminaries to speech analysis: the distinctive features and their correlates,* 2d ed. Cambridge, Mass.: MIT Press.

JAKOBSON, R., and HALLE, M. 1956. *Foundations of language.* The Hague: Mouton.

JENKINS, J. 1964. A mediational account of grammatical phenomena. *J. Communication* 14:86–97.

JENKINS, J. 1966. Reflections on the conference. In *The genesis of language: a psycholinguistic approach,* eds. F. Smith and G. Miller. Cambridge, Mass.: The MIT Press.

JENKINS, J. 1973. Language and memory. In *Communication, language, and meaning: psychological perspectives,* ed. G. Miller. New York: Basic Books.

JENKINS, J. 1974. Remember that old theory of memory? Well, forget it! *American Psychologist* 29:785–95.

JENKINS, J., et al. 1971. An atlas of semantic profiles for 360 words. *American J. Psychology* 71:688–99.

JENKINS, J., and PALERMO, D. 1964. Mediation processes and the acquisition of linguistic structure. In Bellugi, U., and Brown, R. (eds.), *SRCD Monographs* 29:141–69.

JENKINS, J., and RUSSELL, W. 1960. Systematic changes in word association norms, 1910–1952. *J. Abnormal Social Psychology* 60:293–304.

JOHNSON, N. 1965. The psychological reality of phrase structure rules. *J. Verbal Learning Verbal Behavior* 4:469–75.

JOHNSON, N. 1966. The influence of associations between elements of structured verbal responses. *J. Verbal Learning Verbal Behavior* 5:369–74.

JONES, P. 1972. Home environment and the development of verbal ability. *Child Development* 43:1081–86.

KAGAN, J. 1965. Reflectivity-impulsivity and reading ability in primary grade children. *Child Development* 36:609–28.

KAGAN, J. 1967. On the need for relativism. *American Psychologist* 22:131–42.

KAGAN, J. 1968. On cultural deprivation. In *Environmental influences,* ed. D. Glass. New York: The Rockefeller University Press and Russell Sage Foundation.

KAGAN, J. 1969a. Continuity in cognitive development during the first year. *Merrill-Palmer Quarterly* 15:101–19.

KAGAN, J. 1969b. Inadequate evidence and illogical conclusions. *Harvard Educational Review* 39:274–77.

KAGAN, J. 1970. The determinants of attention in the infant. *American Scientist* 56:298–306.

KAGAN, J. 1971. *Change and continuity in infancy.* New York: Wiley.

KAGAN, J., and KOGAN, N. 1970. Individual variation in cognitive processes. In *Carmichael's manual of child psychology,* ed. P.H. Mussem. New York: Wiley.

KAGAN, J., and LEWIS, M. 1965. Studies of attention in the human infant. *Merrill-Palmer Quarterly* 11:95–127.

KAGAN, J., and MESSER, S. 1975. A reply to "Some misgivings about the Matching Familiar Figures Test as a measure of reflection-impulsivity." *Developmental Psychology* 11:244–48.

KAGAN, J., PEARSON, L., and WELCH, L. 1966. The modification of an impulsive tempo. *Journal of Educational Psychology* 57:359–65.

KAGAN, J., ROSMAN, B., DAY, D., ALBERT, J., and PHILLIPS, W. 1964. Information processing in the child: significance of analytic and reflective attitudes. *Psychological Monographs: General and Applied* 78:1–37.

KAPLAN, B. 1961. An approach to the problem of symbolic representation: nonverbal and verbal. *J. Communication* 11:52–62.

KAPLAN, E., and KAPLAN, G. 1970. The prelinguistic child. In *Human development and cognitive processes,* ed. J. Eliot. New York: Holt, Rinehart and Winston.

KASL, S., and MAHL, G. 1965. The relationship of disturbances and hesitations in spontaneous speech to anxiety. *J. Personal Soc. Psychology* 1:425–33.

KATAHN, M., and KOPLIN, J. 1968. Paradigm clash: comment on some recent criticisms of behaviorism and learning theory with special reference to Bregar and McGaugh and to Chomsky. *Psychological Bulletin* 69:147–48.

KAVANAUGH, J., and MATTINGLY, I., eds. 1972. *Language by ear and by eye.* Cambridge, Mass.: MIT Press.

KEENEY, T., CANIZZO, S., and FLAVELL, J. 1967. Spontaneous and induced rehearsal in a recall task. *Child Development* 38:953–66.

KELLAS, G., ASHCRAFT, M., and JOHNSON, N. 1973. Rehearsal processes in the short-term memory performance of mildly retarded adolescents. *American J. Mental Deficiency* 77:670–79.

KELLER, M. 1976. Development of role-taking ability. Social antecedents and consequences for school success. *Human Development* 19:120–32.

KELLOGG, W. 1968. Communication and language in the homeraised chimpanzee. *Science* 162:423–27.

KELLY, G. 1976. Two developmental cognitive processes: performance at the preschool level. Unpublished M.A. thesis. State University of New York, Buffalo.

KELLY, R., and TOMLINSON-KEASEY, C. 1976. Information processing of visually presented picture and word stimuli by young hearing-impaired and normal-hearing children. *J. Speech Hearing Research* 19:628–38.

KENDLER, H. 1971. Environmental and cognitive control of behavior. *American Psychologist* 26:962–73.

KENDLER, H., and KENDLER, T. 1970a. Developmental processes in discrimination learning. *Human Development* 13:65–89.

KENDLER, H., and KENDLER, T. 1970b. An ontogency of optimal shift behavior. *Child Development* 41:1–28.

KENDLER, T., and KENDLER, H. 1959. Reversal and nonreversal shifts in kindergarten children. *J. Experimental Psychology* 58:56–60.

KIRK, S., McCARTHY, J., and KIRK. 1968. *The Illinois test of psycholinguistic ability* (rev. ed.). Urbana: University of Illinois Press.

KLIMA, E. 1965. Negation in English. In *The structure of language,* eds. J. Fodor and J. Katz. Englewood Cliffs, N.J.: Prentice-Hall.

KLIMA, E., and BELLUGI-KLIMA, U. 1969. Syntactic regularities in the speech of children. In *Modern studies in English,* eds. D. Reibel and S. Schane. Englewood Cliffs, N.J.: Prentice-Hall.

KNAPP, M. 1972. *Nonverbal communication in human interaction.* New York: Holt, Rinehart and Winston.

KOCHMAN, T. 1972. Toward an ethnography of black American speech behavior. In *Rappin' and stylin' out,* ed. T. Kochman. Urbana: University of Illinois Press.

KOENIGSKNECHT, R., and LEE, L. 1971. Validity and reliability of developmental sentence scoring: a method for measuring syntactic development in children's spontaneous speech. *Am. J. Speech Hearing Association Convention.*

KOFSKY, E. 1966. A scalogram study of classification development. *Child Development* 37:191–204.

KOHLBERG, L. 1969. Stage and sequence: the cognitive developmental approach to socialization. In *Handbook of socialization theory and research,* ed. D. Goslin. Chicago: Rand McNally.

KOHLBERG, L., YEAGER, J., and HJERTHOLM, E. 1968. Private speech: four studies and a review of theories. *Child Development* 39:691–736.

KOZHERNIKOV, V., and CHRISTOVICH, L. 1965. *Speech: articulation and perception.* Joint Public Research Service 30:543. Washington, D.C.

KRAMER, S. 1976. Performance of four year old iconic and four year old symbolic processors on reversal/nonreversal set shifts. Unpublished M.A. thesis. State University of New York, Buffalo.

KRASNER, L. 1958. Studies of the conditioning of verbal behavior. *Psychological Bulletin* 55:148–70.

KRASNER, L. 1976. Psychology in action: on the death of behavior modification: some comments from a mourner. *American Psychologist* 31:387–88.

LABOV, W. 1965. Linguistic research on nonstandard English of Negro children. In *Problems and practices in New York City schools.* New York: New York Society for the Experimental Study of Education.

LABOV, W. 1966. *The social stratification of English in New York City.* Washington, D.C.: Center for Applied Linguistics.

LABOV, W. 1970a. The logic of nonstandard English. In *Language and poverty: perspective on a theme,* ed. F. Williams. Chicago: Markham Publishing Co.

LABOV, W. 1970b. Stages in the acquisition of standard English. In *English linguistics,* eds. H. Hungerford, J. Robinson, and J. Sledd. Atlanta: Scott Foresman.

LABOV, W. 1972. *Language in the inner city.* Philadelphia: University of Pennsylvania Press.

LABOV, W., COHEN, P., ROBINS, C., and LEWIS, J. 1968. *A study of the nonstandard English of Negro and Puerto Rican speakers in New York City,* vol. 2. New York: Columbia University.

LACEY, J., KAGAN, J., LACEY, B., and MOSS, H. 1963. The visceral level: Situational determinants and behavioral correlates of autonomic resonse patterns. In *Expressions of the emotions in man,* ed. R. Knapp. New York: International University Press.

LADEFOGED, P. 1972a. Phonological features and their phonetic correlates. *Journal of the International Phonetics Association* 2:2–12.

LADEFOGED, P. 1972b. Phonetic prerequisites for a distinctive feature theory. In *Papers in linguistics and phonetics to the memory of Pierre Delattre,* ed. A. Valdman. The Hague: Mouton.

LAHEY, M. 1974. Use of prosody and syntactic markers in children's comprehension of spoken sentences. *Journal Speech Hearing Research* 17:656–68.

LAKOFF, G. 1972. The arbitrary basis of transformational grammar. *Language* 48:76–87.

LAKOFF, G. 1972. Language in context. *Language* 48:907–27.

LAMBERT, W., and MACNAMARA, J. 1969. Some cognitive consequences of following a first-grade curriculum in a second language. *J. Education Psychology* 60:86–96.

LANGACKER, R. 1967. *Language and its structure.* New York: Harcourt.

LAVATELLI, C.S. 1970. *Piaget's theory applied to an early childhood curriculum.* Boston, Cambridge: American Science and Engineering.

LAVATELLI, C. 1971. *Language training in early childhood education.* Urbana: University of Illinois Press.

LAVATELLI, C. ed. 1974. *Preschool language training.* Urbana: University of Illinois Press.

LAWTON, D. 1963. Social class differences in language development: a study of some samples of written work. *Language and Speech.* 6:120–43.

LAWTON, D. 1968. *Social class, language and education.* New York: Schocken.

LEE, L. 1966. Developmental sentence types: a method for comparing normal and deviant syntactic development. *J. Speech Hearing Disorders* 31:311–20.

LEE, L. 1969. *Northwestern syntax screening test.* Evanston, Ill.: Northwestern University Press.

LEE, L. 1974. *Development sentence analysis: a grammatical assessment procedure for speech and language clinicians.* Evanston, Ill.: Northwestern University Press.

LEE, L., and CANTER, S. 1971. Developmental sentence scoring: a clinical procedure for estimating syntactic development in children's spontaneous speech. *J. Speech Hearing Disorders.* 36:315–40.

LEES, R. 1965. *The Grammar of English nominalizations.* Bloomington: Indiana University Press.

LENNEBERG, E. 1967. *Biological foundations of language.* New York: Wiley.

LENNEBERG, E. and LENNEBERG, E., eds. 1975. *Foundations of language development,* vols. I and II. New York: Academic Press.

LEONARD, L. 1972. What is deviant language? *J. Speech Hearing Disorders* 37:427–46.

LEONARD, L. 1973. Teaching by the rules. *J. Speech Hearing Disorders.* 38:174–83.

LEONARD, L. 1975a. Modeling as a clinical procedure in language. *Speech and Hearing Services in Schools* 6:72–85.

LEONARD, L. 1975b. The role of nonlinguistic stimuli and semantic relations in children's acquisition of grammatical utterances. *J. Experimental Child Psychology* 19:346–57.

LEONARD, L. 1976. *Meaning in child language.* New York: Grune & Stratton.

LEONARD, L., BOLDERS, J., and MILLER, J. 1976. An examination of the semantic relations reflected in the language usage of normal and language-disordered children. *Journal Speech Hearing Research* 19:371–92.

LEONARD, L., and RITTERMAN, S. 1971. Articulation of /s/ as a function of cluster and word frequency of occurrence. *Journal Speech Hearing Research* 14:476–85.

LESSER, G. 1976. Applications of psychology to television programming: formulation of program objectives. *American Psychologist* 31:135–36.

LESSER, G., FIFER, G., and CLARK, D. 1965. Mental abilities of children in different social and cultural groups. *Monogr. Society Research Child Development* 30 (serial no. 102).

LEWIS, M. 1967. The meaning of a response or why researchers in infant behavior should be oriental metaphysicians. *Merrill-Palmer Quarterly* 13:7–18.

LEWIS, M. 1970. Attention and verbal labeling behavior: a study in the measurement of internal representations. Princeton, N.J.: Educational Testing Service.

LEWIS, M. 1971. Individual differences in the measurement of early cognitive growth. In *Exceptional Infant,* vol. 2, ed. J. Hellmuth. New York: Brunner/Mazel.

LEWIS, M. 1972. State as an infant-environment interaction: an analysis of mother-infant behavior as a function of sex. *Merrill-Palmer Quarterly* 18:95–121.

LEWIS, M., and FREEDLE, R. 1973. Mother-infant dyad: The cradle of meaning. In *Communication and affect: language and thought,* eds. P. Pliner, L. Krames, and T. Alloway. New York: Academic Press.

LEWIS, M., and GOLDBERG, S. 1969. Perceptual-cognitive development in infancy: a generalized expectancy model as a function of the mother-infant interaction. *Merrill-Palmer Quarterly* 15:81–100.

LEWIS, M., KAGAN, J., and KALAFAT, J. 1966. Patterns of fixation in infants. *Child Development* 37:331–41.

LIBERMAN, A., HARRIS, K., KINNEY, J. and LANE, H. 1961. The discrimination of relative onset time of the components of certain speech and nonspeech patterns. *J. Experimental Psychology* 61:379–88.

LIMBER, J. 1976. Unraveling competence, performance and pragmatics in the speech of young children. *J. Child Language* 3:309–18.

LIMBER, J. 1977. Language in child and chimp? *American Psychologist* 32:280–95.

LOCKE, J. 1970. Subvocal speech and speech. *Asha* 12:7–15.

LOCKE, J. 1976. Personal correspondence.

LONGHURST, T. 1974. Communication in retarded adolescents: sex and intelligence level. *Am. J. Mental Deficiency* 78:607–18.

LONGHURST, T., and BERRY, G. 1975. Communication in retarded adolescents: response to listener feedback. *Am. J. Mental Deficiency* 80:158–64.

LONGHURST, T. and REICHLE, J. 1975. The applied communication game: a comment on Muma's "Communication Game: Dump and Play." *J. Speech Hearing Disorders* 40:315–19.

LONGHURST, T., and SIEGEL, G. 1973. Effects of communication failure on speaker and listener behavior. *J. Speech Hearing Research* 16:128–40.

LORGE, I., and CHALL, J. 1963. Estimating the size of vocabularies of children and adults: an analysis of methodological issues. *J. Exp. Education* 32:147–57.

LOVELL, K., and DIXON, E. 1976. The growth of grammar in imitation, comprehension, and production. *J. Child Psychology Psychiatry* 8:31–39.

LURIA, A. 1961. *The role of speech in the regulation of normal and abnormal behavior.* New York: Pergamon.

LYONS, J. 1968. *Introduction to theoretical linguistics.* London: Cambridge University Press.

LYONS, J. 1970. *Noam Chomsky.* New York: Viking Press.

McCAFFREY, A. 1976. *Talking in the classroom: how can we teach children to use language?* New York Speech and Hearing Association Convention.

McCAFFREY, A. 1977. Talking in class: a non-didactic approach to oral language in the elementary classroom. *Quebec Français* 25.

McCALL, R. 1967. Stimulus-scheme discrepancy and attention in the infant. *J. Experimental Child Psychology* 5:381–90

McCALL, R. 1972. Smiling and vocalization in infants as indices of perceptual-cognitive processes. *Merrill-Palmer Quarterly* 18:341–48.

McCALL, R., and KAGAN, J. 1967a. Stimulus-schema discrepancy and attention in the infant. *Journal of Experimental Child Psychology* 5:381–90.

McCALL, R., and KAGAN, J. 1967b. Attention in the infant: effects of complexity, contour, perimeter, and familiarity. *Child Development* 38:939–52.

McCALL, R., and KAGAN, J. 1969. Individual differences in the infant's distribution of attention to stimulus discrepancy. *Developmental Psychology* 2:90–98.

McCarthy, D. 1930. *The language development of the preschool child*. Institute Child Welfare, Monograph Series, no. 4. Minneapolis: University of Minnesota Press.

McCarthy, D. 1954. Language development in children. In *Manual of child psychology,* 2d ed., ed. L. Carmichael. New York: Wiley.

McCawley, J. 1968. The role of semantics in a grammar. In *Universals in linguistic theory,* eds. E. Bach and R. Harms. New York: Holt, Rinehart and Winston.

Maccoby, E. 1967. *What copying requires.* Washington, D.C.: American Psychological Association Convention.

Maccoby, E. and Bee, H. 1965. Some speculations concerning the lag between perceiving and perceiving. *Child Development* 36:367–78.

Maccoby, E., and Jacklin, C. 1974. *The psychology of sex differences*. Stanford, Calif.: Stanford University Press.

McConnell, F., and McClamroch, M. 1961. Social participation levels of nonlanguage children. *J. Speech Hearing Disorders* 26:354–58.

MacCorquedale, K. 1970. On Chomsky's review of Skinner's *Verbal behavior. J. Exp. Analysis Behavior* 13:83–99.

McDonald, E. 1964. *Articulation testing and treatment: a sensory-motor approach.* Pittsburgh: Stanwix House.

MacDonald, J., and Blott, J. 1974. Environmental language intervention: the rationale for a diagnostic and training strategy through rules, context, and generalization. *J. Speech Hearing Disorders* 39:244–56.

Maclay, H., and Osgood, C. 1959. Hesitation phenomena in spontaneous English speech. *Word* 15:19–44.

Macnamara, J. 1967. The linguistic independence of bilinguals. *Journal Verbal Learning Verbal Behavior* 6:729–36.

Macnamara, J. 1972. Cognitive basis of language learning in infants. *Psychological Review* 79:1–13.

Macnamara, J., and Kushner, S. 1971. Linguistic independence of bilinguals: the input switch. *Journal Verbal Learning Verbal Behavior* 10:480–87.

McNeill, D. 1963. The origin of associations within the same grammatical class. *J. Verbal Learning Verbal Behavior* 2:250–62.

McNeill, D. 1965. Some thoughts on first and second language acquisition. Paper presented to the Modern Foreign Language Title III Conference, Washington, D.C.

McNeill, D. 1966a. Developmental psycholinguistics. In *The genesis of language,* eds. F. Smith and Miller. Cambridge, Mass.: MIT Press.

McNeill, D. 1966b. A study of word association. *Journal Verbal Learning Verbal Behavior* 5:548–57.

McNeill, D. 1970. *The acquisition of language: the study of developmental psycholinguistics.* New York: Harper & Row.

McNeill, D., and McNeill, N. 1968. What does a child mean when he says "No"? In *Language and language behavior,* ed. E. Zale. New York: Appleton-Century-Crofts.

McNemar, Q. 1965. *Psychological statistics.* New York: Wiley.

McNutt, J., and Keenan, R. 1970. Comment on "The relationship between articulatory deficits and syntax in speech defective children." *Journal Speech Hearing Research* 13:666–67.

McReynolds, L. 1970. Contingencies and consequences in speech therapy. *J. Speech Hearing Disorders* 35:12–24.

McReynolds, L., and Engmann, D. 1975. *Distinctive feature analysis of misarticulations.* Baltimore: University Park Press.

McReynolds, L., and Huston, K. 1971. A distinctive feature analysis of childen's misarticulations. *Journal Speech Hearing Disorders* 36:155–66.

MacWhinney, B., and Osser, H. 1977. Verbal planning functions in children's speech. *Child Development* 48:978–85.

MAHL, G. 1958. On the use of "ah" in spontaneous speech: quantitative, developmental, characterological, situational, and linguistic aspects. *Am. Psychologist* 13:349.

MANDLER, G. 1962. From association to structure. *Psychological Review* 69:415–27.

MARATSOS, M. 1973a. Decrease in the understanding of the word "big" in pre-school children. *Child Development* 44:747–52.

MARATSOS, M. 1973b. Nonegocentric communication abilities in preschool children. *Child Development 44:697–700.*

MARATSOS, M. 1973c. The effects of stress in the understanding of pronominal coreference in children. *J. Psycholinguistic Research* 2:1–8.

MARKHAM, E. 1976. Children's difficulty with word-referent differentiation. *Child Development* 47:742–49.

MARKS, L., and MILLER, G. 1964. The role of semantic and syntactic constraints in the memorization of English sentences. *J. Verbal Learning Verbal Behavior* 3:1–5.

MARTIN, B. 1975. Parent-child relations. In *Review of child development research,* vol. 4, eds. F. Horowitz, E. Hetherington, S. Scarr-Salapatek, and G. Siegel. Chicago: University of Chicago Press.

MARTIN, D., and RIGRODSKY, S. 1974. An investigation of phonological impairment in aphasia, part I. *Cortex* 10:317–28.

MARTIN, D., WASSERMAN, N., GILDEN, L., GERSTMAN, L., and WEST, J. 1975. A process model of repetition in aphasia: an investigation of phonological and morphological interactions in aphasia error performance. *Brain and Language* 2:434–50.

MARTIN, E., and ROBERTS, K. 1966. Grammatical factors in sentence retention. *J. Verbal Learning Verbal Behavior* 5:211–18.

MARTIN, E., ROBERTS, K., and COLLINS, A. 1968. Short-term memory for sentences. *J. Verbal Learning Verbal Behavior* 7:560–66.

MAZEIKA, E. 1971. A comparison of the phonologic development of a monolingual and a bilingual (Spanish-English) child. Presented at Biennial Meeting of the *Society for Research in Child Development,* Minneapolis.

MEAD, G. 1934. *Mind, self, and society.* Chicago: University of Chicago Press.

MEHRABIAN, A. 1972. *Nonverbal communication.* Chicago: Aldine-Atherton.

MEICHENBAUM, D. 1971. Implications of research on disadvantaged children and cognitive training programs for educational television: ways of improving *Sesame Street.* Washington, D.C. Am. Psychological Assoc.

MEICHENBAUM, D., and GOODMAN, J. 1969. The developmental control of operant motor responding by verbal operants. *J. Experimental Child Psychology* 7:553–65.

MELLON, J. 1967. Transformational sentences combining: a method for enhancing the development of syntactic fluency in English composition. *Harvard R & D Center on Educational Differences,* Report no. 1.

MELTON, A., and MARTIN, E. 1972. *Coding processes in human memory.* New York: Wiley.

MENN, L. 1971. Phonotactic rules in beginning speech: a study in the development of English discourse. *Lingua* 26:225–51.

MENYUK, P. 1963. Syntactic structures in the language of children. *Child Development* 34:407–22.

MENYUK, P. 1964a. Alternation of rules of children's grammar. *J. Verbal Learning Verbal Behavior* 3:480–88.

MENYUK, P. 1964b. Syntactic rules used by children from preschool through first grade. *Child Development* 35:533–46.

MENYUK, P. 1968. The role of distinctive features in children's acquisition of phonology. *J. Speech Hearing Research* 11:138–46.

MENYUK, P. 1969. *Sentences children use.* Cambridge, Mass.: MIT Press.

MENYUK, P. 1971. *The acquisition and development of language.* Englewood Cliffs, N.J.: Prentice-Hall.

MENYUK, P. 1972. *The development of speech.* New York: Bobbs-Merrill.

MENYUK, P. 1974. Early development of receptive language: from babbling to words. In *Language perspectives: acquisition, retardation, and intervention,* eds. R. Schiefelbusch and L. Lloyd. Baltimore: University Park Press.

MENYUK, P., and LOONEY, P. 1972a. A problem of language disorder: length versus structure. *J. Speech Hearing Research* 15:264–79.

MENYUK, P., and LOONEY, P. 1972b. Relationships among components of the grammar in language disorder. *J. Speech Hearing Research* 15:395–406.

MERCER, J. 1972a. The lethal label. *Psychology Today* 44.

MERCER, J. 1972b. *Labeling the mentally retarded.* Berkeley: University of California Press.

MERCER, J. 1974. A policy statement on assessment procedures and the rights of children. *Harvard Educational Review* 44:125–42.

MESSICK, S. 1968. Children's cognitive and perceptual development: background and theory. In *Disadvantaged children and their first school experience,* eds. S. Anderson et al. ETS-OEO Longitudinal Study.

MILLER, G. 1956. The magical number seven, plus or minus two: some limits on our capacity for processing information. *Psychological Review.*

MILLER, G. 1962. Some psychological studies of grammar. *Am. Psychologist* 17:748–62.

MILLER, G. 1965. Some preliminaries to psycholinguistics, *Am. Psychologist* 20:15–20.

MILLER, G. 1969. The organization of lexical memory: are word associations sufficient? In *The pathology of memory,* eds. G. Tallard and N. Waugh. New York: Academic Press.

MILLER, G. ed. 1973. *Communication, language, and meaning: psychological perspectives.* New York: Basic Books, Inc.

MILLER, G., GALANTER, E., and PRIBRAM, K. 1960. *Plans and the structure of behavior.* New York: Holt, Rinehart and Winston.

MILLER, G., and NICELY, P. 1955. An analysis of perceptual confusions among some English consonants. *J. Acoustical Society of America* 27:338–52.

MILLER, J. 1976. *Clinical application of Piagetian psychology.* New York Speech and Hearing Association Convention.

MILLER, J., and YODER, D. 1974. An autogenic language teaching strategy for retarded children. In *Language perspectives: acquisition, retardation and intervention,* eds. R. Schiefelbusch and L. Lloyd. Baltimore: University Park Press.

MILLER, P., KESSEL, F., and FLAVELL, J. 1969. Thinking about people thinking about people thinking about . . .: a study of social cognitive development. *Child Development* 41:613–23.

MILLIKAN, C., and DARLEY, F. 1967. *Brain mechanisms underlying speech and language.* New York: Grune & Stratton.

MINER, L. 1969. Scoring procedures for the length-complexity index: a preliminary report. *J. Communication Disorders* 2:224–40.

MINIFIE, F., DARLEY, F., and SHERMAN, D. 1963. Temporal reliability of seven language measures. *J. Speech Hearing Research* 6:139–49.

MOELY, B., OLSEN, F., HALWAS, T., and FLAVELL, J. 1969. Production deficiency in young children's clustered recall. *Developmental Psychology* 1:26–34.

MOERK, E. 1974. Changes in verbal child-mother interactions with increasing language skills of the child. *J. Psycholinguistic Research* 3:101–16.

MOERK, E. 1975. Piaget's research as applied to the explanation of language development. *Merrill-Palmer Quarterly* 21:151–70.

MOERK, E. 1976. Processes of language teaching and training in the interactions of hother-child dyads. *Child Development* 47:1064–78.

MOERK, E. 1977. *Pragmatic and semantic aspects of early language acquisition.* Baltimore: University Park Press.

MOFFETT, J. 1968. *An integrated curriculum in the language arts, K–12*. Boston: Houghton Mifflin.

MOORE, D. 1971. Language research and preschool language training. In *Language training in early childhood education*, ed. C. Lavatelli. Urbana: University of Illinois Press.

MOREHEAD, D., and INGRAM, D. 1973. The development of base syntax in normal and linguistically deviant children. *J. Speech Hearing Research* 16:330–52.

MOREHEAD, D., and MOREHEAD, A. 1974. From signal to sign: Piagetian view of thought and language during the first two years. In *Language perspectives: acquisition, retardation, and intervention*, eds. R. Schiefelbusch and L. Lloyd. Baltimore: University Park Press.

MORSE, P. 1974. Infant speech perception: a preliminary model and review of the literature. In *Language perspectives: acquisition, retardation, and intervention*, eds. R. Schiefelbusch and L. Lloyd. Baltimore: University Park Press.

MOSKOWITZ, H. 1970. The two-year-old stage in the acquisition of English phonology. *Language* 46:426–41.

MOSS, H. 1967. Sex, age, and state as determinants of mother-infant interaction. *Merrill-Palmer Quarterly*, 13:19–35.

MOWRER, O. 1952. The autism theory of speech development and some clinical applications. *J. Speech Hearing Disorders*, 17:263–68.

MOWRER, O. 1960. *Learning theory and the symbolic process*. New York: Wiley.

MUELLER, E. 1972. The maintenance of verbal exchanges between young children. *Child Development* 43:930–38.

MUMA, D., and MUMA, J. 1973. Syllabic structure inventory of /s/ syllables for words in *Webster's Elementary Dictionary*. Research Project, Memphis State University.

MUMA, J. 1971a. Syntax of preschool fluent and dysfluent speech: a transformational analysis. *J. Speech Hearing Research* 14:428–41.

MUMA, J. 1971b. Language intervention: ten techniques. *Language, Speech, and Hearing Services in Schools* 5:7–17.

MUMA, J. 1971c. *Parent-Child Development Center*. Conceptualization, Program, Evaluation. Birmingham, Ala.

MUMA, J. 1973a. Language assessment: the co-occurring and restricted structures procedure. *Acta Symbolica* 4:12–29. Republished in *Linguistic analysis of children's speech*, ed. T. Longhurst. New York: MSS Information Center.

MUMA, J. 1973b. Language assessment: Some underlying assumptions. *Asha* 15:331–38. Republished in *Linguistic analysis of children's speech*, ed. T. Longhurst. New York: MSS Information Center.

MUMA, J. 1975a. The communication game: dump and play. *J. Speech Hearing Disorders* 40:296–309.

MUMA, J. 1975b. Review of Schiefelbusch, R., and Lloyd, L., *Language Perspectives: Development, Retardation, and Intervention. Asha* 18:371–73.

MUMA, J. 1977a. Language intervention strategies. *Language, Speech, and Hearing Services in the Schools* 8:107–25.

MUMA, J. 1977b. *Make-Change: A game of sentence sence*. Boston: Teaching Resources (in press).

MUMA, J. In press. Clinical assessment: new perspectives. In *Applied Psycholinguistics*, eds. K. Ruder and M. Smith. Baltimore: University Park Press.

MUMA, J., ADAMS-PERRY, M., and GALLEGHER, J. 1974. Some semantic properties in sentence perception. *Psychological Reports* 35:23–32.

MUMA, J., and BAUMEISTER, A. 1975. Programmatic evaluation in mental retardation. *J. Special Education* 9:293–306.

MUMA, J., and LUBINSKI, R. 1977. Language assessment: data or evidence? (Unpublished manuscript.)

MUNSINGER, H., and KESSEN, W. 1966. Stimulus variability and cognitive change. *Psychological Review* 73:164–78.

MURAI, J. 1963. The sounds of infants, their phonemicization and symbolization. *Studia Phonologica* 3:18–34.

MUSSEN, P., CONGER, J., and KAGAN, J. 1969. *Child development and personality*. New York: Harper & Row.

NAIR, P. 1963. An experiment in conservation. *Annual Report*. Center for Cognitive Studies, Harvard University.

NAKAZIMA, S. 1962. A comparative study of the speech developments of Japanese and American English in childhood. *Studies Phonol*. 2:27–39.

NAKAZIMA, S. 1970. A comparative study of the speech developments of Japanese and American English in childhood (part three). *Studies Phonol*. 5:20–35.

NATION, J. 1972. A vocabulary usage test. *J. Psycholinguistic Research* 1:221–32.

NEISSER, U. 1967. *Cognitive psychology*. New York; Appleton-Century-Crofts.

NELSON, K. 1973a. Some evidence for the cognitive primacy of categorization and its functional basis. *Merrill-Palmer Quarterly* 19:21–39.

NELSON, K. 1973b. Structure and strategy in learning to talk. *Monographs of the Society for Research in Child Development* 38, serial no. 149.

NELSON, K. 1974. Concept, word, and sentence: interrelations in acquisition and development. *Psychological Review* 81:267–85.

NIHIRA, K., FOSTER, R., SHELLHAAS, M., and LELAND, H. 1974. *AAMD Adaptive Behavior Scale*. Washington, D.C.: American Association of Mental Deficiency.

NORCROSS, K. 1958. Effects of discrimination performance of similarity of previously acquired stimulus names. *J. Experimental Psychology* 56:305–09.

NORMAN, D. 1969. *Memory and attention: an introduction to human information processing*. New York: Wiley.

ODOM, R. 1972. Effects of perceptual salience on the recall of relevant and incidental dimensional values: a developmental study. *Journal of Experimental Psychology* 92:285–91.

ODOM, R., and CORBIN, D. 1973. Perceptual salience and children's multidimensional problem solving. *Child Development* 44:425–32.

ODOM, R., and GUZMAN, R. 1970. Problem solving and the perceptual salience of variability and constancy: a developmental study. *Journal of Experimental Child Psychology* 9:156–65.

ODOM, R., and GUZMAN, R. 1972. Development of hierarchies of dimensional salience. *Developmental Psychology* 6:271–87.

O'DONNELL, R. 1967. Personal Communication.

O'DONNELL, R., GRIFFIN, W., and NORRIS, R. 1967. *Syntax of kindergarten and elementary school children: a transformational analysis:* National Council of Teachers of English Research, Report no. 8.

OLIM, E. 1970. Maternal language styles and cognitive development of children. In *Language and Poverty,* ed. E. Williams. Chicago: Markham Press.

OLLER, K., and KELLY, C. 1974. Phonological substitution processes of a hard-of-hearing child. *Journal Speech Hearing Disorders* 39:65–74.

OLMSTEAD, D. 1971. *Out of the mouth of babes*. The Hague: Mouton.

OLSON, D. 1970. Language and thought: aspects of a cognitive theory of semantics. *Psychological Review* 77:257–73.

OLSON, D. 1971. *Cognitive development: the child's acquisition of diagonality*. New York: Academic Press.

OLSON, D. 1972. Language use for communicating, and thinking. In *Language comprehension and the acquisition of knowledge,* eds. J. Carroll and R. Freedle. New York: Wiley.

OLSON, G. 1973. Developmental changes in memory and the acquisition of language. In *Cognitive development and the acquisition of language,* ed. T. Moore. New York: Academic Press.

OLVER, P., and HORNSBY, R. 1966. On equivalence. In *Studies in Cognitive Growth,* eds. J. Bruner and P. Olver. New York: Wiley.

OSGOOD, C. 1957. Motivational dynamics of language behavior. In *Nebraska Symposium on Motivation,* ed. M. Jones. Lincoln: University of Nebraska Press.

OSGOOD, C. 1968. Toward a wedding of insufficiencies. In *Verbal behavior and general behavior theory,* eds. T. Dixon and D. Horton. Englewood Cliffs, N.J.: Prentice-Hall.

OSGOOD, C., SUCI, G., and TANNENBAUM, P. 1957. *The measurement of meaning.* Urbana: University of Illinois Press.

OSSER, H. 1970. Biological and social factors in language development. In *Language and poverty: perspectives on a theme,* ed. F. Williams. Chicago: Markham Publishing Co.

PAIVO, A., ROGERS, T., and SMYTHE, P. 1968. Why are pictures easier to recall than words? *Psychonomic Science* 11:137–38.

PALERMO, D. 1971. Is a scientific revolution taking place in psychology? *Science Studies* 1:135–55.

PALERMO, D. 1972. More about less: A study of language comprehension. *Journal of Verbal Learning and Verbal Behavior,* 12:211–21.

PALERMO, D., and EBERHART, W. 1968. On the learning of morphological rules: an experimental analogy. *J. Verbal Learning Verbal Behavior* 7:337–44.

PALERMO, D., and JENKINS, J. 1964. *Word association norms grade school through college.* Minneapolis: University of Minnesota Press.

PALERMO, D., and LIPSITT, L., eds. 1964. *Research readings in child psychology.* New York: Holt, Rinehart and Winston.

PALERMO, D., and MOLFESE, D. 1972. Language acquisition from age five onward. *Psychological Bulletin* 78:409–28.

PANAGOS, J. 1974. Persistence of the open syllable reinterpreted as a symptom of language disorder. *Journal Speech Hearing Disorders* 39:23–31.

PANAGOS, J., and HOFMANN, J. 1971. Some linguistic parameters of children's unintelligible speech. *Journal Australian College of Speech Therapists* 21:68–72.

PERFETTI, C. 1972. Psychosemantics: some cognitive aspects of structural meaning. *Psychological Bulletin* 78:241–59.

PETERSON, G., and BARNEY, H. 1952. Control methods used in the study of the vowels. *J. Acoustical Society Am.* 24:175–84.

PHILLIPS, J. 1973. Syntax and vocabulary of mother's speech to young chldren. Age and sex comparisons. *Child Development* 44:182–85.

PIAGET, J. 1954. *The construction of reality in the child.* New York: Basic Books.

PIAGET, J. 1961. The language and thought of the child. In *Classics in psychology,* ed. T. Shipley. New York: Philosophy Library.

PIAGET, J. 1962. *Play, dreams, and imitation in childhood.* New York: Norton.

PIAGET, J. 1963. *Psychology of intelligence.* New York: Humanities Press.

PIAGET, J. 1970. Piaget's theory. In *Carmichael's manual of child psychology,* ed. P. Musser. New York: Wiley.

PIAGET, J., and INHELDER, B. 1963. *The child's conception of space.* London: Routledge & Kegan Paul.

PIAGET, J., and INHELDER, B. 1966. *La psychologie de l'enfant.* Paris: Presses Universitaires de France.

PICHE, G., MICHLIN, M., RUBIN, D., and JOHNSON, F. 1975. Relationships between fourth graders' performances on selected role-taking tasks and referential communication accuracy tasks. *Child Development* 46:965–69.

PLUMER, D. 1970. A summary of environmentalist views and some educational implications. In *Language and poverty: perspectives on a theme,* ed. F. Williams. Chicago: Markham Publishing Co.

POLLACK, E., and REES, N. 1972. Disorders of articulation: some clinical applications of distinctive feature theory. *J. Speech Hearing Disorders* 37:451–61.

POOLE, I. 1934. Genetic development of articulation of consonant sounds in speech. *Elementary English Review* 71:159–61.

POSTAL, P. 1966. Underlying and superficial linguistic structure. In *Language and Learning*, eds. J. Emig, J. Flemming, and H. Popp. New York: Harcourt Brace Jovanovich.

POSTMAN, L., and KEPPEL, G. 1970. *Norms of word associations*. New York: Academic Press.

POWELL, J. 1973. *Individualized data base: data system handbook*. San Francisco: Pacific State Hospital Research Center.

PREMACK, D. 1971. Language in Chimpanzee? *Science* 172:808–22.

PRIZANT, B. 1975. Verbal behavior of autistic children: a review of the literature and a guide for parents. Unpublished M.A. Thesis. Buffalo: State University of New York.

PROSHANSKY, H. 1976. Environmental psychology and the real world. *American Psychologist* 31:303–10.

PRUTTING, C., and CONNOLLY, J. 1976. Imitation: a closer look. *Journal Speech Hearing Disorders* 41:412–22.

PUTRAM, A., and RINGEL, R. 1972. Some observations of articulation during labial sensory deprivation. *J. Speech Hearing Research* 15:529–42.

QUAY, L. 1971. Language, dialect, reinforcement, and the intelligence test performance of Negro children. *Child Development* 42:5–15.

QUIRK, R., and GREENBAUM, S. 1973. *A university grammar of English*. London: Longmans.

RAMBUSCH, N. 1962. *Learning how to learn: an American approach to Montessori*. Baltimore: Helicon.

RAMER, A. 1976. The function of imitation in child language. *J. Speech Hearing Research* 19:700–17.

REES, N. 1973a. Auditory processing factors in language disorders: the view from Procrustes' bed. *J. Speech Hearing Disorders* 38:304–15.

REES, N. 1973b. Bases of decision in language training. *J. Speech Hearing Disorders* 37:283–304.

REICH, P. 1976. The early acquisition of word meaning. *J. Child Language* 3:117–24.

REICHLE, J., LONGHURST, T., and STEPANICH, L. 1976. Verbal interaction in mother-child dyads. *Developmental Psychology* 12:273–77.

REITMAN, W. 1965. *Cognition and thought*. New York: Wiley.

RENFREW, C. 1966. Persistence of the open syllable in defective articulation. *Journal Speech Hearing Disorders* 31:370–73.

RIEGEL, K., ed. 1975. The development of dialectical operations. *Human Development* 18:(Parts I and II).

The rights of children (A Special Issue—Part I). 1973. *Harvard Educational Review*. Cambridge, Mass.

The rights of children (A Special Issue—Part II). 1974. *Harvard Educational Review*. Cambridge, Mass.

ROBERTS, P. 1964. *English syntax*. New York: Harcourt Brace Jovanovich.

ROBERTS, P. 1967. *The Robert English series: a linguistic program*. New York: Harcourt Brace Jovanovich.

ROBINSON, W. 1970. Social factors and language development in primary school children. In *Language acquisition: models and methods*, eds. R. Huxley and E. Ingram. New York: Academic Press.

ROCHESTER, S. 1973. The significance of pauses in spontaneous speech. *J. Psycholinguistic Research* 2:51–81.

RODGON, M., and RASHMAN, S. 1976. Expression of owner-owned relationships among holophrastic 14- to 32-month-old children. *Child Development* 47:1219–24.

ROSCH, E. 1973a. On the interval structure of perceptual and semantic categories. In *Cognitive development and the acquisition of language*, ed. T. Moore. New York: Academic Press.

ROSCH, E. 1973b. Natural categories. *Cognitive Psychology* 4:328–50.

Rosch, E., and Mervis, C. 1975. Family resemblances: studies in the internal structure of categories. *Cognitive Psychology* 7:573–605.

Rosenbaum, P. 1967. *The grammar of english predicate construction*. Cambridge, Mass.: MIT Press.

Rosenberg, S., and Cohen, B.D. 1966. Referential processes of speakers and listeners. *Psychological Review* 73:208–31.

Ross, J. 1974. Squishing. In *Festschrift for Martin Joos,* ed. E. Burtinsky. Toronto: University of Toronto Press.

Rossi, S., and Wittrock, M. 1967. Clustering versus serial ordering in recall by four-year-old children. *Child Development* 38:1139–42.

Rossi, S., and Wittrock, M. 1971. Developmental shifts in verbal recall between mental ages two and five. *Child Development* 42:333–38.

Ruder, K., and Smith, M. 1974. Issues in language training. In *Language perspectives: acquisition, retardation, and intervention,* eds. R. Schiefelbusch and L. Lloyd. Baltimore: University Park Press.

Ryan, J. 1974. Early language development: towards a communicational analysis. In *The Integration of a Child into a Social World,* ed. P. Richards. London: Cambridge University Press.

Sachs, J. 1967. Recognition memory for syntactic and semantic aspects of connected discourse. *Perception and Psychophysics* 2:437–42.

Sadock, J. 1974. *Towards a linguistic theory of speech acts*. New York: Seminar Press.

Saltz, E. 1971. *The cognitive bases of human learning*. Homewood, Ill.: Dorsey.

Saltz, E., Soller, E. and Sigel, I. 1972. The development of natural language concepts. *Child Development* 43:1191–1202.

Salus, P., and Salus, M. 1974. Developmental neurophysiology and phonological acquisition order. *Language* 50:151–60.

Savin, H., and Perchenock, E. 1965. Grammatical structure and the immediate recall of English sentences. *J. Verbal Learning Verbal Behavior* 4:348–53.

Scarr-Salapatek, S. 1971. Unknowns in the IQ equation. *Science* 74:1223–28.

Schacter, F., Kirshner, K., Klips, B., Friedricks, M., and Sanders, K. 1974. Everyday preschool interpersonal speech usage: methodological, developmental, and sociolinguistic studies. *Monographs: Society for Research in Child Development* no. 156.

Schachter, F., Fosha, D., Stemp, S., Brotman, N., and Granger, S. 1976. Everyday caretaker talk to toddler vs. threes and fours. *J. Child Language* 3:221–45.

Schank, R. 1972. Conceptual dependency: a theory of natural language understanding. *Cognitive Psychology* 3:552–631.

Schlesinger, I. 1971. Production of utterances and language acquisition. In *The ontogensis of grammar,* ed. D. Slobin. New York: Academic Press.

Schlesinger, I. 1974. Relational concepts underlying language. In *Language perspectives: acquisition, retardation, and intervention,* eds. R. Schiefelbusch and L. Lloyd. Baltimore: University Park Press.

Schuell, H. 1965. *Minnesota test for differential diagnosis of aphasia*. Minneapolis: University of Minnesota.

Schuell, H., Jenkins, J., Jimenez-Pabon, E. 1964. *Aphasia in adults*. New York: Harper & Row.

Schwebel, M., and Raph, J. 1973. *Piaget in the classroom*. New York: Basic Books.

Scollon, R. 1976. *Conversations with a one year old: a case study of the developmental foundation of syntax*. Honolulu: University of Hawaii Press.

Scott, C., and Ringel, R. 1971. The effects of motor and sensory disruptions on speech: a description of articulation. *J. Speech Hearing Research* 14:819–28.

Searle, J. 1969. *Speech acts*. London: Cambridge University Press.

Shannon, C., and Weaver, W. 1949. *The mathematical theory of communication*. Urbana: University of Illinois Press.

SHANTZ, C., and WILSON, K. 1972. Training communication skills in young children. *Child Development* 43:693–98.

SHARP, E. 1969. *Thinking is child's play*. New York: Dutton.

SHATZ, M., and GELMAN, R. 1973. The development of communication skills: Modifications in the speech of young children as a function of listener. *Monographs: Society for Research in Child Development,* no. 152.

SHERMAN, J. 1971. Imitation and language development. In *Advances in child development and behavior,* ed. H. Reese. New York: Academic Press.

SHEWAN, C. 1975. The language-disordered child in relation to Muma's "Communication Game: Dump and Play." *Journal Speech and Hearing Disorders* 40:310–14.

SHIPLEY, E., SMITH, C., and GLEITMAN, L. 1969. A study in the acquisition of language: free responses to commands. *Language* 45:322–42.

SHRINER, T. 1969. A review of mean length of responses as a measure of expressive language development in children. *J. Speech Hearing Disorders* 34:61–67.

SHRINER, T., HOLLOWAY, M., and DANILOFF, R. 1969. The relationship between articulatory deficits and syntax in speech defective children. *J. Speech Hearing Research* 12:319–25.

SHUY, R., ed. 1965. *Social dialects and language learning*. Champaign, Ill.: National Council of Teachers of English.

SHUY, R. 1970. The sociolinguists and urban language problems. In *Language and poverty: perspectives on a theme,* ed. F. Williams. Chicago: Markham Publishing Co.

SHVACHKIN, N. 1973. The development of phonemic speech perception in early childhood. In *Studies of child language development,* eds. C. Ferguson and D. Slobin. New York: Holt, Rinehart and Winston.

SIEGEL, G. 1962. Interexaminer reliability for mean length of response. *J. Speech Hearing Disorders* 5:91–95.

SIEGEL, G. 1969. Vocal conditioning in infants. *J. Speech Hearing Disorders* 34:3–19.

SIEGEL, G. 1975. The high cost of accountability. *Asha* 17:796–97.

SIGEL, I. 1971. Language of the disadvantaged: the distancing hypothesis. In *Language training in early childhood education,* ed. C. Lavatelli. Urbana: University of Illinois.

SIGUELAND, E., and DELUCIA, C. 1969. Visual reinforcement of nonnutritive sucking in human infants. *Science* 165:1144–46.

SIMON, H. 1974. How big is a chunk? *Science* 183:482–88.

SINCLAIR, H. 1970. The transition from sensory-motor behavior to symbolic activity. *Interchange* 1:119–126.

SINCLAIR-DEZWART, H. 1969. Developmental psycholinguistics. In *Studies in cognitive development,* eds. D. Elkind and J. Flavell. New York: Oxford University Press.

SINCLAIR-DEZWART, H. 1971. Sensorimotor action patterns as a condition for the acquisition of syntax. In *Language acquisition: models and methods,* eds. R. Huxley and E. Ingram. New York: Academic Press.

SINCLAIR-DEZWART, H. 1973a. Language acquisition and cognitive development. In *Cognitive development and the acquisition of language,* ed. T. Moore. New York: Academic Press.

SINCLAIR-DEZWART, H. 1973b. Some remarks on the Genevan point of view on learning with special reference to language learning. In *Constraints on Learning,* eds. L. Hinde and H. Hind. New York: Academic Press.

SINGH, S. 1976. *Distinctive features: theory and validation*. Baltimore: University Park Press.

SKINNER, B. 1957. *Verbal behavior*. New York: Appleton-Century-Crofts.

SLOBIN, D. 1966. The acquisition of Russian as a native language. In *The genesis of language,* eds. F. Smith and G. Miller. Cambridge, Mass.: MIT Press.

SLOBIN, D. 1970. Suggested universals in the ontogenesis of grammar. Language Behavior Research Laboratory: Working Paper 32. Revised version: SLOBIN, D. 1973. Cognitive prerequisites for the development of grammar. In *Studies of child language development,* eds. C. Ferguson and D. Slobin. New York: Holt, Rinehart and Winston.

SLOBIN, D. 1971. *Psycholinguistics*. Glenview, Ill.: Scott, Foresman.

SLOBIN, D. and WELSH, C. 1971. Elicited imitation as a research tool in developmental psycholinguistics. In *Language training in early childhood education,* ed. C. Lavatelli. Urbana: University of Illinois Press.

SMITH, E., SHOBEN, E., and RIPS, L. 1974. Structure and process in semantic memory: A featural model for semantic decisions. *Psychological Review* 81:214–41.

SMITH, F. 1971. *Understanding reading: a psycholinguistic analysis of reading and learning to read*. New York: Holt, Rinehart and Winston.

SNIDER, J., and OSGOOD, C. 1969. *Semantic differential technique: a sourcebook*. Chicago: Aldine-Atherton.

SNOW, C. 1972. Mother's speech to children learning language. *Child Development* 43:549–66.

SOKOLOV, E. 1963. *Perception and the conditional reflex*. New York: Macmillan.

SOUNDERS, C. 1972. *Individualized data base: implementation and application*. Conference report. Pacific State Hospital Research Center, San Francisco.

SPIKER, C., GERJUOY, I., and SHEPARD, W. 1956. Children's concept of middle-sizedness and performance on the intermediate size problem. *J. Comparative and Physiological Psychology* 49:416–19.

SPRIESTERBACH, D., and CURTIS, J. 1964. Misarticulation and discrimination of speech sounds. Reprinted in McDonald, E., *Articulation Testing and Treatment: A Sensory-Motor Approach*. Pittsburgh: Stanwix House, Inc.

SROUFE, L. 1970. A methodological and philosophical critique of intervention-oriented research. *Developmental Psychology* 2:140–45.

SROUFE, L., and WATERS, W. 1976. The ontogenesis of smiling and laughter: A perspective on the organization of development in infancy. *Psychological Review* 83:173–89.

STAATS, A. 1969. *Learning, language, and cognition*. New York: Holt, Rinehart and Winston.

STAMPE, D. 1969. The acquisition of phonetic representation. Paper from the Chicago Linguistic Society, 443–54.

Standards for community agencies. 1973. Chicago: Joint Commission on Accreditation of Hospitals.

Standards for residential facilities for the mentally retarded. 1971. Chicago: Joint Commission on Accreditation of Hospitals.

STEPHENS, W., NOPAR, R., and GILLIAM, L. 1971. Equivalence formation by mentally retarded and nonretarded children using pictorial and printed word stimulus items. *Am. J. Mental Deficiency* 76:252–56.

STETSON, R. 1951. *Motor phonetics: a study of speech movement in action*. Amsterdam: North-Holland.

STEVENS, K., HOUSE, A., and PAUL, A. 1966. Acoustic descriptions of syllabic nuclei: an interpretation in terms of a dynamic model of articulation. *Journal Acoustical Society America* 40:123–32.

STEWART, W. 1968. A linguistic approach to nonstandard speech (with special emphasis on Negro dialects). American Speech Hearing Convention.

STODOLSKY, S., and LESSER, G. 1967. Learning patterns in the disadvantaged. *Harvard Educational Review* 37:546–93.

SUCI, G., and HAMACHER, J. 1972. Psychological dimensions of case in sentence processing: action role and animateness. *Linguistics* 89:34–48.

SWINNEY, D., and TAYLOR, C. 1971. Short-term memory recognition search in aphasics. *J. Speech Hearing Research* 14:578–88.

TEMPLIN, M. 1957. *Certain language skills in children: their development and interrelationships*. Minneapolis: University of Minnesota Press.

THOMAS, O. 1965. *Transformational grammar and the teacher of English*. New York: Holt, Rinehart and Winston.

THORNDIKE, E., and LORGE, I. 1944. *The teacher's word book of 30,000 words.* New York: Bureau of Publications, Teachers College, Columbia University.

THORNDIKE, R. 1971. *Reading as reasoning.* Washington, D.C.: Am Psychological Assoc.

TODD, T., and PALMER, B. 1968. Social reinforcement and infant babbling. *Child Development* 39:591–96.

TOFFEL, C. 1955. Anxiety and the conditioning of verbal behavior. *J. Abnorm. Soc. Psychol.* 51:496–501.

TOWNSEND, D. 1976. Do children interpret "marked" comparative adjectives as their opposites? *J. Child Language* 3:385–96.

TREHUB, S., and RABINOVITCH, M. 1972. Auditory-linguistic sensitivity in early infancy. *Developmental Psychology* 6:74–77.

TRUBY, H., BOSMA, J., and LIND, J. 1965. Newborn infant cry. *Acta Paedist. Scand.* Supplement 163.

TRUDGILL, P. 1974. *Sociolinguistics: an introduction.* London: Penguin Books.

TUNKIS, G. 1963. Linguistic theory in the transformationalist approach. *Lingua* 16:384–76.

TURNER, E., and ROMMETVEIT, R. 1967. The acquisition of sentence voice and reversibility. *Child Development* 38:549–660.

TURNURE, C. 1971. Response to voice of mother and stranger by babies in the first year. *Developmental Psychology* 4:182–90.

TYLER, S. 1969. *Cognitive anthropology.* New York: Holt, Rinehart and Winston.

UNDERWOOD, B. 1975. Individual differences as a crucible in theory construction. *American Psychologist* 30:128–35.

UZGIRIS, I., and HUNT, J. 1975. *Assessment in infancy: ordinal scales of psychological development.* Urbana: University of Illinois Press.

VAN RIPER, C. 1963. *Speech correction: principles and methods,* 4th ed. Englewood Cliffs, N.J.: Prentice-Hall.

VENNEMANN, T. 1972. On the theory of syllabic phonology. *Linguist. Ber.* 18:1–18.

VENNEMANN, T., and LADEFOGED, P. 1973. Phonetic features and phonological features. *Lingua* 32:61–74.

VESPUCCI, P. 1975. Two developmental cognitive processes: performance at the kindergarten level. Unpublished M.A. Thesis. Buffalo: State University of New York.

VYGOTSKY, L. 1962. *Thought and language.* Cambridge, Mass.: MIT Press.

WALDROP, M., PEDERSON, F., and BELL, R. 1968. Minor physical anomalies and behavior in preschool children. *Child Development* 39:391–400.

WALES, R., and MARSHALL, J. 1966. The organization of linguistic performance. In *Psycholinguistics paper,* eds. L. Lyons and R. Wales. Chicago: Aldine Publishing Co.

WALSH, H. 1974. On certain practical inadequacies of distinctive feature systems. *Journal Speech Hearing Disorders* 39:32–43.

WARYAS, C. 1973. Psycholinguistic research in language intervention programming: the pronoun system. *J. Psycholinguistic Research* 2:221–37.

WATERSON, N. 1971. Child phonology: a prosodic view. *J. of Linguistics* 7:179–211.

WEBSTER, B., and INGRAM, D. 1974. The comprehension and production of the anaphoric pronouns "he, she, him, her" in normal and linguistically deviant children. American Speech and Hearing Association Convention.

Webster's Elementary Dictionary. 1971. Springfield, Mass.: G. & C. Merriam.

WECHLSER, D. 1975. Intelligence defined and undefined: a relativistic appraisal. *American Psychologist 30:135–39.*

WEIR, M., and STEVENSON, H. 1959. The effect of verbalization in children's learning as a function of chronological age. *Child Development* 30:173–78.

WEIR, R. 1962. *Language in the crib.* The Hague: Mouton.

WELLS, G. 1974. Learning to code experience through language. *J. Child Language* 1:243–69.

WEPMAN, J. 1958. *Auditory discrimination test.* Chicago: Language Research Associates.

WEPMAN, J. 1972. Aphasia therapy: a new look. *J. Speech Hearing Disorders 37:203*–14.

WEPMAN, J. 1976. Aphasia: language without thought or thought without language? *Asha* 18:131–36.

WEPMAN, J., and JONES, L. 1961. *The language modalities for aphasia.* Chicago: University of Chicago Education Industry Service.

WEPMAN, J., JONES, L., BOCK, R., and VAN PELT, D. 1960. Studies in aphasia: background and theoretical formulations. *J. Speech Hearing Disorders* 25:323–32.

WERNER, H. 1948. *Comparative psychology of mental development.* Rev. ed. Chicago: Follett.

WERNER, H. 1957. The concept of development from a comparative and organismic point of view. In *The concept of development,* ed. D. B. Harris. Minneapolis: University of Minnesota Press.

WERNER, H., and KAPLAN, B. 1963. *Symbol formation.* New York: Wiley.

WEST, J. 1971. The application of verbal learning techniques to adult aphasia theory. Chicago: *Am. Speech Hearing Ass.* Convention.

WHITACRE, J., LUPER, H., and POLLIO, H. 1970. General language deficits in children with articulation problems. *Language and Speech* 13:231–39.

WHITE, S. 1965. Evidence for hierarchical arrangement processes. In Lipsitt, L., and Spiker, C. *Advances in child development and behavior* New York: Academic Press.

WHITEHURST, G., and NOVAK, G. 1973. Modeling imitation training, and the acquisition of sentence phrases. *J. Experimental Child Psychol.* 16:332–45.

WHITEHURST, G., and VASTA, R. 1973. Is language acquired through imitation? *Journal Psycholinguistic Research* 4:37–60.

WICKLEGREN, W. 1966. Distinctive features and errors in short-term memory for English consonants. *J. Acoust. Soc. Amer.* 39:388–98.

WICKLEGREN, W. 1969. Auditory or articulatory coding in verbal short-term memory. *Psychological Review* 76:232–35.

WIEMAN, L. 1976. Stress patterns of early child language. *Journal Child Language* 3:283–86.

WIENER, M., DEVOE, S., RUBINOW, S., and GELLER, J. 1972. Nonverbal behavior and nonverbal communication. *Psychological Review* 79:185–214.

WIEST, W. 1967. Some recent criticisms of behaviorism and learning theory with special reference to Breger and McGaugh and to Chomsky. *Psychological Bulletin* 67:214–25.

WILLIAMS, F., ed. 1970. *Language and poverty: perspectives on a theme.* Chicago: Markham Publishing Co.

WILLIAMS, F., and NAREMORE, R. 1969a. On the functional analysis of social class differences in modes of speech. *Speech Monograph* 36:77–102.

WILLIAMS, F., and NAREMORE, R. 1969b. Social class differences in children's syntactic performance: a quantitative analysis of field study data. *J. Speech Hearing Research* 12:777–93.

WINITZ, H. 1969. *Articulation Acquisition and Behavior.* New York: Appleton-Century-Crofts.

WINITZ, H. 1975. *From syllable to conversation.* Baltimore: University Park Press.

WINOGRAD, T. 1972. Understanding natural language. *Cognitive Psychology* 3:1–191.

WITKIN, H., DYK, R., FATERSON, H., GOODENOUGH, D., and KARP, S. 1962. *Psychological differentiation.* New York: Wiley.

WITKIN, H., PATERSON, H., GOODENOUGH, D. and BIMBAUNY, J. 1966. Cognitive patterning in mildly retarded boys. *Child Development* 37:301–16.

WOLFENSBERGER, W., and GLENN, L. 1973. *PASS (Program Analysis of Service Systems): field manual.* National Institute of Mental Retardation.

WOOD, B. 1976. *Children and communication: verbal and nonverbal language development.* Englewood Cliffs, N.J.: Prentice-Hall.

WOZNIAK, R. 1974. Verbal regulation of motor behavior—Soviet research and non-Soviet replications. *Human Development* 15:13–57.

YANDO, R.M., and KAGAN, J. 1968. The effect of teacher tempo on the child. *Child Development* 39:27–34.

YANDO, R.M., and KAGAN, J. 1970. The effects of task complexity on reflection-impulsivity. *Cognitive Psychology* 1:192–200.

YNGVE, V. 1960. A model and an hypothesis for language structure. *Proceedings American Philosophical Society* 108:275–81.

YOUNISS, J. 1974. Operations and everyday thinking: a commentary on "dialectical operations." *Human Development* 17:386–91.

ZAPOROZHETS, A. 1965. The development of perception in the preschool child. *Monograph of the Society for Research in Child Development* 30:82–111.

ZELAZO, P. 1971. Smiling to social stimuli: eliciting and conditioning effects. *Developmental Psychology* 4:32–42.

ZELAZO, P. 1972. Smiling and vocalizing: a cognitive emphasis. *Merrill-Palmer Quarterly* 18:349–65.

ZELAZO, P., HOPKINS, J., JACOBSON, S., and KAGAN, J. 1974. Psychological reactivity to discrepant events: support for the curvilinear hypothesis. *Cognition* 2:385–93.

ZELAZO, P., and KOMER, M. 1971. Infant smiling to nonsocial stimuli and the recognition hypothesis. *Child Development* 42:1327–39.

ZELNIKER, T., COCHAVI, D., and YERED, J. 1974. The relationship between speed of performance and conceptual style: the effect of imposed modification of response latency. *Child Development* 45:779–84.

ZIMMERMAN, B., and BELL, J. 1972. Observer verbalization and obstruction in vicarious rule learning, generalization and retention. *Dev. Psychology* 7:227–31.

ZIMMERMAN, B., and ROSENTHAL, T. 1974. Observational learning of rule-governed behavior by children. *Psychological Bulletin* 81:29–42.

ZIPF, G. 1949. *Human behavior and the principle of least effort.* Cambridge, Mass.: Addison-Wesley.

ZWICKY, F. 1957. *Morphological analysis.* Berlin: Springer.

ZWYCEWICZ, C. 1975. Developmental performance on systematically varied semantic-syntactic contexts. Unpublished M.S. Thesis. Buffalo: State University of New York.

Glossary

Accessibility: in concept development, the availability of a concept for use in thinking. Concepts become increasingly accessible with development.

Accommodation: process in which existing schemata become reorganized or new schemata are produced to incorporate new information.

Accountability: answerable. Clinically, to be answerable to a supervisor, administrator, parent, or someone with a particular interest in appropriateness of assessment-intervention and nature of progress.

Action: performance. An act.

Adaptiveness: ability to deal effectively with one's circumstances. Alternative strategies to cope with one's environment.

Adjectival system: any verbal form that functions as a noun modifier exclusive of the determiner system, e. g., *big* boy, the boy is *big,* the boy *in the tree* is *big,* etc.

Adult words: words used by adults. Have adult meanings.

Adverbial system: any verbal forms that function as adverbs.

Affixes: various bound morphemes attached to the beginning (prefixes) or ending (suffixes) of words. Derivational or inflectional.

Agent: person or thing that initiates or is responsible for action.

Ambiguity: more than one meaning or interpretation.

Anaphoric reference: a grammatical mechanism that notifies a decoder that a previous reference is being used again. The pronominal system's primary function is anaphoric. In the sentence, "He ate Tom's lunch," *he* refers to a previously identified or implied person other than Tom.

Applied fields: various fields, especially education, involved in the application or implementation of information, in contrast to basic research. Refers primarily to general education, special education, vocational training, school psychology, etc.

A priori approaches: clinically, approaches that set basic dimensions of intervention such as content, sequencing, pacing, and reinforcement *before* encountering an individual and appraising his needs. Also, assessment in which categories and responses are determined *before* meeting the individual to be tested.

Appropriateness: relevance, pertinence. Clinically, pertaining to one's readiness, representativeness, needs, and ecological conditions.

Assessment: clinical assessment is an attempt to appraise and understand behavior and attitudes to determine the existence of a problem, the nature of a problem, or changes of a problem.

Assimilation: process in which existing schemata are altered by adding new information.

Associationism: theoretical view that one event is linked to another by a common attribute. Stimulus-response (or S-R) view of behavior. S-R theories of language hold that sentences are chains of associated words. Even the most eminent S-R theorists now concede that S-R explanations of language are inadequate.

Associations: word-associations. Word responses to a stimulus word (see *paradigmatic shift*).

Attribution: awareness of an attribute or feature of something or someone.

Authoritarianism: following an authority's proclamation. Authoritarianism may politicize a profession.

Auxiliary system: component of the verb phrase that contains tense, but may also contain modals, aspect, and negation.

Available reference: actual or presumed reference used in referring to someone or something (see *referent*).

Behavior: attitudes, thoughts, and beliefs, or actions of an individual or group.

Behaviorism: theoretical view of behavior that relies on directly observable events and resists inferring underlying processes, exemplified by behavior modification.

Capacity: see *repertoire*.

Case grammar: grammar about semantic functions and relations of utterances rather than form. Generative semantic grammars.

Categorization: categorize or classify one's experience.

Causality: in cognitive development, awareness of causitive agents. A prerepresentational ability.

Cerebral overflow: clinical expression for mouthing activities and other motor activities that occur when an individual is engaged in a difficult or studied act.

Chunking: cognitive unit. A segment of experience determined by how previous experiences have been categorized. A perceptual unit.

Clinician: individual who intervenes for the purpose of improving a client's clinical problem or condition.

Cluster reduction: simplification of consonant clusters, e.g., ''stop'' becomes ''top.''

Coarticulation: influence of one phoneme on another in perception or production. Feature spreading in phonetic context. Left-to-right influences are forward or carryover coarticulations; right-to-left influences are backward or anticipatory coarticulations.

Code: an organized set of symbols to convey a messsage. To symbolize a message.

Codification: code or place one's thoughts in language.

Cognition: the processes of knowing. Includes sensation, perception, memory, conceptualization, mental operations, thinking, etc.

Cognitive bias: response determined by the perception of inherent features with their typical action patterns.

Cognitive dissonance: conflict of information. Possibly an emotional override of information.

Cognitive distancing: cognitive ability to be increasingly removed from direct experience and more reliant on representation. Operationally: an actual object is cognitively close because action patterns can be used; pictorials are more distant because they give prototypic information; words are even more distant because they are referential.

Communication game—Dump and Play: communicative processes, after a roletaking attitude has been obtained, in which both encoder and decoder actively formulate and issue messages of presumed best fit (dump) and identify and reconcile or resolve communicative obstacles (play).

Communicative: acts and processes in conveying information.

Communicative intent: desired purposes and functions of a communicative effort.

Communicative matrix: complexity of simultaneous codes any of which may dominate a message, e.g., linguistic, nonlinguistic, paralinguistic, etc.

Communicative obstacle: breakdown or barrier in a communicative process, caused by difficult words, complex syntax, etc.

Competence: one's knowledge or abilities. Linguistically, what one knows about his language (psycholinguistic competence) and about using his language (sociolinguistic or pragmatic competence).

Complex: interrelated components. Behavior is complex because it is the result of many underlying processes.

Complexes: unorganized, unstable concepts underlying early labeling.

Complexity-simplicity: complexity pertains to cognitive difficulty. Presumably cognitively simple also means "easy to learn." Things are cognitively easy in a relevant and functional context but relatively difficult when segmented and isolated. Traditionally, things were thought to be easier when isolated. Linguistically, theories of complexity are not yet developed.

Concept formation, concept development: progressive attainment of conceptual features and reorganization of features. Schema development.

Conceptual knowledge: knowledge or cognitive structures one uses to represent his experiences, as contrasted to semantic knowledge.

Conditional: reflecting contextual influences. Behavior is conditional because it is the product of its context.

Conservation: cognitive ability to maintain salient relationships between attributes even though the attributes undergo covariation or transformation.

Constituent: component. Syntactically, immediate constituents are immediately subordinated components of a structure.

Content: substance, material. In language learning, one's language.

Context: linguistically, behavior is the product of its linguistic and referential contexts. Linguistic context is the co-occurring cognitive-linguistic system for a target system. Referential context is the available referents and communicative intent of an utterance.

Convergent thinking: cognitive style. Integration.

Co-occurrence: coexistence of something with something else. Linguistically, the coexistence of various systems within an utterance (horizontal co-occurrence), or various instances of a target system across utterances sampled (vertical co-occurrence). Horizontal co-occurrences define linguistic contexts or conditions (structurally and functionally) for the acquistion/use of a target system. Vertical co-occurrences define the nature of a target system.

Core vocabulary: basic set of words that have high utility for a particular person in his regular activities. A relatively small set of words with considerable potential for someone.

Correlation hypothesis: language space is the same as, and depends on, perceptual space. Development of temporal awareness is correlated to the development of spatial awareness. The acquisition of temporal terms follows that of spatial terms.

Crossover: a shift in the relationship between thought and language in acquisition. In early language acquisition, cognitive development anticipates language development; the crossover function operates when language begins to function in cognitive development and cognitive development continues to influence language learning.

Cumulative complexity: $x + y$ is more complex than either x or y alone. For example, agent-action is more complex than either agent or action alone.

Data: numbers, behavioral sets, or instances. Data are not necessarily evidence.

Dative: recipient of action. Direct object.

Decoder: individual who attends to and deciphers a message, taking into account alternative but simultaneous coding mechanisms, topic, communicative context, and available reference. A decoder may identify communicative obstacles and notify the encoder.

Degenerative processes: breakdown of function or abilities due to aging.

Deixis: ability to code in language the contrastive perspectives of someone else, e.g., this/that, these/those, here/there, etc.

Denial: nonacceptance of a circumstance or event.

Derivation: linguistically, an ability to produce new word forms from old words, phrases, or sentences. "Happiness" can be derived from "happy."

Descriptive assessment: assessment process in which systems and processes available to and used by an individual are described. Can deal with the nature of a problem.

Determiner system: linguistic devices that determine the state of a noun in a noun phrase. Articles, demonstratives, possessive, number, etc.

Developmental profiles: any of a number of age oriented profiles that index presumed acquisition of behavioral categories. Such profiles obscure individual strategies and are categorical rather than process oriented.

Diagnostics: assessment process based on specific patterns of attitudes and behaviors indicative of a particular clinical condition. Diagnostics usually results in a clinical label.

Dialect: grammars of a subgroup of individuals who speak the same language but in whose language differences exist.

Differentiation: developmental process whereby increasing specification becomes realized.

Dimensional adjectives: attributes of things, e.g., color, size, shape, texture, etc.

Dimensional salience (perceptual salience): inordinate orientation on a perceptual domain. Clinically, perceptual salience varies from day to day.

Diminutive: addition of /ɪ/ on the end of nouns in child speech, e.g., doggy, Mommy, Daddy, etc.

Discrepancy: cognitively, a perceived slight difference between what one knows and what he experiences.

Distal: removed physically or cognitively.

Distinctive features: components of phonemes that distinguish phonemes. Components are distinctive in phonemic contexts when they contrast from one segment to the next.

Divergent thinking: cognitive style, thinking about novel functions or applications of something.

Dual listener: listener of *Sesame Street* who is engaged in an activity as he watches the television.

Dump: issuance of a message in a communication game.

Dynamic: change, changing. Linguistically, a dynamic relationship between form (structure) and function (meaning). One word can have many referents and one referent can have many words. A dynamic relationship between thought and language. One thought can be expressed in many ways and one expression can have many thoughts or meanings.

Dynamic attributes: attributes that change, e.g., action, relationships, states, temporal relations, spatial relations.

Ecologically valid: directly relevent or derived from one's natural surroundings. Natural. Ecologically valid assessment-intervention transpires in the home, playground, school, or anywhere else an individual typically functions. Clinical activities may be considered ecologically valid if they can be directly translated to one's natural contexts.

Egocentricity: oriented on oneself.

Elliptic: shorten. Elliptic utterances, for example, are "I can," "He must," "They will."

Encoder: individual who formulates and issues a message of presumed best fit for a particular communicative intent in the context of available reference and perceived requirements.

Evidence: data pertinent or relevant to an issue.

Exemplar: instance of something. There are four of these:

Focal exemplar: exemplar that best represents a category, prototypic.

Peripheral exemplar: exemplar that may be regarded as a part of a category but would more easily be regarded in another category.

Positive exemplar: instance of something consistent with a rule for the category.

Negative exemplar: violation of a rule.

Expansions: natural responses of parents to child utterances. The responses are syntactically expanded versions of the child's utterance.

Faith: to believe without firm evidence.

First language learning: principles and processes in original language learning. Pertains to an individual's control of content, sequencing, pacing, reinforcement, and motivation.

Formal approaches: approaches that rely on specific behaviors elicited from contrived tasks.

Function: use. Functional approaches in language pertain to the uses or purposes of language, e.g., speech acts, case grammars, generative semantics, etc.

General intelligence: traditional notion that intelligence is unitary rather than multidimensional, static rather than dynamic.

Generic: most general. Superordinate. Generic learning begins with the most general and proceeds to increasing levels of specificity.

Glossing: linguistically, a verbal structure that functions for several other structures. For example, "got" may function as a modal, have, or some other verb.

Glued-on listener: listener of "Sesame Street" who is strongly fixed, enthralled, or oriented to the program.

Grammar: one's linguistic rules. Rules that provide the individual a generative capacity to express himself (or understand others) verbally. A finite set of rules that provide an individual an ability to produce (or comprehend) an infinite number and variety of utterances of his language.

Graphemes: written forms or letters that stand for phonemes.

Hesitation phenomena: any of several disruptions in speech production, such as false starts, repetitions, unusual pauses, fillers, particularly "ah," etc.

Heterogeneity: dissimilar. Varied. Clinically, individual differences are outstanding.

Hierarchy, hierarchical: organization with superordinate and subordinate relationships. Developmentally, hierarchical relationships exist because some behaviors must be antecedent to others. Cognitively and linguistically, concepts and utterances manifest hierarchical structure (see *differentiation* and *recursiveness*).

Holophrastic: one-word utterances which have several meanings.

Homogeneity: similarity. Clinically, commonalities exist in non-aberrant aspects.

Hypothesis testing: cognitively, the second phase in attending to a stimulus. Covertly evidenced by cardiac acceleration. Overtly evidenced by smiling and possibly laughter (see *orienting response*). In language development, the manner in which an individual induces the nature of language.

Iconic: imagery, awareness or orientation toward perceptual stimuli. Iconic thought is an orientation toward perceptual attributes such as color, size, shape, position, number, etc. Iconic memory is imagery.

Ideolect: grammar of an individual.

Ideology: beliefs or attitudes that govern alternative actions. Clinically, ideology may account for why a clinician may intellectualize new approaches but not *use* them.

Idiosyncratic meaning: meaning specific to one's limited experiences. Peculiar meaning.

Imagery: see *iconic*.

Imitation: follow an available model. Faithfully emulate. Spontaneous imitation is naturally occurring imitation; induced imitation is elicited by someone else. Spontaneous imitation is of particular significance in language learning and assessment. Deferred or delayed imitation has special significance in cognitive development.

Imperative: utterances in which the subject noun phrase is assumed or implied by context: ''Give it to me.''

Individual differences: idiosyncrasies. Uniqueness. Clinically, individual differences are outstanding. It is all but impossible to find two individuals with exactly the same clinical problems; accordingly, clinical assessment-intervention should be oriented on individual differences rather than similarities.

Induction of latent structure: realization of the nature of one's language through hypothesis testing.

Inflection: linguistic device that modulates meanings, e.g., tense marker, plural, possessive, noun-verb agreement.

Informal approaches: approaches that rely on disciplined observations of natural as opposed to contrived behavior.

Information processing model: model that stresses information processing in terms of input, association, output. Expression, integration, and reception.

Informational: language used to inform others, to convey information.

Innate capacity: biological predisposition. Strong version is that language learning is innate; weak version is that both maturation and environmental determinates operate in language learning.

Instrumental: language used to satisfy one's own material needs. A semantic function. What may be used by an agent in an agent-object relationship.

Intentional meaning: speaker's purpose in uttering a word.

Interactional: language used to establish and maintain contact with significant others.

Intermodality transfer: transfer of information or knowledge in one modality to another. Transfer of oral/aural linguistic abilities to writing/reading.

Intervention: to intercede on one's behalf. Deal with another's behavior and attitudes.

Intonation: rhythm pattern of a string of syllables in an utterance. Intonation patterns are specific to sentence mode, e.g., question intonation, declarative intonation, etc.

Intransitive verb systems: verbalizations that have agent-action relationships.

Invented words: in language learning, children will invent words to serve a grammatic function. As actual words are learned that serve the function of invented words, the invented words are lost.

Isomorphism: one-to-one relationship. In language acquisition and usage, a partial isomorphism exists between thought and language because certain cognitive processes must be realized before linguistic processes can be realized. However, there is no exact one-to-one relationship between a word and underlying thoughts.

Iteration: linguistically, utterances in which "it" is the subject. For example, "It is time to go."

Kinetics: body language.

Label, clinical label: term used by clinicians in a diagnostic process to categorize the clinical behaviors of an individual in terms of a clinical condition or syndrome, e.g., learning-disabled, cultural-familial retardation, mental retardation, delayed language, etc.

Label, labeling: giving a word, phrase, or sentence for an object, action, relationship, state, or event for the purpose of establishing and carrying out any of several intra- or interpersonal functions of speech acts. Codification. In language learning, a label is a speaker's attempt to regulate joint attention or joint action between himself and those he addresses.

Language: theoretical construct about the total number of products (sentences) of a number of people who have essentially the same grammars.

Language acquisition: pertaining to developmental processes and stages in language learning.

Language sample size: size of a language sample. Cannot be *a priori* set. Sample size is determined by the obtained distribution of a target system. When a target system is evidenced in a sufficient quantity to yield a distribution or pattern that is presumably representative, a sample is adequate.

Learned distinctiveness: knowledge that previously undifferentiated concepts can be differentiated.

Learned equivalence: knowledge of a common attribute between seemingly disparate things.

Lexicon, dynamic lexicon, lexical: one's words and the concepts underlying each of the words or labels. One's lexicon is continuously changing by virtue of new experiences. New words are altered and old words change their meanings.

Limbic system: portion of the central nervous system responsible for emotion and basic states such as hunger, thirst, fear, etc.

Linguistic: pertaining to language and the grammar of language.

Linguistic continuum: one's stylistic range of talking—formal, informal, technical, etc.

Linguistic determinism (Sapir-Whorf hypothesis): one's language determines one's thoughts.

Linguistic relativity (Sapir-Whorf hypothesis): groups of people who have the same language think in similar ways.

Linguistic situation: circumstantial variables play a major role in learning language. Language is conditional.

Linguistic variable: linguistic variations are largely the product of sociological influences.

Local rules: situational constraints and influences on the production of utterances.

Locative: adverb of place.

Mainstreaming: attempt to integrate handicapped individuals into their regular community, as opposed to removing them through institutionalization.

Make-Change: educational game in which players have a variety of decisions about sentence making.

Markedness: explanation for how a child may deal with a dimension but not specific or contrastive aspects of a dimension; subsequently he will mark specific aspects.

Marker: linguistically, certain indexing devices. For example, "do" is a tense marker.

Mediation deficiency: failure to have a rehearsal strategy or some kind of mediator to realize a solution or categorization.

Mediator: mental process whereby new information or new behavior may be generated. A stimulus generates an intervening process, thereby establishing the potential for a variety of responses, some of which may be novel.

Memory, memory-span, memory capacity: storage and retrieval of information. Traditionally, clinicians were interested in the notion of memory span in terms of external units such as digits and commands. Clinicians are now interested in memory in terms of rehearsal strategies, iconic/symbolic memory, primacy/ recency functions, and short-term/long-term memory.

Mentalism: theoretical view of behavior that relies on an explanation of underlying mental processes.

Message of best fit: coded message that most appropriately meets the communicative intent of an encoder and the needs of a decoder in a particular situation.

Metaphoric: figurative language—"long" stick, "long" time.

Metareferential: referring to language or code itself. For example, "That was a *big word.*"

Minor physical anomalies: slight physical differences.

Mitigated echolalia: echoic or imitative behavior in which variations appear. Observed in the behavior of retarded and autistic children.

Modal: an optional component of the auxiliary system. Tense is marked on modals. English modals include: can (could), may (might), shall (should), will (would), must.

Modality: verbal form or means. Clinically, the old information processing models had a language modality orientation: expressive language, receptive language, written and oral modalities, speech, listening, writing, reading.

Mode: way or means. Linguistically, may mean utterance mode such as declarative, question, negation, etc., or may have a more specific theoretical meaning, e.g., an utterance has a mode and an argument, or a mode and a proposition.

Modeling: emulate or follow the example of another. Intervention procedure in which models are provided.

Morphology: aspect of syntax that formulates words from morphemes. *Lexical morphemes* are the substantive or contentive aspects of an utterance. *Grammatical morphemes* are the function aspects of an utterance. Morphology pertains to inflectional and some derivational rules.

Motivation: inherent action and purpose. An organism's acts are partly determined in direction and strength by its own nature and internal state.

Nominal system: structures equivalent to a noun phrase, e.g., proper noun, determiner + noun, pronoun, indefinite pronoun, etc.

Nonexistence: something is not exhibited or present when expected.

Nonlinguistic: coding devices not formally governed by verbal rules but that contribute to a message, e.g., smiling, head nodding, posture, gestures, etc.

Nonverbal child: child who does not speak or has limited speech because of socioemotional reasons or lack of verbal abilities.

Normative assessment: assessment process based on norms. Can deal only with the problem/no problem issue for a particular normative category but is inadequate for more substantial aspects of assessment.

Nouns: label of entities. There are animate nouns, inanimate nouns, count nouns, noncount or mass nouns; regular nouns, and irregular nouns.

Numbers game: clinically, the use of numbers to categorize behavior and issue "diagnostic" labels. A process that skirts issues of complexity, dynamism, conditionality, relativity of behavior, and behavioral systems.

Object noun phrase: NP_2. Second noun phrase in a subject-action-object structure, or object in a prepositional phrase.

Object permanence: in cognitive development, awareness that things exist even though they cannot be experienced directly. Ability to represent experience. Without object permanence, awareness becomes out of sight–out of mind.

Old information/new information: old information is context and new information is change in context.

Open-endedness: recursiveness.

Open syllable: consonant-vowel (CV) syllable. Developmentally, earliest syllabic construction.

Operantly determined loci of learning: individual learns the particular aspects of language he is ready to learn, when, where, why, and how he chooses. Learning is determined by one's readiness and his opportunities.

Operantly determined switching loci: individual switches from one aspect of language to another according to his readiness to learn and available opportunities.

Operational: procedural. Available for use.

Orienting response (OR): first phase of two phases attending to a stimulus. Covertly an OR is evidenced by cardiac deceleration; overtly by a reduction of extraneous activity and a fix on the stimulus (see *hypothesis testing*).

Original Thinking Game: term used by Jerome Bruner to encompass all that is entailed in the emergence of cognitive capacities. It has particular reference to stages in cognitive growth (enactive, iconic, symbolic), active processing, and technology of reckoning.

Original Word Game: term used by Roger Brown to encompass all that is entailed in first language learning. It has particular reference to cognitive-socialization processes in language acquisition.

Ostensive terms: labels of observable things, actions, and states.

Overextension: in language learning, child uses a word beyond an acceptable adult usage. Indicates a restricted conceptual development for a word. Also overinclusion, "That's a big doggy (horse)."

Overlearning: something is learned so completely that an individual is duped into thinking he knows all. In open-learning, on the other hand, an individual knows he is learning selected exemplars of a principle and thus seeks new exemplars.

Pacing: amount and rate at which material is incorporated in the learning process.

Paradigmatic shift: developmental shift that occurs at about seven years of age in word-association tasks, younger children give syntagmatic responses (place the stimulus word into a syntactic context) whereas individuals over seven give paradigmatic responses (response words are from the same category as the stimulus word).

Paralinguistic: coding devices superimposed upon a linguistic code, e.g., unusual or special pauses, stress, intonations, inflections, etc.

Parallel play: play in which two individuals do similar things in the same situation but whose activities do not intersect.

Parallel talking: intervention procedure in which a clinician selectively talks about objects, actions, events, attributes, or relations of activities in which a child participates.

Paraphrase: to restate something without changing its meaning.

Parsing: describe a sentence according to its components.

Partial learning: principle of language learning. Linguistic systems are learned in stages.

Patient: person or thing in a given state or change of state.

Peer: one's equal, usually in age and skill.

Perceptual drift: natural shifting of a frame of reference in perception and clinical judgments.

Performance: one's actions. One's usage. Linguistically, the verbal products of one's grammar and intra- and interpersonal constraints.

Personal: language used to express one's individuality and self-awareness.

Phoneme: basic discernible segment in sound patterns of a language. Speech sounds.

Phoneme-grapheme correspondence: relationships between phonemes and their respective graphemes in a language. Some phonemes have a direct relationship such as /p/ and p, /d/ and d, /t/ and t, but others do not, for example, /s/ can be s or c.

Phonemic principle: aspects of speech patterns that index meaning.

Phonetic inventory: one's repertoire of speech sounds.

Phonology: domain of linguistics pertaining to sound patterns of a language. Perception of speech sound patterns is *phonemics* whereas an individual's production of speech sound patterns is *phonetics*.

Phonotactic: developmentally, phonological processes that extend beyond a phoneme, e.g., weak syllable deletion, reduplication, voicing, etc.

Phrase structure rules: aspect of syntax that accounts for phrases. Immediate constituents are identified by phrase structure rules.

Positive term: one of two polar adjectives that usually refers to the dimension of the adjectives, e.g., "big" for bigness rather than "little."

Possession: ownership, genitive.

Postvocalic: following a vowel in a word or syllable.

Pragmatics: psychosociodynamics of language use for an individual.

Prescriptive assessment-intervention: attempt to appraise one's clinical condition and define for a practitioner the things to do in intervention. Operationally, prescription approaches are usually taxonomic.

Presumed message of best fit: coded message that an encoder thinks is the message of best fit.

Prevocalic: before a vowel in a word or syllable.

Primacy function: memory function in which information has been placed into primary storage by a rehearsal strategy. Primacy effect in a serial learning curve is the recall of the initial items.

Probabilistic: probabilities. Likelihood. Not certain, but likely.

Process: a series of operations leading to a result. Grammatical processes result in the production of utterances for communicative (and cognitive) functions.

Process approach: clinically, an appraisal of processes that pertain to an individual's behavior. In assessment, an attempt to define the nature of a problem in terms of systems and processes.

Production deficiency: failure to produce a rehearsal strategy such as a failure to label something or issue action patterns as a means of processing relevant information.

Productive: can be produced. Linguistically, something is productive when it is under the reliable control of a functional rule system. Some early utterances are nonproductive because they are not products or reliably governed by a functional rule system.

Products: results of underlying systems and processes.

Pronominal: any verbal form that stands for an explicit or understood nominal, e.g., I, he, she, one, etc.

Prosodic features: suprasegmentals.

Prototype: a standard. Cognitively, an exemplary concept for a label that an individual constructs from experience.

Proxemics: to study spatial proximity of interaction between people in various circumstances.

Psycholinguistic: pertains to the psychology of language and grammar. The psychological processes employed by an individual as he learns and uses language.

Psychometric: mental measurement. Quantification of mental behavior in a test.

Quantitative approaches: approaches that convert complex dynamic relative conditional behavior into numbers.

Readiness: psychological state of preparedness for learning something new. An individual's readiness is determined by knowledge from past experience, emotional state or set, motivation or desire to learn, and opportunities to become actively involved in the learning process. An individual is always ready to learn something somewhat different from what he knows but not too new—discrepancy.

Reauditorization: nearly simultaneous restating of part of an utterance by a decoder as an encoder speaks. This behavior is apparently to control the rate of encoding and to simplify decoding. Evidenced in aphasia, mental retardation, and language translation.

Recency function: memory function in which information remains in short-term storage. Recency effect in a serial learning curve is the recall of the final items. Recency processing effects refers to performance on the most recently processed information.

Recurrence: awareness that someone or something is experienced again.

Recursiveness: applying a rule again and again. Open-endedness of grammar and counting.

Reductionism: in language learning, a process in which linguistic systems become restricted, usually due to memory processing load.

Reduplication: repetition of syllables, usually open syllables, e.g., mama, dada.

Referent, referential: to direct attention. Linguistically, actual and presumed reference. Actual reference is to directly perceived things whereas presumed reference is to things that are available to one through thought. Usually cued by an utterance.

Referential boundaries: limits of meaning of concept(s) underlying a word. Referential boundaries extend beyond state attributes into dynamic attributes of referential and linguistic contexts.

Referential meaning: conceptual representation expressed by a word, as contrasted with intentional meaning.

Regression effect: phenomenon in using scales in perception and clinical judgments in which judgments tend to be distributed in the middle of the scale. The extremes tend to be ignored.

Regulatory: language used to exert control over the behavior of others.

Reinforcement: strengthening of something. *Behaviorism:* that which increases the occurrence or strength of a behavior. Reinforcers are regarded as external, such as social (''good'') and tangible (edibles, tokens). *Mentalism:* internal psychological process. An act itself is reinforcing if it works as intended. An individual must deem something reinforcing to be reinforcing.

Rejection: refusal.

Relational adjectives: description of where things are in relationship to other things in time or space, e.g., in, on, under, near, far, early, late, etc.

Relational terms: labels of temporal or spatial relationships.

Relative, relativity: related to other things. Behavior is relative, therefore it is necessary to deal with *patterns* (systems and processes) rather than isolated events.

Relevance: traceable, significant, logical connection. Clinically, pertaining specifically to a client's needs.

Reorganization: in cognition, processes become changed by reorganizing. Reorganization occurs in concept formation and language learning. May be the process whereby one can shift from unskilled to skilled acts.

Repertoire: all the behaviors possible for a given person in a particular domain and circumstance. One's capacity.

Representational: having reference. Linguistically, a word or utterance that stands for or represents something (see *referent.*)

Representative: typical of something or someone. Not unusual.

Restricted structures: products of limited or restricted knowledge of a system. Traditional ''errors'' are restricted structures because they reflect restricted knowledge. For example, ''mines hot'' is a restricted possessive.

Retrieval: recall. Recovery of information from memory.

Reversibility: in cognitive development, an ability to reconstruct or reorganize. Linguistically, after cognitive reversibility is obtained, an individual can organize a coherent string of utterances. A discourse paragraph.

Roletaking: communicatively, the cognitive ability of an encoder to take the role of the decoder so he can issue an appropriately coded message and appropriately reckon with any communicative obstacles that may arise. The encoder uses decoder cues to measure the extent to which an intended message is realized.

Scope of grammar: domain, range. Functionally, grammar extends across various cognitive (mediational, representational) functions to various communicative (interact, signify, regulate, inform, etc.) functions. Structurally, grammar extends from one's underlying thoughts to the formulation of words (morphemes) to the organization of words to speech sound patterns or written patterns. It is also possible to deal with the grammar of gestures, body language, and play.

Second language learning: principles and processes in learning a second language or dialect while already possessing a language or dialect. This strategy rests on motivation and similarities and differences between one's functional language and the target language.

Security base: in sociodevelopment, a base of operations which a young child establishes, usually between himself and a significant other (mother, father, etc.). Linguistically, a limited set of linguistic structures and/or functions which an individual knows relatively well and will use as a base from which he extends himself.

Segmental: phoneme. A phoneme with its hierarchy of structure, e.g., syllables, words, phrases, etc.

Segmentation: process of dividing into segments.

Selection rules: contextual constraints on verbal behavior, particularly topical and situational constraints.

Selective imitation: spontaneous imitation. Occurs under certain conditions. For linguistic systems, an individual is ready to learn.

Semantic feature hypothesis: adult meanings of words come about by compiling knowledge of features and the order of acquisition of features, from general to specific.

Semantic functions: substantive meanings of utterances, specifically agent, action, object, locative, dative, instrumental, etc.

Semantic knowledge: meanings entailed in words and linguistic structure as contrasted to conceptual knowledge.

Semantic relations: meanings of utterances that depend upon substantive meaning, specifically rejection, denial, nonexistence, recurrence, possessiveness, etc.

Semantics: domain of linguistics pertaining to meaning.

Separation anxiety: emotional stress or anxiety brought on by a separation or impending separation between an individual and a significant other. Separation anxiety occurs particularly in infancy and preschool ages. Traditional clinicians have usually been ignorant of separation anxiety and its clinical implications (see *stranger anxiety.*)

Sequence: order, series. In language learning, acquisition sequences for specific systems are highly stable but sequences between systems vary greatly from one individual to another.

Sibling: brother or sister.

Sociolinguistics: pertains to sociological influences on language learning and use. Sociological influences on an individual in language learning and use (see pragmatics).

Spatial: pertaining to physical space: front/back, high/low, left/right, proximal/distal.

Spatial awareness: developmentally, topological awareness (point in space), projective awareness (one's perspective imposed on others or things), Euclidean awareness (awareness of the perspectives of others).

Speech acts: all that is entailed in an effort to communicate. In early language learning, the purposes and functions of utterances and their modes. Utterance, proposition or intent, illocutory force.

Speech receptor mechanism: speech perceptual ability reported to be spontaneously available to an infant as young as one month of age.

Spontaneous exploration of available repertoire: active processing of experience by exploring the range of possible alternatives, thereby extending one's repertoire.

Standard English: mythical reference to "typical" English. Linguists cannot agree on what Standard English is. Perhaps school English or textbook English is a better term.

State verb systems: verbalizations that have agent-BE-object/adjectival relationships. Copula verb. Also includes other verbs of state, i.e. Vh, Vs, Vb, etc.

Static attributes: constant attributes, e.g., color, size, shape, etc.

Status: in concept learning, number and organization of attributes of concepts.

Status approach: clinically, appraisal of states as opposed to processes. Identification of variables rather than systems. In assessment, resolution of the problem/no problem issue (see *process approach.*)

Stereotypic behavior: nonpurposeful cyclic behavior, seemingly self-stimulating. Evidenced with autistic and retarded individuals in rocking, head banging, spinning, etc.

Stimulation: arousal of an organism. Traditionally, motivate to learn. Often linked to the term "enrichment."

Storage: memory. To place information in memory.

Story retelling: procedure in which a listener retells a story he has just heard. An exercise in listening and recoding.

Stranger anxiety: emotional stress or anxiety brought on by an encounter with a stranger. Stranger anxiety is not uncommon in clinics and schools (see *separation anxiety.*)

Strategies: alternative principles for the implementation or realization of something.

Stress: energy increase on certain syllables and words that contrasts with other syllables and words. Usually results in increased loudness.

Structuralism: to be structurally oriented. Linguistically, an orientation on syntax.

Structure: form. Structural approaches in language deal with various forms, e.g., "parts of speech," sentence types, complexity, transformational operations, etc. *Surface structure* is the actual words (morphemes) and their organization in an utterance. *Deep structure* is the underlying meaning(s) of an utterance.

Style: linguistically, individuals can talk in different styles, e.g., formally, informally, crudely, western style, northern style, southern style, etc.

Subject noun phrase: NP$_1$. The agent of a sentence.

Suprasegmental: superimposed aspects of verbal behavior, e.g., intonations, stress, inflections, unusual but intentional pauses, etc.

Switching: versatility and dynamics of verbal behavior that provide mechanisms for switching. One can switch topics, codes, modalities, emotionality-rationality, styles, and referents.

Syllabic structure: organization of phonemes in a syllable; the following formula can be used to describe syllabic structure: $\#>CCCVCCC<\#$.

Symbolic: something that stands for or represents something else.

Syntax: domain of linguistics pertaining to organizational rules of morphemes in utterances. Syntax has three major components: phrase structural rules, transformational operations, and morphological rules. Traditional language approaches usually equate grammar with syntax.

System: network or organization. In grammar, mechanisms that function in similar ways comprise a system, e.g., various noun phrase equivalents constitute the nominal system.

Systematic extension of available repertoire: manipulation of presumed antecedents and consequences of a target domain. Modeling, behavior modification.

Tag question: declarative sentence marked either by inflection or by an external marker, e.g., "I go, right?"

Target system: that grammatical system (form or function) of particular interest to a clinician in assessment-intervention. Could also pertain to a particular system an individual seems to be acquiring.

Taxonomic: categorical, classification. Taxonomic approaches in language tally verbal categories, e.g., nouns, verbs, adjectives, etc.

Technician: individual who intervenes for the purpose of improving an individual's clinical problem or condition. Technicians are method oriented; they tend to seek *the* assessment and *the* intervention procedures.

Techniques: methods or procedures.

Technology of reckoning: ability to reckon and deal with an increasing number, type, and varied organization of attributes including the integration of attributes in a conservation task.

Tempo: cognitively, rate of processing information. *Impulsivity* is a fast and inaccurate thinking style. *Reflectivity* is a slow and accurate thinking style.

Temporal: pertaining to time. Sequence. Before/after; past/present/future.

Thematic: having a theme.

Tip-of-the-tongue phenomena (TOT): cognitive state in which an individual cannot think of a word but knows various attributes of the word, e.g., part of speech, number of syllables, initial sound, etc.

Trade-off: in phonological development, the acquisition of a new part of a word may alter the production of another part.

Traditional: body of practices carried on and more or less accepted as typical routine or practice.

Transformational generative grammar: theoretical view that an individual can produce and understand an infinite number and variety of utterances of his language because he knows transformational operations in producing and deriving sentences.

Transformations: in transformational grammar, syntactic operations on phrase structure leading to complex structures.

Transitive verb system: verbalizations or actions that have agent-action-object relationships.

Type I and Type II errors: a Type I error is a conclusion that something—a clinical problem—exists when in fact it does not. A Type II error is a conclusion that something does not exist when in fact it does.

Underextension: in language learning, a child may not permit the use of a word for an adult range of referents. Indicates a restricted conceptual development for a word. Also "underinclusion." "No, that's not a doggy. Fluffy is a doggy."

Unmarked term: in language learning, one of two polar adjectives, usually the positive term, used to refer to a dimension but not a contrastive aspect of the dimension.

Utterance: statement.

Utterance length: number of morphemes or words in an utterance.

Validity: actual, real. In concept development, pertains to successive changes in a concept as it becomes increasingly adult-like. Idiosyncratic concepts become adult concepts.

Verbal: pertaining to language. Linguistic behavior.

Verbial: verb system. Pertaining to the verb and constituents inherent to the verb, exclusive of the auxiliary system, e.g., VI, VT + NP, Vh + NP, Vs + adj, etc.

Vicarious learning: learning by witnessing the learning of someone else.

Vocabulary word: actual words used as differentiated from underlying meaning. In language learning, words initially enter a lexicon as a vocabulary item but subsequently obtain appropriate meanings.

Vocalization period: traditional notion referring to the period of language learning before "true speech." Period in which reflexive utterances, babbling, and echolalia occur.

Vocative: call someone. An utterance used to signal an impending statement.

Voicing: process in early language learning in which the initial consonant is voiced and the final consonant unvoiced, e.g., pig → [bɪк].

Weak syllable deletion: deletion of a weak syllable in speech production, e.g., ''ʌfant'' for elephant.

Wh-question: questions about various constituents in a sentence, e.g., what, when, where, why, how.

Word attack skills: abilities to ''sound out'' written words as a way of pronouncing and reading words.

Word learning: spontaneous learning: meanings of a word are spontaneously known from previously deduced attributes. A new word consolidates past experience. Scientific learning: meaning of a word becomes known by hypothesizing.

Yes/no question: question that can be answered by yes or no.

Name Index

383

Subject Index